THE BILL JAMES GUIDE
to Baseball Managers
from 1870 to Today

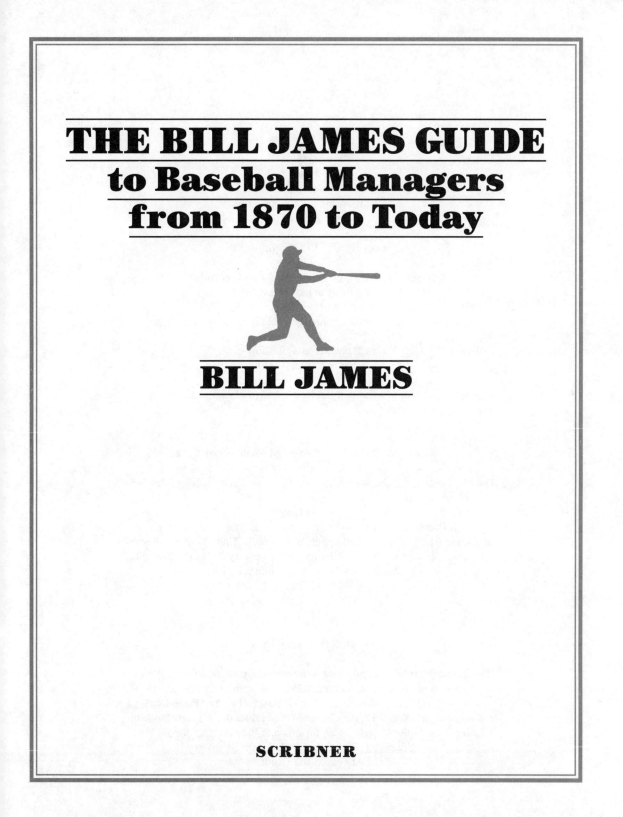

BILL JAMES

SCRIBNER

SCRIBNER
1230 Avenue of the Americas
New York, NY 10020

SCRIBNER and design are trademarks of Simon & Schuster Inc.

Designed by Colin Joh
Set in Century Book

Manufactured in the United States of America

1   3   5   7   9   10   8   6   4   2

Library of Congress Cataloging-in-Publication Data
James, Bill, 1949–
The Bill James guide to baseball managers : from 1870 to today / Bill James.
p.   cm.
Includes index.
1. Baseball managers—United States—Biography. 2. Baseball
managers—Rating of—United States. 3. Baseball—United States—Records.
4. Baseball—United States—History—19th century. 5. Baseball—United
States—History—20th century. I. Title.
GV863.A1J364   1997
796.357'092'2—dc21   97-3103
[B]   CIP

ISBN 0-684-80698-3

The author gratefully acknowledges permission from the following sources
to reprint material in their control: Bettman Archive for the photos of
Casey Stengel, Leo Durocher; National Baseball Hall of Fame Library,
Cooperstown, New York, for photos of Paul Richards, Wilbert Robinson,
Bobby Cox, Miller Huggins, Ralph Houk and Billy Martin, Connie Mack,
Sparky Anderson; and NBC for the photo of
Charlie Dressen and Groucho Marx.

CONTENTS

INTRODUCTION

Hi, I'm Bill James. When not used in connection with baseball, the term "manager" is not normally a title of great distinction. Look around at your life and find the people who have the word "manager" attached to them. You've got office managers, supply managers, production managers, service managers, branch managers, account managers. Do you want any of these jobs? Franchise restaurants have store managers. None of these positions is in the path toward a vice presidency. A manager is not someone who excels; a manager is someone who *copes*. I'll manage somehow.

Your computer has a file manager, and then there is baseball, where the term "manager" has somehow settled onto *both* of the glamour jobs—field manager and general manager. This book is about field managers.

A manager's job, broadly speaking, is to organize the work of all of the members of a baseball team. Whitey Herzog once said that George Brett was the only player he ever knew who didn't need a manager. George kicked himself in the butt every morning; he didn't need somebody to do it for him. This is unusual. Brett found his own weaknesses and directed himself at the task of removing them. This is not common.

Suppose that you have been assigned to hire a baseball manager. You don't get to hire Dave Johnson or Bucky Showalter; you start out knowing nothing or almost nothing about the candidates. What do you look for? Genius? What does genius look like? How do you spot that? You want knowledge of baseball? What, are you going to hire Peter Gammons?

There is one indispensable quality of a baseball manager: The manager *must* be able to command the respect of his players. This is absolute; everything else is negotiable.

This book began to form in the back of my mind about twelve years ago, with an entry I wrote for one of the annual editions of the *Baseball Abstract*. The discussion of baseball managers, I realized at that time, was the most disorganized, unproductive, and ill informed discussion in the world of sports.

And I wasn't helping.

People like to talk about baseball managers, about Tony LaRussa and Bobby Cox and Joe Torre. The talk focuses almost entirely on who is a good manager and who is a lousy manager. The average fan has a one-dimensional image of a manager: He's good, or he's bad. If he's real good, he's a genius. If he's real bad, he's an idiot.

When the discussion turns to why a manager is good or why he is bad, you realize how little solid information is being used. On a talk show, 97% of all explanations as to why the local manager is an idiot will begin with the words "Well, one time he . . ." One time he bunted with the number-six hitter, sent up a pinch hitter, Felipe Alou walked the pinch hitter and then the number-eight hitter grounded into a double play; see, Felipe Alou outsmarted him there. One time he took out his starting pitcher with a three-run lead in the seventh inning, and his relievers didn't have anything.

Much of what the average fan uses to form his impressions of a manager is no doubt valid—for example, if a player fails with one organization, goes somewhere else and succeeds, he may give interviews in which he explains how one manager helped him, and the other didn't. Even if he doesn't, if the fans see that a manager repeatedly takes over players whose careers are going nowhere and gets good performance from them, as Johnny Oates did from almost a dozen players in 1996, the fans may well interpret that to the credit of that manager. Conversely, if a manager lets his star pitcher throw 155 pitches on a cold day and the pitcher pulls up with a sore arm, the fans may connect the dots.

But people who discuss baseball managers—I include fans and professionals—have, in my experience, almost no conceptual framework within which to store these observations. Working with a one-dimensional concept of a manager's job, we use what we learn to push managers up and down the scale, toward the "idiot" pole or toward the "genius" pole. This is all we know.

So when you try to talk about what, specifically, one manager does *different* from another one, the average fan has no way of knowing. My idea, a few years ago, was to back off, disengage from the issue of who was a good manager and who was a bad manager, and to try to organize my own thinking about how one manager was *different* from another. What, *specifically*, does one manager do that another manager would not do? Does he pinch-hit a lot, and if so, under what conditions? Does he like to platoon? Is he aggressive about using his bullpen? Does he hit and run much? Is he prone to bring the infield in? Does he favor the intentional walk? Simple, objective questions which have simple, objective answers.

In a sense, this book is a continuation of the discussion which began at that time. What I have done in this book, in the main, is not to try to say who was a good manager and who was not, but to focus on how one manager was different from another. Having thought about the issue for much of my professional life, and having organized my own thinking about managers to some limited extent, I have written this book in the hope that I can help other people to think a little more clearly about baseball managers.

Managers are fascinating people. Of the twenty-five greatest managers of all time, at least eighteen were alcoholics. Is this a coincidence, or is there a reason for it? Should we, in looking to hire a manager, make sure he has Betty Ford on his resume?

A manager earns his daily bread in the gunsights of 30,000 rifles. The manager meets the press each day and greets us with an icy calm that could easily be mistaken for terror. Although, as a group, they know virtually nothing about math, they look constantly for what they call percentages, and find them in the most improbable places. Good managers, with few exceptions, are notable for their intelligence and personality. They are forceful men, often loud, often crude, sometimes hilarious. They are manipulative, cunning, intense, and selfish. All good managers have a strong need to be the center of attention. They are rarely, if ever, trusting, naive, or open.

   Within that range, they are of infinite variety. In a hundred years, the job description of a baseball manager has changed enormously, yet the men who were good at the job a hundred years ago seem familiar to us now, as if we had just seen them on Channel Eight. This is a book about all of those things—the job, the men who have made the job what it is, the personalities, the percentages, the pratfalls, and the press clippings. The world of a baseball manager is a world of exhilaration and failure, intelligence and stupidity, hope and satisfaction, fear and disgrace. Occasionally there is a John McGraw, a Casey Stengel, a Sparky Anderson—and for every one of those, there are two hundred of the others, the ones who work a lifetime for one moment in the shadows next to glory.

Decade Snapshot: 1870s

Most Successful Managers: 1. Harry Wright
                                          2. Dick McBride
                                          3. Bob Ferguson

Harry Wright was, in essence, the *only* successful manager of the decade, the completely dominant manager. His Boston Red Stockings won the National Association in 1872, 1873, 1874, and 1875, and won the National League in 1877 and 1878.

Most Controversial Manager: Bob Ferguson

Others of Note: George Wright
                           Albert Spalding
                           Cal McVey
                           Bill Craver

Stunts: In the 1870s the rules didn't require the manager to name his lineup until the players actually came to the plate. Cap Anson would often wait to see how the first inning developed before deciding whether he would hit third, fourth, or fifth.

Typical Manager Was: Just an experienced player.

Percentage of Playing Managers: 68%

Most Second-Guessed Manager's Move: I could be wrong about this, but my impression is that the business of second-guessing manager's moves is a relatively late development in baseball history. Nineteenth-century fans had no expectation that the game would pivot constantly on small strategic decisions, and thus no concept of the manager as a chess player.

Until 1905 virtually all games were completed by the starting pitcher, except for a few games when the pitcher was beaten up early and the game was lost. The sacrifice bunt didn't become common until 1890, and pinch hitters were so infrequently used that until 1905, you could lead the league in pinch hits for the season with three.

Lineups were basically constant, and in the 1870s most teams used only one or two pitchers. Without pinch hitting, pinch running, pitching changes, or sacrifice bunting, the second-guesser's field of opportunities was tremendously limited.

Chicago owner John Hart did quarrel openly with Cap Anson about Anson's dislike of the sacrifice bunt, but as a general rule, even when these things did develop, it took some time for fans and reporters to be familiar enough with them that they felt qualified to say what the manager *should* have done.

This is not to say that fans and media of the nineteenth century gave managers a free ride, because they certainly didn't. The nineteenth-century concept of a manager was of a leader, a teacher, and a man who could find good ballplayers and get them to come play for him. If, in the eyes of the fans, the team didn't have much "fire" or didn't make the plays they were supposed to make, that was held against the manager, and the manager was often skewered in the press. But that criticism never focused on strategic decisions in the way that it would in the twentieth century.

Evolutions in Strategy: Far too numerous to discuss. The rules were still changing very rapidly at this time, basic stuff like the number of balls and strikes and the dimensions of the field. Under these conditions, strategies could be dominant one year, obsolete the next. The "fair/foul bunt," a sort of swinging bunt which bounced once in fair territory, then rolled into foul territory, was tremendously important for two or three years, but disappeared when the rules were changed to make it a foul ball if fielded in foul territory.

HARRY WRIGHT IN A BOX

Year of Birth: 1835

Years Managed: 1871–1893

Record as a Manager: 1,225–885, .581
Wright's teams were 225–60 in the National Association, and 1,000–825 in the National League. He managed Boston in the National Association/National League from 1871 to 1881, Providence in 1882 to 1883, and Philadelphia from 1884 to 1893.

Managers for Whom He Played: None.

Others by Whom He Was Influenced: Harry Wright was, in essence, the first manager.

Wright was born in England, but his family moved to the United States when he was a baby. His father, Sam Wright, was a professional cricket player and was employed by a New York City cricket club as a club pro.

In about 1855 baseball had a surge of popularity in New York City. Wright played both cricket and baseball, was a member of the New York Knickerbockers baseball club, and was one of the better players in New York. According to *Baseball in Cincinnati* (Harry Ellard, 1907), "Harry Wright, so well known in baseball circles in the early days, was previous to his coming to Cincinnati the bowler for the New York Cricket Club, working only during the summer at $12 per week, and at his trade (that of jeweler) during the winter, but in August, 1865, he was engaged by George B. Ellard, at a salary of $1,200 a year, to play in the same capacity for the Union Cricket Club, which position he held until November 22, 1867, when he was engaged to act as pitcher for the baseball club at the same salary."

Like his father, Wright had become a club cricket pro. The Union Cricket Club in Cincinnati arranged matches against other teams, both in cricket and baseball. A cricket match goes on for several days, and the public didn't have much taste for that; they drew better when they tried baseball—thus, in 1867, the Unions decided to switch to baseball.

Baseball teams in this time were organized into the National Association of Baseball Players. The NABP extolled amateurism, although many of its players had phantom jobs,

Actors

The three great figures of nine-teenth-century baseball were Harry Wright, Albert Spalding, and Cap Anson.

Anson was two years younger than Spalding; Spalding was fifteen years younger than Wright. Anson played for Spalding; Spalding played for Wright. When the National Association started in 1871, the first thing Harry Wright did was to try to convince the best baseball player he had seen to come join his team. That was Albert Spalding. When the National Association broke up and the National League formed five years later, Spalding did the same with Cap Anson.

They were all handsome men, all outstanding players, all three very bright, all out-standing managers. All three men had imagination on such a scale that it is more properly called vision.

One way to think about them is that Harry Wright was Cary Grant, Spalding was Michael Douglas, and Cap Anson was John Wayne.

Wright's players went along with what he wanted them to do because they liked him, and he always gave sound reasons for what he wanted.

Spalding was a manipula-tor, a man who knew every-body's buttons.

☛

and were in fact professionals. Wright persuaded the Union club, in 1868, to add six of these quasi-professional players.

This gave the Unions the best team in Cincinnati. Wright and some friends designed their uniforms, which had long pants and bright red stockings; the sox would eventually give their name to two major league teams. Flushed with success, Wright approached the new president of the team, a Cincinnati lawyer named Aaron Champion, and attempted to persuade him to abandon the pretense of amateurism, and put together a professional team of the best baseball players in the country.

Champion was uncertain at first, advancing the com-monly held belief that the public would never accept athletes who played for money, and also expressing the fear that the professional team would be blacklisted by the NABP. Wright argued, however, that the NABP rules were pure hypocrisy, since there were dozens of professional players around the country, and also that the Association lacked the ability to enforce its rules.

Wright prevailed, and was authorized to hire a team of professional baseball players, the first openly professional team. Champion financed the venture by selling $15,000 stock in the team, and Wright, by the spring of 1869, had nine baseball players under contract.

In 1869 the Cincinnati Red Stockings went on a grand tour, playing 57 games, 56 of which they won, and the other of which ended in a tie; this is, of course, one of the most cele-brated events in baseball history. This provoked another wave of popularity for baseball, and businessmen from other cities began to bid for the best players as a matter of local pride, trying to build up their teams to compete with Cincin-nati. Major league baseball is an outgrowth of this competition.

The Red Stockings won another 27 games in 1870, finally losing to the Brooklyn Atlantics; they would lose 5 games before the 1870 season was over. They also failed to show a profit, despite their dominance on the field, and Aaron Cham-pion was ousted as president of the club. The team began to break up, the best players being lured away with better offers.

Throughout 1869 and 1870, the rift between the NABP and the amateurs grew increasingly sharp, and on March 17, 1871, Wright and some other prominent baseball men formed a new organization, the National Association of Professional Base Ball Players. Later that spring a group of businessmen in Boston contacted George Wright, Harry's younger brother, and asked him to come to Boston and be the "manager" (meaning captain and business manager) for their team in the new professional league. George Wright, twelve years younger than Harry, was the best player on the Cincinnati team, and probably the best player in baseball at that time. George, however, didn't want to try to be both a player and a manager, and recommended to the men in Boston that they hire Harry to be the manager.

Harry accepted. According to George Wright, in an interview with the New York *Sun* in 1908, "His first move was to go to Rockford, Illinois, and sign A. G. Spalding, the Rockford pitcher, Ross Barnes, their second baseman, and Fred Cohen, their left fielder." Continuing to add outstanding players, and playing cohesively in a way that no other team did, the Boston Red Stockings dominated the National Association, winning the competition by such margins that other teams began gradually to lose interest. In 1875, the last year of the National Association, the Red Stockings were 71–8, 15 games better than any other team.

Characteristics As a Player: He was a center fielder and pitcher, strong, fast, very smart, and with an outstanding arm. He was not a great player; he was good.

He is believed to have been the first pitcher to throw a changeup.

WHAT HE BROUGHT TO A BALL CLUB

Was He an Intense Manager or More of an Easy-to-Get-Along-With Type? Wright was not difficult to get along with. He was competitive, of course, but until 1880 he was more of a "captain" than a modern manager. He was a first-among-equals, a team leader who worked with his men.

According to Lee Allen, "he was a decent, quiet man who did not believe in playing baseball on Sunday. In an uncouth age he had the respect of even the rowdiest players and was, in many ways, much like Connie Mack."

The *1893 Reach Guide*, writing about Harry Wright nearing sixty, said that Wright "has kept himself in step with the new ideas of the game, and never showed a disposition to cling to the things which were primitive or ancient. As a controller of men he has no peer, and in controlling base ball players successfully he shows unwonted powers, because, as a rule, professional ball players are a rather untractable set. It is Mr. Wright's system to never find fault after a defeat. It is when the team wins that he takes occasion to criticize the player's work, because they will then be in a frame of mind to take crit-

And Cap Anson . . . well, Cap Anson could whip any man in the house. People went along with him because their options were limited and unattractive.

These are approximations, of course. Harry Wright did not speak with a British accent, and compared to Cary Grant he was more concerned with values, and less obsessed with sophistication. Still, he was British, urbane, quiet, composed, trim, and elegant.

Spalding was shrewd, calculating, more intense than Wright, less ethical, but he, too, was always in control.

Cap Anson was huge, noisy, arrogant, opinionated, stubborn, and theatrical. He had tremendous courage, and he was probably the hardest-working man in baseball. As far as hard work would get you, that's how far his teams went.

icism kindly. If Mr. Wright, as a manager, has a fault, it lies in an over kindness and a lack of severe methods in dealing with the men."

Was He More of an Emotional Leader or a Decision Maker? More of a decision maker.

Was He More of an Optimist or More of a Problem Solver? He was the ultimate problem solver. He was pro-active in everything, a man who figured out how things *should* be and began to move them in that direction.

HOW HE USED HIS PERSONNEL

Did He Favor a Set Lineup or a Rotation System? He used a set lineup.

Did He Like to Platoon? Never heard of it.

Did He Try to Solve His Problems with Proven Players or with Youngsters Who Still May Have Had Something to Learn? The form of this question assumes a structure. Wright operated in a more open system. Finding good young players was something he liked to do.

How Many Players Did He Make Regulars Who Had Not Been Regulars Before, and Who Were They? Everybody he signed was, of course, a first-time regular in the major leagues.

Did He Prefer to Go with Good Offensive Players or Did He Like the Glove Men? What was most outstanding about his teams was their pitching and defense.

Did He Like an Offense Based on Power, Speed, or High Averages? In 1869, when the Cincinnati team was on tour, baseball was a very high-scoring game. George Wright hit 59 home runs for the Redlegs, in 58 games, and the team scored an average of more than 40 runs per game.

For reasons that I don't fully understand, this changed dramatically in the following few years. Runs-scored totals fell to modern levels, and home runs became relatively rare.

Did He Use the Entire Roster or Did He Keep People Sitting on the Bench? He dealt with ten- to fifteen-man rosters. There wasn't room to have players sitting around.

GAME MANAGING AND USE OF STRATEGIES

Did He Go for the Big-Inning Offense, or Did He Like to Use the One-Run Strategies? One-run strategies weren't really developed until the late 1890s.

Did He Pinch-Hit Much, and If So, When? Nobody used pinch hitters in the 1870s.

Did He Use the Sac Bunt Often? It hadn't been invented.

Did He Like to Use the Running Game? There are no statistics until 1887, near the end of his career.

In What Circumstances Would He Issue an Intentional Walk? Unknown. The intentional walk was used at this time.

Did He Hit and Run Very Often? Hit and run wasn't invented until the 1880s at the earliest, and not common until the 1890s.

How Did He Change the Game? It has been written many times that Harry Wright invented professional baseball. This is an oversimplification; many other men were involved with Wright at each step of the way as baseball made its ten-year transition to open professionalism. Nonetheless, it is certainly accurate to say that Harry Wright made changes in the game far more far-reaching and profound than those of any other manager.

HANDLING THE PITCHING STAFF

Did He Like Power Pitchers, or Did He Prefer to Go with the People Who Put the Ball in Play? The question doesn't really apply to 1870s baseball. Until 1887, the batter could call for a high pitch or a low pitch. In 1870s baseball strikeouts and walks were relatively rare, and players who couldn't throw hard weren't used as pitchers.

Did He Stay with His Starters, or Go to the Bullpen Quickly? In this era, pitchers could be replaced only with the consent of the opposition, so teams had nearly 100% complete games. Wright was an exception; he did like to make pitching changes. In 1876, the first season of the National League, he used 21 relief pitchers in 70 games, whereas the other seven teams combined used only 29 relievers during the season.

Did He Use a Four-Man Rotation? No, but Wright was closer to a pitching rotation than any other manager of his era. In 1876, when most of the other teams in the National League used only one pitcher, Wright used three. He went with one starter in 1877–1878, but as the schedule expanded rapidly in the 1880s, all teams shifted to using more and more pitchers. Wright was always a step ahead in this march. By the early 1890s he was using a three-man rotation.

What Was His Strongest Point As a Manager? He had an almost phenomenal ability to persuade people to go along with his plans.

If There Was No Professional Baseball, What Would He Have Done with His Life? There wasn't any professional baseball. He invented it.

Decade Snapshot: 1880s

Most Successful Managers: 1. Cap Anson
2. Jim Mutrie
3. Charlie Comiskey

Most Controversial Manager: Comiskey
Comiskey's men in St. Louis pioneered the use of rowdy fans as a weapon of combat. Their fans, egged on by Comiskey and his players, were so abusive that they frightened and intimidated opponents.

Others of Note: Frank Bancroft
John Morrill
Gus Schmelz
Pop Snyder
Bill Watkins

Typical Manager Was: A young entrepreneur. The game was divided between country boys, many of them with little or no education, and the eastern, urban descendants of the gentleman's clubs which had dominated baseball in the 1860s. The brighter and more ambitious in each group sometimes became managers.

Some of those, like Cap Anson, stayed in baseball until circumstances forced them out. But more of them, best represented by Monte Ward, were on their way to some other destination.

Percentage of Playing Managers: 41%

Evolutions in Strategy: The Chicago club (under Anson) used a play that they called the "hit and run," although there is dispute about whether this was the modern hit and run play, in which the batter attempts to take advantage of the hole created by a fielder's moving, or something closer to the modern run and hit, a simpler play which just involves the runner moving while the batter swings away.

The Detroit team of 1887, National League champions under Bill Watkins, may have been the first to experiment with the sacrifice bunt. There are other claimants.

Evolution in the Role of the Manager: With the exceptions of Harry Wright and Cap Anson, who were both quite remarkable men, the role of the professional manager was just beginning to take shape in the 1880s. Cap Anson was probably the first hard-ass manager in baseball. The managers of the early 1870s couldn't be too hard on their players, because the players could easily move on to other teams, and thus had all the power in the relationship.

Sorry I Asked

Jim O'Rourke was manager of Buffalo in the National League from 1881 to 1884, and of Washington in 1893. He was known as Orator Jim, for reasons which may be inferred from his answer to one of his players when the player asked for a ten-dollar advance.

"I am sorry," O'Rourke replied, "but the exigencies of the occasion and the condition of our exchequer will not permit anything of the sort at this period of our existence. Subsequent developments in the field of finance may remove the present gloom and we may emerge into a condition where we may see fit to reply in the affirmative to your exceedingly modest request."

Bewildering Options

With a twenty-five-man roster there are 741 billion possible ways for a manager to pick a nine-man lineup. Actually, there are millions of times that many, but what I am saying exactly is that given a set of twenty-five players, there are 741,354,768,000 (741 billion, 354 million, 768 thousand) different ways to choose nine players from those twenty-five.

Once you have chosen the nine players, there are 362,880 options for the batting order, which is nine factorial. Combining these two questions into one, how many ways are there to make a nine-man batting order from a twenty-five-man lineup? The answer is 269 quadrillion—269,022,818,211,840,000 to be exact. One year, Casey Stengel used them all. No, actually, this is approximately the same as the number of seconds which would pass in ten billion years.

We haven't yet considered the defensive alignment; if we allowed for that, the number of options would be . . . well, I don't know, exactly, but trust me, it would be some very large number. For each of the 269 quadrillion possible lineups, there would be, in theory, 362,880 different defensive alignments.

The possible options would shrink considerably if we divided the roster into pitchers and position players. If you have a roster of fourteen position players and eleven pitchers, and you assume that only one pitcher will start, that reduces the options for the starting lineup from seven hundred billion to one billion. If you assume that only certain players can catch, only certain players can play the outfield, etc., that reduces the options further; heck, you can get down to a few million in no time.

Managers get hammered in barroom discussion because, out of the 269 quadrillion options for the batting order, they frequently don't choose exactly the right one. You may wonder what computer analysis has to say about lineup selection, and I will tell you more about the subject a little later. But the first point to make, along that line, is that we can never *really* be sure what the optimal lineup is. The number of options is so large that it overpowers even the largest and most sophisticated computers. The only way to approach the problem is by whittling down the theoretically possible selections into those which seem reasonable, and then evaluating what seem to be the prime alternatives.

The Marshalltown Enfant Terrible

Cap Anson was not only larger than life, but louder, too. It would be the understatement of the week to say that Cap Anson was a natural leader. Anson was so big, so strong, so loud, and so forceful in his opinions that it would have been impossible for anyone else to manage the team while he was around. Even Albert Spalding, in time, would have been pushed aside by the younger man.

Adrian Constantine Anson was born in Marshalltown, Iowa, in 1852; he was the first white child born in that town, laid out and developed the previous year by Anson's father. Henry Anson had settled in 1851 among the Pottawotami Indians in central Iowa.

Anson's mother, according to his autobiography, stood five-foot-ten and a half and weighed over two hundred pounds. She died when Adrian was seven years old, leaving Anson to be raised by a huge, hulking braggart who attempted to drive the world around him with his voice. Baseball fever broke out in Marshalltown in the summer of 1866; the whole town seems to have been playing or watching baseball games every evening. The Marshalltown Stars developed into the best team in the state while Adrian was still young; his father and brother Sturgis were regulars, while Adrian, then fourteen, was on the second team. Adrian eventually made the team as a second baseman, and the Marshalltown Stars with the three Ansons claimed the Iowa state championship for several years.

One of the first professional teams west of the Mississippi was the Forest City Club of Rockford, Illinois, starring Albert Spalding. It isn't a long distance from Forest City to Marshalltown, and in 1870 a match was arranged between the Marshalltown Stars and the Forest City Club. Forest City won 18 to 3 and then won a rematch 35 to 5. A fistfight between Henry Anson and Albert Spalding was narrowly averted.

After that game two members of the Marshall town team turned pro, joining Forest City. When Spalding and Ross Barnes left Forest City in 1871, joining Harry Wright in Boston, the Ansons were invited to try out for the vacancies on the Forest City roster. Henry Anson had a business to run—several businesses, actually—and he kept Sturgis Anson to help him, but allowed Adrian to sign with the professional team. Adrian was paid $66 a month.

Anson's 1900 autobiography, *A Ballplayer's Career*, is full of stories which may perhaps have acquired some character from frequent repetition. One story which I will repeat is that Clinton and Des Moines, Iowa, had a fierce baseball rivalry. They arranged a big match, and the Clinton Group offered Anson $50 to play the game for them. Dying his hair and staining his skin so he would not be recognized, Anson set off for Des Moines, but was intercepted at the railroad station by his father, who asked him what the devil he thought he was doing. Anson explained that there was fifty dollars at stake, but his father would not permit him to take part in the deception.

You know why I believe the story? Because Anson loved to dress up. Throughout his life, this was a constant theme: The man loved to put on funny clothes.

The National Association was organized in 1871 with the Forest City team as one of the nine original members. Without Spalding and Ross Barnes, Rockford was left as the association's weakest team. The nineteen-year-old Anson played third base and hit very well (reportedly .352, although record-keeping in the Association was not reliable.) They called him "Baby" Anson, or "The Marshalltown Infant."

Forest City wanted Anson back in 1872 at the same salary, but the Philadelphia Athletics offered him $1,250. Anson took the offer to Forest City and told them he would have to have at least $100 a month to stay with them. Losing money, they couldn't do it, and Anson left for Philadelphia. Forest City disbanded, and Anson would not see his home town again for several years.

Anson loved Philadelphia, an exciting place for a country boy; he all but lived in the billiard parlors, and took boxing lessons from a championship boxer. In the summer of 1874 the Athletics and Red Stockings played an exhibition tour in England. Anson loved London, too—in fact, for a while he became quite fond of the night life. In a bar one night in 1875, back in Philadelphia, Anson got into a fight with a city cop and was hauled to the police station, covered with cuts and bruises. Fortunately, the president of the Athletics at that time was also the police commissioner.

Retiring to a bar to celebrate his release, he had several rounds and stumbled out the door, at which point he chanced upon a young woman whom he hoped to make Mrs. Anson. She expressed her opinion about men who drank to excess and got arrested in barroom brawls. Anson's life was altered by that moment of humiliation. He stopped going to bars, never again drank excessively, and claimed that he was involved in only one fistfight in the rest of his life, that coming when Anson punched out a man on a streetcar who had insisted that baseball games were fixed.

The woman in question was Virginia Fiegal, the daughter of a Philadelphia hotel and restaurant owner. Anson had met her when she was quite young (twelve or thirteen) and began to court her soon after that; this apparently was not considered remarkable at the time.

As this courtship was progressing, in the summer of 1875, the National Association was disintegrating, and the National League was forming. Four key players from Boston, including Albert Spalding, and one key player from Philadelphia, Adrian Anson, jumped their teams and agreed to play in Chicago. Anson had originally wanted to play in Chicago, which was nearer his home than

Philadelphia, and in the winter of 1875–1876 he agreed to join Spalding, Ross Barnes, Bob Addy, Paul Hines, Deacon White, Cal McVey, and others in Chicago; he was to be paid a reported $2,000.

When he told Virginia that he had signed to play in Chicago there was a scene. Anson assured her that he could purchase his release from his new contract, and traveled to Chicago to meet with William Hulbert, owner of the new White Stockings. He offered to purchase his release; Hulbert refused. Later in the winter he made another trip to Chicago for the same purpose, offering Hulbert $1,000; Hulbert still refused. Early in the season, Anson showed up at the park one day in a Prince Albert coat and striped trousers—the dress of an Eastern gentleman—and played the entire game in that garb.

Concluding that he was stuck in Chicago and had better make the best of it, Anson persuaded Virginia Fiegal that they should be married, and they were.

The White Stockings won the National League in its first season, 1876. At the end of the 1877 season Albert Spalding resigned as manager to devote full time to his sporting goods business, though he remained as part owner and continued to hang around the park. Bob Ferguson managed the team in 1878; he was older than Anson and probably smarter, but hard to get along with. By 1879 Anson was a veteran star at twenty-seven, his hellraising days far behind him.

He was named to manage the White Stockings in 1879. It was the role he was born to play. He became "Cap" Anson, the Captain. He scheduled daily workouts for his players, hard ones. When, in his first year as manager, Spalding came onto the field to express his opinion in a dispute with the umpires. Anson lit into Spalding with a string of obscenities. Spalding retreated.

Six foot tall, maybe six-one, Anson weighed 220 to 240 pounds and was always in perfect shape. He had a bullhorn voice which he used to berate and intimidate umpires, a major strategy of nineteenth-century ball clubs. (The umpires, attempting to work games solo, were subject at this time to constant abuse—tripping, bumping, shoving. It got worse before it got better.) Anson spoke his mind quickly and plainly, absolutely without fear; everybody knew where they stood with Anson. He worked hard himself, giving him the moral authority to insist on the same from his players. He was intelligent, strategically sound and innovative in a game which was still evolving rapidly and therefore had fluid strategy. He was a good judge of ballplayers.

The team improved in 1879, and in 1880 added Mike "King" Kelly, who was to become the most popular player of the early 1880s, and Anson's rival in marquee value. In 1880 the White Sox returned to the top of the National League, posting a 67–17 record. Backed by Spalding's wealth, the White Stockings prospered throughout the early '80s. They won the National League again in 1881, and won a third time in 1882. In 1882 the White Stockings played a postseason series against the Cincinnati team of the American Association, a series sometimes listed as the first World Series. They played two games, and split.

At a baseball clinic in his hometown of Marshalltown in 1883, Anson saw a young man named Billy Sunday and signed him to play with the White Stockings. Sunday was a decent player, a good base stealer, and, at the time, quite a hell-raiser himself. We come then to the events which, as time passes, grow ever larger in the modern image of Cap Anson. In the early 1880s there were a few black players playing professional baseball. Cap Anson was outspoken in his opposition to allowing blacks to play in the majors.

Anson's autobiography does not discuss his role in drawing the color line, but does discuss at considerable length his relationship with a black minstrel named Clarence Duval, whom the team kept as a mascot. He refers to Duval casually as a "little darkie," a "coon," and a "no account nigger." He quotes Duval as saying things like, "Spec's

you's a' right, Cap'n," and tells that on joining the team "Duval was taken out, given a bath, against which he fought with tooth and nail." They treated Duval, in short, exactly as one would treat a dog.

The Toledo team of the American Association (a major league team) had a catcher named Moses Fleetwood Walker, a black gentleman, a college graduate, well spoken and well liked.

On July 20, 1884, in Toledo, the White Stockings were scheduled to play an exhibition game against Toledo. The Chicago team secretary wrote a letter to Charlie Morton, Toledo manager, reminding him of Anson's feelings about black ballplayers. They thought that they had an agreement that Walker would not play.

When the Chicago team got to the ballpark, however, Walker was in uniform. Anson refused to play the game unless "that nigger" was removed from the field. The Toledo management told Anson that he could play against Walker or go home. Anson played the game—but spoke out loudly against it.

This incident is frequently cited as the beginning of baseball's color line—in fact, the version of it usually printed until a few years ago was that Toledo had knuckled under, and Anson had successfully driven Walker from the field. In any case, the engine of discrimination was in motion. Several leagues in the following months passed covenants banning "colored" players from participation. The Toledo team dropped out of the American Association in 1885.

The situation was unresolved. Black players were banned from some leagues, but continued to play in others. There were no blacks in the National League or the American Association, the "major" leagues, but no one knew for sure whether or not he could sign a black player if he chose. Anson resumed his career.

In the spring of 1885 Anson brought his Cubs to Sulphur Dell, Tennessee, for three weeks of spring training. Although teams had gone south for training for many years, even before the beginning of the National League, Anson apparently pushed spring training to new levels of organization, or something, and so is often credited (or miscredited) with having invented spring training.

Teams in the mid-1880s still relied heavily on one starting pitcher, and the decline of the Chicago team in 1883–1884 can be traced to the decline of their number one pitcher, Larry Corcoran. In late 1884 Corcoran was supplanted by a hard-throwing sensation named John Clarkson, who won 53 games in 1885. The White Sox returned to the top of the league with a sensational 87–25 record.

Cap Anson, as a player: He stood with his heels together, very erect at the plate, and swung perhaps the heaviest bat in history. Most of the time he allowed the first pitch to go by; some accounts insist that he almost never swung until there were two called strikes on him, although the advantage in this would be hard even for Ted Williams to explain. He had huge, powerful hands.

Anson as described by Robert Smith: "Anson was six feet two, an erect, square-shouldered, lop-eared man, tightly muscled, of a slightly dour countenance. His eyes were deep and his gaze level and clear. His mouth was firm, his nose curved and badly proportioned, like something a child might draw. There was a fierceness in his nature which took the form of a stubborn honesty and independence, a grim clinging to prejudice, a tendency to express his mind loudly and directly, and a desire to go his own way—and have his own way."

When Anson thought that an umpire had done him wrong, or failing that when he thought an umpire could be intimidated, he roared at the umpires with his remarkable foghorn voice.

He bullied anybody he could bully, starting with the opposition; he would stand on the sidelines and berate the opposition pitcher in loud and offensive language. He was "an acknowledged rough," said Henry Chadwick, and his influence on the conduct of the game was not a healthy one—but he had put together the best team in the National League, and that as he saw it was his job.

The St. Louis Browns, under Charles Comiskey, had emerged as the powerhouse of the rival league, the American Association. The difference between the Browns and the White Sox was that the Browns were even rougher. The two teams arranged to play a series to determine the 1885 World Championship, as had been done in 1884. St. Louis probably won the series, but the second game of the series was stopped in the sixth inning by fights on the field and a near-riot in the stands. The Chicago papers claimed the unfinished game as a victory for Chicago, and thus claimed that the series had ended in a tie.

That argument roared for a year, and grew hotter when both Chicago and St. Louis repeated as champions in 1886. Anson had a great year, driving in 147 runs and hitting .371—but then, Anson always had a great year; the only higher average belonged to his utility superstar, King Kelly, who hit .388. Chris Von der Ahe, owner of the St. Louis team, challenged the White Stockings, by now also called the Colts, to settle the question of the championship once and for all. "We'll play your team," Anson told Von der Ahe, "on one condition—that the winner take every penny of the gate."

Anson looked upon the American Association champions as upstarts. It is impossible, at this late date, to sort out what was really said and done from the press notices sent forward to hype the gate, but in any case a best-of-seven series was arranged, and the public was told that it was winner-take-all. For the first time, the champions of two leagues would meet in a format resembling the modern World Series—seven games, four at one park and three at the other, no games on another field somewhere, no matches tapering off in indecision or indifference. The first three games were played in Chicago, with Chicago winning two of the three. Traveling to St. Louis to play in front of the rowdy, beer-guzzling, insult-belching fans that Comiskey and Von der Ahe had cultivated, the Colts lost games four and five to fall behind, three games to two.

Clarkson started the sixth game for Chicago against Bob Caruthers. Heading into the bottom of the eighth the Colts held a 3–0 lead. The Browns scored; it was 3–1. With runners on first and second and more than ten thousand fans crowding around the field and screaming like maniacs, littering the field with debris, Arlie Latham ripped a triple to left field, tying the game at three. In the tenth inning Chris Welch raced home, sliding in with the winning run—the famous $15,000 slide. The St. Louis Browns were the champions of the world.

Cap Anson would remain a proud and imposing figure until the day he died thirty-five years later, but in a very real sense Anson's life passed its peak at that moment, and was lived forever after on a downward spiral. King Kelly, beloved by the fans but never a favorite of Anson's due to his heavy drinking, was sold to Boston. George Gore, the star center fielder, had fought with the Colts constantly for more money; Anson sold him, too, to the New York Giants. "I'll go," said Gore, "but if I do, you'll never win another pennant."

And he was right. Gore and Kelly would play for championship teams again. Anson never would.

The Colts slipped to third in 1887. In early 1888 Anson signed a ten-year contract as manager of the Chicago Colts; he was also to receive 130 shares of club stock.

The hooves of racism were heard again in the background. In September 1887, the Cuban Giants were scheduled to play a game against the St. Louis Browns. Comiskey's men refused to play the game.

In July 1888, Anson's Colts were scheduled to go to Newark to play an exhibition. The Newark team of the International League had a black pitcher named George Stovey, who had major league ability. Some white players in the International League had been grumbling about playing against blacks. After a meeting of the International League's board of directors on July 14 it was announced that they would "approve no more contracts with colored men." On that same day the *Newark Evening News*, unaware of what was happening at the league meeting in Buffalo, announced that George Stovey would pitch for Newark in an exhibition game against the White Stockings on July 19.

But when the day came, Anson refused to play against Stovey; "Get him off the field," Anson reportedly said, "or I get off." Stovey, wishing to avoid an embarrassing incident, volunteered to withdraw.

By opening day of the 1888 season, the International League had no black players.

The color line had effectively been drawn.

When these incidents are written about today, Cap Anson usually bears the full weight of the responsibility for banning blacks. On a literal level, the portrayal of the color line as being a consequence of Cap Anson's racism is extremely naive.

Anson had no authority by which to ban black players. The notion that Anson "intimidated" the National League into banning blacks is silly. Anson was a great and imposing figure, but the National League at that time was full of great and imposing figures, many of whom had more impact on the decisions of the league than did Anson.

One must remember that at this time Jim Crow laws were being enacted all over the country. According to C. Vann Woodward in *The Strange Career of Jim Crow,* "It was quite common in the 'eighties and 'nineties to find in the *Nation, Harper's Weekly,* the *North American Review* or the *Atlantic Monthly* Northern liberals and former abolitionists mouthing the shibboleths of white supremacy regarding the Negro's innate inferiority, shiftlessness, and hopeless unfitness for full participation in the white man's civilization." A series of Supreme Court decisions between 1873 and 1898 clipped the concept of equality, and cleared the way for the institutional racism. In the very month when blacks were banned from baseball, they were also banned from countless streetcars, theaters, drinking fountains, trains, and restaurants by this little city and that great state and the other private business. It is enormously likely that Jim Crow would have come to baseball even had Cap Anson never been born.

This is not written to mitigate Cap Anson's moral responsibility. When one makes oneself a spokesman for racial intolerance, one becomes morally responsible for the pain that racism inflicts upon its victims. But the weight of Anson's voice was derived entirely from one thing: that he was a spokesman for the *majority* position.

Attempting to promote baseball worldwide, Albert Spalding organized a world tour in the winter of 1888–1889. Anson was a part of the tour, as was Clarence Duval, the mascot. The trip went through Chinatown in San Francisco. Anson's views of "Chinamen" were as enlightened as his views of blacks. Anson's experiences in Australia, France, Egypt, etc., occupy a huge portion of his autobiography.

In 1890 baseball was split by the Brotherhood War, with most of the biggest stars in the game moving over to the Player's League. Anson, a part owner of the Colts, stayed in the National League and denounced those who had left as greedy and disloyal.

The Colts were forced to put together a team of young and inexperienced players, whom sportswriters nicknamed the "Cubs." Anson himself, once known as the "Marshalltown Infant," reached his final stage as "Pop" Anson.

With the aid of Spalding's pocketbook, the assembly of the 1890 team was accomplished fairly well. When the defectors returned in 1891, Anson, like the other managers around the league, was forced to piece the two teams together into one, and again he accomplished this fairly well. But when the American Association folded into the National League in 1892, there was a further com-

pression of the talent. The short-run effect was that the quality of play moved up a notch. The Chicago team did not meet the challenge.

Anson himself, thirty-eight years old by 1890, was still a good player. On September 4, 1891, after some newspaper men had commented on Anson's age, Anson dressed up in a white wig and false white beard that came down to his stomach, and played the entire game in that costume.

Anson was in a creative period. On August 6 of the same season, Anson batted against Kid Nichols. Just as Nichols would get set to pitch, Anson would jump to the other side of the plate, batting left-handed, then right-handed, etc. Nichols looked at him as if he was half-crazy, which wasn't necessarily false, and waited for him to stand in and hit. Anson kept jumping from side to side.

At last the Boston coach asked the umpire to tell Anson to cut it out. The umpire said there was no rule that Anson couldn't do that if he wanted. Nichols refused to pitch, Anson continued to jump around, and the umpire, perhaps intimidated by Anson, refused to order him to stop. At last the umpire sent Anson to first base, ruling that he was entitled to first base since Nichols had refused to pitch to him.

So they made a rule about that, that if a hitter switches positions in the batter's box after the pitcher is set he is called out. This rule is still in the books; you may remember it was the subject of a beer commercial a few years ago.

Anson loved to play games like this; there are several other incidents on record in which Anson tried to exploit a hole in the rules. In the off season, he cashed in on his popularity by working in vaudeville. He had a slapstick routine in which he would wear green whiskers, was squirted in the face with soapy water, had buckets emptied on him, and sang silly songs.

In December 1895, he made Broadway. Charles H. Hoyt, a popular playwright, wrote a play for Anson called *A Runaway Colt*. According to James Mote's wonderful book *Everything*

Baseball, the play involved a minister's son named Manley Manners who was recruited by Anson, as himself, to play for the Colts. It was a melodrama, involving a bad guy's attempts to force Manley Manner's fiancée into an unwelcome marriage. The *New York Dramatic Mirror* reported that Anson's performance was "quite as good as most of the people on the stage with him," but added that "he speaks his lines with the directness of an artillery officer, no matter whether he is accepting an invitation to dinner or defending the good cause of professional baseball." It lasted only a few weeks, but provided the basis of Anson's favorite self-description: a better actor than any ball player, a better ball player than any actor.

Another story from this era, since we're having fun here, involved a swaybacked white horse which the Chicago groundskeeper kept to pull his equipment. The horse's name was Sam, and when not working he browsed in a field behind the clubhouse.

Sam, for some reason, didn't like Anson, and would lay back his ears and snort whenever he saw him. Well, one day a Louisville player grounded the ball to Bill Dahlen, and Dahlen threw wildly to first. The throw hit the stands and bounced toward right field. Anson was chasing the ball up the right field line, when he looked up and saw a horse. Somebody had left Sam's gate open.

Now, Anson was not afraid of any man on earth, but a horse is another matter. Anson and the horse looked at each other for a second. Anson glanced at his glove, as if maybe he would throw that at the horse, but rejected that option and decided instead to run like hell. The horse took out after him. And the batter scored, because there just wasn't any rule that said how many bases you could advance while the first baseman was being chased by a horse.

Anyway, that was 1891, which was maybe the last good year of Cap Anson's life. In May 1892, the Ansons had their third baby boy, and for the third time the child died in infancy. Though the Ansons had four daughters of whom Cap was enormously proud, he idolized his own father, and no doubt very much wanted a son. The *Chicago Post* reported that on one occasion "Adrian Constantine Anson has given the New York Sun a few reflections concerning the duties of womankind . . . Mr. Anson thinks that the average woman cannot attend to her regular knitting and to clubs at the same time, and he fecilitates himself that the ladies of his immediate family have been restrained by his influence and his arguments from wasting time in society work that should belong to the needs of the small and sympathetic domestic circle." Fun guy, Cap was.

Anson began to have trouble with the team's owners. On the round-the-world trip several years earlier, one of the part-owners of the team, James A. Hart, had come along to act as financial manager. Spalding had organized an effort to buy a set of diamond cuff links as a gift for Hart. Everyone on the trip contributed—except Anson. "Why should Hart get a gift like this?" Anson wanted to know. "I'm doing the biggest work around here. He's being well paid for what he does."

In 1891 Spalding resigned as president of the Colts; Hart was elected to replace him. Hart was brave enough to second-guess Anson on such things as Anson's choice of players and Anson's dislike of the bunt, but the most serious problem between the two concerned training habits. Faced with a gradually declining team, Anson attempted to become even stricter, and even more of a disciplinarian. He did not allow his players to drink or smoke. He demanded precise performance of team drills, and would levy fines for drinking, misconduct, or insubordination. Hart would not collect the fines. As the team slipped away throughout the 1890s, Anson began increasingly to quarrel with everyone around him. He fought with his players, the management, the league, the opposition, the press, the umpires. "That ain't no shadow," one of his players remarked, pointing to the ground behind Anson. "That's an argument. Everywhere Cap goes, the argument goes."

A newspaper reporter asked Anson to name his All-Time team. He did, naming himself the first baseman. He was criticized, of course, for his arrogance.

"They wanted my opinion," said Anson. "And I gave it to them."

Jokes about Anson's age became common. A letter to *The Sporting News* in 1897 contained the following verse from a fan:

How old is Anson? No one knows.
I saw him playing when a kid,
When I was wearing still short clothes,
And so my father's father did;
The oldest veterans of them all
As kids, saw Anson play baseball.

In 1897 the ten-year contract Anson had signed in 1888 drew to a close. After a close loss, Anson approached sportswriter Hugh Fullerton of the Chicago *Inter-Ocean* and accused Fullerton of being a coward. Why, Fullerton wanted to know, was he a coward? Because, Anson said, you won't print what I tell you. "You're protecting them," Anson said.

"Protecting who?" Fullerton asked.

"These ballplayers," Anson said, gesturing toward his players. "You're afraid to write the truth."

"And just what is the truth?"

"The truth," said Anson, "is that they're a bunch of drunkards and loafers who are throwing me down."

Fullerton said that if he wrote that he'd get sued. Well then, replied Anson, say that I said it. But what if you deny it, Fullerton asked?

Anson shook his fist under Fullerton's nose. "Do you think I'd deny it?"

"No. You're bullheaded enough to stick to it, and make it worse."

"All right," Anson insisted. "Put it in blackface type at the head of your column."

The next day Fullerton wrote:

CAPTAIN A.C. ANSON DESIRES ME TO ANNOUNCE, IN BLACK TYPE AT THE HEAD OF THIS COLUMN, THAT THE CHICAGO BASE-BALL CLUB IS COMPOSED OF A BUNCH OF DRUNKARDS AND LOAFERS WHO ARE THROW-ING HIM DOWN.

That, of course, was the end for Anson. Remarkably, Anson had survived the ten years not only as a manager, but as a player. Forty-five years old in 1897, he still hit .302—a poor average for a first baseman in that era, but not the worst in the league.

There followed a period of intense politicking, as Anson attempted to find a way to save his job, and succeeded in entangling himself in a bitter feud with Albert Spalding. The short version is that Anson, part-owner of the Cubs, wanted to borrow money to buy more stock, thus hanging onto his job. When he was unable to raise the money, he accused Spalding of leaning on potential lenders, persuading them not to make the loans.

The public was on Anson's side in this dispute. His tirades against his lazy players, however much they might damage the team, were well received. "Baseball as at present conducted is a gigantic monopoly intolerant of opposition," Anson said, "and run on a grab-all-that-there-is-in-sight basis that is alienating its friends and disgusting the . . . public."

Trying to patch things over, Spalding sponsored a fund which was to be collected for Anson as a token of esteem. The goal was to raise $50,000. Anson rejected the offer. "If I need help," Anson said, "I'll go to the county welfare office." Spalding contacted the league office and offered Anson a position as National League Umpire-in-Chief. Anson refused that, too. He accused Spalding of using his name, without his permission, to promote a "Baseball School," which was in reality a scheme to sell some of Spalding's real estate.

Anson managed the New York Giants in 1898, but that lasted only a few weeks, as he couldn't get along with their owners, either. He tried to buy a Chicago franchise for the Western League, but Spalding, who had franchise rights to the Chicago area, refused his consent. "Twenty-two years with that man," Anson said, "and look how he treats me now."

In the spring of 1899 something called the "New American Base-Ball Association" met in Detroit and planned to revive the old American Association. Anson was president of the League's board; they announced plans to launch that summer, and when that failed retrenched and aimed for 1900. This was a different organization from that which founded the American League in 1900–1901, although many of the same people were involved. Anson was offered a chance to be involved with the effort which did result in the American League, but was not offered what he considered an appropriate position, and announced instead that he did not want to dishonor his twenty-plus years in the major leagues by being involved with a minor league team.

By 1900 Anson was slipping toward poverty. He had made a good deal of money, but lost it in bad investments. His father had been a business-man, and Anson, like most athletes, idolized his father, and then too there was the rivalry with Spalding, who parlayed his baseball career into a multimillion-dollar fortune. Anson figured he was just as smart as Spalding and if Spalding could do it he could, too. He invested in billiard parlors, ice rinks, toboggan slides. At one point he owned several bowling alleys. He invested in a golf course and a handball court. He invested in a company which bottled ginger beer, but the bottles kept exploding.

Some reports say that Anson did become chief of umpires in the National League for a while, although I'm not certain of this. He was elected city clerk of Chicago in 1905 and served in that capacity from 1905 to 1907.

He continued to search for ways to market his fame. In 1909–1910, Anson formed a touring team, which played spring exhibitions against major league teams and barnstormed through smaller towns in the summer. Nearing sixty, Anson played with the team.

The venture made no money, and Anson returned to the stage. He formed an act with his daughters, "Cap Anson and Daughters." Years later, his daughter Dorothy recalled the perfor-mances:

We had two pretty fair writers, Ring Lardner and George M. Cohan. Papa wore tails while he deliv-ered a monologue . . . We carried a huge bag filled with papier-mâché baseballs made for us by AG Spalding. As we threw the balls into the audi-ence, we sang "We're going to take you to the game/where dear old Dad won his fame." That was a cue for Pop to appear wearing his old Chicago uniform and carrying a silver bat which had been given to him by Notre Dame alumni.

Anson would set up in his stance, while members of the audience would toss the papier-mâché base-balls at him, and he would hit them back.

This didn't bring in as much money as managing the Cubs, and Anson was forced into bankruptcy. He lost his house. Once again, an effort was launched to raise money for him, and once again he refused it. The National League attempted to establish a pension fund for him. Anson said more emphatically than ever that he could take care of himself, and wanted no charity.

In 1921, in the wreckage of the Black Sox scandal, baseball was looking for its first com-missioner. Anson let it be known that he thought himself well qualified for the post.

Anson died suddenly on April 14, 1922, the victim of an apparent heart attack. He left no estate, only a request that his gravestone read "Here lies a man who batted .300."

The league paid the funeral expenses and established a fund to create a "fitting memorial" for Anson. The body of Anson's wife was removed from its resting place in Philadelphia and brought to lie in Chicago with that of the man who batted three hundred. "It has been meanly stated that this was a 'belated appreciation of Captain

Anson,' " wrote Francis Richter in the 1923 *Reach Guide*. "In justice to the National League let it be stated that the body for many years stood ready to come to Anson's assistance when necessary. That it was not necessary was due to the fact that the independent old man would not accept a pension, in default of which no position could be created that he could fill satisfactorily owing to his disposition which was self-opinionated and brooked neither advice or order."

Now *that* should have been on his tombstone.

(This is an edited version of a much longer article by the author which was originally published several years ago. Sources for this article, in addition to Anson's autobiography, include Anson's obituaries in the 1923 *Reach* and *Spalding* Guides, Robert Smith's books *Baseball* and *The Hall of Fame*, Ira Smith's *Baseball's Famous First Basemen*, *The Strange Career of Jim Crow*, by C. Vann Woodward, and *They Gave Us Baseball*, by John M. Rosenberg, as well as many other articles, histories, and newspaper articles.)

Decade Snapshot: 1890s

Most Successful Managers: 1. Frank Selee
2. Ned Hanlon
3. Patsy Tebeau

Most Controversial Manager: Patsy Tebeau. Tebeau, given less talent than Hanlon, tried to outrowdy him. He had some success, keeping Cleveland over .500 from 1892 to 1898. In 1900 he managed McGraw and Wilbert Robinson in St. Louis. They hated him.

Others of Note: Buck Ewing
Arthur Irwin
King Kelly
Bill McGunnigle
Monte Ward

Stunts: Chris Von der Ahe, the eccentric owner of the St. Louis Cardinals, also managed them for one game in 1895, two games in 1896, and fourteen games in 1897.

Typical Manager Was: The typical 1890s manager was finished by the time he was forty. More than 80% of the managers of the 1890s were in their thirties. There were a few guys in their late twenties, and a handful in their early forties, although most of them quit or were fired by that age. No one who managed in the 1890s was fifty years old, except for Harry Wright, who was still managing in the early part of the decade, and a few guys who filled in for part of a season.

Percentage of Playing Managers: 51%

Player Rebellions: The Chicago Cubs, by 1897, had had it up to here with Cap Anson. See "The Marshalltown Enfant Terrible," page 21.

Evolutions in Strategy: Throughout the 1870s and 1880s, baseball's rules changed so much that it would have been difficult for strategies to become strongly entrenched.
The concept of strategy began to gain traction in the late 1890s. The sacrifice bunt became an accepted part of the game, and managers began occasionally to use pinch hitters, or even to bring in a new pitcher when the starting pitcher faded.

Evolution in the Role of the Manager: Baseball in the 1890s was atavistic, meaning that it was evolving backward. After two decades of expanding markets, exciting races, and rapidly increasing incomes, baseball in the 1890s went through a bitter retrenchment. The pennant races were undermined by syndicate ownership arrangements which knifed one team in the back to feed another. Baseball on the field became a crude, violent game dominated as much by intimidation as by skillful play, granting that strategies and "scientific baseball" did continue to evolve through this phase.

This atavism also infected baseball managers. Twenty years earlier, Harry Wright had chosen "baseball manager" as his profession, just as Tony LaRussa and Gene Mauch and Bobby Cox would do in the late twentieth century. The managers of the 1890s were, in the main, *not* professional managers. They were mature players, in their late thirties, who shepherded herds of ruffians from one hotel to the next. None of the prominent managers of the 1890s were still managing in 1910, when almost all of them would have been about fifty years old.

Hanlon and Selee

Ned Hanlon and Frank Selee were exact contemporaries. Hanlon was born in 1857 and managed in the major leagues from 1889 to 1907. Selee was born in 1859 and managed in the major leagues from 1890 to 1905. Teams managed by one of them or the other won the National League pennant every year from 1891 to 1900—five pennants for Hanlon, five for Selee, granting that it is sometimes difficult to figure out who won what in the 1890s. Each man won about 1,300 games as a manager.

Selee's record is significantly better than Hanlon's, or vastly better, depending on how you rank them. By the scoring system I set up for managerial accomplishments (see "Ranking Managers," page 139), Selee ranks as the twelfth greatest manager of all time, Hanlon as the seventeenth. Selee's career winning percentage was .598; Hanlon's was .530. Among managers who managed 1,000 or more major league games, Selee ranks fourth in winning percentage; Hanlon ranks thirty-third.

Selee's teams won 422 games more than they lost (1,284–862); he also ranks fourth all-time in this regard. Hanlon's teams were 149 games over .500 (1,313–1,164); he ranks thirty-first.

Despite this, Hanlon is much more famous than Selee. Hanlon was elected recently to the Hall of Fame; Selee hasn't been, and won't be. Hanlon played for the Detroit Wolverines in the 1880s and became the leader of the Baltimore Orioles in the 1890s.

> We knew that they were good, that legend said they were the greatest team of all time until the 1927 Yankees came along (McGraw said they were better than the Yanks) . . . For three decades sportswriters had been telling and retelling stories about the Old Orioles . . . how they invented the hit-and-run, the sacrifice bunt, the squeeze play, the double steal and other strategic ploys . . . how they developed "inside baseball."
>
> —Bob Creamer, *The Ultimate Baseball Book*

The 1894 Orioles had six Hall of Famers in their everyday lineup—Dan Brouthers, Hughie Jennings, John McGraw, Willie Keeler, Joe Kelley, Wilbert Robinson. They were aggressive to the border of criminality:

> Ned Hanlon's Baltimore Orioles of the 1890s filed their spikes in front of opponents, then used them on them . . . He storm-trooperd the Orioles to three National League championships.
>
> —Charles B. Cleveland,
> *The Great Baseball Managers*

But the 1894 Orioles were not the greatest team before the 1927 Yankees, nor even the greatest team of their own generation. The 1897 Boston Beaneaters were the greatest team of the nineteenth century, and the 1906 Chicago Cubs were the greatest team before the 1927 Yankees.

What those teams have in common is that both teams were built by Frank Selee. Selee's Beaneaters battled Baltimore to a draw in the 1890s. He left Boston after a couple of .500 seasons and was hired to manage the Cubs, who had been floundering since the retirement of Cap Anson several years earlier. They had gone 53–86 in 1901.

Deciding to start at shortstop, Selee invited a dozen shortstops to come to camp with the Cubs in 1902. One of them was Joe Tinker. Later in the summer, Selee purchased the contract of another young shortstop, Johnny Evers, and put him at second base. He had two young catchers, Johnny Kling and Frank Chance. He moved Chance to first base, brought in Three Finger Brown and Ed Reulbach, and edged the team forward to 68–69 in 1902, just 6 games behind Hanlon's men in Brooklyn. They improved to 82–56 in 1903 (11 games *ahead* of Hanlon's team), and 93–60 in 1904 (37 games ahead of Hanlon's last team in Brooklyn).

Early in 1905, however, the Cubs were sold. According to Bob Richardson in *Nineteenth Century Stars* (SABR, 1989), Selee retired at that time because he had developed tuberculosis. Other sources say that the new owner fired Selee because he wanted to bring in his own man. In any case, the magnificent team which Selee had spent three and a half years constructing was handed over to Frank Chance, who would do very well with it, indeed.

Frank Selee is one of my favorite men in baseball history. He was cheated out of the chance to manage his second great team in their greatest years, and the memory of his first great team, in Boston, was obscured by the legends spun by three members of the old Orioles, Wilbert Robinson, Hughie Jennings, and John McGraw, who spent a total of sixty-six years managing in the majors, most of them in New York City. McGraw and Robinson claimed credit for inventing everything except shoe leather, and the simple fact that it wasn't true (many of the things they claimed the old Orioles invented existed before 1890, and others were clearly in use in Boston before they were invented in Baltimore) wasn't going to prevent any sportswriter from making use of a good story.

Selee was a gentleman; Hanlon, a ruffian. Selee's philosophy as a manager was "if I make things pleasant for the players, they reciprocate." He expected his players to be temperate and responsible, and he wouldn't take on players who were not. Nonetheless, while I like Selee a great deal more than Hanlon, Selee has no real legacy in the modern major leagues, while Ned Hanlon is the great-grandfather of most modern major league managers.

All major league managers, essentially, come from one of three families—the Connie Mack family, the Branch Rickey family, and the Ned Hanlon family. The Hanlon family is the largest of the three; most major league managers today can be traced back to Ned Hanlon. Let us take, for example, Lou Piniella.

Lou Piniella was probably most influenced, as a potential manager, by Billy Martin. Billy Martin was unquestionably most influenced by Casey Stengel. Stengel was probably most influenced by John McGraw, and John McGraw was the chief proponent of the legend of the old Orioles in the days of Ned Hanlon.

Stengel never actually *said* that he was most influenced by John McGraw. What Stengel actually said on the subject, in his autobiography *Casey at the Bat*, was this:

> Some ballplayers, when they get a chance at managing will copy another manager. That's a very serious mistake. You can take some of a man's methods, but don't ever think you can imitate him . . . I played (for) John McGraw, and when I started managing, everybody said, "I'll bet he's going to copy McGraw." Well, there's been anywhere from fifteen to fifty men that tried to imitate McGraw and never made it.

But if not McGraw, who else? Stengel came to the majors with Brooklyn in 1912, where he played for Bill Dahlen, who had played for Cap Anson—and Ned Hanlon. Dahlen was replaced by Wilbert Robinson, McGraw's longtime teammate and erstwhile buddy, and the other major source of the legend of the old Orioles; Stengel played for him for four seasons.

After he left McGraw and the Giants, Stengel played for Dave Bancroft, who had been McGraw's shortstop. So anyway you cut it, Stengel, as a manager, is the grandson of Ned Hanlon. Billy Martin is the great-grandson of Ned Hanlon, as a manager, and Lou Piniella is his great-great-grandson.

Or take Tony LaRussa. LaRussa was probably most influenced, as a manager, by his fellow Tampa native, Al Lopez. I don't know that; that's a guess. Anyway, Lopez has said many times that he learned more about baseball from Casey Stengel than from anyone else. Lopez played for Stengel in both Brooklyn and Boston, and managed against him for many years, with some success.

Apart from Stengel, the largest influence on Lopez as a manager was probably the man who brought him to the major leagues in 1930 and managed him his first couple of years: Wilbert Robinson.

But maybe LaRussa *wouldn't* cite Lopez as his number one managerial influence. He might cite his own first major league manager. That would be Ed Lopat—who had his best years in the majors with the Yankees in the early fifties. For Casey Stengel. Or LaRussa might cite Bill Rigney, of whom, I know, he is also very fond. Rigney came to the major leagues in 1946, and played for three years for Mel Ott, who had been more or less adopted, as a seventeen-year-old, by John McGraw.

Rigney later played several years for Leo Durocher. The only major league managers Rigney played for were Ott and Durocher, and he eventually replaced Durocher as manager of the Giants. A December 1955 article in the *Baseball Digest* introduced Bill Rigney, new manager of the Giants, as "part Ottie, park Lip."

Durocher is an interesting case. The largest influence on Durocher, as a manager, was unquestionably Miller Huggins:

> Durocher learned his baseball under Miller Huggins . . . "Huggins liked me," Durocher explained. "He'd talk to me all the time. He said, 'You'll never be a great hitter but you could bat .275 to .280' . . . He said, 'Be smart. Be a "take charge" guy. There is only one place to play, and that's in the majors.' Huggins gave me a notebook and I studied every hitter. Miller used to move his men around, and I took notes. I got an idea of where to play every hitter. I used to sit on the bench next to him and watch him give signals to Artie Fletcher and the other coaches."
>
> —Charles B. Cleveland,
> *The Great Baseball Managers*

So Durocher, as a manager, is the son of Miller Huggins. Miller Huggins came to the majors in 1904, where he played for Joe Kelley. Joe Kelley was the left fielder for the 1894 Baltimore Orioles. After two years, Kelley was replaced as manager—by Ned Hanlon himself. Huggins played two years for Hanlon.

In 1910, Huggins was traded to St. Louis, where he played for Roger Bresnahan. Bresnahan thought John McGraw was God. He had played several years for McGraw; he was McGraw's favorite player.

So Miller Huggins unquestionably goes back to Ned Hanlon, one way or the other. Huggins's best buddy and longtime coach was Art Fletcher—who had played virtually his entire career for John McGraw.

The other major influence on Durocher, as a manager, was Frankie Frisch, who managed the Gashouse Gang in St. Louis. Frisch also liked Durocher, and thought he was a very underrated player. Frisch said that Durocher could get rid of the ball quicker, as a shortstop, than anybody he ever saw. One time Shanty Hogan, a big fat catcher who was said by some to be slower than Ernie Lombardi, hit a ground ball to Durocher. Durocher rushed the throw to first and threw it into the seats. Frisch was livid. "What are you doing?" he yelled at Durocher. "You could autograph the damn ball and still throw out Hogan! The next throw like that will cost you three hundred dollars."

"Three hundred dollars?" asked Durocher. "It ought to be five hundred."

Anyway, Frisch, of course, never played in the minors. Like Mel Ott, he was signed as an amateur and brought straight to the majors by John McGraw, who taught him how to play baseball. So, again, anyway you look at it, Tony LaRussa's lineage goes back to Ned Hanlon. You can do it this way:

Tony LaRussa

◇

Al Lopez

◇

Casey Stengel

◇

John McGraw

◇

Ned Hanlon

Or you can do it this way:

Tony LaRussa

◇

Ed Lopat

◇

Casey Stengel

◇

Wilbert Robinson

◇

Ned Hanlon

Or you can do it this way:

Tony LaRussa

◇

Bill Rigney

◇

Mel Ott

◇

John McGraw

◇

Ned Hanlon

Or you can do it this way:

Tony LaRussa

◇

Bill Rigney

◇

Leo Durocher

◇

Miller Huggins

◇

Ned Hanlon

But almost any way you do it, you're going to wind up with Tony LaRussa as the great-great-grandson of Ned Hanlon. Lou Piniella's fifth cousin.

Let's do Davey Johnson. Dave Johnson was brought to the major leagues in 1965 by Hank Bauer. Bauer, of course, played almost his entire major league career for Casey Stengel, so we can see where that one is going.

Johnson, however, probably wouldn't cite Hank Bauer as the largest influence on him, as a manager. My guess is that he would cite Earl Weaver, who replaced Bauer, and who also had managed Johnson in the minor leagues.

Weaver is hard to classify, because he never played in the majors, and had a peripatetic minor league career in which he played for almost everybody. Worse yet, if asked to cite his largest influence as a manager, Weaver might cite George Kissell, a longtime minor league manager who also never played in the majors.

Weaver, however, grew up in St. Louis and was an obsessive baseball fan at a young age. His father did the dry cleaning for the Gashouse Gang, also for the St. Louis Browns, and Weaver used to get to go into the Cardinals' clubhouse, which was a big thrill for him as a young boy. When asked why he screamed at umpires the way he did, Weaver said that he didn't really know, but his hero as a kid was Leo Durocher, and so when he got a chance to manage, he just kind of acted like Durocher.

So probably the most accurate way to classify Weaver, as a manager, is to describe him as a descendant of Leo Durocher and Frankie Frisch. That, of course, puts you back in the line to Ned Hanlon. Or if it doesn't, consider this line, from Earl Weaver's *It's What You Learn After You Know It All That Counts*:

I got to see over a hundred ball games every year at Sportsman's Park, where both the St. Louis teams played. . . . So throughout my childhood I sat in the stands and studied baseball day after day, second-guessing one of the game's greatest managers, Billy Southworth of the Cardinals.

This is discussing the years when Weaver was a little older, in his teens; Billy Southworth managed the Cardinals from 1940 to 1945.

Southworth had played for John McGraw. Southworth, as I mentioned somewhere else in the book, didn't much like McGraw, and in several ways tried to do things exactly the way McGraw *didn't* do them. But who else did Southworth play for? He played for Hugo Bezdek, a football guy who didn't know anything about baseball, but who was an effective leader, and who taught Southworth to communicate with his players. And he (Southworth) played for Fred Mitchell, a pitcher who had a short and undistinguished major league career in which he played for Frank Selee. And Ned Hanlon.

So Dave Johnson leads back to Ned Hanlon, one way or the other. Don Baylor, of course, was brought to the majors and managed the first half of his career by Earl Weaver. In the minors, Baylor played two years for Joe Altobelli, who had played for Al Lopez; is this beginning to sound familiar?

Felipe Alou, the brilliant manager of the Montreal Expos, was brought to the majors in 1958 by Bill Rigney, whom we've already covered. Rigney was succeeded by Alvin Dark, who had played for Durocher and Billy Southworth.

In 1965, Alou was traded to Milwaukee, where he played for Bobby Bragan, who had played for Durocher. Bragan also played for several other managers. Bragan played, for example, for Hans Lobert—who had played for Hanlon, and also for John McGraw.

I don't know who Mike Hargrove would cite as his biggest influence; he played for everybody. He was brought to the major leagues by Billy Martin, which puts us, at least arguably, back in the Hanlon family.

Another arm of the Hanlon phenomenon for many years was Hughie Jennings, who managed Detroit from 1907 to 1920 and who himself managed many managers. Fred Haney, for example, was influenced by Ty Cobb, who played most of his career for Jennings.

Donie Bush, a significant manager in his own right, played many years for Jennings. Pie Traynor thought highly of Donie Bush.

The Jennings line, however, appears to have largely died out by now, except as a supporting influence. None of Jennings's managerial sons became a *great* manager, although many of them took a shot at it.

Then there was Fielder Jones, another Hanlon disciple who managed the White Sox in 1906, defeating Selee's old Cub team in their finest season. I don't mean to overstate the argument; there are at least two other families of managers which permeate baseball history, the Connie Mack family, and the Branch Rickey family. The Branch Rickey family is formed by the formidable system established by Rickey at Brooklyn in the late 1940s, and which I think constitutes a seminal experience comparable in its impact to the Ned Hanlon/John McGraw group.

The Connie Mack family is smaller and nearly extinct by now, but that's another story. Connie Mack also played for Ned Hanlon, at Pittsburgh (then called Pittsburg) in 1891:

> "Hanlon was one of the really great managers of baseball," said Mack, "and I am proud that I once played under him. He later was fortunate in getting such great—and brainy—players as John McGraw, Hugh Jennings, Joe Kelley, and Willie Keeler; but Hanlon was smart, one of the great generals of baseball. He thought up many of the plays which McGraw, Jennings, and Keeler executed. All three had been around the league for several seasons before Hanlon brought out their full ability."
>
> —Fred Lieb, *Connie Mack*

There's no evidence that Hanlon had tremendous influence on Mack, and I'm not putting Mack in the Hanlon family.

Frank Selee was every bit as smart as Ned Hanlon, and his teams, in their time, were as noted for brains as were Hanlon's, probably more so. For some reason, none of Selee's players became outstanding managers except Frank Chance, and his influence as a manager dissipated quickly.

Johnny Evers was known as the smartest player in baseball, and he managed a couple of years, but he just couldn't stand to sit still on the dugout bench.

Joe Tinker managed for a couple of years, but his wife was not well, and he moved to Florida for her health.

Frank Chance, of course, is in the Hall of Fame, but Chance didn't particularly like Selee, and didn't do anything to spread his reputation.

Bobby Lowe, Selee's second baseman in Boston, managed just part of one season, with no success.

Fred Tenney, Selee's first baseman in Boston, managed for four seasons with the same team, but he had no talent to work with, and his managerial record is among the worst in history.

Chick Stahl, Selee's right fielder in Boston, managed for 18 games and committed suicide.

Jimmy Collins, his third baseman, managed for several years with good success, but did not succeed in fathering any other managers.

Hugh Duffy, Selee's left fielder, managed four major league teams, but with no success.

John Ganzel, another one of his outfielders, managed two major league teams, a year at a time.

Kid Nichols, one of Selee's best pitchers, managed a year and a half, with no success.

Pat Moran, probably Selee's best shot at establishing a royal lineage, drank himself into an early grave.

As a minor league manager, Selee tried to sign Connie Mack, but Mack received two offers simultaneously, and chose the other one.

Without a John McGraw to carry on his reputation, without a Wilbert Robinson, a Miller Huggins, or a Hughie Jennings, there is no Leo Durocher or Frankie Frisch or Casey Stengel in the generation following.

Selee died of tuberculosis in July 1909, in Denver, Colorado. His great shortstop, Herman Long, also died of tuberculosis, also in Denver, just a few months later. Hanlon, who had made good money in baseball and saved it, retired to an estate by the sea, and would outlive John McGraw, Wilbert Robinson, Hughie Jennings, Miller Huggins, and Fielder Jones.

NED HANLON'S
All-Star Team

		G	AB	R	H	2B	3B	HR	RBI	BB	SO	SB	Avg	SPct
C	Wilbert Robinson, '94	109	414	69	146	21	4	1	98	46	18	12	.353	.430
1B	Dan Brouthers, 1894	123	525	137	182	39	23	9	128	67	9	38	.347	.560
2B	DeMontreville, 1898	151	567	93	186	19	2	0	86	52		49	.328	.369
3B	John McGraw, 1894	124	512	156	174	18	14	1	92	1	12	78	.340	.436
SS	Hugh Jennings, 1896	130	521	125	209	27	9	0	121	19	11	70	.401	.488
LF	Joe Kelley, 1895	131	518	148	189	26	19	10	134	77	29	54	.365	.546
CF	Steve Brodie, 1894	129	573	134	210	25	11	3	113	18	8	42	.366	.464
RF	Willie Keeler, 1897	129	564	153	239	27	19	1	74	35		64	.424	.544

		G	IP	W–L	Pct.	H	SO	BB	ERA	GS	CG	ShO	Sv
SP	Bill Hoffer, 1895	41	314	31–6	.838	296	80	124	3.21	38	32	4	0
SP	Joe McGinnity, 1900	44	347	29–9	.763	350	93	113	2.90	41	38	4	2
SP	Tom Hughes, 1899	35	292	28–6	.824	250	99	119	2.68	35	30	3	0
SP	Doc McJames, 1898	45	374	27–15	.643	327	178	113	2.36	42	40	2	0

FRANK SELEE'S
All-Star Team

		G	AB	R	H	2B	3B	HR	RBI	BB	SO	SB	Avg	SPct
C	Johnny Kling, 1903	132	491	67	146	29	13	3	68	22		23	.297	.428
1B	Frank Chance, 1903	125	441	83	144	24	10	2	81	78	6	7	.327	.440
2B	Bobby Lowe, 1894	133	613	158	212	34	11	17	115	50	25	23	.346	.520
3B	Jimmy Collins, 1897	134	529	103	183	28	13	6	132	41	1	4	.346	.482
SS	Herman Long, 1896	120	501	108	172	26	8	6	100	26	16	36	.343	.463
LF	Billy Hamilton, 1896	131	523	152	191	24	9	3	52	110	29	83	.365	.463
CF	Hugh Duffy, 1894	124	539	160	236	50	13	18	145	66	15	49	.438	.679
RF	Tom McCarthy, 1894	127	539	118	188	21	8	13	126	59	17	43	.349	.490

		G	IP	W–L	Pct.	H	SO	BB	ERA	GS	CG	ShO	Sv
SP	John Clarkson, 1891	55	461	33–19	.635	435	141	154	2.79	51	47	3	3
SP	Kid Nichols, 1892	53	454	35–16	.686	404	187	121	2.83	51	50	5	0
SP	Jack Stivetts, 1892	53	415	35–16	.686	346	180	171	3.04	48	45	3	1
SP	Vic Willis, 1899	41	343	27–8	.771	277	120	117	2.50	38	35	5	2

Decade Snapshot: 1900s

Most Successful Managers: 1. Fred Clarke
2. John McGraw
3. Frank Chance

Most Controversial Manager: John McGraw

The key figure in the elimination of the "Rowdy Ball" of the 1890s was Ban Johnson. Johnson was president of the new American League, which made a pledge of clean baseball, and won over the fans by keeping that promise.

McGraw, who was employed in the American League in 1901–1902, resisted Johnson's efforts to clean up the game, and by so doing made himself the spokesman for dirty baseball. He was also the most outspoken opponent of peace between the two leagues, and refused to play the World Series in 1904 because of his dislike for the American Leaguers.

Others of Note: Jimmy Collins
Clark Griffith
Hughie Jennings
Fielder Jones
Nap Lajoie

Typical Manager Was: Fielder Jones. Fielder Jones had played for Ned Hanlon, as did most of the top managers of this time, and was a playing manager, as were 57% of the managers during the decade. There were more playing managers in this decade than in any other since 1880.

Percentage of Playing Managers: 57%

Most Second-Guessed Manager's Move: Baseball in the first decade of this century had many marvelous pennant races and World Series, and hundreds of controversial events. The press in this era was very aggressive, and would crucify a *player* who made a misplay at a critical moment, or who played poorly in a World Series. They did this, for example, to Honus Wagner, who played poorly in the 1903 World Series; to Jack Chesbro, who won 41 games in 1904, but threw a fatal wild pitch on the last day of the season; to nineteen-year-old Fred Merkle, who failed to touch second base in a game on September 23, 1908; and to Harry Coveleski, who was accused of collapsing due to teasing by enemy batters in 1909.

And yet, as I mentioned in an earlier comment, this criticism never seemed to target *managers;* always players. Managers, when attacked, would be attacked because their teams didn't play hard. Typical was this comment by Hooks Wiltse in the New York *American* on August 9, 1908:

Bob Allen

Robert G. (Colonel Bob) Allen was a nineteenth-century shortstop who managed the Cincinnati Reds in 1900.

Allen was the son of a banker, and a childhood friend of Warren G. Harding. A light hitter but a brilliant fielder, Allen played in the National League from 1890 to 1894. Out of the majors a few years, he attracted the attention of Reds owner John T. Brush by managing Indianapolis to the championship of the Western Association.

Allen's managerial season was attended by misfortunes. The Reds' park burned down, and they acquired the rights to a young pitcher named Christy Mathewson, but traded him to New York before he reported.

After leaving Cincinnati Allen purchased the Knoxville team in the Southern Association, which he owned and operated for many years with great success. From Rudy York's letter to his son, in the first *Fireside Book of Baseball*, "Somebody told Colonel Bob Allen in Knoxville about me. This Colonel Allen . . . was known as a smart baseball man . . . But Colonel Allen made a mistake. He released me. If he had held onto me another year, he could have sold me for $50,000 or more."

Allen died in Little Rock in 1943.

Frank Chance's braves are not possessed of the proper spirit, in my estimation. Everything was lovely while the Windy City lads were showing a stern chase to the rest of the company. But when collared the Cubs have proved quite docile.

This is quoted from G. H. Fleming's marvelous book, *The Unforgettable Season.* McGraw *could* have been criticized for putting Merkle into the game to commit his famous boner, but by and large wasn't; the criticism fell on Merkle. The concept of a manager as a chess player still was not common. The manager, up until 1910, was still seen largely as a field leader and instructor, not as a tactical strategist.

Clever Moves: In 1909 the Pittsburgh Pirates won 110 games for Fred Clarke. Their pitching staff included Howie Camnitz (25–6), Vic Willis (22–11), and Lefty Leifield (19–8) as well as a pair of thirty-seven-year-old veterans of the 1903 World Series, Sam Leever (8–1), and Deacon Phillippe (8–3).

Crossing up everybody, Clarke decided to start Babe Adams, a twenty-seven-year-old rookie, in the first game of the World Series. Adams had also pitched brilliantly down the stretch, finishing 12–3, but, because of his inexperience, no one thought he would start in the World Series.

Clarke, however, was listening to National League President John Heydler. Heydler had seen a game in which Dolly Gray, a mediocre pitcher for Washington, had been very effective against the American League champion Detroit Tigers. Heydler thought that Adams's delivery and pitching style was similar to that of Dolly Gray,

Adams stopped the Tigers 4–1 in Game One of the series, came back in Game Five to beat them again (8–4), and, on two days rest, shut them out in Game Seven, vaulting overnight to superstar status.

Evolutions in Strategy: The sacrifice bunt, in use since the 1880s, swept the baseball world shortly after the turn of the century, becoming far more common than it was before, or has been since.

The assumption that the starting pitcher would finish every game began to deteriorate, as Frank Chance, John McGraw, and Clark Griffith began to use their best pitchers to finish out the wins of their second-line pitchers, and McGraw began to experiment with pitchers who were primarily relievers.

The number of pinch hitters used increased enormously.

Dode Criss, in St. Louis, became the first player commonly used as a pinch hitter, as he pinch-hit 147 times between 1908 and 1911. The manager who defined this role for him was Jimmy McAleer.

Evolution in the Role of the Manager: The role of a baseball manager changed tremendously in the first fifteen years of this century. First, the rapid development of in-game strategies such as bunting, pinch hitting, and relief pitching greatly increased the number of game decisions that a manager was required to make.

Second, it was during this period that teams first hired coaches. The hiring of coaching staffs changed the relationship of the manager to his team, forcing the manager to become a kind of chief of staff, as opposed to a hands-on teacher.

Third, press attention to baseball exploded between 1900 and 1915, which forced managers to devote vastly more of their time and attention to the role of press spokesman.

Fourth, an equally rapid growth in the minor leagues changed the way that managers acquired talent and forced managers into a permanent competition to find, evaluate, and acquire the best talent buried in the bush leagues. Since scouts or other emissaries had to be used to accomplish that, this again required managers to spend time and energy organizing the work of other people.

Because of these changes, professional managers, of whom there was only one in the nineteenth century (Harry Wright) suddenly appeared in significant numbers. The average length of time that a manager held his job increased steadily.

FRED CLARKE'S
All-Star Team

		G	AB	R	H	2B	3B	HR	RBI	BB	SO	SB	Avg	SPct
C	George Gibson, 1909	150	510	42	135	25	9	2	52	44		9	.265	.361
1B	K Bransfield, 1901	139	566	92	167	26	16	0	91	29		23	.295	.398
2B	Claude Ritchey, 1899	147	536	65	161	15	7	4	71	49		21	.300	.377
3B	Tommy Leach, 1907	149	547	102	166	19	12	4	43	40		43	.303	.404
SS	Honus Wagner, 1901	140	556	100	196	39	10	6	126	53		48	.353	.491
LF	Fred Clarke, 1897	128	518	120	202	30	13	6	67	45		57	.390	.533
CF	G Beaumont, 1903	141	613	137	209	30	6	7	68	44		23	.341	.444
RF	Owen Wilson, 1912	152	583	80	175	19	36	11	95	35	67	16	.300	.513

		G	IP	W–L	Pct.	H	SO	BB	ERA	GS	CG	ShO	Sv
SP	D Phillippe, 1903	36	289	24–7	.774	269	123	29	2.43	33	31	4	2
SP	Sam Leever, 1903	36	284	25–7	.781	255	90	60	2.06	34	30	7	1
SP	Howie Camnitz, 1909	41	283	25–6	.806	207	133	68	1.62	30	20	5	3
SP	Jack Chesbro, 1902	35	286	28–6	.824	242	136	62	2.17	33	31	8	1

Decade Snapshot: 1910s

Most Successful Managers: 1. John McGraw
                                       2. Connie Mack
                                       3 (tie) Pat Moran
                                                   Bill Carrigan

Most Controversial Manager: Roger Bresnahan
Bresnahan played several years for John McGraw, after which McGraw sold St. Louis owner Stanley Robison on the idea that Bresnahan would be a great player/manager. Most of Bresnahan's managerial career was consumed in one sort of controversy or another. Bresnahan got the St. Louis job in 1909 and was okay for a year or two, but by 1912 Robison had died, and the Cardinals weren't doing a whole lot better. Robison's niece, Lady Bee Britton, inherited the Cardinals.

According to Fred Lieb's *The St. Louis Cardinals*, Bresnahan "was as truculent and as much of a battler with umpires and rival players as was (McGraw) . . . Bresnahan, reared by McGraw in a tough baseball school, wasn't particular about his language. He talked to Lady Bee Britton as he would have talked to Frank DeHaas or Stanley Robison." Lady Bee fired him.

Others of Note: Pants Rowland
                            Jake Stahl
                            George Stallings
                            Joe Tinker

Stunts: The New York Highlanders finished last in the American League in 1908. In 1909 they hired George Stallings to be their manager, and improved by 24½, to 74–77. By late 1910 they had improved another 11 games, to 78–59, to second in the American League.

The Highlanders' first baseman was Hal Chase. Chase went to the team owner, Frank Farrell, and complained about Stallings's management, said that all the players were unhappy with him. Farrell fired Stallings and hired Hal Chase to manage the team.

In two years they were back in last place.

Typical Manager Was: Either a player/manager or a man in his forties who had played for Ned Hanlon in the 1890s. Managers were becoming much more professional.

Percentage of Playing Managers: 44%

Most Second-Guessed Manager's Move: Horace Fogel, owner of the Philadelphia Phillies, was inclined to drink too much and make indiscreet remarks. At the close of the 1912 season Fogel alleged that Roger Bresnahan had rolled over for the New York Giants, not playing his strongest lineup against them. This allowed John McGraw, whom Bresnahan idolized, to win the pennant.

Fogel was banned from baseball for making this remark. A pertinent note: Bresnahan's sixth-place Cardinals had in fact beaten the Giants seven times in 1912, whereas Fogel's Phillies, who finished fifth, beat them only five times. The Cardinals had posted a better record against the Giants than fourth-place Cincinnati, fifth-place Philadelphia, seventh-place Brooklyn, or last-place Boston.

Clever Moves: In September 1915, Whitey Appleton of the Dodgers was pitching against the St. Louis Cardinals. The game was tied in the seventh inning, but the Cardinals had a runner on third and two out.

Cardinal manager Miller Huggins, coaching at third, yelled to Appleton, "Hey, Bub, let me see that ball." The rookie pitcher threw the ball to Huggins, who stepped aside and let the ball roll up the third base line as the winning run dashed home.

It's irrelevant to the present story, but if you ever see a picture of Casey Stengel, there's a prominent scar coming out of his bottom lip and running jaggedly down the left side of his jaw. Whitey Appleton gave that to him. Appleton was Stengel's roommate that summer. One day they went to visit a couple of nice young ladies at their home on Coney Island, had too much to drink, and got into a terrible fight on the way back to their apartment. Appleton got his fingers inside Stengel's cheek and gave a yank, tearing Stengel's face wide open.

Player Rebellions: St. Louis (A), 1917, vs. Fielder Jones.

Evolutions in Strategy: In 1914 George Stallings platooned at all three outfield positions. His team, the Braves, had finished last in the league in 1910, 1911, and 1912, sixth in 1913. They were dead last in late July 1914, but stunned the baseball world by surging to the 1914 National League pennant, then defeating Connie Mack's mighty A's in four straight.

This event had tremendous impact on other managers, almost revolutionary impact, as opposed to evolutionary. Managers had platooned, a little bit here and there, since the 1880s, but it was very rare, the sort of thing that somebody would try once or twice a decade for a few weeks.

From 1915 to 1925, basically all major league teams platooned at one or more positions.

The baseball of 1915–1919 was choking in strategy. Runs were scarce, and every one-run strategy (sacrifice bunts, stolen base attempts, issuing intentional walks, drawing the infield in, etc.) was used with great frequency. Combined with platooning and greatly increased use of pinch

Wilbert Robinson: Living the Good Life

hitters and relief pitchers, this put the game into the hands of managers
in a way that it never had been before.

Evolution in the Role of the Manager: By 1919, major league managers were highly professional. At the start of the 1919 season, not one
of the sixteen major league managers was a player/manager, although two
managers were fired during the season, and in both cases veteran players were assigned to take over the team. Those sixteen managers include
eight Hall of Famers, all of whom were selected to the Hall of Fame largely
for their contributions as managers or executives (Miller Huggins,
Hughie Jennings, Ed Barrow, Clark Griffith, Connie Mack, John McGraw,
Wilbert Robinson, and Branch Rickey.) One of the other eight, Hugo
Bezdek is in the college football Hall of Fame. Five of the remaining seven
(Pat Moran, George Stallings, Fred Mitchell, Lee Fohl, and Kid Gleason)
were successful or highly successful managers, although they are not in
the Hall of Fame.

Of these sixteen managers who began the 1919 season, at least
seven had played for Ned Hanlon, and at least three of the others had
played for some other manager who had played for Ned Hanlon.

The managers of 1915–1920 are as impressive a group as you would
find in any era of baseball history.

JOHN MCGRAW IN A BOX

Year of Birth: 1873

Years Managed: 1899, 1901–1932

Record As a Manager: 2,784–1,959, .587

Managers for Whom He Played: Ned Hanlon, Billy Barnie, Patsy Tebeau.

Characteristics As a Player: Extremely high on-base percentage. Fast, aggressive, fearless. Quick fielder with quick release, arm not outstanding.

McGraw's career on-base percentage, .465, is the third-highest ever among players with 4,000 career at bats, behind only Ted Williams and Babe Ruth. He was a .334 hitter who walked almost once a game.

WHAT HE BROUGHT TO A BALL CLUB

Was He an Intense Manager or More of an Easy-to-Get-Along-With Type? He was very intense. According to Rogers Hornsby in *My War With Baseball*, "If players thought I was mean they should have spent a little time under John McGraw . . . He'd fine players for speaking to somebody on the other team. Or being caught with a cigarette. He'd walk up and down the dugout and yell, 'Wipe those damn smiles off your face.'"

Was He More of an Emotional Leader or a Decision Maker?

He was both. McGraw was a master of detail. Casey Stengel remembered that McGraw would go over the meal tickets at the team hotel, checking to see what his players were eating. If a player wasn't eating right, McGraw would talk to him about it.

According to Hornsby, McGraw had an 11:30 curfew, and somebody would knock on your door every night at exactly 11:30. And you'd better answer.

Was He More of an Optimist or More of a Problem Solver?

One key thing that McGraw brought to a team was *direction* and order. An awful lot of what happens on a baseball team is wasted effort due to chaos and disorder. McGraw was such a powerful figure that he organized the world around him by his mere presence. If John McGraw traded for you, you knew why he had traded for you and what he intended for you to do. If you were a young player, you knew what his plans for you were. The rules were well understood. This put his teams ahead of most of the other teams.

HOW HE USED HIS PERSONNEL

Did He Favor a Set Lineup or a Rotation System? A set lineup, with the exception noted below. McGraw used his bench players *less* than the typical major league manager during his time, but in more well-defined roles.

Did He Like to Platoon? McGraw adopted platooning after it was popularized by George Stallings in 1914, as did almost all of the managers. He was never ahead of the curve on platooning, and was not aggressive in its use, but he did normally platoon at one or two outfield positions for the rest of his career, 1915–1932.

Did He Try to Solve His Problems with Proven Players or with Youngsters Who Still May Have Had Something to Learn? John McGraw lived to teach young men how to play baseball. I mean, he loved the horses, he loved the stage, he loved his cigars, and he loved his whiskey, but teaching young men to play baseball was what he *did*.

Consider this, from *Frankie Frisch: The Fordham Flash*, by J. Roy Stockton:

> McGraw gave me a lot of personal attention . . . He saw to it that I was given a chance to hit during batting practice. He used to play the infield himself and he personally took charge of polishing up my fielding. He would hit grounders for hours. He'd hit them straight at you and he'd hit them to either side . . . McGraw even hit to the infield in the pre-game warm-up. If you didn't make a play the way McGraw wanted it, he'd hit you another, five more, ten more, until the play was made the way he wanted it.

Over the course of his career, he took on many, many young men with no minor league experience or very little minor league experience, and worked with them until they became outstanding players. His list includes Mel Ott, Fred Snodgrass, Fred Merkle, Freddie Lindstrom, Larry Doyle, Ross Youngs, George Kelly, and Travis Jackson.

Johnny Evers

Johnny Evers, the scrappy little leader of the Cubs, was, during the 1913 season, the same bundle of nerves and ginger as of old. He probably carried his aggressiveness even further than he formerly did, because of a healthier and stronger constitution. The Evers who suffered a nervous breakdown in 1911 was not the Evers of 1913. The Trojan declared recently that he did not care much about managing a club from the bench. Said he:

"There is too much fretting about it. I pity men like Clarke and McGraw—this is, if they look at things the way I do when I am not in there working. I would sooner play in a double-header than watch one game from the bench. I tried it once this season. We were playing two games at St. Louis. I did not play in the first game, in which Cheney had a tough battle with Sallee, beating him eventually, 2 to 1. I was all worn out when it was over and made up my mind that there would be no bench managing for mine as long as I was able to kick in and play myself. I played in the second game, and it went 10 innings and proved a much more uncertain battle. But I enjoyed it and pulled through it much better. Watching a game from the bench is tiresome, and I don't know how some of them do it. I believe that Fred Clarke often pines for the days when he was in there himself instead of sitting on the bench and pulling for others."

—*1914 Reach Guide*

Rube Foster's Ox

Rube Foster was the greatest manager in the history of the Negro Leagues, not to mention a leading pitcher, the owner of the American Giants, and the de facto commissioner of Negro baseball. Foster usually had a pipe in his mouth, even when he was in the dugout, and like most pipe smokers, he wasn't going to take the thing out of his mouth to talk to you unless he actually had something to say. When he had a young player who didn't give quite the appropriate effort, Rube would take him aside and tell him this story.

A farmer had a donkey and an ox, which he worked as a team. It was hard work, and one day the ox decided just to stay in his stall all day and eat. When the donkey got back to the barn that night, the ox asked him, "What did the boss say about me?"

"Didn't say nothing," said the donkey.

The ox slept well that night, and when the farmer came out the next morning, the ox again balked at leaving the barn. When the donkey came back that night, he asked again, "What did the boss say?"

"Didn't say nothing," the donkey answered, "but he visited the butcher."

The next morning the ox

He was incredibly tenacious in teaching young players. He thought nothing of taking on a young player, and working with him every day for three years, gradually breaking him into the lineup. Of course, many times these kids didn't pan out. Over the years he had countless young players like Eddie Sicking, Joe Rodriguez, Tillie Schaefer, Andy Cohen, Gene Paulette, and Grover Hartley whom he would work with for a year or two, and then decide that they weren't going to make it.

If he couldn't develop his own player, he wasn't opposed to trading for or purchasing an established player from somebody else; he also did that many times. But most of his stars were homegrown. His first option was always to spot a hole developing two or three years down the road, and start getting some twenty-year-old kid ready to move in there.

How Many Players Did He Make Regulars Who Had Not Been Regulars Before, and Who Were They? Too many to name. In addition to those named above, one could add Bill Terry, Buck Herzog, Art Fletcher, Art Devlin, Chief Meyers, Josh Devore, Jeff Tesreau, Carl Hubbell, and Freddie Fitzsimmons.

Did He Prefer to Go with Good Offensive Players or Did He Like the Glove Men? He wouldn't risk his defense to get a slugger in the lineup, because he never thought he had to.

Like most managers, McGraw was a control freak, and as such perpetually battling against anything that represented a loss of control. If a player doesn't make the plays he is supposed to make, that's a loss of control. He didn't get much out of Hack Wilson, for example, because he was concerned about the stocky Wilson's ability to play the outfield. He rejected a young Earl Webb, a career .306 hitter who holds the major league record for doubles in a season, because he didn't like Webb's defense. He got rid of Rogers Hornsby after one year. He used George Kelly, who had the defensive ability of a middle infielder, as a first baseman. There's a story about Bill Terry (below) which also reflects on this issue.

Did He Like an Offense Based on Power, Speed, or High Averages?

McGraw's teams commonly led the league in batting average—a total of eleven times in his career. Until 1920, McGraw's teams were speed dominated. His 1911 team still holds the major league record for stolen bases, and five of the top ten teams all-time were McGraw's teams.

When the game changed in 1920, however, McGraw understood the change and adapted to it more rapidly than any other established manager.

Did He Use the Entire Roster or Did He Keep People Sitting on the Bench? He kept kids sitting around, waiting to earn playing time, and also he liked to pick up a veteran player who maybe had had an injury or who had gotten out of shape, and just keep him sitting around playing twice a month until he could get him in shape. Jack Scott, for example, was released by Cincinnati in early 1922 and reportedly contacted every major league team, asking for a chance to pitch. McGraw said okay, come work out with us for a while, and we'll see what we can do. By the end of the year he was 8–2, and pitched a shutout in the World Series.

But he also used *specialists* much more than any other manager of his time. He had several players that he used as full-time pinch runners. In 1914, for example, he kept Sandy Piez on the roster all year as a pinch runner. In 1913 he used Claude Cooper in that role, in 1919 he used Lee King, and in 1923 Freddie McGuire. He had Jim Thorpe for several years, and used him to pinch-run, and he would often use one of his young projects as a regular pinch runner.

Most intriguingly of all, one year he had Tony Kaufman. Tony Kaufman was a veteran pitcher, had been in the league for years, but his arm went dead and he was released by St. Louis in 1928. McGraw took him on and used him in 1929 as a pinch runner and defensive replacement in the outfield, just killing time hoping his arm would come back. It never did.

He also used pinch hitters probably more than any other manager of his time, and he absolutely loved to have a pitcher who could also pinch-hit. In 1923 he was thrilled when he was able to purchase Jack Bentley from the great Baltimore minor league team. Bentley had hit .371, .412, and .351 at Baltimore the previous three years, playing everyday at first base, and also filled in on the mound, going 16–3, 12–1, and 13–2 the same three years. McGraw made him mostly a pitcher, and in 1923 he went 13–8 for the Giants, also hitting .427, and leading the National League in pinch hits.

Did He Build His Bench Around Young Players Who Could Step into the Breach If Need Be, or Around Veteran Role-Players Who Had Their Own Functions Within a Game? More of the latter. He always had kids on

was out of his stall early, waiting by the yoke when the farmer appeared.

"You might as well go back to your stall," the farmer told him. "I've already sold you to the butcher."

the bench, but he had a timetable in mind for them, and he wasn't going to rush them in just because somebody got hurt. He liked to keep around two or three players who had been regulars for some other team, like Casey Stengel, Billy Southworth, and Beals Becker, who was a regular in Boston in 1909, and a bench player for McGraw from 1910 to 1912.

GAME MANAGING AND USE OF STRATEGIES

Did He Go for the Big-Inning Offense, or Did He Like to Use the One-Run Strategies? McGraw made very sparing use of the sacrifice bunt after 1908. He used the running game a lot.

Did He Pinch-Hit Much, and If So, When? He pinch-hit more than other managers of his era, at conventional times. He would pinch hit for his pitcher or his number-eight hitter when he was behind in the late innings.

An anecdote in the October 1956 edition of the *Baseball Digest* begins, "Probably the best pinch batter in the history of the major leagues was Harry Elwood (Moose) McCormick of John J. McGraw's fabled Giants." When Macmillan's *Baseball Encyclopedia* was compiled in the late 1960s, we learned that McCormick had a career total of 28 pinch hits. He was, however, a regular pinch hitter for McGraw in 1912 and 1913, at a time when few managers used a regular pinch hitter.

Was There Anything Unusual About His Lineup Selection? It was conventional. In McGraw's time, catchers always hit eighth. McGraw's catcher, Chief Meyers, led his team in hitting in 1911 (.332), 1912 (.358), and 1913 (.312), and McGraw finally relented and moved him to seventh in the order. That was as radical as he got in this area.

One of McGraw's least-known stars was a leadoff man named George Burns, who was the absolute model of a leadoff hitter, hitting .300 several times, leading the league in walks five times, leading the league in stolen bases twice, and leading the league in runs scored five times. McGraw purchased him from Utica, where he was being used as a catcher.

Did He Use the Sac Bunt Often? Early in his career, McGraw's teams bunted a great deal. His 1903 and 1904 teams led the National League in sacrifice hits, with totals of 185 and 166.

About 1909, however, McGraw appears to have changed his opinion of the bunt, and from 1909 on the Giants bunted less often than any other National League team. The Giants were *last* in the league in sacrifice hits in 1909, 1912, 1913, 1915, 1920, 1925, 1926, 1931, and 1932. In almost all the other years, they were near the bottom of the league.

In part, McGraw's teams could dispense with the bunt because they had so much speed. In pre-1920 baseball moving the runners was central to the game, much more so than later. The question wasn't *if* the manager would do something to move the runner; the question was, what would he do? Teams bunted more, stole bases more often, and used the hit-and-run more often. Playing station-to-station baseball just wasn't done. McGraw's teams had outstanding speed, and they probably had fewer bunts simply for that reason.

There is a good deal of discussion about McGraw and the bunt in *The Glory of Their Times*. The thrust of this discussion is that, while the sportswriters perceived John McGraw to be an absolute dictator who determined every detail of strategy, in fact he wasn't; he gave his players a great deal of leeway. The players themselves, at least prior to 1920, would put the hit-and-run on, or the batter would signal to the runner that he intended to bunt, without waiting for a signal from McGraw. McGraw expected them to know how to play baseball, and they did.

Post-1920, McGraw did become more of a dictator.

Did He Like to Use the Running Game? A great deal, yes, particularly before 1920. When the lively ball era arrived, he cut back on his base stealing.

In What Circumstances Would He Issue an Intentional Walk? In 55 World Series games, McGraw's men issued four walks which were certainly intentional, plus a dozen or more other walks which may have been ordered from the bench. Of the four clearly intentional walks, two came in situations which would now be regarded as odd.

Both of the odd intentional walks were issued by a man who hardly ever walked anybody, Christy Mathewson. In Game Two of the 1913 World Series, against Connie Mack's Athletics, Mathewson intentionally walked Amos Strunk to pitch to Jack Barry, with the game scoreless in the fourth inning. Christy Mathewson, afraid to pitch to Amos Strunk? In the fourth inning?

That's odd enough, but the even odder one was in Game Eight of the 1912 World Series, against Boston. In the tenth inning the score was tied 2–2, runners on second and third, one out. Mathewson intentionally walked Duffy Lewis to pitch to Larry Gardner. Gardner hit a sacrifice fly to win the game.

The walk to Lewis set up a force at every base and created the opportunity for Mathewson to get out of the inning with a ground ball. But on the other hand:

a) Gardner had hit .315; Lewis, .284, and

b) Gardner was left-handed; Lewis, right-handed.

With the game on the line, Mathewson intentionally walked a right-handed hitter to get to a left-handed hitter who was also a better hitter.

This event provides good evidence that, prior to 1914, no one was really paying much attention to the platoon differential. Managers were aware of the theory that a left-hander would hit better against a right-hander, had been since the 1870s, but I think at the time it was nothing more than that—a theory.

Did He Hit and Run Very Often? A lot. He expected his players to be able to hit and run.

Were There Any Unique or Idiosyncratic Strategies That He Particularly Favored? Pinch running was unusual in his time; he used pinch runners religiously. He was the first manager to have a pitcher who was used mostly in relief, that being Doc Crandall.

How Did He Change the Game? It's in the details.

McGraw certainly did more to establish the *profession* of managing than anyone else in history. He helped to ease the way for relief pitchers and professional bench players, but really, relief pitching was inevitable, and I doubt that McGraw caused it to develop any sooner than it otherwise would have.

McGraw was the first manager to hire a coach, although that, too, was probably inevitable.

John McGraw was not a great innovator, and in many ways, he was a dinosaur. He was a part owner/operator, a species which wasn't common when he started, and was becoming rare. He personally evaluated young players, personally signed them, and personally taught them to play baseball. This was the exception in 1920, and by 1940, that kind of manager was gone.

But McGraw's legacy is in those hundreds of people that he taught to play baseball, in the tiniest details of what he taught them—where you plant your foot when you pivot on the double play, where you place a bunt under what circumstances, who backs up what base on which play, what you do on the sixth day of spring training, and what the baserunner looks for when he decides whether to break for second or get back to first. McGraw and Connie Mack established orthodoxy in all of these things. He took his job seriously, and he was good at it. He changed it from a young man's job to a job that required the wisdom of a few gray hairs.

HANDLING THE PITCHING STAFF

Did He Like Power Pitchers, or Did He Prefer to Go with the People Who Put the Ball in Play? Control pitchers. He never had any use for a hard-throwing pitcher who didn't throw strikes. Again, McGraw was always afraid of losing. He figured a wild pitcher would lose the game for him.

No John McGraw team ever led the league in walks allowed. Eleven of McGraw's teams led the league in *fewest* walks allowed.

Did He Stay with His Starters, or Go to the Bullpen Quickly? From the beginning of his career to the end, McGraw went to the bullpen more quickly than almost any other manager of his era.

In McGraw's time, a pitcher's stamina was considered a moral quality. I say this in dead earnest, and without a trace of irony. A pitcher who was unable to finish a game was looked down upon, disparaged. He was a "seven-inning pitcher," meaning that he didn't have what it took to pitch when it really counted, when the game was on the line.

When McGraw began managing, almost 90% of starts ended in complete games. By the time he retired, less than 50% of starts were completed—yet the perception that the starting pitcher failed if he could not complete the game was, if anything, even stronger in 1932 than it had been in 1900. Pitchers were taken out when they *lost*, or when they were behind. Or when, God forbid, they "lost their stuff."

Part of the secret of John McGraw is that he saw through that. McGraw understood that the practical consequence of confusing physical stamina with moral courage was that tired pitchers would be on the mound when the game was on the line, when fresh pitchers would be available.

"Saves" did not exist in McGraw's time—not as a statistic,

not as a concept. But when saves were figured retroactively, many years later, McGraw's teams had led the league in saves seventeen times—in 1903, when the Giants led the majors with 8 team saves, in 1908, when they led with 18, in 1921, when they led again with 18. Only in his last few seasons did the league catch up to McGraw in this respect.

This was probably worth at least five games a year to his teams. I don't have statistics to prove this—it hasn't been studied—but I would bet that a typical team in the early 1920s probably blew 20 to 25 leads in the late innings. McGraw's teams probably blew 15 to 20.

Did He Use a Four-Man Rotation? Never for any sustained length of time, except possibly in 1921.

Did He Use the Entire Staff, or Did He Try to Get Five or Six People to Do Most of the Work? Early in his career, McGraw rode his two best pitchers like they were mules. In 1903 Mathewson and McGinnity pitched 800 innings, 63% of the team total. Of course, starting pitchers pitched more innings then than they do now, but even in 1903, few teams got 50% of their innings out of two pitchers, and no one else was close to the innings pitched by Matty and the Iron Man, who were 1–2 in the majors in innings pitched.

But as time passed, this became less and less true. The last McGraw pitcher to lead the league in innings pitched was Mathewson, in 1908. McGraw managed twenty-four years after that. After 1920, few of McGraw's pitchers were even listed among the league leaders in innings pitched.

He became, in this respect, the manager that Casey Stengel emulated—a man who kept lots of pitchers around and used each of them in his own role. In 1924, when McGraw won his last pennant, Virgil Barnes led the team in starts, with 29. He had six pitchers with 16 to 29 starts apiece, and six other pitchers who started one game or a few games. Barnes led the team in innings, with 229; no one else threw more than 188.

McGraw probably went overboard in this respect. One *could* interpret it this way: that as McGraw became more and more arrogant in his later years, he began to see himself as the center of the Giants' team and began to see his pitchers as interchangeable parts. That's an oversimplification, of course, but there probably is an element of truth there. One of the things that Bill Terry did that got the Giants back to first place in 1933 was to give Carl Hubbell enough innings to allow him to dominate the league.

How Long Would He Stay with a Starting Pitcher Who Was Struggling? Not long.

Was There Anything Unique About His Handling of His Pitchers? Several things—his willlingness to use his bullpen, his willingness to use his sixth starter, his fondness for using one pitcher to pinch-hit for another one.

What Was His Strongest Point As a Manager? Organization. Foresight. Vision.

Call it what you will, McGraw had a plan, and he stuck to it. Frank Graham, in *McGraw of the Giants*, tells an innocuous little story about Bill Terry in the spring of 1924. It's not even an anecdote; it's just something Graham remembered and wrote about twenty years later. George Kelly was entrenched as the Giants' first baseman, and Terry was frustrated about sitting on the bench. "Try me in the outfield," said Terry.

McGraw snorted. "You think I want you to get hit on the head and killed?" he asked.

"I played the outfield at Shreveport," said Terry.

"This isn't Shreveport," said McGraw.

Something showed in Terry's face, irritation or despair. "Take it easy," said McGraw. "Stick to first base. You'll be a big-league first baseman some day. Forget about the outfield."

I would suggest that, with almost any other manager, this incident would have ended differently. You've got a talented young hitter here, can't get in the lineup, and he's frustrated. "Let me play the outfield," he says. Almost any manager is going to figure, "Well, why not? We need another bat; if I can use this kid in the outfield, that gives me another option. He wants to play; I don't want him to sit around and get frustrated and get impatient with me. Sure, let him play the outfield."

But McGraw didn't. McGraw had a plan, and he stuck to it. His plan was for Bill Terry to replace George Kelly at first base when the time came, and that's exactly what happened.

If I had been asked to explain John McGraw's success, before I began work on this book, I would have given an answer something like this. McGraw had inherent advantages on the rest of the league. He was in New York, and he had

Hugo Bezdek

Hugo Bezdek managed the Pittsburgh Pirates from 1917 to 1919. Bezdek was the football coach at Penn State for many years, and, as I mentioned, is a member of the College Football Hall of Fame. According to Casey Stengel, who played for Bezdek, Bezdek didn't know much about baseball and didn't claim to, but did a competent enough job of managing by relying on his veteran players. He would ask Vic Saier, who had played with the Cubs, "How did Frank Chance handle that play?" Or he would ask Bill McKechnie, who had played for McGraw, what McGraw would have said about it.

Bezdek knew about conditioning athletes, and he knew a lot about handling men. He'd ask for guidance, and then he'd say, "Okay, this is what we're going to do." He did as well as could be expected with the talent he had.

money behind him. He was part owner of the Giants. He wasn't going to be fired. The Giants could make money, so they could spend money. When he wanted a good young player, he could get him. The Giants had Christy Mathewson before they had McGraw. He was a good manager, but with another team, he was probably just another good manager.

But when you look closely at McGraw's teams, that's really not it. McGraw had Mathewson and Bill Terry and Frankie Frisch, yes, but the other teams had some good players, too. Mathewson was great, but he was no more than the equal of two contemporaries, Walter Johnson and Pete Alexander. Frisch was great, but he wasn't Honus Wagner, either. He wasn't even Eddie Collins. McGraw never had an outfielder like Tris Speaker or Ty Cobb or Babe Ruth, or even Zack Wheat or Harry Heilmann.

McGraw accomplished an awful lot with players like Doc Crandall, Buck Herzog, and Walter Holke. In McGraw's career, there were a few times when he purchased players that his team critically needed, like Art Nehf or Dave Bancroft, and there were times when he bought young players in a bidding war, like Rube Marquard, Benny Kauff, and Jack Bentley. But there were many, many *more* times when he worked out anonymous young kids, liked what he saw, and built them into baseball players.

In McGraw's time the minor leagues were all independant operators, and there was always some hotshot rookie who was being hyped as the greatest thing since gravy. McGraw was generally just not interested in those guys. If you compare the talent going into the system, the Philadelphia Phillies probably acquired more talent in McGraw's time than the Giants did. The Phillies had Pete Alexander, Gavvy Cravath, Fred Luderus, Tom Seaton, Dave Bancroft, Cy Williams, Pinkie Whitney, Lee Meadows, Jimmie Ring. The Boston Red Sox certainly had more star players to work with than the Giants did. What they didn't have was the *depth* in quality players, and the reason they didn't have that is because they didn't build it.

If There Was No Professional Baseball, What Would He Probably Have Done with His Life? McGraw would have been a businessman, a good one. He'd have made a lot of money running a midsize business, a steel mill or a mine or something. He would also have made a good military officer.

JOHN MCGRAW'S
All-Star Team

		G	AB	R	H	2B	3B	HR	RBI	BB	SO	SB	Avg	SPct
C	Chief Meyers, 1912	126	371	60	133	16	5	6	54	47	20	8	.358	.477
1B	Bill Terry, 1930	154	633	138	254	39	15	23	128	57	33	8	.401	.619
2B	Rogers Hornsby, '27	155	568	133	205	32	9	26	125	86	38	9	.361	.586
3B	Fred Lindstrom, '30	148	609	127	231	39	7	22	106	48	33	15	.379	.575
SS	Dave Bancroft, 1921	156	651	117	209	41	5	4	60	79	27	16	.321	.418
LF	Irish Meusel, 1922	154	617	100	204	28	17	16	132	35	33	12	.331	.509
CF	Mike Donlin, 1905	150	606	124	216	31	16	7	80	56		33	.356	.495
RF	Mel Ott, 1929	150	545	138	179	37	2	42	151	113	38	6	.328	.635

		G	IP	W–L	Pct.	H	SO	BB	ERA	GS	CG	ShO	Sv
SP	C. Mathewson, '08	56	391	37–11	.771	285	259	42	1.43	44	34	12	5
SP	Joe McGinnity, 1904	51	408	35–8	.814	307	144	86	1.61	44	38	9	6
SP	Jeff Tesreau, 1914	42	322	26–10	.722	238	189	128	2.38	40	26	8	1
SP	Rube Marquard, '12	43	295	26–11	.703	286	175	80	2.57	38	22	1	1
RA	Ferdie Schupp, 1916	30	140	9–3	.750	79	86	37	0.90	11	8	4	1

Mack's Marks

Connie Mack was a *great* manager. There is a lot of misunderstanding about this, because Mack stayed too long, and in the end he lost more games than he won. He had some great teams, but he had a bunch of terrible teams, too, and I believe that the general impression is that he didn't really do too much that any other manager wouldn't have done if he'd owned the team and been able to manage for fifty years.

If I had a baseball team, and I could hire any manager ever to manage that team, Connie Mack would be on the short list.

John McGraw managed in 1899, then managed from 1901 to 1932. Connie Mack managed in 1894–96, and then managed from 1901 to 1932, and beyond.

John McGraw's record is the best of any manager who ever lived. If you look at Connie Mack's record in the same years, up to 1932, it's not as good as John McGraw's, but it's 90% as good. From 1901 to 1932, Mack

a) won eight pennants,

b) won five World Series,

c) finished over .500 twenty-one times, and

d) was 274 games over .500.

CONNIE MACK IN A BOX

Year of Birth: 1863

Years Managed: 1894–1896, 1901–1950

Record As a Manager: 3,731–3,948, .486

Managers for Whom He Played: Mack played for John Gaffney, Walter Hewett, Ted Sullivan, John Morrill, Arthur Irwin, Jack Rowe, Jay Faatz, Ned Hanlon, Bill McGunnigle, Al Buckenberger, and Tom Burns. Many of these men were large figures in nineteenth-century baseball. Sullivan is believed to have coined the term "fan." Irwin was the first man to put padding in a baseball glove.

Others by Whom He Was Influenced: The strongest influence on Mack was his mother, Mary (McKillop) McGillicuddy. He was also influenced by his first minor league manager, whose name was Tom Reilly. His boyhood hero was Cap Anson.

Characteristics As a Player: Mack was a light-hitting catcher, had a reputation as a smart player, but didn't do anything particularly well as a player.

Mack, tall and very thin, was a catcher. The idea that catchers should be short, squat men does not appear to have developed until about 1910.

WHAT HE BROUGHT TO A BALL CLUB

Was He an Intense Manager or More of an Easy-to-Get-Along-With Type? He was easygoing. He was a gentleman.

Was He More of an Emotional Leader or a Decision Maker? By his own choice, Mack was a decision maker. He was a team architect, a man who made decisions about ballplayers and then attempted to help those men play as well as they could.

At the same time, Mack unquestionably set the emotional tone for his clubhouse, not only because all managers do, but because Mack was so different from most baseball men in his era.

Was He More of an Optimist or More of a Problem Solver? Mack was an optimist. He tried to give every player a full opportunity to work through his difficulties.

HOW HE USED HIS PERSONNEL

Did He Favor a Set Lineup or a Rotation System? A set lineup.

Did He Like to Platoon? I am not aware that Mack ever used a traditional platoon. He did use a kind of platoon at second base for several years, Jimmie Dykes and Max Bishop. Dykes was a regular-at-several-positions, like Frankie Frisch.

Did He Try to Solve His Problems with Proven Players or with Youngsters Who Still May Have Had Something to Learn? He always used youngsters. The only veterans that he brought in, with a few exceptions, were superstars on their last legs, whom he liked to keep around as an influence on the young stars.

How Many Players Did He Make Regulars Who Had Not Been Regulars Before, and Who Were They? Too numerous to mention. The Hall of Famers and near Hall of Famers that he developed include Jimmie Foxx, Mickey Cochrane, Eddie Collins, Eddie Plank, Lefty Grove, Al Simmons, Bob Johnson, Jimmie Dykes, Chief Bender, Jack Coombs, Home Run Baker, Wally Schang, Stuffy McInnis, Bullet Joe Bush, Herb Pennock, Bob Shawkey, Rube Bressler, Eddie Rommell, Wally Moses, Joe Dugan, and George Kell.

Did He Prefer to Go with Good Offensive Players or Did He Like the Glove Men? Mack's best teams had so much talent that he was never forced to try to get extra offense at a position by skimping on defense. There were several times in his career when he did use marginal defensive players in the infield to get their bats in the order—for example, Home Run Baker was not a great defensive third baseman, Maxie Bishop was not much of a second baseman, and in 1933 Mack's shortstop was Dib Williams, a good hitter (.289 with 11 homers, 73 RBI), but a very erratic fielder. Later, Mack tried unsuccessfully to use Jimmie Foxx as a third baseman or a catcher, and to use Bob Johnson, a slugging outfielder, at second base.

In the middle of that record is a ten-year abscess (1915–1924), which is completely attributable to Mack's inability to pay competitive salaries.

McGraw, in the same period, won ten pennants and three World Series, and was over .500 twenty-seven times. If you leave out the ten-year dead spot attributable to the lack of money, Mack's record is a lot *better* than John McGraw's.

After 1932 Mack had to sell off his players again, and by the time that drought was over, Connie was old and out of touch with the game, so his career ends with eighteen years of miserable baseball, a weighty anchor which sinks his career record. You can talk about that if you want to, but my point is that the Connie Mack who was good was very good indeed.

What made him good? Three things, one of which is so obvious we can dismiss it quickly. Like John McGraw, Mack had a staggering command of the details of the game.

The two other things:

1) From 1900 to 1930, the manager's job began with bringing talent into the system. I've written about it other places, but the manager was responsible for signing young players, and

for making trades. Mack didn't make many trades, although he did bring in a few key players that way.

Because the manager had to bring in young players, he had to network, to use the 1990s term, with the entire baseball world. Whenever there was a young man who might be good anywhere in the baseball world, the manager needed to hear about him, and he had to make a decision about him, and if he was really good then he had to acquire him.

Connie Mack was better at that game than anybody else in the world. People liked Mack, respected him, and trusted him, and there were times when Mack got players for that reason. Mack answered every letter and listened patiently to every sales job, and there were times when he got players for that reason.

And he knew a young ballplayer when he saw one. Mack personally scouted Mickey Cochrane. He was so impressed, he purchased the team which owned Cochrane's contract, just to get Cochrane. He personally scouted Al Simmons, overlooked his odd batting stance, and acquired his contract. This wasn't all that easy. Mack was in his sixties by the time he saw those two

Did He Like an Offense Based on Power, Speed, or High Averages? He used a structured offense—leadoff men with very high on-base percentages, middle-of-the-order men with power. Thirteen of Mack's teams led the league in home runs, whereas only nine of them led in batting average, and only two in stolen bases.

Did He Use the Entire Roster or Did He Keep People Sitting on the Bench? He used his bench little, with the exception of a couple of bench players who became quasi-regulars.

Did He Build His Bench Around Young Players Who Could Step into the Breach If Need Be, or Around Veteran Role-Players Who Had Their Own Functions Within a Game? Mack's handling of Jimmie Foxx was exactly the same as John McGraw's handling of Mel Ott. He took on Foxx as a seventeen-year-old kid and worked with him for four years until Foxx was ready to be a regular. His handling of Eddie Collins is similar to McGraw's development of Frankie Frisch. But as a generalization, John McGraw liked to take on young kids and develop them slowly. Mack took on players two or three years older, often college men, and slapped them straight into the lineup.

Mack's bench was generally composed of older players, often minor league veterans, whose basic function was to protect him from injuries and to pinch-hit. He was much less creative in the use of his bench than was John McGraw.

GAME MANAGING AND USE OF STRATEGIES

Did He Go for the Big-Inning Offense, or Did He Like to Use the One-Run Strategies? He was a big-inning manager.

Did He Pinch-Hit Much, and If So, When? Not much, and conventionally. He would use his fourth and fifth outfielders to pinch-hit for his pitcher when he was behind in the late innings.

Was There Anything Unusual About His Lineup Selection? For years he used Eddie Collins, who had leadoff-hitter type–skills, as a number-three hitter. Also, it was Mack who broke the convention of hitting the catcher eighth. Of course, he had Mickey Cochrane, who was the best-hitting catcher since Buck Ewing, so I would assume that almost any manager would have done the same.

Did He Use the Sac Bunt Often? Very little.

Did He Like to Use the Running Game? Very little. He had some good individual base stealers, but only two of Mack's teams ever led the league in stolen bases, and one of those was in 1950, when Mack's lieutenants were in complete charge of the team.

In What Circumstances Would He Issue an Intentional Walk? In 43 World Series games, Mack issued only two intentional walks, both in conventional circumstances—late innings, score tied. The two intentional walks were in 1914, Game Three, and 1930, Game Six.

Did He Hit and Run Very Often? Not much.

Were There Any Unique or Idiosyncratic Strategies That He Particularly Favored? His handling of his starting pitchers in World Series games was very odd, and is essentially inexplicable. In 1910 he used only two pitchers, Jack Coombs and Chief Bender, not using his veteran superstar Eddie Plank (16–10) or anyone else. In 1911 Plank went 22–8—and still pitched very little in the World Series. Again, he used only three pitchers in the series.

In 1913 he had five starting pitchers who won 14 games or more, yet he again used only three pitchers in the World Series.

In 1929 he didn't start the best pitcher in baseball, Lefty Grove, instead starting Howard Ehmke in Games One and Five, George Earnshaw in Game Two and again in Game Three, and forty-five-year-old Jack Quinn in Game Four. Grove pitched relief.

In the main, Mack was a straightforward strategic manager. He did not believe that baseball revolved around managerial strategy.

How Did He Change the Game? Mack was one of the first managers to work hard on repositioning his fielders, shifting to one side if he didn't feel this batter could pull this pitcher, telling the third baseman to guard the lines/not guard the lines, etc.

young players, and his team didn't have too many days off. But when he had a day off, he got out and saw a game somewhere.

2) Better than any other manager, Mack understood and promoted intelligence as an element of excellence.

Mack looked for seven things in a young player: physical ability, intelligence, courage, disposition, will power, general alertness, and personal habits. He knew that if he got men who had these qualities, everything else would fall into place.

This is an oversimplification, but John McGraw wanted empty vessels, into which he could instill his own concept of how baseball was to be played. If a player was intelligent, in McGraw's world, that was great; that meant that he could soak up McGraw's teachings more rapidly.

Connie Mack also wanted intelligent players. Mack wanted young people who would learn from experience, and who would learn from each other. He preferred educated players. He preferred self-directed, self-disciplined, self-motivated players. He preferred gentlemen.

Not that everybody on Mack's teams was Eddie Collins or Sam Chapman, but that was what he was looking for. Yes, he had Ty Cobb, who was certainly not a gentleman, but Ty Cobb

a) was extremely bright,

b) worked extremely hard, and

c) knew as much about playing baseball as anybody in the world.

Yes, he had the manchild Rube Waddell, and he had Lefty Grove, who was a hothead, but there just was something he couldn't resist about a left-hander with a 100-MPH fastball. He had Jimmie Foxx, who was a big bumpkin, but Jimmie Foxx could hit a fastball 500 feet. Mack wasn't stupid; he knew that you couldn't overlook those things.

But he also knew that he would get more out of those guys if he surrounded them with intelligent players than if he surrounded them with dull-witted men who were just burrowing through their careers.

There is an element of elitism in this. Although Mack and McGraw were products of essentially the same cultural background, McGraw would eagerly have signed black players, had he been able to. Mack might not have.

But at the same time, it wasn't all about winning. Winning was the end product of doing the right things.

Like McGraw, Mack was something of an anomaly in his own time and did not have the broad, sweeping impact of a Branch Rickey or a Harry Wright. His greatest impact was in establishing orthodoxy in how the game was played.

An odd thought—Mack *would* have had greater impact on succeeding generations, if college baseball had achieved greater popularity in the 1920s and 1930s. Mack liked college players, and for that reason many of his players became college coaches. Jack Coombs, Mack's best pitcher in 1910–1911, became a college coach, and wrote the most popular "How-to-Play-Baseball" type of book published between 1900 and 1940. Andy Coakley, a twenty-game winner for Mack in 1905, was the longtime coach at Columbia, where he coached Lou Gehrig. Dick Siebert, who played for Connie Mack from 1938 to 1945, also wrote the most popular How-to-Play-Baseball type of book in his era.

HANDLING THE PITCHING STAFF

Did He Like Power Pitchers, or Did He Prefer to Go with the People Who Put the Ball in Play? His best pitchers had exceptional fast balls. Rube Waddell, Jack Coombs, Lefty Grove, Bullet Joe Bush—these were among the hardest throwers of their time. George Earnshaw was a hard thrower.

On the other hand, he had Eddie Rommel, a knuckleball pitcher, and Eddie Plank, whose strongest points were control and composure.

Did He Stay with His Starters, or Go to the Bullpen Quickly? He was more inclined to stay with the starter. He got as far as using his top starting pitchers to finish out the wins of the other starters. Mack did that, as most managers did, in the years 1925–1940. He never really got beyond that.

Did He Use a Four-Man Rotation? Probably for some portions of a season, but never for a full season. The A's didn't really go to a four-man rotation until after he retired.

Did He Use the Entire Staff, or Did He Try to Get Five or Six People to Do Most of the Work? He got as much as he could out of his top pitchers.

How Long Would He Stay with a Starting Pitcher Who Was Struggling? In a crucial game, not long at all. Early in the season, a long way.

What Was His Strongest Point As a Manager? See "Mack's Marks," page 60.

If There Was No Professional Baseball, What Would He Probably Have Done with His Life? He would have become manager of the shoe factory in Brookfield, Massachusettes, where he worked as a youth.

If Howard Ehmke had gone to John McGraw and asked for a chance to pitch in the 1929 World Series, McGraw would have said no, because McGraw was obsessively afraid of losing. He would have seen the idea of pitching Ehmke as being a chance to lose a game by not using his best pitcher. Mack wasn't afraid of losing.

McGraw's philosophy was, you have to control every element of the player's world and get rid of everything in there that might cause you to lose a game. Mack's philosophy was, you get good people, you treat them well, and you'll win. McGraw's approach was and is much more common among managers and coaches in all sports. But Mack won just as often, and his approach has another advantage.

If you do it Connie Mack's way, you won't drink yourself into an early grave.

CONNIE MACK'S
All-Star Team

		G	AB	R	H	2B	3B	HR	RBI	BB	SO	SB	Avg	SPct
C	Mickey Cochrane, '32	139	518	118	152	35	4	23	112	100	22	0	.293	.510
1B	Jimmie Foxx, 1932	154	585	151	213	33	9	58	169	116	96	3	.364	.749
2B	Nap Lajoie, 1901	131	543	145	229	48	13	14	125	24		27	.422	.635
3B	Home Run Baker, '12	149	577	118	200	40	21	10	130	50		40	.347	.541
SS	Eddie Joost, 1949	144	525	128	138	25	3	23	81	149	80	2	.263	.453
LF	Wally Moses, 1937	154	649	113	208	48	13	25	86	54	38	9	.320	.550
CF	Al Simmons, 1930	138	554	152	211	41	16	36	165	39	34	9	.381	.708
RF	Bob Johnson, 1938	152	563	114	176	27	9	30	113	87	73	9	.313	.552

		G	IP	W–L	Pct.	H	SO	BB	ERA	GS	CG	ShO	Sv
SP	Jack Coombs, 1910	45	353	31–9	.775	248	224	115	1.30	38	35	13	2
SP	Lefty Grove, 1931	41	289	31–4	.886	249	175	62	2.05	30	27	4	5
SP	Rube Waddell, 1905	46	329	26–11	.703	231	287	90	1.48	34	27	7	4
SP	Eddie Plank, 1912	37	260	26–6	.813	234	110	83	2.21	30	24	3	2
RA	Joe Berry, 1944	53	111	10–8	.556	78	44	23	1.94	0	0	0	12

Decade Snapshot: 1920s

Most Successful Managers: 1. Miller Huggins
2. John McGraw
3. Bill McKechnie

Most Controversial Manager: Rogers Hornsby

Others of Note: Donie Bush
Bucky Harris
Wilbert Robinson
Tris Speaker

Stunts: Judge Emil Fuchs was the owner of the Boston Braves in the late 1920s. He had once been a night magistrate in New York City, and had been the biggest investor in a syndicate formed around Christy Mathewson. When Mathewson died, Fuchs took over as the acting partner.

In 1929 Fuchs, who had never played baseball well enough to talk about, named himself to manage the team. Amazingly, the perennial losers started out 10–2. "Why don't you quit now?" asked a reporter. "You're leading the league."

"I will," said Fuchs. "I want to hire a new manager on this next road trip." He offered the job to Rabbit Maranville, but Maranville, who had managed the Brooklyn Dodgers several years earlier and had gotten released as a player for his troubles, didn't want to have anything to do with it, so Fuchs continued to sit in the manager's chair.

As a practical matter, Johnny Evers ran the team that summer. Fuchs held the title of manager, but Evers made out the lineups, and made essentially all of the in-game decisions. They finished with 98 losses.

As a consequence of this and other fiascos, the leagues eventually passed a bylaw prohibiting owners from managing their teams.

Typical Manager Was: A second- or third-generation Ned Hanlon disciple with a baritone voice and the volume cranked permanently on high.

Percentage of Playing Managers: 24%

Most Second-Guessed Manager's Move: 1925, Bucky Harris left Walter Johnson in the seventh game of the World Series to fritter away leads of 4–0, 6–3, and 7–6, ultimately losing 9–7. American League president Ban Johnson joined in the witch hunt, sending Harris a telegram denouncing the committment to Walter as "sentimental," and adding that "sentiment has no place in a World Series."

Clever Moves: 1924, Bucky Harris started Curly Ogden in Game Seven of the 1924 World Series (see "Beard," page 81).

Bloodlines

Connie Mack and John McGraw were both the sons of Irish immigrants.

Both were close friends of George M. Cohan, who could be described as the Mike Nichols of his era. Cohan started as a songwriter, and grew to be the biggest fish on Broadway. Cohan and Mack were childhood friends in Brookfield, Massachusettes. Cohan and McGraw were both members of the Lambs, a theatrical men's club.

Mack married Margaret Hogan on November 2, 1887; she died in 1893, and he remarried in 1910. McGraw married Minnie Doyle on February 3, 1897; she died in 1899, and he remarried in 1902.

1929, Connie Mack started Howard Ehmke in Game One of the World Series

Player Rebellions: 1926, Pittsburgh; see "The Clarke Affaire." page 83.

Evolutions in Strategy: Babe Ruth changed everything. The number of runs scored per game in the major leagues increased from 3.59 in 1917 to 5.19 in 1929, while the number of home runs per game quadrupled. Sacrifice bunts per game dropped precipitously (we don't know exactly how much because of a wrinkle in the record-keeping), and stolen bases per game decreased by about 50%.

Platooning, common in the first half of the 1920s, faded away in the second half. While complete games continued to decline, experiments with full-time relievers essentially ended after Firpo Marberry in 1925. Every pitcher in the late 1920s was a starter/reliever.

Evolution in the Role of the Manager: Until 1920, a major league manager was expected to find young players and bring them into the organization. Established managers built up networks of friends, associates, coaches, minor league managers, writers, and traveling salesmen who assisted them in finding prospects, very much like a real estate agent in the modern world. It was a personality business. In some ways, the pre-1920 manager was like a college coach today, scouring the country for prospects, except of course that the manager held the cards, and wasn't really expected to kiss some eighteen-year-old kid's ass to get him to come play for him.

When a manager heard about a young player who intrigued him, he might send a scout out to take a look, or he might send the kid train fare to come to the city and work out before a game. The great strength of Connie Mack and John McGraw is that they were better at this business than anyone else was. Connie Mack got Jimmie Foxx, for example, because one of his old players (Home Run Baker) was playing with Foxx on a local team and sent Connie excited telegraphs telling him what this kid could do. Connie said bring him by; I'll sign him on your say-so.

John McGraw got Frankie Frisch in a similar way; one of his old players was Frisch's college coach, at Fordham.

Between 1920 and 1935, with the development of farm systems, the responsibility for finding young players shifted away from the manager, and to the front office, the general manager, and the scouts who assisted him. This transfer of responsibility is the most fundamental shift in the role of the manager in the history of baseball.

MILLER HUGGINS'S
All-Star Team

		G	AB	R	H	2B	3B	HR	RBI	BB	SO	SB	Avg	SPct
C	Wally Schang, 1921	134	424	77	134	30	5	6	55	78	35	7	.316	.453
1B	Lou Gehrig, 1927	155	584	149	218	52	18	47	175	109	84	10	.373	.765
2B	Tony Lazzeri, 1929	147	545	101	193	37	11	18	106	69	45	9	.354	.561
3B	Joe Dugan, 1924	148	610	105	184	31	7	3	56	31	32	1	.302	.390
SS	Rogers Hornsby, '17	145	523	86	171	24	17	8	66	45	34	17	.327	.484
LF	Bob Meusel, 1921	149	598	104	190	40	16	24	135	34	88	17	.318	.559
CF	Earle Combs, 1927	152	648	137	231	36	23	6	64	62	31	15	.356	.511
RF	Babe Ruth, 1921	152	540	177	204	44	16	59	171	144	81	17	.378	.846

		G	IP	W–L	Pct.	H	SO	BB	ERA	GS	CG	ShO	Sv
SP	Bill Doak, 1914	36	256	19–6	.760	183	118	87	1.72	33	16	7	1
SP	Waite Hoyt, 1927	36	256	22–7	.759	242	86	54	2.64	32	23	3	1
SP	Carl Mays, 1921	49	337	27–9	.750	332	70	76	3.04	38	30	1	7
SP	Joe Bush, 1922	39	255	26–7	.788	240	92	85	3.32	30	20	0	3
RA	Wilcy Moore, 1927	50	213	19–7	.731	185	75	59	2.28	12	6	1	13

WILBERT ROBINSON'S
All-Star Team

		G	AB	R	H	2B	3B	HR	RBI	BB	SO	SB	Avg	SPct
C	Al Lopez, 1930	128	421	60	130	20	4	6	57	33	35	3	.309	.418
1B	Jack Fournier, 1925	145	545	99	191	21	16	22	130	86	39	4	.350	.569
2B	Milt Stock, 1925	146	615	98	202	28	9	1	62	38	29	8	.328	.408
3B	Jimmy Johnston, '21	152	624	104	203	41	14	5	56	45	26	28	.325	.460
SS	Glenn Wright, 1930	139	532	83	171	28	12	22	126	32	70	2	.321	.543
LF	Zack Wheat, 1924	141	566	92	212	41	8	14	97	49	18	3	.375	.549
CF	Johnny Frederick, '29	148	629	127	206	52	6	24	75	39	34	6	.328	.545
RF	Babe Herman, 1930	153	614	143	241	48	11	35	130	68	56	18	.393	.678

		G	IP	W–L	Pct.	H	SO	BB	ERA	GS	CG	ShO	Sv
SP	Dazzy Vance, 1924	35	309	28–6	.824	238	262	77	2.16	34	30	3	0
SP	Burle Grimes, 1920	40	304	23–11	.676	271	131	67	2.22	33	25	5	2
SP	Jeff Pfeffer, 1916	41	329	25–11	.694	274	128	63	1.91	37	30	6	1
SP	Dutch Ruether, 1922	35	267	21–12	.636	290	89	92	3.54	35	26	2	0
RA	Jack Quinn, 1931	39	64	5–4	.556	65	25	24	2.66	1	0	0	15

Bill McKechnie

Bill McKechnie hit .134 in 44 games for the New York Yankees in 1913, but something good happened to him. Frank Chance took a liking to him and had him sit next to him on the bench when he played. Fred Lieb, covering the team for the New York *Press*, asked Chance why he was so fond of a .134 hitter.

"Because he's the only son-of-a-sea-cook on this club who knows what it's all about," Chance said, at least if you believe Lieb's story. "Among this bunch of meatheads, his brain shines like a gold mine."

Despite the endorsement, a few days later McKechnie was playing second base on a muddy field in a rainstorm. The ball skidded into shallow right field, where McKechnie lost it in a large puddle of muddy water, allowing a runner to score from first. Chance was incensed, accused McKechnie of loafing, fined him, and sold him to a minor league team. McKechnie always remembered how unfair that was, as a manager, and always reminded himself to hear the player's side before he took any action.

McKechnie got a chance to manage in the Federal League in 1915, when he was only twenty-eight years old, and apparently decided then that he wanted to manage. He retired as a player after a pretty good 1918 season and went to work in a factory in Ohio. The Pirates were left weak at third base. Barney Dreyfuss, owner of the Pirates, contacted McKechnie and asked him to return to the team in 1920. McKechnie agreed to return as a player/coach, under George Gibson; there may have been a tacit understanding that he would get the next chance to manage the team. He did, anyway, becoming manager of the Pirates after a year back in the minors.

He inherited a very good team and kept them in contention from 1922 through 1924. In 1925 they won the National League by 9 games, ending John McGraw's four-year hold on the championship. In 1926, however, the team was ripped apart by infighting over Fred Clarke (see "The Clarke Affaire," page 83), which made McKechnie's position untenable. He was fired after that season, coached with the Cardinals in 1927, and was hired to manage St. Louis in 1928.

And he won the pennant in St. Louis.

And he was fired again.

This is among the truly strange events in baseball history, but apparently St. Louis owner Sam Breadon and Branch Rickey had a difference of opinion as to who should manage the Cardinals, and McKechnie became a Ping-Pong ball between the two of them. After the 1928 season, in which the Cardinals won the pennant but lost the World Series, Breadon fired McKechnie, and gave the Cardinals' job to Billy Southworth, who had been managing the Cardinals' top minor league franchise at Rochester.

Breadon asked McKechnie to accept the Rochester job and, surprisingly enough, McKechnie accepted. Southworth wasn't yet ready to manage in the majors, and by midseason (1929) McKechnie was back in control.

After the season, though, McKechnie was anxious to get out of that zoo, and he accepted a five-year contract to manage the Boston Braves. The Braves had lost 98 games in 1929, under owner/manager Emil Fuchs, and had been an awful team for ten years, but Fuchs promised to provide a blank check to buy young players to build the team up.

The blank check disappeared in a matter of weeks, but McKechnie stayed the five years and beyond, managing the Braves until 1937. He never won them the pennant, but his record there is much better than anyone else who managed the team between the wars. In 1937 the Braves started out 21–36, rallied to finish 79–73, and McKechnie won *The Sporting News* Major League Manager of the Year Award.

McKechnie was a hot property then; at least three teams contacted the Braves, asking permission to talk to their manager. The Braves by this time were under new management, and the new management said they would not stand in McKechnie's way. He accepted an offer from the Cincinnati Reds for $25,000 a year, plus an attendance bonus, a substantially better salary than he had been making in Boston.

McKechnie took the Reds from last to first in two years, winning the National League title in 1939 and repeating in 1940. For many years McKechnie was the only man to win pennants with three different teams, although he was eventually joined by Dick Williams and Billy Martin. McKechnie stayed in Cincinnati until 1946, the last six seasons of which were a kind of death march.

McKechnie was a coach with the Cleveland Indians in 1948, reportedly the highest paid coach in baseball history at that time. He retired from baseball following the 1950 season.

Fundamentals

Joe McCarthy's first major league team, the 1926 Chicago Cubs, was also the first team in major league history to have more double plays than errors.

When organized baseball began, fielders wore no gloves, and defensive play favored the erratic, an average team committed about six errors per game and turned about one double play for each two games—a ratio worse than ten to one.

This flattened out gradually over the years, as double plays became more common, and errors less. By 1900 a normal ratio was between 3–1 and 4–1. By 1920 teams were down to about one and a half errors per game, and double play totals were in excess of a hundred a year.

Still, in order to cross over (to have more double plays than errors), McCarthy's men in 1926 had to lead the league in both categories, and by solid margins. No other team in the National League that year turned more than 161 double plays, or committed less than 183 errors. The American League champion Yankees, the Ruth/Gehrig Yankees of 1926, had barely half as many double plays (117) as

☞

BILL MCKECHNIE IN A BOX

Year of Birth: 1886

Years Managed: 1915, 1922–1926, 1928–1946

Record As a Manager: 1,896–1,723, .524

Managers for Whom He Played: John McGraw, Frank Chance, George Stallings, Fred Clarke, Bill Phillips, Christy Mathewson, Hugo Bezdek, George Gibson.

Others by Whom He Was Influenced: Despite playing for almost all of the great managers of his time, McKechnie once said that he learned more from Honus Wagner than from anyone else. He played the infield beside Wagner for three years; Wagner was always telling where he should play each hitter and why.

Another influence was Joe Cantillon, for whom he played at Minneapolis in 1921.

The 1918 Pirates were a fourth-place team, but had three of the greatest managers of all time on their roster—McKechnie, Casey Stengel, and Billy Southworth.

Characteristics As a Player: McKechnie was a good defensive third baseman who ran fairly well, but hit more like a shortstop or second baseman, at which positions he also filled in.

WHAT HE BROUGHT TO A BALL CLUB

Was He an Intense Manager or More of an Easy-to-Get-Along-With Type? He was very easy to get along with. Edwin Pope wrote that McKechnie was "more nurse than Boss." He liked to say, "You'll catch more flies with honey than you will with vinegar."

Was He More of an Emotional Leader or a Decision Maker? He was a decision maker; he specifically didn't believe in rah-rah do-it-for-the-team type of stuff. This was what got him fired a lot. Front offices in McKechnie's era, accustomed to John McGraw–style in-your-face managers, thought that McKechnie was too flat emotionally, and too easy on the players. McKechnie said, "The average ballplayer plays for himself. He isn't hustling for the manager or the owner, but for his own contract, his family, his future."

Was He More of an Optimist or More of a Problem Solver? He was an optimist. He would stick with a player as long as he reasonably could, rather than make a change.

Once, when Johnny Vander Meer was struggling and had walked a couple of hitters, McKechnie walked to the mound and said, "John, just remember one thing. These guys are a lot more afraid of you than you are of them."

HOW HE USED HIS PERSONNEL

Did He Favor a Set Lineup or a Rotation System? Except for platooning and switching catchers, he used a set lineup.

Did He Like to Platoon? He did, yes; McKechnie was one of the few managers who continued to platoon through the 1930s, when platooning was out of fashion. One of his favorite sayings was, "If you take care of the percentages, the percentages will take care of you."

Did He Try to Solve His Problems with Proven Players or with Youngsters Who Still May Have Had Something to Learn? If it was an actual problem—something that needed to be fixed right now—he almost always used a veteran. But when he had a young player with ability, he would give him every chance to play. His record of young players developed is quite impressive.

How Many Players Did He Make Regulars Who Had Not Been Regulars Before, and Who Were They? Among others, Pie Traynor, Kiki Cuyler, Remy Kremer, Paul Waner, Glenn Wright, Chick Hafey, Wally Berger, Elbie Fletcher, Vince DiMaggio, Lou Fette, Jim Turner, Frank McCormick, Harry Craft, Mike McCormick, Debs Garms, Johnny Vander Meer, Eddie Joost, Elmer Riddle, Joe Beggs, Grady Hatton, Frankie Baumholtz, Ewell Blackwell, and at least four people named "Moore."

In his own words, McKechnie looked for three things in a young player:

1. Can he run?
2. Can he throw?
3. Can he swing?

errors (210). The Cubs' ratio was 174–162.

In modern baseball, most (but not all) teams have more double plays than errors.

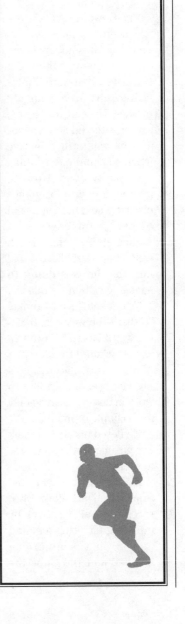

Ehmke

The most brilliant managerial stratagem in the history of baseball occurred in 1929, when Connie Mack named Howard Ehmke to start the first game of the 1929 World Series.

The Howard Ehmke story has been told hundreds of times, and it is not my intention to repeat it here. In broad detail, Howard Ehmke was a thirty-five-year-old pitcher. He had had a fine career, with 166 career wins, and he was still effective when he could pitch, which was hardly ever. After he pitched a couple of games his arm would hurt, and he'd be out for three weeks. In August 1929, Connie Mack called Ehmke aside, and told him that he was going to have to give him his release.

"Mr. Mack," said Ehmke. "If that's the way it is, that's the way it has to be. But I've always wanted to pitch in a World Series, and if this is my last season, I'd like to work in this one, maybe only for a couple of innings."

He flexed his arm. "I think I've got one more good game in there."

Mack thought about it, and finally he said okay. Both races were all but over by mid-August; the A's had locked up the American League, and the Cubs the

"Swing" did not mean "hit." He figured if the player had a good swing, he would eventually hit.

Did He Prefer to Go with Good Offensive Players or Did He Like the Glove Men? Glove men, all the way, and this is the easiest answer in the book.

Almost his entire career, McKechnie used shortstops at second base. If a player was a good first baseman but a marginal outfielder, he played first base. If he had a player who could hit but couldn't play the field, he wouldn't play him. He was almost certainly the most extreme and consistent manager in baseball history in preferring defensive players over offensive players.

When McKechnie took over in Pittsburgh, Pie Traynor was playing shortstop and third base. McKechnie immediately made him a full-time third baseman. When the Pirates purchased Glenn Wright, who had a tremendous arm, McKechnie moved his shortstop, Rabbit Maranville, to second.

A year later (1925) the Pirates traded for George Grantham, a career .302 hitter with speed and some power, who had been playing second base for the Cubs. Grantham was an awful second baseman, but McKechnie moved him to first, where he platooned with Stuffy McInnis, one of the best defensive first basemen of all time. In the outfield the Pirates had two Hall of Fame center fielders, Max Carey and Kiki Cuyler, and another center fielder on the bench, Carson Bigbee.

The 1925 Pirates were probably the best defensive team in baseball history up to that time. After McKechnie was fired, the Pirates released McInnis and tried to get an extra bat in the lineup by switching Grantham back to second.

McKechnie was on to St. Louis. Rabbit Maranville, the punchless glove man whom McKechnie had traded away in Pittsburgh, became his favorite player. Maranville was a notorious carouser. McKechnie, in Pittsburgh, assigned himself to room with Maranville, to keep an eye on him. They were an odd couple, but they got along great. Maranville, released by Brooklyn in 1925, would play another ten years in the majors, almost all of them for McKechnie.

McKechnie got Rabbit a job with the Cardinals, then made him his regular shortstop in 1928, although he hit just .240, one of the lowest averages in the majors in 1928. The Cardinals didn't think that was all that smart, and when they fired McKechnie they sold Maranville to Boston. McKechnie joined him in Boston a year later and kept him in the lineup for four years. Even in 1933, when Maranville was forty-one years old and hit .218 with no homers, McKechnie played him almost every day at second base. Rabbit broke his leg in spring training the next year and had to take the whole year off, but when he was able to walk around again in 1935, McKechnie tried to put him back in the lineup. He hit .149 in 23 games.

There are countless other examples of McKechnie's fondness for defensive players. In 1928, McKechnie's year in St. Louis, he wouldn't play Spud Davis, a terrific hitting young catcher. Instead, he traded Davis plus another player to Philadelphia for Jimmie Wilson, a weaker hitter but a much better defensive catcher. (Years later, the teams reversed the trade, sending Wilson back to Philadelphia for Davis-plus. When McKechnie got to Cincinnati in 1938 Davis was there, and he traded him again.)

In Boston, McKechnie re-created his three-shortstops-in-the-infield trick, with Rabbit Maranville, Billy Urbanski, and Fritz Knothe, all natural shortstops, playing second, short, and third.

McKechnie's greatest success as a manager was in Cincinnati, where he took over a last-place team and won the pennant in two years. As his first move, he purchased Lonnie Frey, who had played shortstop in the National League for five years. Frey was a good hitting shortstop, but his career was degenerating because he wasn't much of a defensive shortstop. McKechnie made him his second baseman.

The Reds had a minor league first baseman named Frank McCormick, a .300 hitter and an exceptional glove man, who had been bouncing up and down to the minors since 1934 because he didn't hit the home runs that first basemen were expected to hit in that era. McKechnie made him an everyday, never-comes-out-of-the-lineup type of player. He led the National League in hits for three straight years, drove in 100 runs a year on singles, doubles, and an occasional home run, and won the MVP Award in 1940.

The additions of Frey and McCormick, as well as Billy Werber, enormously improved the Reds infield. In center field, he made a major leaguer out of Harry Craft; Craft led the National League in putouts in his first season.

On the other hand, McKechnie wouldn't use Hank Sauer, a tremendous hitter, even though Sauer unquestionably would have been the Reds' best hitter in the early 1940s. This decision contributed to the team's decline in those years. In 1928 at St. Louis, he wouldn't use Pepper Martin, because Martin's defense wasn't up to his standard.

In the 1940 All-Star game, McKechnie started Max West in right field over Mel Ott, explaining to reporters that right field

National. Mack assigned Ehmke to stay on the East Coast when the A's went west, and get tickets to see the Cubs play in Philadelphia, New York, and Brooklyn. Ehmke was to send Mack reports on the Cub batters—and also, without telling anyone, to prepare himself to pitch the opening game of the World Series.

When Mack named Ehmke to start the opener, the public was shocked. Mack had two 20-game winners, a lefty and a righty, plus an 18-game winner. The fans had been debating which 20-game winner would get the call. When Ehmke was announced, people thought that Mack was risking the World Series on a sentimental call.

Ehmke pitched one of the best games in World Series history, striking out 13 Cub batters and shutting the team out until the ninth inning. Ehmke, who struck out only 20 batters all season, got 65% of that total in nine innings.

Connie Mack's decision to let Ehmke pitch that game was unique, gutsy—and had every probability of succeeding. Ehmke could still pitch; he was 7–2 in 1929, with an ERA a run better than the league. Mack knew

☞

that with a month to get ready for his next start, Ehmke's arm would be fine.

A month to get ready, and all the time he needed to study the upcoming opponent, to figure out exactly what to do with each hitter. A smart veteran pitcher, with a month to think: This is the biggest game of my life. I must get ready to win this one game. How could it go wrong?

No one has ever really tried to duplicate this trick, but did you ever notice that there are always old pitchers around who pitch great for two or three starts after they get off the disabled list? What if you took, let us say, Fernando Valenzuela, and you stopped pitching him three weeks before the end of the season. Instead, you figured out who you might be playing in the NLCS, and you sent Fernando to watch them for three weeks. What if you told Fernando that, win or lose, this is it; we're going to release you after the World Series. Don't you reckon, under those conditions, that Fernando would pull it all together and pitch a four-hit shutout?

I know, of course, that there are practical problems with the theory. Whoever Fernando is pitching for isn't

would be the sun field later in the afternoon, and he wanted the veteran outfielder out there for defense in the later innings. West hit a three-run homer, leading to a 4–0 win.

As a consequence of this, McKechnie's teams often didn't score all that many runs. But throughout his career, he would get tremendous performances out of pitchers whose careers were going nowhere until they joined up with McKechnie. In 1937, for example, he brought two veteran pitchers out of the minor leagues, Lou Fette and Jim Turner, both in their thirties. They won 20 games each as rookies. A few others:

•Johnny Vander Meer was 3–5 as a rookie in 1937. In the rotation for McKechnie the next year, he went 15–10 and threw two no-hitters.

•The Reds purchased Bucky Walters in June 1938; he had gone 11–21 in 1936, 14–15 in 1937, and was 4–8 in 1938. For McKechnie, he went 11–6, 27–11, and 22–10 in his first three seasons.

•Paul Derringer went 19–19 in 1936, 10–14 in 1937, with ERAs of 4.02 and 4.04. In his first two seasons for McKechnie he went 21–14 and 25–7, with ERAs of 2.93 each year.

•Ed Brandt was 9–21 in 1928, 8–13 in 1929, and 4–11 in 1930, his first season under McKechnie. But in his next four seasons he went 18–11, 16–16, 18–14, and 16–14.

•Danny MacFayden's career foundered from 1932 to 1935, with records of 8–15, 3–2, 4–3, and 6–15. For McKechnie in 1936 he went 17–13.

The exceptional defense of McKechnie's teams made the work of his starting pitchers enormously easier, cut a full run off of their ERAs, and thus enabled many of his pitchers to make sudden leaps to join the league's elite starters.

Did He Like an Offense Based on Power, Speed, or High Averages? He liked .300 hitters, speed more than power. None of McKechnie's teams ever led the league in home runs.

Did He Use the Entire Roster or Did He Keep People Sitting on the Bench? He used a set lineup. His bench players did not play a whole lot.

Did He Build His Bench Around Young Players Who Could Step into the Breach If Need Be, or Around Veteran Role-Players Who Had Their Own Functions Within a Game? Mostly veterans.

GAME MANAGING AND USE OF STRATEGIES

Did He Go for the Big-Inning Offense, or Did He Like to Use the One-Run Strategies? He used one-run strategies.

Did He Pinch-Hit Much, and If So, When? He almost always had two left-handed hitting outfielders on the bench, and those two would always be among the league leaders in pinch hitting attempts.

Was There Anything Unusual About His Lineup Selection? His use of shortstops at second base was certainly idiosyncratic. Another thing was, he used an exceptional number of players named "Moore"—Eddie Moore, Gene Moore, Randy Moore, Whitey Moore.

Did He Use the Sac Bunt Often? Very often.

Did He Like to Use the Running Game? Average or slightly above average amount.

Did He Hit and Run Very Often? Yes.

Were There Any Unique or Idiosyncratic Strategies That He Particularly Favored? He liked to let his hitters swing away 3 and 0. He always said if you can't hit a pitcher when you're ahead 3 and 0, you're never going to hit him.

HANDLING THE PITCHING STAFF

Did He Like Power Pitchers, or Did He Prefer to Go with the People Who Put the Ball in Play? He preferred veteran pitchers, all things being equal.

Did He Stay with His Starters, or Go to the Bullpen Quickly? He worked his starters very hard. Nine of McKechnie's teams led the league in complete games, far more than led the league in any other category.

Did He Use a Four-Man Rotation? He did; he was one of the first managers to use a fixed rotation. As I've said, the circumstances of the game through most of this era simply did not permit managers to use a four-man rotation, but McKechnie was religious about starting his best two or three pitchers every fourth day when he could.

going to be 10 games ahead in August, and they'll need to use every pitcher they've got. Even if they *were* 10 games ahead, they wouldn't be able to figure out three weeks ahead of time who they would be playing in the NLCS, round one.

But that's the beauty of what Connie Mack did. He was in a unique situation, and he figured out a way to take advantage of it. By so doing, he pulled a game out of thin air and saved his best pitchers for Game Two. It wasn't a strategy devised to get him an *out,* or a *base,* or a *base runner;* it was a strategy designed to get him a *game,* a World Series Game. We'll never see it again—but if we did, I would bet dollars to doughnut holes that it would work again.

Did He Use the Entire Staff, or Did He Try to Get Five or Six People to Do Most of the Work? He got all he could out of his best pitchers.

What Was His Strongest Point As a Manager? First, McKechnie was a gentleman, and the players liked him and respected him.

Second, McKechnie knew exactly what he wanted to do. He had a plan: He wanted outstanding defensive players at every position, he wanted as many .300 hitters as he could get without sacrificing defense, and he wanted veteran pitchers who could go to the well every fourth day. He wanted two left-handed outfielders on the bench to pinch-hit. There wasn't any effort wasted on his teams while the manager was trying to define roles for his players.

If There Was No Professional Baseball, What Would He Probably Have Done with His Life? Like Connie Mack, he would have become a plant manager. A hands-on executive.

Minor League McGraw

Spencer Abbott never managed in the major leagues, but won 2,180 games as a minor league manager, and was recommended by Wilbert Robinson to be his successor as manager of the Brooklyn Dodgers.

Born in Chicago in 1877, Abbott's astonishing managerial career began in 1903 with Fargo in the Northern League, and ended in the Tri-State League in 1947. His story of how he became a manager:

"I was a pitcher, but my arm petered out and so I went about the country trying to land a job of any sort. Finally I hit Fargo, North Dakota, and that team needed a first baseman. I hit pretty well, and got to be manager of the club. George Tebeau, who owned the Kansas City club, heard something about an Abbott and he supposed it to be some youngster. I had known him earlier and he had concluded I had quit when my arm became useless. Kansas City acquired me by the draft route, Tebeau paying $300, a good deal of money in those days. I won't forget the look on his face when I walked into his office.

"'Why, how are you, Abby, old fellow,' he said. 'I thought you were dead. What are you doing?'"

"I'm your new first baseman," Abbott replied. "You just paid $300 for me."

Tebeau put Abbott in the lineup and, according to Abbott, tried to sell him to every team that Kansas City played. Finally he had a good game against Topeka, and the Topeka team bought him to be their player/manager.

At this time there were a huge number of minor league teams. Abbott managed in small leagues in Kansas from 1904 through 1911, managing Topeka, Hutchinson, Wellington, and Lyons, Kansas, in the Missouri Valley League, the Western Association, and the Kansas State League. In his first ten years as a manager he almost always had a losing record. "When I first started out I had a bad failing," he would recall years later. "During games I would lose my temper. I found out how it was to the players at times, and started trying to curb it."

In 1914 baseball attendance collapsed, dozens of minor leagues folded, and Abbott was out of baseball for five years. Somehow he caught on as manager of the Tulsa team in 1919. He had a good ball club in Tulsa, and the Western Association at that time was an exciting league, with many players just a step away from the major leagues. In 1920 the lively ball era came to the Western League as it did to the majors, and a catcher named Yam Yaryan hit .357 with 41 home runs. Yaryam had been playing for Wichita for several years, without impressive results, before 1920. Anyway, leading Wichita 8–5 in the ninth inning, Abbott saw Yaryan come to the plate with the bases loaded. "Now I get a flash of genius," Abbott would say. "I tell my pitcher to give Yam an intentional pass. It forces in a run, of course, but we get the next guy out and win, eight to six. Now I'm expecting I'll get a pretty good write-up for my strategy. Know what the headlines said next day? 'Yellow Abbott Walks Yaryan!'"

After winning the Western Association with Tulsa in 1920, Abbott jumped to Memphis in the Southern Association, where he hit big again, finishing with a 104–49 record. A part of a minor league manager's job in that time was to hype his players to help sell them to the higher leagues. In 1924, managing a rather poor Reading team in the International League, Abbott's top star was a slugging outfielder named Shags Horan. In an exhibition game against the Dodgers, Horan belted a pitch through the window of a schoolhouse beyond the left-field fence. "Does it all the time," Abbott yelled to the Brooklyn writers. "They've got a special monitor in the class room who watches the game from the window and yells, 'Under the desks, kids, Horan is up!'"

Abbott was able to sell Horan and a veteran pitcher (Al Mamaux) to the Yankees and infielder Rhodie Miller to their top competitors at the moment, the Senators. "One of the best deals I ever made," he said. "I got about seventy thousand dollars all told for the three of them in August and had them all back in Reading with me the next spring." Abbott got fired a couple of months into the 1925 season, but then it was on to the next job, Kansas City in 1926.

Abbott was always a difficult man to play for. Tom Meany wrote that he "probably put verbal blow-torches to even more players than John McGraw." When he was hired by the Kansas City Blues in the spring of '26, Blues president George Muehle-bach said "I want a manager who will make the players work."

"The average fan has the conception that Spencer Abbott is a slave driver," reported a KC writer. "A despot hard upon his men, a ruler whose scepter is wielded savagely." The Kansas City dugout had a low roof. Once KC lost a game when the tying run was picked off first base. Abbott yelped and leaped off the bench, whacking his head on the dugout roof so hard that he knocked himself out. A young player tried to revive him.

"Let the old sonuvabitch lay there," said a veteran. "At least we'll be able to dress in peace."

"There have been times when I would have liked to commit murder," Abbott acknowledged. "At that, I believe they should pass a rule permitting a manager to carry a shotgun."

Abbott lasted one year in Kansas City and then on to the next job, Jersey City, in 1927. He managed in the top minor leagues almost continuously from 1919 through 1943, though he never spent more than three years in any job, and usually only one. When Wilbert Robinson left the Dodgers in 1931 he recommended Abbott as his replacement, but Abbott was only a few years younger than Robinson, and the Dodgers chose Max Carey instead. In 1935 Abbott coached with the Senators, then went back to the minors. Managing Williamsport in the early war years, Abbott lost three second basemen in one year to the draft. "I guess they're going to fight this damn war around second base," Spence concluded.

Out of baseball for three years, the sixty-nine-year-old Abbott returned as manager of Charlotte in the Tri-State League in 1946, leading that team to a rout of the pennant race with a 93–46 record and a win in the playoffs. Retiring as a manager after 1947, Abbott was hired to scout for the Washington Senators, and died in Washington in 1951.

Beard

In the seventh game of the 1924 World Series, Bucky Harris started a right-handed pitcher. His name was Curly Ogden, but that's not really the point; the reason Ogden started was that he was right-handed. Harris was trying to get Bill Terry out of the game. Terry, a rookie, was a left-handed platoon player; he had hit .500 in the series (6 for 12), but he sat down when a lefty came in. Harris's idea was to list Ogden as the starting pitcher, get Terry in the lineup, then bring in a lefty and force him to sit down. Then, when it was time for Harris to go to his relievers (Firpo Marberry and Walter Johnson), Bill Terry would be unavailable for comment.

It worked. John McGraw listed Terry in the starting lineup. Harris let Ogden face two batters, then switched to a left-handed pitcher. McGraw left Terry in to go 0 for 2 against the lefty. When Terry was due to bat with none out, two on in the sixth, however, McGraw blinked. He pinch-hit for Terry, and Harris immediately switched to his right-handed pitchers. New York grabbed a 3–1 lead, but the two right-handers, not having to face Terry, shackled New York for six innings, allowing Washington to win in twelve.

This gambit has been used a few other times. In 1990, for example, Jim Leyland started Ted Power in the sixth game of the NLCS, for essentially the same reason. The question I wanted to pose, though, is why *isn't* this a normal part of the game? Why isn't a "beard" or "cover pitcher" used more often? If the other team platoons at three positions, you could gain the platoon edge, in theory, for twelve at bats. If the other manager refuses to grant you that advantage, then you can drain his bench before the game gets to crunch time. Managers routinely make moves, offensively and defensively, which get them the platoon edge for only one hitter. Why *don't* they make a move which has the potential to reshape the game?

I can think of four reasons why they might not choose to use this move.

1. It wouldn't work.
2. It might work, but might backfire.
3. It might work when it is not anticipated, but fail to work when it is anticipated.
4. Not using it is a kind of gentleman's agreement.

I think the strategy *would* work, or at the very least I think the use of a cover pitcher would have a higher probability of gaining an advantage for the team naming him than many other common strategies. I've seen people use the strategy in table-game leagues, and it works there.

There are two ways the move could backfire. First, you could find yourself in a situation in which you need to use the pitcher that you burned by naming him to start the game. Second, the other manager could list the wrong hitters, forcing you to stick with the pitcher you were only intending to fake with, who might not be the best pitcher you have.

Neither of those, however, seems to be all that big a problem. Anytime you use a player, you might wish later that you had saved him; that's just a normal part of the game. And, since the opposing manager can only negate the advantage by using players he would not normally use, it's hard to see how the danger of losing to that set of players could outweigh the danger of losing to the other set of players.

Perhaps this might be a good strategy when it is sprung upon the other team unexpectedly, but not otherwise. But I don't think that's the right explanation, either, for two reasons. First, if an average team did this, let's say, five times a season, that would seem to be infrequent enough to preserve the element of surprise. It's used about once every thirty years. There is no way the need to keep the strategy a surprise is going to drive the frequency of use *that* low.

And second, so what if the other manager suspects what you're up to? What can he do? If it's Greg Maddux's turn to pitch and you list some left-handed rookie with an ERA about Cecil Fielder's belt size, that's not much of a fake, but you wouldn't do that, would you? As long as the fake starter has credibility, then the only way to avoid taking the fake is to list the wrong hitters, the ones who cede the platoon advantage to the pitcher. That leaves the manager who used the cover pitcher with a credible pitcher *who has the lineup stacked in his favor.* Some risk.

So why don't they do it?

It's a gentleman's agreement. Everybody understands that if I did this to the other guy, he would do the same to me. The advantage I gain today, I would forfeit tomorrow. The result would be that every manager's job would be a lot more complicated, and everybody would have one more damn thing to worry about. The job is hard enough as it is. If we complicate those semiroutine things like setting your lineup to face a lefty and scheduling regular work for your bench players, it just adds pressure to the job. Who needs it?

The Clarke Affaire

One of the most famous player mutinies in baseball history involved not an effort to discredit the manager, but a misdirected effort to support the manager. It happened in Pittsburgh in August, 1926, and centered around Fred Clarke.

Fred Clarke was the most successful manager of the early years of this century. He was the same age as McGraw, give or take a few months, started managing a year and a half sooner, and by 1909 he was 250 wins ahead of John McGraw. This is a large number of wins. McGraw won less than 3,000 games in his career; if Clarke had kept managing, McGraw would never have caught him. Clarke's Pirates won four pennants between 1901 and 1909, and won 90 or more games nine times in his career.

Clarke's ability as a manager decreased significantly as soon as Honus Wagner began to grow old, however, and he was forced out after the 1915 season. He retired to his ranch in Kansas, where oil was discovered on his property, the best break he'd had since he hooked up with ol' Honus. By the early 1920s he was a millionaire gentleman, able to deal with Pirates' owner Barney Dreyfuss more or less as a social equal.

Clarke was well liked by press, public, and the Dreyfuss family, which owned the team. He was a hero in Pittsburgh second only to Wagner. He invested some of his money in the Pirates and rejoined the team as a vice president/minority partner. Despite the VP title, Clarke sat on the bench, in a suit, during the games. Nobody saw any reason why he shouldn't do this, as he was more than qualified to be a coach.

The Pirates in 1925 won their first World Series since 1909, with Fred Clarke once more in the dugout. For the moment everybody was happy, but there was a suspicion even then that Clarke was trying to position himself to take credit for the team's success.

Only two men remained with the Pirates who had played for Clarke—Babe Adams, star of the 1909 World Series, and Max Carey, who had become the team captain. Both liked Clarke well enough, and

had welcomed him back, but as the 1926 season progressed, some members of the team began to feel that Clarke was angling to get back in the manager's chair.

The Pirates were playing well, holding first place. In Boston on August 7, the team was shut out in a doubleheader by the Braves, a bad team. Max Carey, fighting a sinus infection, had a bad day at the end of a string of bad days, and Clarke suggested to Bill McKechnie that he ought to put somebody else in center field. McKechnie asked who else he could play in center field, probably with a tone of voice that suggested "You're not going to bring up this shit about Kiki Cuyler playing center field again, are you?"

"Put in the bat boy," said Clarke in annoyance. "He can't be any worse."

Carson Bigbee, an outfielder who had been with the team for years, reported the remark to his friend Max Carey. The insulted team captain talked to several other players. He found a number of players whom he believed to be nursing grudges over things Clarke had said. He asked Babe Adams what he ought to do. Adams was a soft-spoken man in his mid-forties, the village elder. "The manager is the manager," Adams shrugged. "Nobody else should interfere."

Max Carey, speaking for the players, asked that Fred Clarke be removed from the bench. The newspapers got wind of the dispute almost immediately, forcing players to choose sides. Adams and Bigbee stood with Carey publicly on the issue. Carey felt that he represented the majority of the players, maybe all of them, and that as team captain he was acting properly as a spokesman for the players in support of their manager. They met with McKechnie before going public with their statement.

McKechnie at first seemed to appreciate the support, but then studied the situation and found himself between a brick wall and baseball bat. If he supported his players, he was in effect criticizing the management of the team. He was forced to denounce the players' "attempt to meddle in the administration of the team."

Fred Clarke announced publicly that he would not return to the bench until heavy penalties were inflicted upon the offenders.

Headlines flew. Barney Dreyfuss was vacationing in France, leaving the club in the hands of his son Sam, who was universally hated by the players. Exchanging telegrams with Paris, the Pirate front office met August 12 in a crisis atmosphere. They scheduled a meeting the next day with the players. The players held their own angry meeting on August 12, and while it is not clear exactly what happened, there was a notable shortage of people willing to stand up in support of Max Carey and the other dissidents. Reportedly, a resolution to demand the removal of Clarke was supported by only six players.

The World Champion Pittsburgh Pirates were in chaos.

Sam Dreyfuss began the meeting of August 13 with the announcement that "I'll do all the talking here."

Bigbee and Adams were given their unconditional release. Max Carey was put on waivers and suspended without pay; Pie Traynor replaced him as team captain.

Expecting support from two sides, the dissidents had been cut off at the knees when neither arrived. Meeting in Pittsburgh on August 15, the three appealed to Commissioner Landis for a hearing of their grievance. "We have been unjustly treated and penalized without a hearing," they said in a telegram. Landis agreed that there should be a hearing, but asked National League president John Heydler to conduct the hearing, which was held in Pittsburgh on August 17.

"I cannot go back of the right of the officials of a league club to release, suspend or ask waivers on any of its players," said Heydler in his report, "nor would I wish to do so if I had the right; but it is my opinion, after a most complete and thorough hearing of this case, that none of the three players—Carey, Bigbee and Adams—has been guilty of willful subordination or malicious intent to disrupt or injure his club." In effect, Heydler had cleared the players' names, but refused to reinstate them.

The historical import of the controversy is twofold. First, it obstructed the development of a dynasty in Pittsburgh.

The Pirates, divided by the confrontation, collapsed to a third-place finish. McKechnie was fired after the season and Clarke removed from the bench. In view of the fact that the Pirates were World Champions in 1925 and added several outstanding players in the next few years (including the Waner brothers), it may well be that the crisis prevented the Pirates of the late 1920s from becoming one of the game's great dynasties. The rift deprived the Pirates of an outstanding manager. They replaced McKechnie with Donie Bush, who won another pennant, but had conflicts with his players.

Even more significantly, this incident did a great deal to define the roles played by coaches and executives in the modern front office.

The front office in 1926 was at a critical point in its evolution. Branch Rickey moved into the Cardinal front office in 1925; Billy Evans in 1927 became the first man to wear the title "General Manager." Baseball was leaving the era of the major league owner/operator, the guys who ran their own teams with a treasurer, a secretary, a manager, and a couple of part-time scouts. In a few years, there would be farm directors and scouting supervisors and executive vice presidents with Rolodexes and reservations for lunch. Never again would there be a coach/vice president. The Clarke affair exposed the dangers in doing that. Placing an executive on the field, below the manager but also above him, fatally undercut the man in charge. In effect, this incident built a wall between front office and field level management, a wall through which the manager was—and is—the only door.

Max Carey moved on to the Dodgers, where he played, coached, and managed for several years. Bill McKechnie would manage three more teams, with great success. The major league careers of Carson Bigbee and Babe Adams had come to an end. "A series of misunderstandings," Heydler said, which it was beyond his power to undo.

Speaker and Cobb

Ty Cobb managed the Tigers from 1921 to 1926, finishing over .500 every year except the first one. Tris Speaker managed the Indians from 1919 to 1926, winning the pennant in 1920, and finishing over .500 six of eight seasons.

On November 2, 1926, Ty Cobb resigned as manager of the Tigers and was released as a player. This was hard to explain, as the 1926 Tigers had a decent enough year, and Cobb, although pushing forty, had hit .339.

Rumors circulated about that for a month, and then on December 2 the other shoe dropped. The same exact thing happened to Tris Speaker. This was truly inexplicable, in that Speaker, a year younger than Cobb, had hit 52 doubles in 1926, and his team had finished second, their best season in years.

The newspapers tugged at the corners of the story for a few weeks, and eventually the commissioner's office had to come clean. It was the last gasp of the Black Sox scandal. Dutch Leonard, a former American League pitcher, had accused Cobb and Speaker of participating in fixing a game at the end of the 1919 season. Leonard turned over to authorities two letters, one from Joe Wood and one from Ty Cobb, which seemed to corroborate their participation in the scam. American League president Ban Johnson, paying a reported $20,000 for the letters, had ordered the dismissal of the two great center fielders.

The commissioner had no choice but to get involved. He held a hearing and released a report (more than a hundred pages long) exonerating Cobb and Speaker of anything more serious than long-ago bad judgment. Cobb and Speaker, he stated, were free to sign with any team that wanted them.

However, neither Cobb nor Speaker ever managed again. There has always been a suspicion, among baseball historians, that while Cobb and Speaker were publicly acquitted and allowed to stay in the game as players, Judge Landis gave a private order that they were never to manage again.

I have thought about this issue for years, and I have reached the conclusion that there was no such order. Why? Because there isn't any evidence against Tris Speaker.

We have a tremendous willingness, as Ogden Nash observed, to believe the worst of our fellow men. The assumption of innocence is a legal posture; as a practical matter, no one who is accused of wrongdoing can ever really clear his name.

Our willingness to accept the guilt of the accused has few more vivid examples than that of Tris Speaker. When baseball historians speak of this issue, many or most will casually assume that of course Speaker did participate in fixing the game.

But based on what? I agree that there is significant evidence (Wood's letter) that Joe Wood bet against his own team that day, and there is some evidence (Cobb's letter) that Cobb may have known that the Indians were laying down for them, although Cobb's letter is vague, and Cobb's 1926 interpretation of it is as reasonable as Leonard's.

But I defy anyone to show me any credible evidence that Tris Speaker was involved. Neither letter produced by Leonard makes any mention of Speaker, and neither makes any mention of any third party who reasonably could have been Tris Speaker. Cobb's letter discusses Wood's role in the affair, and Wood's letter discusses Cobb's role. Neither mentions Speaker. Isn't that odd?

Dutch Leonard did claim in 1926 that Speaker was involved, but

a) Leonard was nursing a grudge against Speaker, and

b) Leonard refused to repeat his allegations under oath.

Speaker swore that he knew nothing about the matter. Both Wood and Cobb, although acknowledging some role in betting on the game, said that the conversation related by Leonard, which is the only thing which involved Speaker, never took place.

Given that factual basis, there is just no possible way that Landis could have authorized any action against Tris Speaker.

Further, while Speaker never managed again in the major leagues, he did manage again in the minor leagues. Judge Landis always insisted that, as far as matters of ethics and propriety were concerned, the standards for minor leaguers were exactly the same as the standards for major leaguers.

So to assume that Speaker was allowed to manage in the minors, but wouldn't have been allowed to manage in the majors, you have to assume that Landis was a hypocrite. Of course, this isn't a big hurdle for many people, because there are always people around who will say that any authority figure is a hypocrite, and if you're willing to believe the worst of Tris Speaker, you're probably going to be willing to believe the worst of Judge Landis, too.

But there isn't any evidence that Landis was a hypocrite. That portrayal of him is just random cynicism, a reaction to the contemporary efforts to portray him as a crusading knight determined to defend the honor of Organized Baseball. As a practical matter, there is much better evidence that he was a crusading knight defending the honor of Organized Baseball than there is that he was a hypocrite.

Is it strange that Cobb and Speaker, both of whom have pretty good records as managers, never managed again?

Well, maybe. Speaker and Cobb were forced out of their positions by American League president Ban Johnson, who in turn was forced out of his position for so doing. I am a great admirer of Ban Johnson's, but it was appropriate to ask him to leave the game at that point. There was no justification for Johnson to force the resignation of Cobb and Speaker. It was a witch hunt.

But by the time Landis stepped in and attempted to straighten it out, their jobs were gone. Cobb was probably near the end of the line as a manager, anyway. His players didn't like him, and his team was slipping backward by two games a year. Speaker was coming off a good year—and two bad years before that.

Pie Traynor's record, as a manager, is as good as Cobb's or Speaker's, yet when he was fired by Pittsburgh in 1939, he never managed again. Is that strange? Walter Johnson's record is as good as Cobb's or Speaker's, maybe a little better, but his career was just as brief. Is that strange? Nap Lajoie's winning percentage as a manager was .550, the same as Johnson's, better than Cobb or Speaker's. He managed the Naps from 1905 to 1909, was fired in 1909, and never managed again. Is this strange?

There is a pattern, I think, of underrating the managerial performance of outstanding players. The record, to me, is clear. Cobb and Speaker left the game on the same terms as Pie Traynor and Walter Johnson and Nap Lajoie. If somebody had wanted to hire them to manage, Landis would not have stood in the way.

Miller Huggins

Miller Huggins was born in Cincinnati, Ohio, May 27, 1880, and he got his major league start there with the Reds after he had been purchased from St. Paul in 1903. He played second base for the Reds until 1910, when he was sold to the Cards. When Roger Bresnahan was released as manager of the St. Louis club in 1913, Huggins was made manager and met with only fair success. When Colonels Ruppert and Huston bought the Yankees they started on the quest for a manager and they went after Huggins, with the result that he was transferred out of the National League and became the pilot of the Yankees. Huggins is not quite popular in New York, and is the constant subject of adverse, and often unjust, criticism.

With the team chock full of prima donnas, Huggins has had the worst managerial task in the major leagues. The players dislike him and the fans ignore him. Regardless of adverse sentiment, Huggins deserves a lot of credit for the victory of the Yanks. It is his ball club. Helped by a willing pair of owners, he opened wide the pursestrings.

Huggins built up the Yankees from nothing. He has had them consistently near the top and has now won two successive pennants, where they used to be a second division club. Much of his unpopularity is due to his retiring nature and partly to poor health. He does not mix with the fans off the field and keeps in the background. Huggins is one of the smartest men in base ball and just about the wisest trader in the big leagues. Huggins is in the unfortunate position of having every one analyze his work to find faults. The bugs never criticise McGraw, because they don't look at him critically.

—Joseph Vila, *New York Evening Sun,*
quoted from the *1923 Reach Guide*

MILLER HUGGINS: The Managing Leprechaun

Decade Snapshot: 1930s

Most Successful Managers: 1. Joe McCarthy
                                       2. Bill Terry
                                       3. Charlie Grimm

Others of Note: Mickey Cochrane
                          Joe Cronin
                          Frankie Frisch
                          Walter Johnson
                          Gabby Street

Typical Manager Was: Younger and more pleasant than in the 1920s.

Percentage of Playing Managers: 32%

Most Second-Guessed Manager's Move: 1934, Bill Terry's sarcastic remark gave Brooklyn something to play for in the closing days of the season.

In 1933 Earl Whitehill (22–8) was scheduled to start the opening game of the World Series for Washington. At the last minute Whitehill was pulled, and Lefty Stewart (15–6) started the game. Stewart was hammered, setting up a five-game rout for the Giants.

It is generally thought that Whitehill reported to the park that day in no condition to pitch. An irony is that the only Senator pitcher to win a game during the series, Whitehill, was blamed for the defeat. Whitehill pitched a shutout in his only start.

Evolutions in Strategy: 1930s baseball did not involve a lot of maneuvering by the managers. It was dominated by straightforward, in-your-face baseball. That was dominated by Joe McCarthy, who was called the Pushbutton Manager (by Jimmie Dykes, another manager).

Platooning in this era was uncommon, and for many years I was puzzled about why the strategy went into a twenty-five-year remission after its widespread use from 1915 to 1925. I finally realized that what happened was that the players disliked platooning so much that managers were reluctant to impose it on them.

I was curious, for example, about whether Joe McCarthy platooned Bill Dickey, because when you look at his records, it looks like he was platooning, but nobody ever says that he was. We took several months of Yankee games, and studied them. Conclusion: Dickey started 42% of the games against left-handers, 82% of the games against right-handers. McCarthy was careful not to say that he was resting Dickey because of the left-hander. What would happen was, they would have a couple of tough left-handers coming up, and Dickey would suddenly turn up with a mild case of influenza. In August.

Dickey, of course, didn't want to admit that he didn't hit left-handers as well as he hit right-handers, and Joe McCarthy wasn't going to force him to admit it. Openly acknowledging that you were platooning was like confessing to a weakness in your player, a kind

Tracer

I can remember one game very distinctly. The Giants had a pitcher by the name of Roy Parmelee, a wild, hard-throwing right-hander. He was pitching against us in the Polo Grounds, the bases were loaded, and Glenn Wright was up. Parmelee threw him a fastball; his fastball had a natural sliderlike break to it. Glenn started to swing, saw the pitch breaking away, and kind of half threw his bat at the ball, almost one-handed. He got out in front of it and hit it down the left-field line . . . just hard enough for the ball to drop in for a grand-slam home run.
—Al Lopez, *The Man in the Dugout*

Lopez tells this same story, through William Mead, in *Two Spectacular Seasons*. The point of his story is that he believes this incident led rather directly to the ball being made less lively in 1931. McGraw threw up his hands in the dugout when Wright's soft fly slipped into the seats, and he said, "What kind of baseball is this?" As Lopez remembers, "The way I understand it, that was the beginning of softening the ball up a bit."

In fact, however, Glenn Wright never hit a home run off of Roy Parmelee, either in the Polo Grounds or in some other park, either with the bases full or with them empty, either in 1930 or in some other season.

The incident that Lopez remembers, or half-remembers, very distinctly may have contained elements of two events. On August 28, 1930, Glenn Wright did hit a home run at the Polo Grounds, not off of Parmelee but off of Carl Hubbell. If you think about it, Hubbell's famous screwball broke away from a right-handed hitter, exactly as Lopez describes the pitch, and Wright might very well have been fooled by a pitch, got a poor swing as Lopez describes, and still hit the ball over the short left-field fence in the Polo Grounds. It was a two-run homer, not a grand slam, but it was an important hit, giving Brooklyn a 5–4 lead, in a game they won 8–7. The game story the next day specifies that Wright's homer was hit to left field, as Lopez remembers, and the New York Times reported that the ball "lofted" into the left-field stands, implying that it was not well hit.

By August 28, however, McGraw had been yelling about the lively ball making a farce out of the game for at least four months, so that incident could not have been the beginning of any movement to silence the lively ball.

of an insult. The players hated it, and managers for a long time just decided to go along and get along.

Evolution in the Role of the Manager: The percentage of managers who were playing managers increased in the 1930s, whereas it has decreased throughout most of the century, probably because the development of front offices from 1925 to 1940 shifted various responsibilities away from managers, and thus made it seem more practical for a player to also serve as manager.

JOE MCCARTHY IN A BOX

Year of Birth: 1887

Years Managed: 1926–1950

Record As a Manager: 2,125–1,333, .615

McCarthy's only losing record as a manager was at Lousiville in 1922. In the minors he managed one year at Wilkes-Barre (1913), playing .600 ball, and seven years at Louisville (1919–1925), posting winning records in six of the seven seasons. In the majors he managed the Cubs for five years, posting winning records all five times, the Yankees for sixteen seasons, posting winning records all sixteen times, and the Red Sox for three seasons, posting winning records all three years.

McCarthy's career winning percentages were .579 with the Cubs, .627 with the Yankees, and .606 with the Red Sox.

The Cubs improved by 14 games his first season in Chicago. The Yankees improved by 8½ games his first season in New York. The Red Sox improved by 12½ games his first season in Boston.

Managers for Whom He Played: McCarthy never played in the majors, and never played for a famous manager in the minors that I am aware of.

Others by Whom He Was Influenced: McCarthy grew up in Philadelphia and was a great admirer of Connie Mack. By nature he was a different man than Mack—more intense and more moody. He was less restrained by nature, but emulated Mack's restraint. He always tried to think twice before he said anything that might hurt someone's feelings, although this did not come naturally to him, as it did to Connie.

Characteristics As a Player: He was a fairly typical minor league second baseman; his records look exactly like Earl Weaver's, except that he didn't walk as much as Weaver. He hit around .260 with no power, usually reached double figures in triples.

McCarthy's batting records, as printed in *The Sporting News* books, contain an obvious error, which has nonetheless gone uncorrected for over fifty years. They show him hitting .325 at Wilkes-Barre in 1913, with 36 doubles and 6

The other game that may have contributed to Lopez's memory was the game of April 28, 1930, in which Brooklyn beat the Giants, at the Polo Grounds, by the remarkable score of 19–15. Parmelee did pitch in that game, and in fact was the most effective pitcher in the game, giving up six runs in seven innings of relief work. He also gave up a home run, and it was hit into the left field stands at the Polo Grounds, but it was hit by a left-handed hitter, Babe Herman.

This was also a big hit. Brooklyn had jumped to a 13–0 lead, knocking out four New York pitchers in the first two innings and bringing Roy Parmelee into the game. Parmelee was the last man on the Giants' bench, just a wild kid who McGraw realized might be a pitcher sometime later on. He never pitched when it meant anything.

Parmelee was effective this day, however, and the Giants scrambled back into the game, trailing 16–12 in the fifth. Babe Herman's home run, with Al Lopez and another guy on base, put the Giants back in a deep hole, at 19–12. Lopez was on third base when this home run was hit, and thus would have been looking ☛

into the Giants' dugout, perfectly positioned to see McGraw's reaction.

Within days of the 19–15 farce there were stories in the newspaper about McGraw being upset with the liveliness of the baseball. Whether McGraw had any impact on the subsequent decision of the National League is an open question. Al Lopez, a twenty-one-year-old rookie at the time, may have regarded John McGraw as a powerful, near-mythic figure whose opinion carried great weight. The National League owners may have regarded him as a cranky old bastard who was always bitching about something. In any case, the National League did act after the season to make the balls a little bit less "lively," and National League batting statistics were much more normal for the rest of the decade.

homers, but only 13 RBI. The New York State League didn't record RBI at that time; the "13" was his stolen bases.

WHAT HE BROUGHT TO A BALL CLUB

Was He an Intense Manager or More of an Easy-to-Get-Along-With Type? He was somewhat intense, but a long way from being John McGraw. Through most of the 1930s, the public image of Joe McCarthy was that of a gentleman, a man who treated his players well and was well liked by the press. He appears to have gotten somewhat cranky about 1943, and after that the things that happened in his salad days were reinterpreted to make him appear more intense than he really was. An apocryphal story about his breaking a card table with an ax, for example, was picked up and repeated ad infinitum, creating the impression that he was a theatrical dictator in the John McGraw tradition.

Was He More of an Emotional Leader or a Decision Maker? A decision maker and a disciplinarian. He set great store by the concept of professionalism, but apart from that he made less effort to be an emotional leader than any other great manager except perhaps Bill McKechnie.

Was He More of an Optimist or More of a Problem Solver? He was very much a problem solver. He was *not* a man to sit and wait for a problem to solve itself. Edward Barrow said that the best thing about him was that he always saw problems coming two years down the road.

HOW HE USED HIS PERSONNEL

Did He Favor a Set Lineup or a Rotation System? A set lineup.

Did He Like to Platoon? He occasionally platooned at one outfield position—for example, in 1927 he platooned Earl Webb with Pete Scott, and in 1948 he platooned Stan Spence with Sam Mele. He didn't platoon a lot.

Did He Try to Solve His Problems with Proven Players or with Youngsters Who Still May Have Had Something to Learn? Joe McCarthy got more distance out of "second chance" players and problem players than anyone else in baseball history. His 1929 National League Champion Cub team was almost entirely built out of players who had failed their first major league trials or who had been cast away by other teams because of conflicts with the manager: Hack Wilson, Riggs Stephenson, Kiki Cuyler, Rogers Hornsby, Zack Taylor, Charlie Root, Hal Carlson. With the Yankees he had a stronger stream of talent coming along, and thus less need to rely on those players.

McCarthy's philosophy was that there were a very few players who had exceptional skills, but otherwise there were a lot of guys who could play baseball, some of them in the majors and some of them in the minors. He had definite ideas about how everything was supposed to be done, and if you didn't want to do things his way, the hell with you, he'd get somebody else who would appreciate the opportunity to play.

As a rookie manager in 1926, McCarthy inherited a last-place team with one superstar, Pete Alexander. In the first month of the season, McCarthy and Alexander had a shouting match in the locker room. A few weeks later, Alexander missed (or ignored) curfew, and McCarthy put him on waivers.

He was ridiculed for doing this, by the press and by Rogers Hornsby, who took Alexander and rode him to the pennant in St. Louis. The derogatory nickname "Marse Joe" was hung on him as a result of this incident, but he knew what he was doing. "Alex always obeyed the rules," he said, "the only problem was, they were Alex's rules." McCarthy was patient with players who had drinking problems—as long as they obeyed his rules. He released Alexander, but by the end of the year he had a better staff than he started with, plus he had established a principle: We're going to do this my way.

What I'm saying is, his basic orientation wasn't "young" or "old"; it was "Do it right or I'll look at the next guy." With the Yankees, who had Paul Krichell out there turning up players left and right, the next guy was almost always a youngster.

How Many Players Did He Make Regulars Who Had Not Been Regulars Before, and Who Were They? At least forty such players, among them Riggs Stephenson, Hack Wilson, Woody English, Joe DiMaggio, Charlie Keller, Red Rolfe, Frank Crosetti, Joe Gordon, Tommy Henrich, Phil Rizzuto, Billy Goodman.

The most impressive part of his record with youngsters is with rookie pitchers. Of the 3,487 major league games managed by McCarthy, I would bet that more than 30% were started by rookie pitchers or pitchers who had less than five wins heading into the season. He almost always had a pitcher who had been in the minors the year before winning 15 or more games.

Faux Pas

If you're going to lose a pennant race by a game or two, I would recommend that you lose it from behind. Make a list of the most famous teams in history that blew the pennant race—the 1934 Giants, the 1951 Dodgers, the 1962 Dodgers, '64 Phillies, '69 Cubs, '78 Red Sox, the '95 Angels . . . well, make your own list. What do they all have in common?

They all lost from ahead.

There is an unwritten rule of sports journalism, which applies to pennant races, to series, and to single games in all sports. If you get behind early, come up strong at the end and lose by a thin margin, you've shown great character in dealing with adversity. But if you play well early and lose at the end, you blew it. You choked. You lost a race (or a game) that you should have won.

It is ironic that Bill Terry, who never said three words when two would do, should be remembered for a careless remark.

New York lost the championship to St. Louis on the last day of the season. Ordinarily such a finish would have brought forth loud expressions of admiration for both clubs. In this case, however, it provoked nothing but chagrin and a feel-

☛

ing almost of resentment against the losers, who were beaten after they seemed to have the pennant as good as won.

—John B. Foster,
1935 Spalding Guide

Blowing a pennant brings forth the urge to scapegoat, and Foster chose George Watkins. "The Giants," wrote Foster, "made one great mistake in trading George Davis, an outfielder, to St. Louis for Watkins. The latter was not as good a batter as Davis and did not add any strength to the club. It was not very long before he demonstrated how weak he had really become, and then the manager was left in the sorry plight of experimenting in his outfield. Had Watkins shown anything like the spirit that moved him during his first year at St. Louis he might have won the championship for New York, as a good batter was all that was needed to swing a half-dozen games."

Foster was relaying the gospel according to Bill Terry. Terry, looking for someone to share the credit for his team's collapse, had focused on poor George Watkins, a minor league veteran who got a chance with the Cardinals in 1930 and hit .373 as a rookie. He followed that up with a couple

Did He Prefer to Go with Good Offensive Players or Did He Like the Glove Men? Basically, with hitters. McCarthy believed in fundamentals. As long as a player did things the right way, McCarthy would use him, even if his defensive skills were limited. Riggs Stephenson, for example, couldn't throw, because of an arm injury suffered playing football at the University of Alabama. Hack Wilson didn't really have a center fielder's speed or arm, and Vern Stephens did not have the agility or quickness of a traditional shortstop. They made the plays they were supposed to make, and that was good enough for McCarthy.

Did He Like an Offense Based on Power, Speed, or High Averages? Power. Thirteen of his teams led the league in home runs, only two in batting average, and only four in stolen bases.

Did He Use the Entire Roster or Did He Keep People Sitting On the Bench? He relied mostly on his frontline players. He didn't use the bench much.

Did He Build His Bench Around Young Players Who Could Step into the Breach If Need Be, or Around Veteran Role-Players Who Had Their Own Functions Within a Game? Veterans.

GAME MANAGING AND USE OF STRATEGIES

Did He Go for the Big-Inning Offense, or Did He Like to Use the One-Run Strategies? The big-inning.

Did He Pinch-Hit Much, and If So, When? The numbers aren't large, because he was normally ahead, but he pinch-hit aggressively when he was behind or tied in the late innings. In the 1936 World Series, for example, he pinch-hit with Red Ruffing in Game Three, but then used a left-hander to pinch-hit *for* Ruffing in Game Five.

Was There Anything Unusual About His Lineup Selection?

1) In 1940, when the Yankees lost by 2 games, McCarthy led off Frankie Crosetti almost all year, although Crosetti hit .194. It may be the lowest batting average of all time for a lead-off man, and certainly was for that era, when a lot of runs were scored. His 1940 Yankees, despite leading off a .194 hitter, still scored 817 runs.

2) This probably reflects available talent rather than strategy, but all of his career, McCarthy got phenomenal power production out of his second basemen. His 1929 second baseman, Rogers Hornsby, hit .380 with 39 homers and drove in 149 runs. In New York he had Tony Lazzeri, who drove in 100 runs a year, and replaced him with Joe Gordon, who also drove in 100 runs a year. At Boston he had Bobby Doerr, who hit 27 homers and drove in 111 runs in 1948, drove in 109 runs in 1949, and drove in 120 runs in 1950. His 1944 second baseman, Snuffy Stirnweiss, had 125 hits, 205 hits, 16 triples, and 55 stolen bases.

Actually, the one position at which McCarthy *didn't* get rather phenomenal offensive production was third base. Until about 1930, second base was more of a power position than was third base. If you look back at 1915 or 1920, you'll find that the top second basemen hit more than the top third basemen did. This shifted about 1925—but not on McCarthy's teams.

Did He Use the Sac Bunt Often? No.

Did He Like to Use the Running Game? No.

In What Circumstances Would He Issue an Intentional Walk? Seems standard. He would sometimes use the intentional walk to load the bases and set up a force at home plate.

Did He Hit and Run Very Often? No.

Were There Any Unique or Idiosyncratic Strategies That He Particularly Favored? McCarthy's basic idea, on offense, was to wear the pitcher down by taking pitches, taking pitches, taking pitches, until the pitcher started to crack. This was before modern bullpens, remember. He'd make the pitcher throw about 150 pitches, and about the seventh inning the pitcher just wouldn't have enough left to get out of trouble.

How Did He Change the Game? In many small ways. McCarthy was the first manager to divide his pitching staff into starters and relievers, ending a fifteen-year period in which all pitchers did both.

I believe that McCarthy, as a part of his "professional image" campaign, was the first manager to insist on a dress

of seasons of solid-to-good performance, but he was thirty years old before he made the Show, and in his mid-thirties by the time he put on a Giants uniform.

January 1934. McGraw had retired, but the Giants remained the proudest team in baseball. The Dodgers were their little brothers, comical and frustrated. Envious. The Giants had won the pennant in 1933, and Bill Terry was confident they would repeat. In a meeting with several members of the press, Terry picked Pittsburgh, St. Louis, and Chicago as the teams to beat in '34. "What about Brooklyn?" asked Rud Rennie of the *Herald-Tribune*.

"Brooklyn?" said Terry. "Is Brooklyn still in the league?"

Sarcasm, like murder, was invented by Cain. "Am I my brother's keeper?" Brooklyn was still in the league and, as a matter of fact, still in town. "Never kick the office boy in the shins," wrote Paul Gallico. "You never can tell when you will come to work some morning and find him sitting at the vice president's desk with three telephones and a beautiful blond secretary." The Giants played well, despite George Watkins, and had a 5 game lead with three weeks to play. With 4 games left to play, they still led by 2½.

Unfortunately, they had to play their little brothers. New York baseball fans at that time generally did not travel to the rival's park, but they would make an exception for special circumstances. The 1934 schedule concluded with the Dodgers playing a two-game series at the Polo Grounds. Terry found his friendly bleachers filled with hostile fans. The Dodgers won both games, giving St. Louis the pennant, and Bill Terry an epitaph.

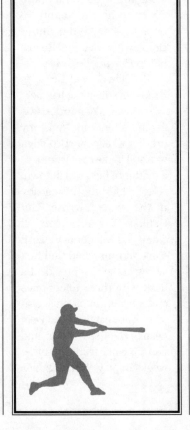

code for his team when they were traveling. This is now standard among coaches in all sports, especially college coaches.

HANDLING THE PITCHING STAFF

Did He Like Power Pitchers, or Did He Prefer to Go with the People Who Put the Ball in Play? He liked power pitchers. Within reason, he was willing to put up with pitchers who did not have outstanding control.

Did He Stay with His Starters, or Go to the Bullpen Quickly? Early in his career, McCarthy did not use his bullpen. In his first two seasons with the Cubs (1926–1927) McCarthy had no pitcher with more than two saves (figured later, of course). He had no bullpen in his early years with the Yankees.

In 1936 he split his staff into starters and relievers, with Pat Malone and Johnny Murphy leading the relief corps. The 1936 Yankees had 21 saves, far more than any other American League team. Murphy was McCarthy's relief ace for several years after that—in a sense, the first career relief ace. Yankee save totals built up over the years, and they led the league in saves several times under McCarthy.

Not to make too much of this, but managers are often forced out of the profession when the game passes them by. In McCarthy's era there were managers who continued to expect their best pitchers to win the game, and never did adapt to the idea of using relievers. McCarthy adapted.

Did He Use a Four-Man Rotation? It wasn't really possible to do so in McCarthy's era. His best starting pitchers in the late thirties, Lefty Gomez and Red Ruffing, usually started no more than 30 times a year. In 1941 and again in 1942 he had seven starting pitchers who started 13 to 27 times apiece.

Did He Use the Entire Staff, or Did He Try to Get Five or Six People to Do Most of the Work? He didn't ride his top starters real hard; he used all of the starters. The workload of his relievers, including Johnny Murphy, was very light.

How Long Would He Stay with a Starting Pitcher Who Was Struggling? If it was one of his best pitchers, a long time. Several of McCarthy's teams led the league in both complete games and saves.

What Was His Strongest Point As a Manager? I believe that Joe McCarthy was the greatest manager in baseball history. He had a tenacious memory, never forgot any little thing that an opposing player might do, for example. He was well organized. Unlike McGraw, who tried to handle every detail of his team's routine, from hitting ground balls for teenagers to checking the hotel receipts to see what his players were eating, McCarthy hired good coaches and relied upon them.

He had definite ideas of what kind of players he wanted, and what he wanted them to do. He was tolerant of diverse players—drinking men, players who had the reputation for being trouble. He laid out clear expectations for how they were to behave, and as long as they were within those guidelines, they were okay. He did not like players who were "colorful" or who wanted to be the center of attention. He didn't like players who were emotional. He wanted players who were calm, mature, and focused on the job.

McCarthy communicated well with his players—not by talking a *lot*, but by talking very little. McCarthy's absolute conviction that there was no shortage of good players gave him the upper hand in his relationship with his players. That conviction was based on two things:

1) McCarthy could see ability in a player who hadn't done anything in the past.

2) He had no fear of using a young player.

If you want one example of what made McCarthy successful, the best answer is in Hack Wilson. For New York in 1925, Hack Wilson hit .239, and was sent out. The Cubs drafted him off a minor league roster that winter.

There is a story, which is printed in several books, about how the Giants lost Hack Wilson . . . it has something to do with a roster foul-up, somebody was supposed to protect Wilson and didn't. It's just that: a story. After Wilson got to be good, writers would ask John McGraw how he let Hack Wilson get away, and he'd tell this CYA story about how some team secretary or minor league franchise operator messed up on him. If you know anything at all about John McGraw, the idea of his sending a young player he liked to the minors to let somebody else teach him to play baseball is ludicrous. The fact is, McGraw had concluded that Wilson couldn't play.

Hack Wilson hit .239 the season before McCarthy got ahold of him; he drove in 30 runs, and his career high remained 57. He played for McCarthy for five years, during

which his averages were .321, .318, .313, .345, and .356. He played almost every game, led the National League in home runs four times, and his RBI counts were 109, 129, 120, 159, and 190.

McCarthy left, and the next year Wilson hit .261 with 13 homers and 62 RBI. He never hit .300 again, never came close to leading the league in home runs or RBI again, and drove in 100 runs only one more time.

If you look at Vern Stephens, twenty-some years later, the pattern is almost the same: Stephens was vastly better for McCarthy than he ever was before or after.

What made him that way? Hack Wilson's biography, by Robert S. Boone and Gerald Grunska, gives two hints:

> When reporters asked Hack the reasons for his 1931 eclipse, he replied that Hornsby had locked his bat on 3-1 and 2-0 counts. "Joe McCarthy always had me hitting. That gave me an edge over the pitchers." (Page 112)

> McCarthy not only knew that Wilson should be allowed to swing when he wanted, but he also understood that his slugger had an unusual need for public approval. If the crowds failed to applaud, McCarthy would take their place. McCarthy also brought a toughness to the Cubs organization. (Page 62)

Well, the right to swing away may have had something to do with it, but I think the key was that McCarthy laid down rules and enforced them. Wilson was a player who needed those rules. McCarthy *knew* what time his players went to bed. If Wilson stayed out late one night he might not say anything, but if he did it again it was time to sit him down and have a talk with him.

It was people skills, in short—not people skills like Chuck Tanner, where everybody liked him and did whatever the hell they wanted to, but *practical* people skills. Chuck Tanner knew what his players *wanted*. Joe McCarthy knew what his players *needed*.

If There Was No Professional Baseball, What Would He Probably Have Done with His Life? He'd have become the chief of the Philadelphia Fire Department.

Pie Traynor

Pie Traynor was discreet enough not to stick needles under another team's fingernails, but then, Pie Traynor didn't have an army of local reporters looking for a story, either. The chronology of the 1938 Pirates closely parallels that of the 1934 New York Giants. Both teams, at various points, had records of 8–3, 13–10, 43–25, 48–28, 52–30, 57–32, and 61–35. Both teams had five-game leads in early September, and both teams still held the lead with a few games to play. Both teams lost the pennant by 2 games.

There is an exception to every rule, and the 1938 Pirates are the exception to the rule that the press will fry you if you get ahead and then lose a pennant race at the last minute. The Pirates, 62–35 on August 9, went 24–29 down the stretch, and were beaten by a Chicago team which is arguably the worst championship team the National League has ever had. In spite of this, the pennant race has been written into history not as a collapse by the Pirates, but as a victory by the Cubs. The "Homer in the Gloaming" is essentially all that is now remembered of that pennant race.

The *1939 Spalding Guide* blamed the collapse of the Pirates on their starting pitchers:

> There was not much fault to find with the batting of the team. The trouble was with the staying power of the pitchers. They could travel along at a good gait until toward the close of a game, when they would show a tendency to weaken.

The Pirates had finished almost last in the league in complete games, with 57. In the 1930s this was considered a character flaw. Mace Brown, a reliever, led the team in wins, with 15. It was the first time in baseball history a pure reliever had led his team in wins.

The 1938 Pirates were 34 runs better than the league average in runs scored, 43 runs better than average in runs allowed—thus, the statement that the batters were good but the pitching failed is incorrect. Forbes Field was essentially a neutral park at this time, with a small tendency to favor hitters, rather than pitchers.

What did happen to the team? Reversing John Foster's appraisal, I would give Pie Traynor good marks for his handling of the pitching staff. He got above-average performance out of an undistinguished pitching staff by giving his bullpen a chance to help Fout. He was ahead of his time in the handling of his pitching staff.

But, like Leo Durocher in 1969 and Don Zimmer in 1977, Traynor rode his starting lineup into the ground. All of his regulars except the catcher had more than 600 plate appearances, and all played more than 90% of the team's games. His catcher, Al Todd, caught 132 games, more than anyone else in the major leagues. The guy wasn't even very good; why couldn't Traynor afford to give him a day off now and then? A player's stats look much more impressive with 600 at bats than they do with 450, so this gives the impression that the Pirate offense was strong. The Pirates scored 4.90 runs per game through August 9, but slumped badly in the closing weeks, while the team ERA actually improved.

That was Pie Traynor's fourth full season as manager of the Pirates, and the fourth time he had kept the team in contention. The team had gone 86–67, 84–70, 86–68, and 86–64. They had an off season in 1939, and Traynor never managed again.

Power Shifts

Unlike most of their modern counterparts, the major league managers of 1934 all had been, or were still, outstanding players. The playing credentials of seven of them were good enough for admission into baseball's Hall of Fame.

—G. H. Fleming, *The Dizziest Season*

Fleming is, of course, drifting out to left field when he says that all of the managers of 1934 had been outstanding players. Joe McCarthy never played in the major leagues, and several of the other managers (Connie Mack, Casey Stengel, Bill McKechnie) were certainly not outstanding players.

As long as there have been managers, there have been managers who were not outstanding players. In 1885 there were twenty-one men who managed major league teams for ten or more games, eight of whom had never themselves played in the major leagues:

	1885
Outstanding Players	3
Good Players	5
Fringe Players	5
Didn't Play in the Majors	8
Good or Outstanding:	38%

This count is somewhat misleading, for two reasons. First, the leagues at that time were very new. Probably some of the managers of 1885 had been good players or even tremendous players, but were finished or nearly finished before the the two major leagues of 1885 (the National League and the American Association) were organized. Second, the job of "manager" was not as well defined then as it is now, so that at times it is even somewhat difficult to say in retrospect whom we should consider the "manager." There were, in the 1880s, bench coaches, playing coaches, owners-who-also-ran-the-team, and people who were called "managers," but whose duties were more in line with what we now consider a traveling secretary.

But we have to start somewhere. The use of outstanding players as managers became more common over time, so that by 1945 about 82% of major league managers had been good or outstanding players:

	1885	**1901**	**1916**	**1930**	**1945**
Outstanding Players	3	7	7	6	8
Good Players	5	2	5	3	6
Fringe Players	5	5	14	7	2
Didn't Play	8	2	2	1	1
Good or Outstanding	38%	56%	43%	53%	82%

To draw up this chart, we made arbitrary decisions about who was a good player, who was a fringe player, etc. You would agree with 95% of these classifications; they're mostly obvious. In both 1930 and 1945, the one major league pilot who hadn't played in the majors was Joe McCarthy. So to some extent, Fleming is on track. The managers of that time *did* include many men who had been outstanding players.

For the last fifty years, we've gone in the other direction. The percentage of major league managers who were outstanding players has steadily declined:

	1945	1960	1975	1990
Outstanding Players	8	6	5	3
Good Players	6	6	7	10
Fringe Players	2	8	13	12
Didn't Play in the Majors	1	1	5	8
Good or Outstanding	82%	57%	40%	39%

To have a major league manager who hadn't played at all in the major leagues was still uncommon until the early 1970s. By 1990, the last point of our study, 61% of the managers were either fringe players or had not played in the majors. The three 1990 managers who were listed as outstanding players were Frank Robinson, Joe Torre, and Red Schoendienst, although arguments can be made that Davey Johnson and Lou Piniella would also deserve to be called outstanding.

It may be that the percentage of managers who had been outstanding players was pushed downward from 1950 to 1990 because many of the best players were blacks and Latins, who were almost never hired to manage. In recent years Felipe Alou, Cito Gaston, Don Baylor, and Dusty Baker have all gotten a chance to manage, and have all had some success. Thus, it may be that the number of managers who were outstanding players is now headed *upward*, not downward.

Master

Of the fourteen highest-scoring teams since 1900, nine were managed by Joe McCarthy.

Six of those nine teams were Yankee teams. The 1931 Yankees, McCarthy's first New York team, scored 1,067 runs, the most of any team since 1900. The 1936 Yankees scored 1,065, second-most since 1900, and the 1932, 1937, 1938, and 1939 Yankee teams are also among the top fourteen teams in runs scored.

But of the five highest-scoring *non*-Yankee teams since 1901, three were also managed by Joe McCarthy. The most runs ever scored by a non-Yankee team were 1,027, by the 1950 Red Sox, managed by Joe McCarthy for the first half of the season. The 1930 Cubs, managed by McCarthy until the closing days of the season, scored 998 runs, missing the modern National League record by only six runs. The 1929 Cubs, despite an injury to Rogers Hornsby which basically wiped out the season of the greatest right-handed hitter in National League history, still scored 982 runs. This is the third-highest total in modern National League history— but the ninth-best total for a team managed by Joe McCarthy.

JOE McCARTHY'S
All-Star Team

		G	AB	R	H	2B	3B	HR	RBI	BB	SO	SB	Avg	SPct
C	Bill Dickey, 1937	140	530	87	176	35	2	29	133	73	22	3	.332	.570
1B	Lou Gehrig, 1934	154	579	128	210	40	6	49	165	109	31	9	.363	.708
2B	Rogers Hornsby, '29	156	602	156	229	47	8	39	149	87	65	2	.380	.679
3B	Red Rolfe, 1939	152	648	139	213	46	10	14	80	81	41	7	.329	.495
SS	Vern Stephens, 1949	155	610	113	177	31	2	39	159	101	73	2	.290	.539
LF	Ted Williams, 1949	155	566	150	194	39	3	43	159	162	48	1	.343	.650
CF	Joe DiMaggio, 1937	151	621	151	215	35	15	46	167	64	37	3	.346	.673
RF	Babe Ruth, 1931	145	534	149	199	31	3	46	163	128	51	5	.373	.700
DH	Hack Wilson, 1930	155	585	146	208	35	6	56	190	105	84	3	.356	.723

		G	IP	W–L	Pct.	H	SO	BB	ERA	GS	CG	ShO	Sv
SP	Lefty Gomez, 1934	38	282	26–5	.808	223	158	96	2.33	33	25	6	1
SP	Charley Root, 1927	48	309	26–15	.634	296	145	117	3.76	36	21	4	2
SP	Mel Parnell, 1949	39	295	25–7	.781	258	122	134	2.77	33	27	4	2
SP	Spud Chandler, 1943	30	253	20–4	.833	197	134	54	1.64	30	20	5	0
RA	Johnny Murphy, 1941	35	77	8–3	.727	68	29	40	1.98	0	0	0	15

JIMMIE DYKES'S
All-Star Team

		G	AB	R	H	2B	3B	HR	RBI	BB	SO	SB	Avg	SPct
C	Johnny Romano, 1961	142	509	76	152	29	1	21	80	61	60	0	.299	.483
1B	Zeke Bonura, 1936	148	587	120	194	39	7	12	138	94	29	4	.330	.482
2B	Don Kolloway, 1942	147	601	72	164	40	4	3	60	30	39	16	.273	.368
3B	Eddie Yost, 1959	148	521	115	145	19	0	21	61	135	77	9	.278	.436
SS	Luke Appling, 1936	138	526	111	204	31	7	6	128	85	25	10	.388	.508
LF	Gus Zernial, 1953	147	556	85	158	21	3	42	108	57	79	4	.284	.559
CF	Mike Kreevich, 1937	144	583	94	176	29	16	12	73	43	45	10	.302	.468
RF	Al Simmons, 1934	138	558	102	192	36	7	18	104	53	58	3	.344	.530

		G	IP	W–L	Pct.	H	SO	BB	ERA	GS	CG	ShO	Sv
SP	Bobby Shantz, 1952	33	280	24–7	.774	230	152	63	2.48	33	27	5	0
SP	Thornton Lee, 1941	35	300	22–11	.667	258	130	92	2.37	34	30	3	1
SP	Vern Kennedy, 1936	35	274	21–9	.700	282	99	147	4.63	34	20	1	0
SP	Monty Stratton, 1937	22	165	15–5	.750	142	69	37	2.40	21	14	5	0
SP	Ted Lyons, 1942	20	180	14–6	.700	167	50	26	2.10	20	20	1	0
RA	G Maltzberger, 1943	37	99	7–4	.636	86	48	24	2.46	0	0	0	14

Nasty Little Man

To be or not to be, that is the question (Alva) Bradley has been asking himself and his Indians ever since taking them over a dozen years ago. Usually rated one-two at the start, it's always the shadow of another club that darkens the payoff window. Maybe this is Alva's year. And it certainly looks like it—on paper.

—*Who's Who in the Major Leagues, 1939*

Alva Bradley was the president of the Cleveland Indians for many years. The Indians were purchased for $1 million in 1927 by a consortium of local businessmen. Bradley was apparently the big money; anyway, he was delegated to act for the group. He hired Billy Evans, an old umpire, to be the general manager, incidentally the first man in baseball to be called the general manager. Evans, in turn, hired Cy Slapnicka to be his chief scout. Along with Barrow and Krichell in New York, they represented the most professional front office of the time.

Bradley told the team to spend whatever it took to contend. Evans was aggressive, and Slapnicka had a great eye for talent. They brought in Earl Averill, Wes Ferrell, Mel Harder, Johnny Allen, Odell Hale, Joe Vosmik, Hal Trosky, and Bob Feller, among many others. Lou Boudreau, Ken Keltner, Jeff Heath. The team, unfortunately, developed a habit of finishing third. They finished third or fourth in 1929, 1930, 1931, '32, '33, '34, '35, and '37. In 1936 they finished fifth, but that was a fluke, with four teams huddled between 80 and 83 wins. They were 3 games out of second place.

The Indians were managed for years by very nice men—first by Roger Peckinpaugh, who was well liked, and then by Walter Johnson, who was even a nicer guy, and then by Steve O'Neill, who was, if anything, even nicer. By the late 1930s they were getting tired of this. The feeling around town was that the Indians were as good, on paper, as anybody in baseball, and maybe the manager just wasn't getting enough out of the

boys. Joe McCarthy, after all, had never been accused of being excessively pleasant.

Oscar Vitt had faced that accusation, but it had been a few years. Born in San Francisco in 1890, Vitt was headed for a career as an architect, but first he wanted to play a little baseball. He had enough ability to draw offers, but his father refused to give permission. The San Francisco earthquake of 1906 moved his father's opinion, and Vitt signed with Oakland in the California State League.

In ten years in the majors, Vitt rubbed shoulders with Ty Cobb and Babe Ruth. Cobb once threatened to blow his frigging head off, but then, that was just Ty's way of making you feel welcome. Vitt was a character—a fighter, a practical joker, a storyteller, known for his perpetual smile. Ronald Mayer's book, *The 1937 Newark Bears*, contains a marvelous profile of Vitt, and is the source of much of my information here. After dropping out of the majors Vitt had several good years at Salt Lake City and was hired to manage the Salt Lake City team.

As a manager he was more intense, and more successful. He managed for eleven years in the Pacific Coast League, with Salt Lake City, Hollywood, and Oakland. At Salt Lake City he signed Tony Lazzeri, tutored him for a couple of years, and eventually sold him for $50,000 to his old friend Ed Barrow, for whom he had played in Boston.

He managed nine years in Hollywood, winning 100 games almost every year, and was repeatedly within inches of landing a major league job. In 1934, when Bucky Harris was dismissed in Detroit, Vitt was certain that he had the ticket. It went instead to Mickey Cochrane. Vitt, irritated to the point of unreasonableness, demanded a big raise from his owner in Hollywood, and the owner fired him.

He managed a year in Oakland and then was hired by Ed Barrow to take over the Newark Bears. The 1937 Newark Bears are believed by many people to be the best minor league team in history, mostly because they played in the New York area, and the New York media can't stand not to have the best of everything. They were a good team, anyway, won 109 games, two rounds of playoffs, and the Junior World Series.

The Indians were looking for a manager, and Oscar by this time had long since worn out the nice-guy label. "I don't want any lazy players on my club," Vitt said at the press conference annoucing his selection. "If the boys won't hustle, out they go."

They finished third—third in 1938, third again in 1939. The team was marginally better under Vitt than they had been under the nice guys. They won 86 games in 1938, the most they had won since 1932, and 87 games in 1939. Nobody was sending flowers.

The team that Vitt inherited had more than its share of talent, and more than its share of characters. His catcher was Rollie Hemsley. On a train ride in early 1939, Rollie and a couple of friends raised such a commotion, marching up and down the aisles with a trumpet stolen from the luggage of a *New York Times* reporter, that the traveling secretary stuck his head out of an upper berth to complain. The next time down the aisle Rollie opened the gentleman's berth and tossed in a handful of lighted matches, and on the subsequent journey, a few cups of water.

Cy Slapnicka by this time was the general manager. When the train got to Cleveland, Slapnicka brought two large strangers to meet the train. The group took command of Hemsley, and marched him off to a meeting of Alchoholics Anonymous; it was what we would now call an "intervention."

Well, Hemsley got to like A.A., became an enthusiastic spokesmen for them, and reportedly convinced several of his teammates to attend with him. One who wouldn't go along was Johnny Allen. Allen was among the most talented pitchers in baseball. Jimmie Foxx said that Johnny Allen was by far the toughest pitcher he ever faced. By the

spring of 1939 he had been in the league for six years, with a career record of 99–38.

But Allen, in the words of Franklin Lewis, "had the temper of seventeen wildcats." Allen was probably the model for Gil Gamesh, the hot-tempered pitcher in Philip Roth's *The Great American Novel*. It was known that he could lose his composure on the mound, and the other teams had ideas on how to nurture Johnny's temper. In 1937 the heckling became so pervasive that Slapnicka wrote a letter to the league president, protesting the poor sportsmanship of Allen's tormentors and asking the league to direct the umpires to help control it. This backfired, of course, and the razzing intensified. Allen littered the 1930s with famous tantrums, smashing up barrooms and hotel lobbies, and once attacked the other team's third-base coach in mid-inning.

On June 7, 1938, Allen was pitching in Boston, pitching well. Red Sox hitters complained that a thread dangling from Allen's uniform was distracting them, and home plate umpire Bill McGowan ordered Allen to cut the thread. Allen flew into a rage and refused to remove the offending string. McGowan told him to cut the thread or leave the mound. Allen left the mound. Vitt ordered him to return; Allen still refused. Vitt fined him $250.

Now the confrontation was between Allen and Vitt. Allen thought the manager should have stood up for him. They exchanged insults for a couple of days, and Allen was suspended. Alva Bradley eventually defused the situation by having his brother, who ran a department store, purchase the sweatshirt for $250 and display it in a glass showcase. The sweatshirt today is the property of the Hall of Fame.

Then there was Bob Feller, the phenomenal young talent whose high school graduation ceremony had been broadcast on national radio, and who had the self-image one would expect of a twenty-year-old kid whose high school graduation ceremony was national news.

The team never warmed up to Vitt. Perhaps this is inevitable, as Vitt had been brought in to whip a collection of talented losers into shape. Vitt, the players alleged, was a nasty little man who would sit on the bench while the team was in the field, bitching about the pitch selection, the mechanics, the glove work, the umpiring, everything and anything. When the players came back to the bench, he wouldn't say anything about it. The players lost respect for him.

Vitt criticized his players in the press; he also criticized his front office. Once, when Slapnicka asked Vitt to cooperate in a promotion, Vitt refused, saying "You run the front office, and I'll run the ball club." By the end of 1938, Vitt and Slapnicka were almost in open warfare.

On June 11, 1940, Mel Harder was hit hard in Boston. The team had had a difficult road trip, dropping out of first place. Harder was a hard-working, soft-spoken player who had been with the team more than ten years. Vitt had to go to the mound and get him. "When are you going to start earning your salary?" he asked Harder sarcastically.

"I always gave you the best I had," said Harder softly.

When the Indians returned to town, a delegation of twelve veteran players requested a meeting with Alva Bradley. They were led by Bob Feller, Al Milnar, Mel Harder, Hal Trosky, and Rollie Hemsley, although Trosky's mother died that morning, and he left for home before the sitdown. The players gave Bradley a litany of complaints about the manager. He had ridiculed his players to the newsmen, the fans, to opposing players and managers. He was sarcastic. He was insincere. He was a "wild man" on the bench, running up and down, making caustic comments on players' mistakes. He made everybody nervous. He had made the team a laughingstock among other teams. He constantly compared the Indians to the 1937 Newark Bears, who, he insisted, never made these kind of mistakes.

Alva Bradley stared somberly at the players.

"Who else knows about this?" he asked the men. The players shifted and stared at their feet.

"If word of this gets out," said Bradley, "you will be ridiculed for the rest of your lives."

The Indians went into full retreat, but the Cleveland *Plain Dealer* already had the story. They ran it as a front page, eight-column headline, followed by foot after foot of type detailing the conflicts between Vitt and his players. The players got all the worst of it. According to *The Cleveland Indians*, by Franklin Lewis (Putnam, 1949), "There never had been a story like it. The tag 'Cry Babies' was attached to the Indians immediately."

Alva Bradley, placed in an impossible position, decided to publicly support his manager. Bradley was well liked by the players. He met with the team and asked them to withdraw their allegations. All but three men agreed to go along, and signed a petition attempting to cancel out the earlier action.

The press, fans, and players from other teams, however, were not ready to let sleeping papooses lie. For the rest of the year the Cry Babies were taunted in opposing parks by fans waving baby bottles, sucking their thumbs and wearing white bonnets, waving crying towels and diapers and oversize diaper pins. It was a team that, for two years, didn't dare complain about *anything*. Opposing players would wipe their eyes in mock sympathy; umpires would dismiss them with icy silence.

The standard interpretation of the Cry Babies is that this incident cost the team dearly as they struggled to win their first American League pennant in twenty years. As Dick Bartell said in *Rowdy Richard*, "Blaming your failure to win a pennant on the manager before the season was even half over was the tactic of a bunch of losers. It backfired on them so bad it probably cost them that pennant."

But as I see it, the Cry Babies incident almost certainly worked to the advantage of the team in the 1940 race. If any team had something to play for, this team had. Goaded and defamed, the Indians fought bravely to clear their names. A hot streak in late June propelled them into first place, and they held first into September. It was one of the wildest pennant races ever. Fans in each town would greet the train at the station or the opposing team at their hotel and welcome them with truckloads of ripe tomatoes and rotten eggs.

The Indians pulled together, not including Vitt. In early September the Tigers surged even, then ahead. Johnny Allen and Rollie Hemsley called a team meeting one night in Allen's hotel room. Vitt wasn't using the hit and run enough, said one player. He didn't know when to call a pitchout.

The players made up their own signals, unknown to Vitt, and began to call their own plays. On September 19, Vitt pulled Mel Harder out of a game after seven and two-thirds innings, leading 4–1. Vitt wanted to switch to Bob Feller, although Feller had pitched two days before, and had told Vitt his arm was tired. Feller surrendered the lead. The newspapers roasted Vitt.

One of the greatest pennant races ever ended on the last day of the season, when a rookie named Floyd Giebell, who won a total of 3 major league games, beat Bob Feller 2–0. Cleveland's 89–65 record was the team's best mark between 1921 and 1947—but one game short of Detroit.

Vitt was fired after the season. Johnny Allen was sold to St. Louis, for the waiver price. The Indians went back to Roger Peckinpaugh, the first of the three nice guys who had managed them at the beginning of the Bradley administration. The team collapsed, winning only 75 games for Peckinpaugh, 75 the year after that for Lou Boudreau.

The story of Ossie Vitt is a syllable-for-syllable match for the story of Vern Rapp, 1977–1978.

Both men were tremendously successful minor league managers who narrowly missed several shots at a major league job. Each man was forty-eight years old when his chance finally came—Vitt, after winning a minor league manager of the year award with the Newark Bears, and Rapp, after winning the same award with the Denver Bears. Both men replaced popular, low-pressure managers and attempted to discipline veteran ball clubs. Both men were confronted by clubhouse revolts, but both men were objectively successful, doing better with their teams than the teams had done in the previous years. In both cases, the fact of the team's success was obscured by the controversy surrounding the players' resistance.

Both men were accused by their players of being sarcastic and negative, yet both men had been extremely well liked by those who had played for them in the minor leagues. In both cases, the team essentially collapsed after the manager was fired and was replaced by a more popular manager.

Vitt tended to blame Bob Feller for his problems. I have some sympathy for anybody who had to manage the twenty-two-year-old Bob Feller, but Vitt was a teammate of Babe Ruth when Ruth was twenty-one, and Ty Cobb when Cobb was twenty-six, so he should have known a little bit about the Leviathan egos of young superstars.

What happened here, I think, is something that any schoolteacher can relate to. Sometimes a class just gets away from you. Sometimes a classful of kids will love you; sometimes they'll hate you. You go in the first day, smile when they do good, look at them sideways when they act up. Sometimes they decide you're fun; sometimes they decide you're a pain. There's not a lot you can do about it.

BILL MCKECHNIE'S
All-Star Team

		G	AB	R	H	2B	3B	HR	RBI	BB	SO	SB	Avg	SPct
C	Ernie Lombardi, '38	129	489	60	167	30	1	19	95	40	14	0	.342	.524
1B	Jim Bottomley, 1928	149	576	123	187	42	20	31	136	71	54	10	.325	.628
2B	Frankie Frisch, 1928	141	547	107	164	29	9	10	86	64	17	29	.300	.441
3B	Pie Traynor, 1923	153	616	108	208	19	19	12	101	34	19	28	.338	.489
SS	Glenn Wright, 1925	153	614	97	189	32	10	18	121	31	32	3	.308	.480
LF	Kiki Cuyler, 1925	153	617	144	220	43	26	17	102	58	56	41	.357	.593
CF	Wally Berger, 1930	151	555	98	172	27	14	38	119	54	69	3	.310	.614
RF	Chick Hafey, 1928	138	520	101	175	46	6	27	111	40	53	8	.337	.604

		G	IP	W–L	Pct.	H	SO	BB	ERA	GS	CG	ShO	Sv
SP	Bucky Walters, 1939	39	319	27–11	.711	250	137	109	2.20	38	31	2	0
SP	Paul Derringer, 1939	38	301	25–7	.781	321	128	35	2.93	35	20	5	0
SP	Johnny Morrison, '23	42	302	25–13	.658	287	114	110	3.49	37	27	2	2
SP	Wilbur Cooper, 1922	41	295	23–14	.622	330	129	61	3.18	37	27	4	0
RA	Joe Beggs, 1940	37	77	12–3	.800	68	25	21	1.99	1	0	0	7

JOE CRONIN'S
All-Star Team

		G	AB	R	H	2B	3B	HR	RBI	BB	SO	SB	Avg	SPct
C	Rick Ferrell, 1936	121	410	59	128	27	5	8	55	65	17	0	.312	.461
1B	Jimmie Foxx, 1938	149	565	138	197	33	9	50	175	119	76	5	.349	.704
2B	Buddy Myer, 1935	151	616	115	215	36	11	5	100	96	40	7	.349	.468
3B	Jim Tabor, 1940	126	498	65	139	29	3	16	101	36	48	17	.279	.446
SS	Joe Cronin, 1938	143	530	98	172	51	5	17	94	91	60	7	.325	.536
LF	Ted Williams, 1941	143	456	135	185	33	3	37	120	145	27	2	.406	.735
CF	Dom DiMaggio, 1941	144	584	117	165	37	6	8	58	90	57	13	.283	.408
RF	Bob Johnson, 1944	144	525	106	170	40	8	17	106	95	67	2	.324	.528

		G	IP	W–L	Pct.	H	SO	BB	ERA	GS	CG	ShO	Sv
SP	General Crowder, '33	52	299	245–15	.615	311	110	81	3.97	35	17	0	4
SP	Wes Ferrell, 1935	41	322	25–14	.641	336	110	108	3.52	38	31	3	0
SP	Boo Ferrisds, 1946	40	274	25–6	.806	274	106	71	3.25	35	26	6	3
SP	Tex Hughson, 1942	38	281	22–6	.786	258	113	75	2.59	30	22	4	4
RA	Jack Russell, 1933	50	124	12–6	.667	119	28	32	2.69	3	2	0	13

Bambino, Go Home

One way to get an idea of the magnitude of Joe McCarthy's accomplishments is to use *The Sports Encyclopedia: Baseball*, and choose an All-Star team of the best seasons by McCarthy's players.

At catcher, McCarthy had two of the best-hitting catchers of all time (Gabby Hartnett and Bill Dickey), so you have to choose among .360 seasons and 37-homer campaigns at catcher. At first base he had Lou Gehrig, so the task there is just to decide between the triple crown year and the 184-RBI season. At second base, you have to choose among a dozen or so 100-RBI guys, but even so, Rogers Hornsby is a pretty obvious choice.

When you get to the outfield, though, you realize how almost bizarre the situation is. You wind up having to kick Babe Ruth out of the outfield—Babe Ruth not in his *best* season, but in a season when he still drives in 163 runs. McCarthy managed Hack Wilson when Wilson drove in 190 runs, so that season kind of has to be in the outfield. He managed DiMaggio in DiMaggio's best season, 1937, when DiMag hit 46 homers and drove in 167 runs, so with his defense it's pretty hard to put Joe on the bench.

McCarthy managed dozens

The Batting Order

There is probably no subject within the province of managing which draws more comment than batting order. Whaddaya think, should Olerud be batting cleanup for Toronto, or is it time to slide Delgado in there? Why did Brady Anderson hit leadoff for the 1996 Orioles, when they had Robby Alomar? The Orioles wound up a few games behind the Yankees. Maybe, if Anderson hadn't hit thirty-some homers with the bases empty, they might have won a couple of games along the way.

My local manager, Bob Boone, is the target of constant criticism because he shuffles his batting order from day to day. One day Jose Offerman will hit leadoff, the next day seventh, the next day second.

It drives the fans batty, but what does it actually amount to? How many runs can a manager cost his team by misaligning his batting order? Is it a big item? Is it one of the most important things a manager does? How many games, over the course of a season, can be turned by improper lineup selection? And what is the proper order? Bobby Bragan used to talk about leading off Henry Aaron, and actually did it a few times, on the theory that Aaron would get 50 more at bats a season batting leadoff than he would batting cleanup.

Some managers clearly think that the subject is important. Others seem to imply that it isn't. Billy Martin, at least once, put the names of his players in a hat and drew them out at random, trying (successfully) to shake his team out of a slump. Some people think it is crucial to get speed at the top of the order. Casey Stengel often used leadoff men like Bob Cerv and Elston Howard who couldn't get out of their own way, but did a good job of getting on base.

Let's start with the broadest question: How much difference does it make? I programmed a computer to simulate games played by the Chicago Cubs in 1930, with this lineup:

SS	Woody English
LF	Riggs Stephenson
RF	Kiki Cuyler
CF	Hack Wilson
C	Gabby Hartnett
3B	Les Bell
1B	Charlie Grimm
2B	Footsie Blair
P	Pitchers

The 1930 Cubs had a classic offense, one of the best ever. The leadoff hitter, Woody English, had 214 hits, drew 100 walks, and scored 152 runs. The cleanup hitter, Hack Wilson, hit 56 homers and drove in 190 runs. Many other members of the lineup had impressive hitting stats. The lineup above was more-or-less the team's regular lineup, although Footsie Blair usually hit second, and Bell and Stephenson were in the lineup and out of it. The team scored 998 runs, one of the highest totals in major league history.

With that lineup in place, I then ran the team through 100 simulated seasons, 16,200 games, to see how many runs they would score.

Then I took the same set of players, and put them in what, it seemed to me, would approximate the worst possible sequence in which the players could be arranged. I had the pitchers bat leadoff, while Hack Wilson, with his 56 homers and .356 average, was assigned to hit ninth. I put Les Bell, a .278 hitter with few walks and little speed, batting eighth, so that Wilson would be following the weakest available hitter, and otherwise tried to place the better hitters toward the end of the order, but without putting them together so that their bats could interact with one another. This was the "illogical" lineup:

P	Pitchers
2B	Footsie Blair
SS	Woody English
1B	Charlie Grimm
LF	Riggs Stephenson
C	Gabby Hartnett
RF	Kiki Cuyler
3B	Les Bell
CF	Hack Wilson

Then I ran that team through 100 seasons, to see how many runs they would score. The best order, and the worst order, you see, although (for reasons I explained before) we can't really be sure what the best order or the worst order might be.

How much difference was there between the "correct" batting order, and the same players in an obviously irrational order? Surprisingly enough, very little. The "normal" batting order scored 99,766 runs in the 16,200 games, or 6.16 per game. The screwy batting order, with Hack Wilson batting ninth, scored 94,800 runs, or 5.85 per game. The difference is 5%, or 50 runs per season.

of outfielders who had seasons like Kiki Cuyler in 1930 (.355, 50 doubles, 17 triples, 134 RBI, 37 stolen bases) or Riggs Stephenson in 1929 (.362, 110 RBI) or Ben Chapman in 1931 (.317 with 17 homers, 61 stolen bases, 122 RBI, 120 runs scored). When you work through them, you come down to Babe Ruth, 1931, or Ted Williams, 1949. Williams hit .343 with 43 homers, 159 RBI, but Ruth has better triple-crown numbers all around: 46, 163, .373. Still, Williams's triple crown numbers are decent enough, and when you add in the 39 doubles, 150 runs scored, and 162 walks, his season seems to me to be a little bit better.

I decided to add a DH.

I am little reluctant to report this study, because I know that most of you aren't going to believe me anyway. I am not the first person to study this issue in approximately the same way. Dick Cramer, twenty years ago, programmed a computer to simulate offenses. Dick constructed a lineup of six pitchers and three Babe Ruths. He then put this lineup in what seems like the most logical order (the three Babe Ruths hitting one, two, and three), and then in the most illogical order (the three Babe Ruths hitting three, six, and nine). By spacing out the three Babe Ruth lines among a string of unproductive hitters, he minimized the interaction between the only good hitters on the team.

I'm uncertain whether Dr. Cramer's study was ever published, and I can't quote specific data from it, but I know essentially what he found: the same thing I found, twenty years later. It doesn't make much difference what order you put the hitters in. I know that you're not going to believe me, because when Dr. Cramer told me about his study, I didn't believe him, either. It's counterintuitive. What do you mean, it doesn't make much difference? We can all think of a thousand reasons why it *should* make a difference what order you put the hitters in.

Let me explain as best I can why it doesn't. In the "good" model, Hack Wilson batted 64,237 times, hitting 6,082 home runs and driving in 20,818 runs, or .3241 RBI per at bat. (In real life he had .3248 RBI per at bat.) By moving Hack to ninth in the batting order, we took almost 8,000 at bats away from him, dropping him to 56,310 at bats. As a consequence of that, we cut him back to 5,490 home runs. By putting a weaker hitter batting ahead of him, we reduced his RBI per at bat from .324 to .294. Thus, we cut Wilson from 20,818 RBI to 16,558.

The thing is, though, that *you can't move everybody down in the batting order.* When you move one guy down, you have to move somebody else up. And you can't put everybody hitting behind the weakest hitters in the lineup. When you put Hack Wilson hitting behind one of the weakest hitters in the lineup, you have to put somebody else batting behind Riggs Stephenson (.367), and somebody else batting behind Kiki Cuyler (.355).

Of course, the loss on Hack Wilson is greater than the gain on the other hitters, because we moved the *best* hitter to the *worst* spot. We succeeded in eliminating 20% of Hack Wilson's RBI—but 75% of those RBI were picked up by other hitters. And in the final analysis, the team lost only 5% of its total run production by having the hitters in the worst order that I could come up with.

With the "logical" lineup, the best innings start when the leadoff hitter leads off, and the second-best innings are when the second-place hitter leads off. In this study, Woody English led off in 31,251 innings, during which the team scored 27,849 runs, or .891 per inning. When the second hitter (Riggs Stephenson) led off, the average was .817 per inning:

Innings Started By	Leadoff Innings	Runs Scored/Inning
#1 (Woody English)	31,251	.891
#2 (Riggs Stephenson)	11,410	.817
#3 (Kiki Cuyler)	12,049	.749
#4 (Hack Wilson)	15,149	.646
#5 (Gabby Hartnett)	14,220	.530
#6 (Les Bell)	14,369	.510
#7 (Charlie Grimm)	15,187	.545
#8 (Footsie Blair)	15,300	.627
#9 (Pitchers)	14,657	.754

There is a logic to that. Woody English not only led off the *best* innings, but also the *most* innings—in fact, he led off twice as many innings as any other player. On a typical team, the number five hitter is second on the team in innings led off. On this team that wasn't true because they had so many great hitters that they tended to push those second-inning leadoff opportunities down further in the lineup.

With the "illogical" lineup, we got these results:

Innings Started By	Leadoff Innings	Runs Scored/Inning
#1 (Pitchers)	27,636	.549
#2 (Footsie Blair)	14,972	.641
#3 (Woody English)	13,211	.740
#4 (Charlie Grimm)	15,936	.692
#5 (Riggs Stephenson)	18,123	.771
#6 (Gabby Hartnett)	13,322	.722
#7 (Kiki Cuyler)	13,464	.674
#8 (Les Bell)	12,940	.596
#9 (Hack Wilson)	14,609	.607

Now the players who lead off most often are the worst leadoff hitters, the pitchers. This creates fewer runners, and fewer runs.

But when you work through the math, the net loss in runs is small. Charlie Grimm now has Stephenson, Harnett, and Cuyler coming up behind him, rather than Blair and the pitchers, so the innings in which Grimm leads off now yield .692 runs per inning, whereas in the earlier study they yielded .545. Gabby Hartnett is not a natural leadoff man, but the innings in which Hartnett leads off now yield .722 runs/inning, rather than .530, because Kiki Cuyler is now batting behind him, and Hack Wilson is now the cleanup hitter in Hartnett's innings. The innings led off by English, Cuyler, Stephenson, Wilson, and the pitchers are less productive than they were before, but the innings led off by Blair, Hartnett, Grimm, and Bell are more productive.

With the "good" lineup, this team scored 14,366 runs in the first inning (in 16,200 games). With the "bad" lineup, they scored only 9,147 first-inning runs—down 36%.

But in the *second* inning, the "good" lineup scored only 9,740 runs. The "bad" lineup scored 11,647—up 20%.

In the third inning the ill-constructed lineup is worse off by 13%, because the top of the order is up again.

But in the fourth inning, they're up by 7%.

So if you add that together, what do you have? Down 36, up 20, down 13, up 7; that's a total of down 22, for four innings. That's a little more than five per inning. Actually, it's a little more than that; it's 9% through the first four innings—but 2% in innings five through nine. I've given you the numbers you need to run the math if you want to, but when you add everything up, the net loss in runs is only 5%.

Now, if the difference between a reasonable batting order and a completely unreasonable batting order is only 5%, what do you suppose the difference would be between two reasonable batting orders? That's right: it's nothing. You take any two reasonable batting orders for any team, put them on a computer and play a hundred seasons, and you'll find they score just as many runs one way as they do another.

Of course, there is no legal requirement for you to accept the findings of the computer. This is an offensive simulator of reasonable sophistication. You might wonder, for example, whether the offensive simulator might miss the value of speed by some clumsy process of routinely sending all runners from first to third on a single, or no runners from first to third on a single. We have been assiduously gathering information on the play-by-play of major league games for more than ten years now, and we have good information on how often runners go from first to third on a single, and on how speed affects that outcome. That information is built into the model. The fast runners go from first to third on a single much more frequently than do the slow runners.

The model is sophisticated enough to specify which field the ball is hit to, and thus is sophisticated enough to send a runner from first to third slightly more often on a single by a left-handed hitter than on a single by a right-handed hitter, because the left-handed hitter is more likely to pull the ball into right field than is the right-hander.

At the same time, real baseball games remain vastly more complex than our statistical models of them. For that reason, it is quite possible that some portion of the difference we are attempting to measure here is eluding us. Many people would argue, for example, that when there is a fast runner on first the hitter at the plate is much more likely to see a fastball, and thus more likely to get a hit. If the first baseman has to hold the runner on, people will tell you, this increases the size of the hole on the right side, and thus increases the batting average of a left-handed hitter in that situation. Thus, they would argue, there is a synergistic interaction between speed and hitting. Our model does not simulate any such interaction.

Our model does not simulate any such interaction, because there is no evidence that such an interaction occurs. The evidence, in point of fact, is the opposite. If you look at a *real* base stealer, and you check the batting averages of the man who bats after him, you will normally find that that average goes *down* with a man on first base, whether the hitter is right-handed or left-handed. Why? Because the batter is often taking a pitch to allow the runner to steal, and for that reason is often hitting behind in the count, whether the runner attempts to steal, or whether he doesn't.

Still, on the more general point, our model assumes that a .355 hitter is a .355 hitter, regardless of where you put him in the lineup (except for the small effects of sacrifice plays). Many people would argue that this is not true, that there might be any number of possible interactions between hitters which are not represented in the model. Our model is far from perfect, and it is absolutely possible that in the future, more sophisiticated models will be developed which will yield different results.

But for now, this discussion has two groups. On the one hand, you have the barroom experts, the traditional sportswriters, the couch potatoes, and the call-in show regulars, all of whom believe that batting orders are important. And then, on the other hand, you have a few of us who have actually studied the issue, and who have been forced to draw the conclusion that it doesn't make much difference what order you put the hitters in, they're going to score just as many runs one way as another. You can believe whoever you want to; it's up to you.

Stengel and Southworth

Billy Southworth was the most successful manager of the 1940s; Casey Stengel, of course, was the most successful manager of the 1950s.

The two men have many things in common. Stengel was born in Kansas City in 1890; Southworth was born in a small town in Nebraska in 1893, but was raised in Columbus, Ohio.

Both were National League players, both outfielders, both left-handed hitters. Stengel reached the major leagues in late 1912; Southworth played one game with Cleveland in late 1913, then went back to the minors for a few years.

The Pittsburgh Pirates traded for Stengel in January 1918, expecting him to play right field. Stengel didn't play well, however, complained about his salary, fought with umpires, had some minor injuries, and was frequently booed by the fans. With World War I going on in Europe, Stengel quit the team in June and joined the navy.

Southworth got his job. Playing well in the minors, Southworth was purchased by the Pirates and reported to them on July 1, 1918. He played tremendously well until the season's early end, hitting .341 in 64 games, and was listed in some contemporary publications as the National League batting champion.

Thus, when Stengel rejoined the Pirates the next season, he was unable to get back in the lineup full time. Stengel was traded to Philadelphia, and from then on to New York. Southworth didn't play as well after his brilliant beginning, so a year later he was traded to Boston. (Stengel, incidentally, was traded for *Possum* Whitted. Southworth was traded for *Rabbit* Maranville. The Pirates were apparently intent on collecting a menagerie.)

Anyway, Stengel spent two years as a platoon player for John McGraw, 1922–1923, after which he was traded to Boston—for Billy Southworth.

It was a trade which hurt both teams. In retrospect, one wonders why either team made the move. Stengel liked McGraw, or if he didn't was at least smart enough not to say so. He played very well in the Polo Grounds, hitting .368 and .339. Southworth, playing regularly in Boston, had hit .319 and scored 95 runs, but McGraw apparently intended from the beginning to slip Southworth into Stengel's platoon slot, in which case it is hard to see what Southworth might have been expected to do that Stengel wasn't already doing.

Southworth and McGraw didn't get along, and Southworth didn't play well. The Boston fans, who had adored Southworth, were slow to accept Stengel as his replacement, and Stengel didn't play well—thus, both of their careers went into a tailspin.

Both Southworth and Stengel were hustling, aggressive players, generally popular with the fans, Southworth more so than Stengel. Both were combative men, Stengel more so than Southworth. It would be hard to say who was a better player, overall; they were essentially the same. Southworth had 1,296 hits, a .415 career slugging percentage, 138 career stolen bases, 402 walks and 561 RBI. Stengel had 1,219 hits, a .410 slugging percentage, 131 stolen bases, 437 walks, and 535 RBI. Southworth played for five major league teams in thirteen seasons; Stengel played for five teams in fourteen seasons.

Both men went from being major league players one year to being minor league managers the next, Stengel starting at Worcester in 1925, Southworth at Rochester in 1928. Both were failures in their first shot at managing in the majors. Southworth took over a championship team in 1929, did nothing with it, and went back to the minor leagues for ten years to reestablish his credibility. Stengel failed in Brooklyn, failed in Boston, but went back to the minors to reestablish his credibility.

Both Stengel and Southworth managed the Boston Braves in the 1940s, Stengel unsuccessfully; Southworth, successfully.

Both managers liked to platoon. Platooning was common in 1915–1925, when Stengel and Southworth played, but fell out of favor until the 1940s. Both Stengel and Southworth were instrumental in reestablishing the strategy. Both were tremendously successful for ten years, dominating the game, and then both were essentially finished, although Stengel tried to manage again.

As personalities, they were very different. Stengel was loud, funny, charming, always the center of attention. Southworth was quiet, warm, and agreeable, if occasionally self-righteous. Stengel played hunches; Southworth was very reasonable, very logical. Stengel admired John McGraw, and emulated McGraw as a manager. Southworth, though he made peace with McGraw after he was traded away, always tried not to do things the way McGraw had done them. He felt that McGraw didn't communicate with his players, didn't explain what he was doing; he made it a point to make sure that his players knew what he was doing and why he was doing it. Stengel's players often had little idea what Casey was doing, or why he was doing it. Southworth's troubles with McGraw came to a head when he felt that McGraw second-guessed him on a play in the field, and for that reason he was obsessive about not second-guessing his own men.

Southworth's teams dominated the National League in the 1940s almost to the same extent that Stengel's dominated the American League in the 1950s. Southworth's record in the 1940s was 890–557, a .633 winning percentage; Stengel in the 1950s was 955–582, a .636 percentage. Southworth's teams won 106, 105, and 105 games in consecutive seasons, and won 90 or more six times; Stengel never won more than 103, but won 90 or more nine times. Southworth's record is more impressive, in that he did it with two teams, neither of which was strong before he took over, but Stengel's record is more impressive in that he won twice as many pennants in his decade (eight to four) and three times as many World Championships (six to two).

Southworth's career reached an abrupt end. Like most of the great managers, Billy was an alcoholic. After he failed in his first shot at managing, with the Cardinals in 1929, his drinking got out of control, and he hit bottom in 1933, out of baseball. He stopped drinking then, pulled his life together, got a second wife, and earned a second chance in baseball. He lectured his teams on the virtues of temperance, restraint, and self-discipline. From his perspective, he was trying to warn his players that they were doing things that might cost them their careers, their marriages, or their money. The lectures were not always appreciated, and this created conflicts with his players.

By August 1949, Southworth was in danger of a nervous breakdown. He took the last six weeks of the 1949 season off to recuperate, and tried to come back in 1950. The team didn't play well, and his career was over just as Stengel's was beginning to take off.

Decade Snapshot: 1940s

Most Successful Managers: 1. Billy Southworth
2. Joe McCarthy
3. Leo Durocher

Most Controversial Manager: Leo Durocher

Others of Note: Lou Boudreau
Eddie Dyer
Steve O'Neill
Luke Sewell
Burt Shotton

Stunts: In *The Fordham Flash,* Frankie Frisch recalled something that happened while he was managing the Pittsburgh Pirates, probably about 1946. There was a gentleman who sat behind his dugout every game in a box seat and offered his advice about when to bunt, when to hit and run, etc.

One day before the game, Frisch approached the grandstand manager and made his dreams come true:

> I told him we were going to let him direct the Pirates that day. . . . Well, he wasn't too bad a manager, at that. I changed pitchers at his suggestion and signaled for the hit-and-run a couple of times for him and used the pinch hitters he suggested. But we lost the ball game, about 7 to 4. . . .
>
> "We enjoyed having you work with us today," I told him (after the game), "By the way, what business are you in?"
>
> He told me he was in the brokerage business and I said, "All right, Mr. Dinwiddie, I'll be down at your office in the morning with my two coaches and we'll tell you how to run your business."

Typical Manager Was: Completely different at the beginning of the decade than at the end. The typical manager until the end of the war was a holdover from the 1920s and 1930s more secure, made gentle by age.

After the war, the older managers were replaced by younger men who had played in the 1930s or early 1940s, who were more aggressive, more intense, generally more inclined to play percentage baseball.

The change in Brooklyn from Burt Shotton to Charlie Dressen, although it didn't occur until 1951, was fairly typical of the transition. Shotton, who had played from 1909 to 1923, was ridiculed by Dick Young as KOBS, Kindy Old Burt Shotton. Dressen wasn't young, but he was fourteen years younger than Shotton, and a lot edgier.

Percentage of Playing Managers: 19%

Most Second-Guessed Manager's Move: 1948, the American League pennant race ended in a tie. Joe McCarthy elected to start Denny Galehouse, rather than Mel Parnell, in the playoff game—a decision for which he is still being second-guessed today.

In the fourth game of the 1946 World Series, Bill Bevens of the Yankees was working on a no-hitter with two out in the ninth inning. The score was just 2–1, however, and the tying run was on second base due to a walk and a stolen base. Apparently trying to protect the no-hitter, Bucky Harris ordered an intentional walk to Pete Reiser. This went against "the book," which prohibits putting the potential winning run on base. A pinch hitter doubled off the wall, giving Brooklyn a 3–2 victory.

Player Rebellions: Cleveland, 1940, vs. Ossie Vitt; Brooklyn, 1943, vs. Leo Durocher.

Evolutions in Strategy: The peculiar baseball of the war years forced adjustments, which reshaped the postwar game. Without star pitchers, almost every team began using an old guy like Jittery Joe Berry, Ace Adams, Gordon Maltzberger, or Joe Heving as a relief ace.

The stolen base, moribund during the 1920s and 1930s, made a brief revival, as the dead baseballs of the war era reduced batting averages and all but eliminated home runs in some parks. (In 1945 the only home run hit by the Washington Senators in Griffith Stadium was an inside-the-park home run by Joe Kuhel on the last day of the season.)

Platooning, uncommon since 1925, returned due to the advocacy of Billy Southworth and Casey Stengel.

Evolution in the Role of the Manager: In the first fifty years of major league baseball, the manager was almost entirely responsible for the personnel on his roster. In the 1920s and 1930s, the responsibility for finding and developing *young* players shifted to the front office, but until about 1940, making trades remained a function of the manager. Bill Terry made his own trades; Joe Cronin made his own deals unless the deal involved a sizable hunk of Tom Yawkey's money. Even Frankie Frisch, working for Branch Rickey in St. Louis, had latitude to get the players he wanted and get rid of those he didn't.

About 1940, general managers began to assume responsbility for making trades. Larry MacPhail was probably the first general manager to take full responsibility for the roster, effectively telling the manager to get used to the idea or look for another job.

To a large extent, I think this was an inevitable transition. Every October, some teams would fire their managers. In 1930, when a team fired one manager they would rush to hire the next one, so that the new manager would have time to make his own deals. At some point, General Managers were bound to realize that all they had to do was wait a couple of months to hire the new manager, and the power to make trades would fall to them by default.

Of course, general managers in 1997 still usually make personnel moves in close consultation with their managers. There was also a profound change, after the war, in the after-hours relationship of the manager and his player. It's hard to draw any solid conclusions about this, because nobody wrote about it until Bouton in 1970, but managers in John McGraw's time closely supervised the private lives of their ballplayers. There is a story about a rookie who was so terrified of McGraw that one time a reporter asked him whether he was married, and kid stammered out "I-I-I don't know, sir; you'd better ask Mr. McGraw."

At some point the managers surrendered this control. When exactly did baseball players, including the married ones, start keeping girlfriends in every city? I'm sure there was always some of that, but the practice seems to have exploded in the late 1940s. This was a source of conflict between Billy Southworth and his men in Boston, and also, I believe, between Frankie Frisch and his team in Pittsburgh.

In part, this change occurred because supervising the players became logistically complicated after the war. The cities became larger, and transportation around the cities became more convenient. Rogers Hornsby said, "When I played, the only entertainment for players was movies or baseball or a speakeasy if you could sneak in one."

Night baseball rendered the traditional 11:30 curfew obsolete. More significantly, the culture changed. The new generation of players did not accept the right of employers to supervise their off-hours activities. Sexual mores changed, and more women began to throw themselves at the players.

Not that everything happened at once—some managers still have curfews for some situations in the 1990s—but I believe the fundamental paradigm shift in this area occured about 1948. Leo Durocher became the norm, rather than the exception. The older generation of managers—McCarthy, Mack, Shotton, Southworth, Frisch—were pushed aside, in part, by this change.

LEO DUROCHER IN A BOX

Year of Birth: 1905

Years Managed: 1939–1946, 1948–1955, 1966–1973

Record As a Manager: 2,010–1,710, .540

Managers for Whom He Played: Miller Huggins, Dan Howley, Gabby Street, Frankie Frisch, Burleigh Grimes.

Others by Whom He Was Influenced: Unlike any other manager I can think of, Durocher was heavily influenced by one of his own coaches, Charlie Dressen. Dressen, hired by Larry MacPhail at the same time as Durocher, was seven years older than Durocher, and had experience as a manager. Durocher came to depend on Dressen, and much of what Durocher accomplished, as a manager, is probably due to Dressen's influence.

Characteristics As a Player: Durocher was a better player than sportswriters generally wrote that he was. He was the third-best shortstop in the National League of the 1930s, behind Arky Vaughan and Dick Bartell.

Durocher did not have a good arm, but he was quick, reliable, and alert. He would have been the Gold Glove shortstop of his time, had there been such an award, and he wasn't an awful hitter, hitting .260 with 70 RBI in 1934, .265 with 78 RBI in 1935, and .286 with 58 RBI in 1936.

He wasn't a *good* hitter, either, but he played 1,509 games at shortstop in the major leagues, which ranks forty-eighth on the all-time list. He was a key player on an outstanding team. He made every play that he was supposed to make, and in any sport, you just cannot overstate the importance of having smart players in the middle of the field.

WHAT HE BROUGHT TO A BALL CLUB

Was He an Intense Manager or More of an Easy-to-Get-Along-With Type? He was extremely difficult to get along with.

Was He More of an Emotional Leader or a Decision Maker? He was both, but he was *essentially* an emotional leader.

What made Durocher successful was his intensity, his ability to communicate to his players the urgency of winning *this* game *now!* Durocher would publicly humiliate a player who, in Durocher's opinion, failed to give him his best effort. If a player made a bonehead play on the bases, Durocher might come out on the field and scream at him as he returned to the dugout. He once described one of his pitchers, Luke Hamlin, as "the gutless wonder" to a group of reporters.

Early in his career, Durocher would make a clubhouse production out of "taking a man's uniform" if he thought the player wasn't hustling. He did this about once a year, but in 1943, with the Dodgers not playing well and Charlie Dressen banished by the front office, he turned on Joe Medwick and Bobo Newsom in separate incidents, throwing them both off the team in theatrical temper tantrums. The team rebelled on him. After the tirade directed at Bobo Newsom, Arky Vaughan handed Durocher his uniform and said, "Here. If you want his uniform, you can have mine, too." Durocher was flabbergasted, and his career as a Dodger manager almost ended right there. It took him a year and a half to get back in control of his team.

Was He More of an Optimist or More of a Problem Solver? He was a problem solver.

HOW HE USED HIS PERSONNEL

Did He Favor a Set Lineup or a Rotation System? A set lineup. If his team wasn't playing well, Durocher would change his lineup frequently, but not on a day-to-day basis. He would fix a lineup and give it a few weeks; if it didn't work out, he would try something else or somebody else. Everybody on his teams was clearly either a regular or a substitute, but the designations as to who was the regular and who was the substitute might change three or four times a season.

Did He Like to Platoon? He never platooned in the starting lineup that I know of. He did pinch hit to gain the platoon edge in a key situation, and he was the first major league manager to place an emphasis on having a lefty in the bullpen.

Did He Try to Solve His Problems with Proven Players or with Youngsters Who Still May Have Had Something to Learn? Veterans.

Joe Kuhel

Joe Kuhel's face was halfway between clownish and movie-star handsome. He had large ears and a nose that raced in front of him as if testing its own engine. His natural smile was almost too wide, his color almost too bright, his eyes almost too lively. Had his shoulders stooped just a little bit, a small paunch gathering above his belt, he would have tipped backward into clownishness. Instead, he was trim, erect, energetic, and natty. He looked like a visiting God.

Joe Kuhel was hired to manage the Washington Senators in 1948.

If Walter Alston had gotten the job, you would never have heard of him, either.

Durocher would play a young player only if the young man had exceptional ability, and he had room for about only one at a time (in the lineup). With the sole exception of Pete Reiser, his great 1941–1942 Brooklyn team was entirely built of players cast aside by or purchased from other teams. His 1951–1954 Giants team contained many of the same type of players, plus some mid-career imports from the Negro Leagues, and his late '60s Cubs consisted mostly of players who were in the lineup before Durocher arrived in Chicago.

Durocher believed (accurately, in my opinion) that he could get more out of a player than another manager could, in part by teaching him and showing him things that he was doing wrong, and in part by getting better effort from him. Jim Hickman (1970) would be the best example of this—a player in his mid-thirties who had been around the league for ten years before Durocher got him, and who gave Durocher performance far beyond what anyone else thought he was capable of.

But Durocher had no long-term plan. Next year was next year; two years down the road was something he'd worry about two years down the road.

How Many Players Did He Make Regulars Who Had Not Been Regulars Before, and Who Were They? Very few. Durocher was proud of his ability to work with young players, and his work in developing Willie Mays is one of the things he is most remembered for. But in his twenty-four years as a major league manager, he put less than fifteen players in the lineup who hadn't been regulars before, and no more than half of those fifteen became quality players. His big hits were Mays and Pee Wee Reese, whom the Dodgers drafted from the Red Sox organization. He also made a regular out of Pete Reiser (1940), Whitey Lockman (1948), Monte Irvin (1950), Wes Westrum (1950), Don Mueller (1950), Hank Thompson (1950), Davey Williams (1952), Randy Hundley (1966), and Adolfo Phillips (1966).

He broke in some outstanding pitchers, too, most notably Hugh Casey (1939), Sal Maglie (1950), and Ferguson Jenkins (1966), all of whom had just limited experience before joining Durocher.

The most interesting phase of his career, in this regard, is what he did with the 1948–1950 Giants. Durocher with the Giants took over a collection of sluggers who had hit 221 home runs for Mel Ott in 1947, a major league record at the time, but had finished fourth. He experimented with them for a year and a half, keeping many of the same players in the lineup, but getting a few at bats for Monte Irvin, Wes Westrum, Don Mueller, and Hank Thompson. In 1950 he entirely turned over his lineup, putting all four of those players in the lineup, joined by Tookie Gilbert (a rookie who failed), and two trade acquisitions (Eddie Stanky and Al Dark). This planted the fuse for the mid-1951 explosion, which was lighted by the return of Sal Maglie, who had been banished for pitching in the Mexican League, and the sudden development of Willie Mays.

But most of these players had *obvious* ability. Durocher worked with veterans, and with young players who had obvious ability. If the ability wasn't obvious, he didn't see it.

Did He Prefer to Go with Good Offensive Players or Did He Like the Glove Men? A balance. There is no clear pattern. There were times when Durocher would stretch a player defensively to get an extra hitter in the lineup—for example, in 1951 he moved an outfielder to third base (Bobby Thomson) to make room for both Mueller and Irvin.

With the arguable exception of Don Kessinger, Leo Durocher never used a Leo Durocher–type player as a regular. He expected everybody in the lineup to make an offensive contribution.

Did He Like an Offense Based on Power, Speed, or High Averages? Four of Durocher's teams led the league in home runs, while only two led in stolen bases, and only one led the league in batting average. Eight of Durocher's teams led the league in walks drawn, far more than any other category.

Did He Use the Entire Roster or Did He Keep People Sitting on the Bench? He used about ten players and about seven pitchers. The rest of the guys just pinch-hit and played in blowouts.

Did He Build His Bench Around Young Players Who Could Step into the Breach If Need Be, or Around Veteran Role-Players Who Had Their Own Functions Within a Game? Almost 100% veterans, except for the 1948–1949 team. Dusty Rhodes, pinch hitter, was the best bench player Durocher ever had.

In general, Leo's bench was his dog house. His bench

**Dick Young on
Leo Durocher**

You and Durocher are on a raft. A wave comes and knocks him into the ocean. You dive in and save his life. A shark comes and takes your leg. Next day, you and Leo start out even.

players had very little role on the team, other than to try to figure out how to get back on Durocher's good side.

GAME MANAGING AND USE OF STRATEGIES

Did He Go for the Big-Inning Offense, or Did He Like to Use the One-Run Strategies? Neither to an extreme degree.

Did He Pinch-Hit Much, and If So, When? He did, yes. His first couple of years as a manager, he had no pinch-hitting specialist. But Lew Riggs gave him a good year as a pinch hitter in 1941, and after that he was always looking for somebody to come off the bench and get a hit for him. Among his notable successes were Jack Bolling, Bobby Hofman, Dusty Rhodes, and Willie Smith.

Was There Anything Unusual About His Lineup Selection? His lineup selection was standard.

This probably doesn't have anything to do with lineup selection, but Durocher had the opportunity to work with four great young center fielders—Pete Reiser, Willie Mays, Adolfo Phillips, and Cesar Cedeno. (It seems absurd now to put Adolfo Phillips in a class with Willie Mays, but he could run and he had power, and at the time, it looked like he was going to be good.) Another thing notable about his teams is good bats at second base—Billy Herman, Eddie Stanky, Glenn Beckert. In Houston he had Joe Morgan for a few games, but the team traded Morgan away that winter, possibly at Durocher's urging.

Durocher usually had one guy on his team who drew a tremendous number of walks. The most notable examples are Eddie Stanky (148 walks for Brooklyn in 1945, 137 in 1946, 144 walks for the Giants in 1950) and Wes Westrum, a catcher who in 1951 had only 79 hits, but drew 104 walks, giving him a .219 batting average but an on-base percentage of .400. Other Durocher players who led the league in walks include Dolf Camilli (1939), Augie Galan (1943–1944), and Ron Santo (1966–67–68).

Did He Use the Sac Bunt Often? Average amount.

Did He Like to Use the Running Game? Not much. Average/below average.

In What Circumstances Would He Issue an Intentional Walk? Mostly to avoid a hot hitter.

I checked the play-by-play of the three World Series in which Durocher participated. He used the intentional walk frequently, and was burned by it several times. In Game Five of the 1951 World Series, he intentionally walked Johnny Mize to pitch to Gil McDougald, loading the bases with two out in the third inning, 1–0 game. McDougald hit a grand slam home run, by far the biggest hit of the Series.

There is no official IBB data from Durocher's salad days, but the data from the Cubs in the late 1960s confirms that Durocher was liberal with the intentional walks.

Did He Hit and Run Very Often? He did, yes. He managed three of the best hit-and-run men in baseball history— Billy Herman, Don Mueller, and Glenn Beckert.

Were There Any Unique or Idiosyncratic Strategies That He Particularly Favored? Durocher was famous for playing hunches. He sometimes did things that didn't seem to make sense, like putting a slow runner in motion, bunting when several runs behind, or using a light-hitting infielder as a pinch hitter when a better-hitting outfielder was available. He would explain these moves by saying he just had a hunch.

Partly, of course, it wasn't a hunch. The optimal strategy is never a predictable strategy. By doing the seemingly irrational, Durocher was doing the unexpected, which prevented the opposition from getting comfortable in the field.

How Did He Change the Game? As to details, Durocher was the first manager to routinely use several pitchers in a game, and the first manager to regularly switch to a left-hander out of the bullpen when the opposition had a big left-handed hitter up with the game on the line. His largest strategic impact was in leading the way toward more aggressive use of the bullpen.

On a larger scale, when Durocher was hired, he was not an established managerial "type." He was an original, a new mold. He was hired by Larry MacPhail, an inspired, half-crazy, half-genius general manager who had once, during World War I, attempted to kidnap Kaiser Wilhelm. Without orders. Nobody but MacPhail would ever have thought to make Durocher a manager.

There were managers before Durocher who drank, swore,

chased women, bet horses, and screamed at umpires—but they were, in some fundamental way, "responsible" men. They were men who obeyed the rules and asked the world for respect.

Durocher didn't give a shit what you thought of him. He didn't make any pretense to being a nice person. Until the 1950s, he didn't make any pretense to being a family man. He was a rogue. He dressed in flashy clothes, drove flashy cars, drove too fast, took a punch at anybody who crossed him, made a pass at every woman he took a liking to, and bragged when he scored.

Durocher, who grew up essentially fatherless, once said that he had spent his life looking for father images. In a sense, all managers in the generation before Durocher (and most managers after) were *paternal* managers, surrogate fathers for their players. Durocher was more like an older brother, not all that much older, and certainly not much more responsible. Other managers did bed checks. Durocher, in effect, gave his players permission to hit the bars and woo the women until all hours, so long as they were ready to play ball at game time. And if you weren't ready to play ball at game time, God help you.

And because he was so successful, Durocher opened up the field for a certain number of managers to follow—Billy Martin, most obviously. He changed the image of what a manager *could* be, took some of the starch out of it.

Before Durocher, managers tended to be stars. After Durocher, they tended to be scrappy middle infielders.

HANDLING THE PITCHING STAFF

Did He Like Power Pitchers, or Did He Prefer to Go with the People Who Put the Ball in Play? Durocher liked a hard-throwing pitcher who threw strikes and worked inside. His idea was that if you could find a pitcher who had a good arm and convince him to back the hitter off the plate with an inside fastball, then nail the outside corner, you'd have something.

He had tremendous success in turning around pitchers with this philosophy. Whitlow Wyatt was thirty-one years old when he joined the Dodgers, and had a career record of 26 wins, 43 losses. For Durocher, he went 8–3, 15–14, 22–10, 19–7 and 14–5. Kirby Higbe was 27–34 in his career before joining the Dodgers, but went 22–9, 16–11, 13–10, and 17–8 in his four full seasons under Durocher. Sal Maglie was thirty-three years old and had five career wins before he joined Durocher.

Durocher made him a household name. Johnny Antonelli was 17–22 in his career before Durocher. In his first season for Durocher, he went 21–7 with a 2.30 ERA.

With the Cubs, Durocher developed Ken Holtzman and Ferguson Jenkins, plus Bill Hands. Holtzman had obvious promise, and his development was widely anticipated, but absolutely no one foresaw that Ferguson Jenkins had Hall of Fame potential.

Durocher also had good luck with knuckleball pitchers. He got a sensational year out of Freddie Fitzsimmons in 1941, when Fitzsimmons went 16–2 as a spot starter. Fitzsimmons taught the knuckleball to Larry French, whose career was almost over, and French went 15–4 with a 1.83 ERA in 1942. Ten years later, Durocher brought Hoyt Wilhelm to the major leagues.

Did He Stay with His Starters, or Go to the Bullpen Quickly? In the 1940s and early 1950s, Durocher went to his bullpen more readily than any other major league manager. But with the Cubs near the end of his career, he was leading the league in complete games.

In 1946 Durocher used 223 relievers in 157 games; this led the National League. In 1967 he used 244 relievers in 162 games, but the National League Average was 254.

Did He Use a Four-Man Rotation? He did after the war when the schedule permitted it, yes. Before the war he had the usual combination of two starters and five starter/relievers making fifteen starts apiece, but when the schedules became more regular after the war, he went to a four-man rotation.

Did He Use the Entire Staff, or Did He Try to Get Five or Six People to Do Most of the Work? He worked his best pitchers hard, probably too hard. He had many pitchers who led the league in games, starts, and innings.

How Long Would He Stay with a Starting Pitcher Who Was Struggling? Not long.

What Was His Strongest Point As a Manager? That his teams gave such great effort.

To finish the thought from before, in many ways Durocher was a new type of manager, but in many ways he was also an anachronism. The public humiliation of players who failed him, the intimidation of the opposition, the manipulation of players through a volatile combination of friendship and fear—all of this was more characteristic of the John McGraw–era manager than of the modern steward.

I don't endorse this gamesmanship, I don't admire it, and I wouldn't hire a manager who treated people that way. That's beside the point, because somebody who did the kind of stuff Durocher did couldn't manage in the 1990s. The players wouldn't respond to it.

But it did produce a wonderful effect on his ball club. Durocher's teams came to beat you. They hustled, they fought, they looked for every opening and every edge. Like Casey Stengel, he was a master manipulator. And he was a great manager.

If There Was No Professional Baseball, What Would He Probably Have Done with His Life? He'd have been a show business agent.

LEO DUROCHER'S
All-Star Team

		G	AB	R	H	2B	3B	HR	RBI	BB	SO	SB	Avg	SPct
C	Wes Westrum, 1950	140	437	68	103	13	3	23	71	92	73	2	.236	.437
1B	Johnny Mize, 1948	152	560	110	162	26	4	40	125	94	37	4	.289	.564
2B	Eddie Stanky, 1950	152	527	115	158	25	5	8	51	144	50	9	.300	.412
3B	Ron Santo, 1967	161	586	107	176	23	4	31	98	96	103	1	.300	.512
SS	Alvin Dark, 1951	156	646	114	196	41	7	14	69	42	39	12	.303	.454
LF	Billy Williams, 1970	161	636	137	205	34	4	42	129	72	65	7	.322	.586
CF	Willie Mays, 1954	151	585	119	195	33	13	41	110	66	57	8	.345	.667
RF	Monte Irvin, 1951	151	558	94	174	19	11	24	121	89	44	12	.312	.514

		G	IP	W–L	Pct.	H	SO	BB	ERA	GS	CG	ShO	Sv
SP	John Antonelli, 1954	39	258	21–7	.750	209	152	94	2.29	37	18	6	2
SP	Fergie Jenkins, 1971	39	325	24–13	.649	304	263	37	2.77	39	30	3	0
SP	Sal Maglie, 1951	42	298	23–6	.793	254	146	86	2.93	37	22	3	4
SP	Larry Jansen, 1951	39	279	23–11	.676	254	145	56	3.03	34	18	3	0
RA	Hoyt Wilhelm, 1952	71	159	15–3	.833	127	108	57	2.43	0	0	0	11

BILLY SOUTHWORTH'S
All-Star Team

		G	AB	R	H	2B	3B	HR	RBI	BB	SO	SB	Avg	SPct
C	Walker Cooper, 1943	122	449	52	143	30	4	9	81	19	19	1	.319	.463
1B	Johnny Mize, 1940	155	579	111	182	31	13	43	137	82	49	7	.314	.636
2B	Eddie Stanky, 1949	138	506	90	144	24	5	1	42	113	41	3	.285	.358
3B	Bob Elliott, 1947	150	555	93	176	35	5	22	113	87	60	3	.317	.517
SS	Marty Marion, 1944	144	506	50	135	26	2	6	63	43	50	1	.267	.362
LF	Stan Musial, 1943	157	617	108	220	48	20	13	81	72	18	9	.357	.562
CF	Johnny Hopp, 1944	139	527	106	177	35	9	11	72	58	47	15	.336	.499
RF	Enos Slaughter, 1942	152	591	100	188	31	17	13	98	88	30	9	.318	.494

		G	IP	W–L	Pct.	H	SO	BB	ERA	GS	CG	ShO	Sv
SP	Warren Spahn, 1947	40	290	21–10	.677	245	123	84	2.33	35	22	7	3
SP	Johnny Sain, 1948	42	315	24–15	.615	297	137	83	2.60	39	28	4	1
SP	Mort Cooper, 1942	37	279	22–7	.759	207	152	68	1.77	36	22	10	0
SP	Johnny Beazley, 1942	43	215	21–6	.778	181	91	73	2.14	23	13	3	3

Rolling in the Grass

In the March 1948, issue of *Sport* magazine, Ralph Kiner confessed that he didn't much like to bunt. Kiner had hit 51 homers the previous season. A *Sport* reader named Bob Wilson ripped out an angry letter to the editor. "Kiner says he doesn't like to bunt. Well, isn't that too bad. It looks like Mr. Ralph Kiner doesn't care whether or not a bunt will help his team, he just wants a homer or nothing."

To bunt, in the 1940s, was not merely a strategic option. Like standard grammar, the sacrifice bunt had grown into a moral imperative. Everybody bunted, and everybody was *expected* to bunt. The 1948 Boston Braves, champions of the National League, laid down 140 sacrifice bunts, almost one per game. Every major league team bunted at least 56 times, with Ralph Kiner's Pirates having the fewest.

Decades pass, and the sacrifice bunt has fallen into disfavor. George Orwell's classic *1984* was written in 1948; Orwell just reversed the last two digits of the year. By 1984 the number of sacrifice bunts (per game) had fallen by more than 40% since the end of World War II. Ralph Kiner had only 9 sacrifice bunts in his career. Harmon Killebrew had 9 fewer.

If I had been asked what happened to the sac bunt, without research, I would have pointed to:

a) the reemergence of the stolen base,

b) artificial turf, and

c) the designated hitter rule.

The stolen base and the sac bunt are competing options. You don't bunt with Rickey Henderson on first base. When speed came back into the game, the number of situations in which the bunt was in order was reduced. Artificial turf is difficult to bunt on, as everybody has been told, because the ball won't roll dead in the grass, and the DH rule took the bat out of the hands of the guys who bunted most often.

* * *

Unfortunately, none of this fits the facts. More specifically, none of it fits the time line. The number of sacrifice bunts per game

• declined more than 20% between 1948 and 1957,

• was fairly constant from 1957 to 1981, and

• dipped by another 20-plus percent in the early 1980s.

The rise in stolen bases, the arrival of artificial turf, and the adoption of the designated hitter rule all came in the middle of that long stretch, when the number of sacrifice bunts per game changed hardly at all.

A better explanation is that the sacrifice bunt was pushed toward oblivion first by the long ball (1948–1957), and second by logical arguments against the bunt (1981–1984).

Between 1948 and 1957 home runs in the major leagues increased by more than 40%. The increase in power worked against the bunt on several levels, which can be summarized in this statement: that not only do you not bunt with Harmon Killebrew, but you also don't bunt with the guy who bats *ahead* of Harmon Killebrew. For many years, with offenses based around line drive hitters, managers had thought about *scoring position*, getting the runner *in scoring position*. But Harmon Killebrew doesn't hit that many singles anyway, so "scoring position" is really not a meaningful concept for him. All you're doing, by bunting ahead of Killebrew, is inviting an intentional walk.

As home run hitters flooded into the game in the 1950s, bunting opportunities went out. So power, not speed, was the first thing that happened to the sacrifice bunt.

The second decline in bunting, twenty-five years later, is attributable to a higher power: the power of ideas. The most successful American League manager of the 1970s was Earl Weaver. About 1980, Weaver grew into something of a prophet, an

Old Testament Prophet, perhaps, spitting baseball wisdom as freely as tobacco juice. I'm a great admirer of Earl Weaver's, and I don't mean any disrespect.

Anyway, Weaver didn't like the sacrifice bunt. As he put it in *Weaver on Strategy*, his fine 1984 book with Terry Pluto, "If you play for one run that's all you'll get." That was the fifth of Weaver's ten commandments, which he called "laws" because he didn't want people comparing him to Moses. His sixth law was "Don't play for one run unless you know that run will win a ballgame," and his fourth law was "Your most precious possessions on offense are your twenty-seven outs." All of which means pretty much the same thing: The bunt is for losers.

It was a great day to be a baseball writer, and many writers picked up on Weaver's ideas. "Baseball is a game of big innings," wrote Thomas Boswell. Boswell pointed out that in some very large percentage of games (I forget the number), the winning team scores more runs in one inning than the losing team does in all nine. Dan Okrent took the reader inside Earl Weaver's strategy in *Nine Innings*.

At the same time, sabermetric research, which had built up unpublished for twenty years, was bursting into the light. The research at that time tended to advance the same notion: that the bunt was a bad play. In fact, that's a direct quote from *The Hidden Game of Baseball*, also published in 1984:

> The sacrifice bunt . . . is a bad play, as several modern-day managers—but not enough of them—have concluded.
>
> —*Thorn and Palmer*

In my own *Baseball Abstracts*, I was skeptical about the value of the bunt. Earl Weaver clearly had an impact on the thinking of younger managers. Whether the rest of us had any impact, or whether we were just piling on, is an open question. I remember another image from that time, a dugout confrontation between Reggie Jackson and Billy Martin. It happened when Martin signaled for a bunt. Reggie, drawing on his genius for irritating theatrics, attempted unsuccessfully to bunt, and at the same time clearly conveyed to the entire stadium that it was an insult for a hitter of his stature to be asked to lay one down. Words followed; fists, blood, suspensions, threats to resign. The power hitter's dislike of the bunt, an infant to be scolded in the time of Ralph Kiner, had matured into an ugly adult.

Cynically, we could argue that managers backed away from the bunt because (unlike Billy Martin) they lacked the stones to confront their power hitters. More charitably, there was a battle of ideas. The bunt was seen most often as a bad idea.

Time passes; there are other books and other prophets. The number of bunts per game has gradually increased since 1984, reaching as high as 80 per hundred games (1993). And I've had second thoughts, and I've done some additional research. I am no longer convinced that the sacrifice bunt is a poor percentage play.

Let's take the Palmer/Thorn argument. Pete Palmer argued that the sacrifice bunt is a bad play because it tends to create a *worse* situation for the offensive team, rather than a better situation. With a runner on first and no one out, for example, a major league team can usually expect to score .783 runs (that is, if a team is in that situation 1,000 times, they can be expected to score about 783 runs). With a runner on second and one out, on the other hand, the expected runs would be .699. Thus, by bunting 1,000 times, a team could expect to score 84 runs *fewer* than if they didn't bunt at all.

For most of the situations in which a bunt may be used, Palmer argued, it will result in a net *loss* of runs scored.

As I've thought about it over the years, however, I've become less convinced by this argument. First, runs scored one at a time are obviously somewhat more valuable than runs scored in big innings. How much more valuable? Perhaps as much as 50% more.

Suppose that you take two teams, one of which scores runs only one at a time, and the other of which scores runs only in groups of three. Earl Weaver's ultimate team: nothing but three-run homers. One team scores in 50% of all innings, one run per inning; that's 4.50 runs per game. The other team scores in only one-sixth of its innings, but scores three runs at a time; that also is 4.50 runs per game.

When these two teams play against one another, who will win? The team which has the big innings will win some games 15–2, but will be shut out in 19% of its games. The team which scores one run at a time can't score more than nine in a game, but will be shut out only once in 500 games. Because of this, the team which scores runs one at a time will win 55% of the games—actually, 55.2816% of the games.

This is a significant advantage. In 162 games, the one-run team would win 90. The big-inning team, scoring exactly as many runs, would win 72 games. Depending on how one wishes to phrase it, runs scored one at a time are 11% to 24% more powerful than runs scored in three-run groups. The winning percentage of the one-run team, playing constantly against the big-inning team, is .553, which is 11% above .500. On the other hand, scoring exactly the same number of runs, the one-run team wins 24% more games than the big-inning team.

But wait a minute. This is based on the assumption that the one-run team always plays for one run, even in situations in which it would make no sense to do so. This is the advantage of a one-run strategy not at a time when a manager would actually use a one-run strategy, but simply at an indiscriminate moment. Trailing 6–1 in the seventh inning, the one-run team still can score only one run at a time. Suppose that we altered the study so that the one-run team didn't bunt when they were behind by two or more runs.

I wrote a simple computer program to simulate this contest. Team B, the big-inning team, scores runs only in three-run groups, and scores once every six innings. Team A scores runs only one at a time, except when Team A is behind by two or more runs. In that case, Team A performs the same as Team B. Both teams score 4.50 runs per nine innings.

The winning percentage of Team A in this simulation was .595 (.603 in home games, .587 on the road). Scoring exactly the same number of runs, the team which usually played for one run won 47% more games than the team which always played for the big inning. This still is not choosing carefully when to play for the big inning, and when to play for one run; this is just using a little bit of discretion. Choosing more carefully when to play for the big inning, the one-run team might win 50 or 60% more games than the big-inning team.

Plug that back into Palmer's research. Palmer concluded that a team had a run expectation of .783 before a bunt and .699 after a successful bunt—a 12% advantage for the "before" situation. But if one-run innings are as much as 50% more powerful one-for-one, we might still conclude that one should bunt early and bunt often.

This is just one of the problems with the analysis. The .783 "run potential" for a man on first/none out situation is not a fixed value, constant for all occasions; rather, this is the center of a range of values which represents many such situations. With Frank Thomas at the plate, the team's expected number of runs would be much higher than .783. With Manny Alexander at bat, the number would be much lower.

So the real question is, do the run-potential ranges ever overlap? The .783 figure would often be lower than .783; the .699 figure would often be higher than .699. Would there ever be real-life situations in which the expected runs would be higher after the bunt?

Well, unless the ranges of run potential are

awfully narrow, they'd have to overlap, wouldn't they? .783 isn't that much higher than .699, considering that

a) the largest variable in a more careful evaluation of the specific situation would be the quality of the hitter, and

b) the variation in run-producing abilities of various hitters is much more than the 12% difference between .783 and .699.

So what this research proves, it seems to me, is not that the bunt is a bad play, but merely that with a runner on first and no one out, there are more situations in which one should not bunt than situations in which one should bunt. Teams should bunt less than 50% of the time. Since teams do bunt less than 50% of the time in that situation, this is hardly a revelation.

In the 1990 edition of the *Baseball Scoreboard*, from STATS Inc., the editors of this exceptional publication studied the value of sacrifice bunts in an article entitled "Do Sacrifices Sacrifice Too Much?" Working with a database of all major league games played in a three-year period (1987–1989), STATS editors Don Zminda and John Dewan sorted out all innings in which teams had a runner on first and no one out. They then split that large group of innings (about 40,000 innings over the three seasons) into two classes—innings in which there was a bunt attempt, and innings in which there was no bunt attempt. Actually, they split the data a lot more ways than that; I'm simplifying.

The study provided an empirical validation of Pete Palmer's theoretical results. Teams do, in fact, score more runs in innings when they don't bunt than in innings in which they do bunt.

This study, however, has the same problem, in a different guise. Suppose that the 1927 New York Yankees have 200 situations in which there is a runner on first and no one out. In 100 of those situations Babe Ruth or Lou Gehrig is up to bat; in the other hundred situations, the batter is Joe Dugan

or Cedric Durst or Ray Morehart. Suppose that the team bunts 50 times in those 200 situations. Would we expect the Yankees to be equally likely to bunt with Babe Ruth at bat, or Cedric Durst?

Of course not. What would happen is that the team would not bunt with Gehrig or Ruth, but might bunt very often with Dugan, Durst, or Morehart.

If studied after the fact, as STATS did, all of the at bats in which Ruth or Gehrig was at the plate would be sorted into the "nonbunt" category. Many of the at bats with weak hitters at the plate would go into the "bunt" category. Of course the runs scored would be higher in the "nonbunt" category than they would in the "bunt" group. This doesn't do anything to show that the bunt is a bad play.

I asked Pete Palmer, who is a friend of mine, whether he had tried to determine values for his model with individual players, rather than overall averages. His reply was that he had studied it based on batting-order positions—that is, with a typical number-three hitter at bat, a typical number-seven hitter, etc. The model still produced more runs without bunts than with them.

This doesn't do much to solve the problem, however, because the variation between individual players is vastly greater than the variation between typical batting-order positions. In the National League in 1993, for example, a typical number-two hitter hit .279 with 10 homers, 64 RBI, a .388 slugging percentage. A typical number-three hitter wasn't a whole lot better, hitting .291 with 19 homers, 94 RBI, a .439 slugging percentage. In the typical case, the sacrifice bunt would transfer the RBI opportunity to a player whose batting average was only 12 points higher, and whose slugging percentage was only 51 points higher.

In real cases, however, the data is very different. Four National League teams that year actually got better performance out of their number-two hitters than their number-three hitters. For the St. Louis

Cardinals, on the other hand, the number-two hitter was usually Ozzie Smith, and the number-three was Gregg Jefferies. His batting average was 54 points higher than Smith's, his slugging percentage 129 points higher.

Further, in real situations, other factors frequently will operate to accentuate those differences. The .280 hitter at bat may actually be a .260 hitter if the opposition has switched to a left-handed pitcher, while the .340 hitter on deck may actually be a .350 hitter. A player with a 1-in-30 chance of hitting a home run in theory might have a 1-in-15 chance if the game is in Colorado, but 1-in-40 in St. Louis. If the wind is howling in from right field, it might be half that. A hitter may be nursing a minor injury, which might make him vulnerable to a double play.

So the variation in performance between batting-order prototypes is not representative of the factors at play in a real-life situation, and therefore what is true in the model might very probably not be true in many real-life situations.

Perhaps an easier way to explain why this argument is unconvincing is simply to apply the same logic to another strategic option, that being the intentional walk. In Palmer's model, of course, the intentional walk would always be a bad play, since it would always increase the expected runs for the opposition.

No one believes that having runners on first and second with one out is a better deal (for the defense) than having just a man on second with one out. But if Barry Bonds is at the plate, and Rikkert Faneyte is on deck, you still might order the walk. The advantage you're going for doesn't reside in the inherent situation; it resides in the identity of the hitter. The same might well apply to the sacrifice bunt.

Another issue raised by the Palmer/Thorn and Dewan/Zminda studies is that the bunt might "fail." Palmer and Thorn concede that the bunt, in theory, might be a good play in certain situations if it works—for example, with runners on first and second, no one out, and the home team behind by one run in the seventh inning:

> . . . the successful bunt (in this situation) raises the win probability slightly, from .529 to .546; however, a failure, leaving men at first and second with one out, lowers the chance of winning substantially, to .432. Using the break-even point formula, we discover that such a play must succeed 85.1% of the time—an improbable rate of accomplishment for this difficult play.

The STATS *Scoreboard* study uses a similar method, relaying the results when the sacrifice bunt succeeds, and when it fails.

This approach, however, assumes that there are two possible outcomes from a bunt attempt—a successful sacrifice bunt, or a failure. Suppose that we use Palmer's data and Palmer's method, but we ask this question instead: *If the batter attempts to bunt for a hit, and gets the sac bunt as a consolation prize, how often must he succeed in order for it to be a good gamble?*

The answer, as it turns out, is "not very damned often." Using Palmer's data, the expected runs for the team with a runner on first, no one out, are .783. With a runner on second, one out, the expectation is .699. But with runners on first and second, no one out, the expected runs increase to 1.380.

Asked this way, how often does the bunter have to "succeed" in order for the bunt to be a good play? Answer: 12.3% of the time. If he can get a base hit one time in eight, and get the sacrifice bunt the other seven times, the team can expect to score more runs with than without the bunt.

A good bunter, like Brett Butler or Otis Nixon, can bunt for a .300 or .350 average with the bases empty, maybe higher. Steve Garvey, who ran about as well as Bill Clinton, used to bunt for a hit ten times every year. If you send the runner from first, the defense isn't going to get a force out, although there is some risk of a pop fly double play. The question is, can the batter bunt .123 with a runner on first? If he can, the bunt is probably a good play.

Is it fair to evaluate the bunt by considering a base hit and a successful sacrifice to be the only two possibilities? It is probably as fair as it would be to consider the only possibilities to be a sac bunt and a failed bunt. One cannot evaluate the impact of the sacrifice bunt, without dealing with the full range of possible outcomes.

Well, what is the full range of possible outcomes? In two editions of the *Scoreboard*, STATS published lists of how many times everything happened in major league play. In 1990, for example, there were 469 foul fly outs, 844 runners thrown out advancing, and 31 cases of batter obstruction. There were 20 times when a runner was caught stealing, but safe on an error.

Although this data is not precise in all the details we need, it is useful for modeling the problem. There appear to be seven outcomes of a sacrifice bunt attempt which are relatively common. Those are:

- a base hit
- an error
- a fielder's choice/all safe
- a fielder's choice/failed bunt
- a successful sacrifice bunt
- a forceout
- a pop out
- a double play

The STATS data doesn't give full details on all of these; for example, it doesn't say how many times a player may have bunted for a hit in a possible sacrifice situation. We must assume that this did happen, but those occurrences are buried in the general category "singles," and we don't know how many of them there might have been. This is an important omission, and there are other things which are also unclear. There is a category entitled "Bunt Pop Out," but it isn't clear whether this includes only sac bunt attempts, or perhaps also attempts to bunt for a single.

Anyway, this is the best data we have, so let's work with it. We can estimate, based on the STATS data, that the frequencies of these events are:

Successful Sacrifice Bunt	71%
Pop Out	10%
Bunt into Forceout	7%
Base Hit	5%
Sac Bunt Plus Error	3%
Fielder's Choice, All Safe	2%
Bunt into Double Play (GIDP)	1%
Pop Out, Runner Doubled Off	1%

About 19% of bunt attempts fail, with about 10% of those (2% of the total) being double plays. The 5% figure for base hits is just a guess.

I have a computer program which simulates baseball games, sort of like a perpetual APBA game. Suppose that we take a team, a kind of average team, and we run them through a hundred simulated seasons in which they don't bunt.

Then we build the information on the chart above into the simulation program, and we put the bunts back in, and we run them through 100 seasons with sacrifice bunts. Will they be better with the sacrifice bunts, or without?

The realistic bunt information isn't all that easy to put into practice, because you can't put things in on a random basis. I worked it out as best I could and ran the simulations. The studies don't show what I thought they might show. I thought the teams might perform better with the bunts than they did without. If they had, then I could argue that the sabermetricians who have studied this before were just wrong, and that the sacrifice bunt really *is* a good play if you use it well.

What I have instead is a mixed picture. I ran three teams through 100 seasons each with and without sacrifice bunts, a total of 600 simulated seasons. All three teams did better without the sacrifice bunt than with the bunts.

But looking carefully at the details of the study, it still appears to me that a case can be made on behalf of the bunt. While all three teams did better overall without the bunt, two of the three actually did better *in home games* when the bunt was in. Team C, for example, had a .521 winning percentage without the bunt, which was the same at home and on the road. When I put the bunts in, their winning percentage went to .515 on the road, but .524 in home games.

Suppose, then, that I just shut off the bunt in road games; what would we have then? Then we'd have .524 at home, and .521 on the road—a better overall record with the bunt (in half the games) than with no bunts at all.

And if you think about it, one of the oldest saws of managing is what? Play for a tie at home; play to win on the road. Never play for a tie on the road.

Isn't that really almost the same thing? What does the expression "never play for a tie on the road" really mean, in practice? It means "if you're behind and you're on the road, don't bunt."

So it may be that what is indicated by the study is not that the bunt is a poor percentage play, but that *I didn't do a good enough job of instructing the computer when to bunt.*

Well, that's easy to understand. I had the computer bunting about fifty times a season, and I put the bunts in on a kind of a commonsense basis—don't bunt with the three/four hitters except in unusual circumstances, bunt mostly with your best bunters, don't bunt with the middle of the order coming up in the early innings, don't bunt when you're two runs behind, etc.

The computer produces bunts in *reasonable* circumstances, but there's also a random component to the decision. It is extremely difficult to teach a computer to think like a major league manager, as anyone who has ever tried it can verify. It seems likely to me that if the computer had done a better job of picking when to bunt, it would probably have posted a better winning percentage with the bunt than without it.

There are other details in the study which sug-

gest the same conclusion. The program keeps track of the number of runs scored per inning, sorted by who the leadoff hitter was. While the number of runs scored dropped overall, the runs scored in the innings started by the seven, eight, and nine hitters did increase in all three studies. Again, this suggests that if the computer had done a better job of picking when to bunt, the results very well might have been different.

So what am I really saying here, other than that I don't know how to tell a computer when to bunt? Am I saying that the 1940s managers, who bunted 100 times a season, were making the right decision?

Certainly not.

Am I saying that Palmer and Thorn were wrong when they said flatly that the bunt was a bad play?

No, I can't say that they were wrong.

What I'm saying is that I think it's an open question.

One way to phrase the question would be to ask for a number. How many times are there, during a season, when a team *should* bunt?

Billy Southworth thought that the answer was somewhere near 150.

Gene Mauch thought that it was over a hundred.

Earl Weaver thought it was more like 30.

Palmer and Thorn's work would suggest that it was near zero.

What I'm saying is that I simply do not know. The answer, dear class, is rolling in the grass. I don't think the right number is zero, and I doubt that it's near zero, but I don't know what it is. Having thought about the issue at great length, having worked hard to analyze the math involved, I can only tell you that there is no definitively correct mathematical answer at this time. Earl Weaver may have been right; Billy Southworth may have been right. Maybe each of them had the right answer for his own team. The rest of us need to keep an open mind.

Bill Meyer

In '47, full of woe
    The Pittsburgh Pirates finished low
But in '48, under Billy Meyer,
    They'll very likely finish higher.
        —Max Salva, *Baseball* magazine,
                March 1948

The Pirates did indeed finish higher under Billy Meyer—in fact, more than 20 games higher. Billy Meyer, after almost forty years in professional baseball, was an overnight sensation, a genius for a day. *The Sporting News* named him the Major League Manager of the Year.

A small, singles-hitting catcher, Meyer played in one game with the White Sox in 1914, then spent two years as a third catcher for Connie Mack. That failing, he was sold to Louisville of the American Association, where he would spend eleven seasons.

Joe McCarthy became manager of the Louisville Colonels in 1919 and set about building a powerhouse. The Colonels won the minor league World Series in 1921. In 1925, after another 102-win season, McCarthy was hired to manage the Cubs. Billy Meyer inherited the Louisville manager's job, probably at McCarthy's recommendation.

For one season they carried on as before, winning 105 games in their first season under Meyer. In 1927 the team fell onto hard times, losing 103 games in 1927, 106 in 1928. Meyer was fired, and at the same time released as a player. He was thirty-six years old, and had played for nineteen seasons.

Meyer returned to his home in Knoxville, Tennessee. There had always been another game tomorrow, another contract next year; now he was thrown back on his wits. Out of baseball for three years, he looked back on his years as the Louisville manager and realized that he had done nothing to discipline himself, let alone his players. He had made good money and wasted it. The depression hit, and money was suddenly scarce.

Meyer looked to get back in baseball. He got married in the spring of 1932 and got a job as a minor league manager, at Springfield in the Eastern League. It wasn't the American Association, but he was back in the game. He had the Springfield team in first place with a record of 53–26 when, on July 17, the league disbanded.

The depression had hit baseball, too.

Meyer was hired to manage Binghamton in the New York–Pennsylvania League, another step down.

At the pace of modern justice, he began to work his way back toward the majors. He took over a seventh-place team in Binghamton, and dragged them to a 34–28 record the rest of the season. He won the pennant there in '33, his third minor league pennant, counting Springfield. The league adopted a split schedule in '34; Meyer's teams won half the pennant each year in '34 and '35.

In 1936 he went to the Pacific Coast League, where he managed the Oakland Oaks. After two years of indifferent results in the PCL, he ran into George Weiss at the winter meetings. Meyer asked Weiss about a place in the Yankee system, and Weiss agreed to ask Joe McCarthy about him. McCarthy gave Meyer an enthusiastic recommendation, and Meyer was hired to manage the Kansas City Blues in 1938.

The highest minor league classification at this time was Double A. The Yankees had two Double A teams, one at Newark and one in Kansas City. Both teams were extremely strong. Meyer managed those two teams for the next ten seasons—Kansas City for four years, Newark for four years, then Kansas City for two more. In the ten years his teams won four pennants and finished second four times, posting only one losing record. His Kansas City teams of 1939–1940 are among the best minor league teams of all time, finishing 107–47 in 1939, and he played a role in the development of many major league stars. Like McCarthy, he was a disciplinarian without being a screamer, a student of the game with a perpetually active mind.

In the 1990s a manager with such a record might get a shot at a major league job within a couple of years. In the mid-1940s there were more minor league teams, fewer major league teams, and the major league teams strongly preferred star players. Meyer was fifty-six years old when Pittsburgh finally hired him for the 1948 season.

The Pirates, a strong franchise until 1945, had slipped badly in 1946–1947, losing over 90 games each year. Ralph Kiner came to the team in 1946, and, as a rookie, led the league in home runs, with 23. Hank Greenberg the same year led the American League in home runs and RBI, with 44 and 127. Greenberg talked seriously about retiring, which forced the Tigers to make him available. The Pirates put together a big-money package and acquired Greenberg to bat behind Kiner. They had visions of first place.

They finished last. Billy Herman, taking over the team in 1947, had recommended that the team trade Kiner, saying that they had Greenberg to bat cleanup now, and he didn't believe Kiner was really that good. Kiner hit .313 with 51 homers. Maybe Herman was right. As Branch Rickey told Kiner in negotiations the following spring, they could have finished last without him.

Anyway, Greenberg retired, and Meyer was hired to fix the mess. The flaws of the 1947 team are in retrospect obvious. They had no left-handed hitting, no speed, and a group of old pitchers who couldn't throw strikes.

Meyer put into the lineup several players who had been hanging around the league for years, not playing much. Stan Rojek, Ed Stevens, Danny Murtaugh; they weren't any better than the guys they had replaced, but they balanced the lineup left/right, and they were hungry. The team stolen base total more than doubled. Bob Chesnes, purchased from the Pacific Coast League, became the Pirates' best pitcher of 1948, at 14–6. The Pirates finished 83–71, just 8½ games out of first place.

Billy Meyer was a genius for the day. The next year, the Pirates fell into their old ways. They loaded up their roster with a bunch of guys who had been good before the war—Ernie Bonham, Kirby Higbe, Walt Judnich, Hugh Casey, Dixie Walker. Murtaugh and Rojek, a brilliant double-play combination in '48, fell off badly. Chesnes slipped to 7–13. A trade with Brooklyn, a short-term winner in 1948, turned into a long-range disaster. The Pirates slipped to 71–83 in 1949.

It got worse. They went 57–96 in 1950, lost 90 more in 1951. By 1952 the Pirates had become one of the worst teams of all time, losing 112 games, against only 42 wins. They finished 54½ games out of first place.

How did the Pirates sink so low? What happened to Billy Meyer, after he managed so well in 1948? Why was he unable to solve any of the Pirates' escalating problems in the following seasons?

There was a story in *Sport* magazine, ten years later, that the Pirates team rebelled against Meyer after he mishandled a question at a postgame press briefing in midseason, 1949. He had given a player a hit-and-run sign, and the player ran into a pitchout. Asked about it after the game, he allowed the press to draw the conclusion that the player had run on his own. A writer wrote something about the incident, and the player felt betrayed. The team lost respect for Meyer, and he was never able to regain their confidence.

Well, that's just a story. Meyer's first team, the Louisville team of 1926, played well for one season, then collapsed. His Pirates did the same. The 1952 Pirates, at the end of Meyer's leash, were unnecessarily bad because Branch Rickey, who had been hired to rebuild the Pirates, wanted to start by taking a long look at some young players who were obviously not ready to play in the major leagues. Meyer was relieved of his command at season's end—the first time he had been fired since 1928. He would be dead within a few years.

Ranking Managers

The ten most successful managers of all time are John McGraw, Connie Mack, Joe McCarthy, Casey Stengel, Walt Alston, Sparky Anderson, Earl Weaver, Harry Wright, Bill McKechnie, and Leo Durocher. I can make this statement because

a) I have studied the issue,

b) I like making definitive statements on subjects about which no reasonable person could claim to have definitive information,

c) It's my book and you can't stop me, or

d) All of the above.

What this book is definitely not about is who is a good manager and who is a bad manager. It is occasionally useful to have a frame of reference. Jimmy Collins, for example, enjoyed a certain degree of success as a manager just after 1900. He managed for six seasons, keeping his first five teams over .500. He managed the first modern World Champions in 1903, and defended his league title the next season, when John McGraw chickened out of a World Series. But in the context of history, what is that? Are there a hundred guys who have achieved this level of success, or 25, or 500? How would you balance his accomplishments against those of, let us say, Gil Hodges or Bobby Cox?

The easiest way to rank managers is just to rank them according to how many games they won, or how many games their teams won while they were at the helm. Let's do that. The top ten managers of all time according to games won through 1996 are:

1.	Connie Mack	3,731
2.	John McGraw	2,784
3.	Sparky Anderson	2,194
4.	Bucky Harris	2,157
5.	Joe McCarthy	2,125
6.	Walt Alston	2,040
7.	Leo Durocher	2,008
8.	Casey Stengel	1,905
9.	Gene Mauch	1,902
10.	Bill McKechnie	1,896

Jimmy Collins, with 455 career wins, ranks as the one hundred eleventh most successful manager of all time in this list. Bobby Cox is thirty-first.

The problem with this, of course, is that it considers four seasons of 50 wins to be the same as two seasons of 100 wins. Win totals without losses are not particularly instructive, and when you put the wins beside the losses, you discover that the number-one man, Connie Mack, is actually behind the league:

Rank	Manager	Won–Lost	Pct
1.	Connie Mack	3,731–3,948	.486
2.	John McGraw	2,784–1,959	.587
3.	Sparky Anderson	2,194–1,834	.545
4.	Bucky Harris	2,157–2,218	.493

CONNIE MACK
Dickey Pearce Taught Me to Do It This Way

5.	Joe McCarthy	2,125–1,333	.615
6.	Walt Alston	2,040–1,613	.558
7.	Leo Durocher	2,008–1,709	.540
8.	Casey Stengel	1,905–1,842	.508
9.	Gene Mauch	1,902–2,037	.483
10.	Bill McKechnie	1,896–1,723	.524

Three of the top ten men had more losses than wins.

As a second try we could rank managers according to won–lost percentage. Ranked according to pure won–lost percentage, the top three managers of all time are Mel Harder (3–0), Dick Tracewski (2–0), and Clyde Sukeforth (2–0). (Incidentally, ranked according to either of these methods, the *worst* manager of all time was George Creamer, one of five unfortunates to have skippered the Pittsburgh Alleghenys in 1884. He had the job for eight games, all of which the Alleghenys lost.) If we require a minimum of ten games managed, the ten top managers would then be:

Rank	Manager	Won–Lost	Pct
1.	George Wright	59–25	.702
2	Heinie Groh	7–3	.700
3.	Mase Graffen	39–17	.696
4.	Jack Clements	13–6	.684
5.	Count Campau	27–14	.659
6.	Mike Walsh	68–40	.630
7.	Albert Spalding	78–47	.624
8.	Will White	44–27	.620
9.	Lou Knight	127–7	.620
10.	Joe McCarthy	2,125–1,333	.615

If you've never heard of these men, they're mostly nineteenth-century guys who managed a season or a part of a season when they weren't busy doing something else. The worst manager of all time, requiring ten games, would be Malachi Kittridge of the 1904 Washington Senators—1 and 16. Bobby Cox ranks eighty-fifth on this list, at .539, and Jimmy Collins ranks sixty-sixth.

If you want a list of real managers, you need to require at least a thousand games managed. That list would be:

Rank	Manager	Won–Lost	Pct
1.	Joe McCarthy	2,125–1,333	.615
2.	Jim Mutrie	658–419	.611
3.	Charles Comiskey	839–540	.608
4.	Frank Selee	1,284–862	.598
5.	Billy Southworth	1,044–704	.597
6.	Frank Chance	946–648	.593
7.	John McGraw	2,784–1,959	.587

8.	Al Lopez	1,410–1,004	.584
9.	Earl Weaver	1,480–1,060	.583
10.	Cap Anson	1,292–945	.578

The twelfth man at the moment would be Davey Johnson. This is a list of legitimately outstanding managers, but it is also a ranking method that places a premium on quitting while you're ahead. Does Frank Chance, who managed for eleven seasons, really deserve to rank ahead of John McGraw, who managed three times as long and had almost the same career winning percentage?

Well, what about ranking managers by games over or under .500? Frank Chance was 298 games over .500; John McGraw was 825 games over. Ranked according to games over .500, the race for the distinction of the greatest manager ever is a two-man contest. John McGraw and Joe McCarthy are almost even; nobody else is on the screen:

Rank	Manager	Won–Lost	Pct	Advantage
1.	John McGraw	2,784–1,959	.587	+825
2.	Joe McCarthy	2,125–1,333	.615	+792
3.	Walt Alston	2,040–1,613	.558	+427
4.	Frank Selee	1,284–862	.598	+422
5.	Fred Clarke	1,602–1,181	.576	+421
6.	Earl Weaver	1,480–1,060	.583	+420
7.	Al Lopez	1,410–1,004	.584	+406
8.	Sparky Anderson	2,194–1,834	.545	+360
9.	Cap Anson	1,292–945	.578	+347
10.	Billy Southworth	1,044–704	.597	+340

Bobby Cox is now ranked twenty-fourth, Jimmy Collins forty-eighth. An interesting note: there are only 36 managers in baseball history who finished their careers 100 games over .500. If you can have a couple of good years, you can move up the list in a hurry. The *worst* manager of all time, either by winning percentage (with a minimum of a thousand games) or by wins minus losses, was Jimmie Wilson, who managed the Phillies in the 1930s and the Cubs in the 1940s.

The flaw in this, as a ranking method, can be seen by looking at the bottom of the list. The most unsuccessful managers of all time, by this method, would be:

Rank	Manager	Won–Lost	Pct	Advantage
1.	Jimmie Wilson	493–735	.401	-242
2.	John McCloskey	190–417	.313	-227
3.	**Connie Mack**	**3,731–3,948**	**.486**	**-217**
4.	Fred Tenney	202–402	.334	-200
5.	Patsy Donovan	684–879	.438	-195
6.	Preston Gomez	346–529	.395	-183
7.	Doc Prothro	138–320	.301	-182
8.	Billy Barnie	632–810	.438	-178
9.	Zack Taylor	235–410	.364	-175
10.	Jimmy McAleer	736–889	.453	-153

Connie Mack, who won more games than anyone else ever born, is now listed as the third least-successful manager, more than 300 notches behind Ted Turner, who was 0–1. Another note: Of the 581 men who have managed in the major leagues through 1996, slightly less than one-third have winning records. 33% of all managers have winning records, 64% have losing records, 3% are right at .500.

It's a sobering thought, if you're a young man who would like to be a manager some day: The odds are two to one against you. I suspect this is probably true throughout the coaching profession. If you studied college basketball coaches, for example, I'm certain you would find that many more have losing records than winning records, for the simple reason that those who win keep their jobs much longer than those who lose. The same is true of baseball pitchers: Most of them have losing records. They have to, because some of them get to be a hundred games over .500, but nobody gets to a be a hundred games *under* .500.

College or high school basketball coaches, college or high school football coaches . . . this can be generalized to any competitive profession, from acting to running a barber shop. About 70% of small businesses fail within two years. Could a government policy designed to help small businesses change that percentage? No, for the same reason. Money coming in and money going out can be seen as wins and losses. Businesses and people exchange money with one another; if you have more going out than coming in, you're failing. Those which succeed will force those which fail out of business, which will mean that the turnover among failures has to be much faster than the turnover among successes, which means that over time there have to be more failures than successes. No policy can change this. The Peter Principle notwithstanding, failure is commonplace, but not enduring.

Anyway, at last report we had Connie Mack ranked 300 notches behind Ted Turner, which anyone except perhaps Jane Fonda and the Florida Democrats would recognize as a flawed ranking system. Connie Mack's teams won five World Championships. This is not something that just inevitably happens to you if you hang around long enough.

If a team wins the pennant in one season, whatever they do in the following season does not take that away from them. This is the flaw in the ranking system: It fails to recognize the winning of pennants and World Championships as a permanent accomplishment.

Well then, we could simply count the number of World Championships won. That ranking of the greatest managers ever would start with Casey Stengel and Joe McCarthy:

Joe McCarthy	7
Casey Stengel	7
Connie Mack	5
Walt Alston	4
Sparky Anderson	3
Miller Huggins	3
John McGraw	3
Eleven men with	2

Our problem now is that we have Leo Durocher ranked even with Joe Altobelli. Al Lopez, a wonderful manager in anyone's book, is now ranked even with you and me, since both of his pennant-winning teams lost the World Series. This extends the principle above to absurd proportions: everyone is a failure except the one guy standing at the end of October.

We're on the right track now, but we need a system which recognizes levels of success. What are the things that a manager can do which would cause the rest of us to describe him as successful?

Well, if a manager has a winning season, that's a mark of success—the lowest mark, but a starting point. Nothing below that can be considered an accomplishment. Winning a division title is beyond that, winning the league championship beyond that. I established a system which recognized six types of accomplishment for a season:

- Posting a winning record
- Winning the division
- Winning the league
- Winning the World Series
- Winning 100 games
- Finishing 20 games over .500

The first four of those are the four basic levels, and are scored as 1, 2, 3, and 4. If you win the World Series, that's a four-point season. If you win the league but lose the World Series, that's a three-point season. If you win your division but not the league, that's a two-point season. If you finish over .500 but don't win the division, that's a one-point season.

To these four levels, we add one point if the team finishes 20 games over .500, and a second point if they win 100 games. Thus, a perfect season—a season in which the team wins the World Championship *and* wins 100 games—is worth six points. Winning the World Championship but with less than 100 wins is worth five points. Winning the World Championship but with a record less than 20 games over .500 is worth four points.

Or, on the other hand, winning 100 games but not even winning your division, like the San Francisco Giants did in 1993, that's worth three points—one for having a winning record, plus one for being 20 games over .500, plus one for winning 100 games.

How good a manager someone is is a largely subjective question. How much success a manager has enjoyed is a relatively objective question. Is Sparky Anderson a good manager, or a lucky stiff who came along in the right organization at the right time? Everybody's got an opinion, and there's no way to prove one or the other. But either way, Sparky Anderson enjoyed a considerable amount of success as the manager of the Cincinnati Reds. All I'm trying to do here is to fix that objective observation in a number.

This system is the basis of the "most successful manager" notes which occur in each Decade Snapshot—the most successful manager of the 1870s was Harry Wright, etc. I buried the article about it here, in the middle of the book, in the vain hope that this would discourage reviewers from thinking that that was what the book was all about.

Anyway, let me defend my system and apologize for it. What I *can't* tell you is that there is any compelling logic to this system, or that this is any reason why this system is right, and another system is wrong. Why should a team get one point for finishing 19 games over .500, and two points for 20? Why is a "perfect season" six points, rather than seven? It's arbitrary.

I would argue, however, that

a) the arbitrary cutoffs are reasonable, and

b) any similar system, designed to measure the successes of major league managers, would yield almost identical rankings for the top 15 or 20 managers, regardless of precisely where cutoffs were established, or how different accomplishments were weighted.

So then, the 52 most successful managers of all time, through 1996, are:

	Points			Points
1. John McGraw	79		28. Hughie Jennings	24
2. Connie Mack	72		Charlie Comiskey	24
3. Joe McCarthy	71		30. Danny Murtaugh	23
4. Casey Stengel	52			
5. Walt Alston	51		Davey Johnson	23
			32. Steve O'Neill	22
6. Sparky Anderson	49		33. Jim Mutrie	21
7. Earl Weaver	42		Joe Cronin	21
Harry Wright	42		35. Bill Terry	19
9. Leo Durocher	38			
Bill McKechnie	38		36. Clark Griffith	18
			37. Pat Moran	17
11. Miller Huggins	37		Gene Mauch	17
12. Frank Selee	36			
13. Fred Clarke	35		39. Red Schoendienst	16
14. Cap Anson	34		Charlie Dressen	16
15. Tommy Lasorda	33		Alvin Dark	16
			Cito Gaston	16
16. Al Lopez	32		Frankie Frisch	16
17. Dick Williams	31		Fielder Jones	16
Ned Hanlon	31			
19. Billy Southworth	30		45. Wilbert Robinson	15
20. Billy Martin	29		Chuck Tanner	15
			47. Lou Boudreau	13
Bobby Cox	29		Bill Carrigan	13
22. Frank Chance	28		Patsy Tebeau	13
Charlie Grimm	28		Jimmy Collins	13
Whitey Herzog	28		Mickey Cochrane	13
Tony LaRussa	28		Lou Piniella	13
26. Ralph Houk	25			
Bucky Harris	25			

The modern manager, in this system, has both advantages and disadvantages compared to earlier eras. The modern manager can earn points for winning his division, which were not available to managers pre-1969—but on the other hand, the number of teams competing for those "championship points" is greater now than it was then. The season is longer now, giving teams an advantage in the race for 100 wins—but there is more competitive balance than there was through much of baseball history, so that in fact there are *not* more teams winning 100 games a season, but fewer. My intention, in laying out the system, was to be fair to managers of all eras.

Anyway, of the top ten men on the manager's list, all are in the Hall of Fame except Sparky Anderson, who I would assume will go in as soon as he's eligible. Of the second ten, five are in, and five are not, but two of those who are in (Fred Clarke and Cap Anson) may have been selected largely as players. After the twentieth spot, all of the managers who are in the Hall of Fame were also outstanding players, with the arguable exception of Wilbert Robinson (and even Robby may have been selected as much for his playing contributions as for his managing).

So that answers, in one form, the question of what a manager has to do to get into the Hall of Fame: He needs about thirty points in this system. If Tony LaRussa has one more good year at St. Louis, he'll probably be in the Hall of Fame. As it is, he's on the bubble. Bobby Cox and Davey Johnson are in a similar position: They've accomplished a lot, but they're not certain Hall of Famers at this point. In five years, they might be.

Another way that managers could be ranked is by comparing their won–lost records to their team's expected wins, based on runs scored and runs allowed. I did that for contemporary managers in one of the *Baseball Abstracts*, and a gentleman named Bob Boynton did it on a wider basis in a recent SABR publication. The theory is that if the team scores 650 runs and allows 650 runs, but finishes 5 games over .500, the manager must have done a good job, whereas if they finish 72–90 he couldn't have been said to have gotten the most wins out of what he had to work with. If they win the close games, they'll come out better than expected.

Boynton studied this issue for 39 long-term and 65 short-term managers, comparing each season's won–lost record to the expected won-lost record based on runs scored and runs allowed. He summarizes this relationship in a "D score"; if the manager done good, his D score is high.

His conclusion:

> Not surprisingly, there is a positive relation between D scores and winning percentage. The exception—and it is a huge one—is Joe McCarthy . . .
>
> There is no intention here to minimize McCarthy's success in the all-important win department. Nevertheless, the evidence seems clear that the teams he managed consistently lost more relatively close games than they won. A likely explanation for this is that, with a rich and continuously replenished pool of top-notch Yankee talent at his disposal, winning required little managerial maneuvering of the sort employed by most managers in an attempt to eke out victories.

This conclusion is completely false; McCarthy's teams did *not* "los(e) more relatively close games than they won." The conclusion results entirely from a flaw in Boynton's method.

Boynton based his win expectations on runs scored per game as opposed to opposition runs per game. If a team scored 1.000 runs per game more than their opponents, he expected them to post a winning percentage of .600. If a team outscored their opponents by 2.500 runs per game, he would expect them to post a .750 winning pecentage.

Within normal ranges of runs scored and runs allowed, this works well enough. But as the run margin increases, the value of each run decreases. What would happen if a team was outscored by, let us say, six runs a game? By Boynton's method, they would have an expected winning percentage *less than zero*. If they outscored their opponents by five runs per game, he would expect them to win every game. If they scored more runs, winning every game wouldn't be enough.

As a team begins to score more and more runs, it becomes impossible for them to win as many games as Boynton expects them to win. The 1939 Yankees, for example, outscored their opponents by 2.72 runs per game; thus, Boynton expects them to win 77.2% of their games. When they actually won "only" 70.2% (they finished 106–45), he gives them a D score of minus 70 (702 minus 772 equals minus 70). He believes they should have finished 117–34. "Although the 1939 season is an extreme case, McCarthy's (record) indicates that the tendency to lose relatively close games was a consistent one throughout his career."

In fact, though, the 1939 Yankees had a *good* record in close games—22–15 in one-run games, and 50–32 in games decided by three or less. The '39 Yankees won 15 games by ten or more runs, a phenomenal accomplishment in itself, including three wins by twenty or more runs. Obviously, they weren't going to *lose* games by twenty or more runs. They were 24–0 in games decided by more than six runs. These are normal expectations for such a team. If you studied minor league teams which scored seven runs a game, you'd find the same types of performance for them.

This problem doesn't have much effect on anyone except Joe McCarthy, because no one else's teams scored so many runs. But there is another problem. Boynton's method predicts a .600 winning percentage if a team outscores their opposition by one run per game—ten to nine, or three to two. Obviously, this is not accurate. The expected winning percentage of a team which outscored their opponents ten to nine would be .552; the expected winning percentage of a team outscoring their opponents three to two would be .692. Walter Alston comes out looking great in Boynton's system, because, in a run-starved environment, his run advantage means much more than projected.

I could have repeated the study with a better formula, I suppose, but I decided to pass. The theory, while intriguing, is just too speculative. It measures the manager *against* the individual accomplishments of his players, when in the real world, a manager has to work *through* the talent he's got. Let's take something really stupid that a manager might have done. Jack McKeon in 1974 with the Kansas City Royals

a) didn't think George Brett was ready to play in the majors, and wanted to keep playing Paul Schaal, and

b) ruined Steve Busby's arm by having him throw about 200 pitches in a game one time when his catcher was telling him Busby wasn't right.

The mistake on Busby, the best young pitcher in baseball at that time, cost the Royals dozens of wins over a period of years, and the mistake on Brett (and Frank White—McKeon didn't think he could play, either) could have cost the Royals countless runs. But how would either of these things have altered the ratio between runs scored, runs allowed, and wins?

If a manager does a good job of keeping his team focused on winning, how will that cause them to have a better ratio of wins to runs scored/runs allowed? It's hard to see. If he tears the team apart with petty battles over irrelevant rules, how will this be reflected in the wins versus expected wins? I can't see it. The theory of it is just too much of a reach.

There is another way of establishing "win expectation," however. Another way to establish expected wins is to look at the performance of this team in previous seasons and establish from that how many games we would expect the team to win this year.

The best way I have found to establish expected wins for a team based on previous seasons is to combine four elements, which are the records of the team in the previous three seasons, and a .500 record. The record of the team in the last season is 50% of the load. The .500 record is 25%, since all teams have a pronounced tendency to drift toward .500. The records of the team the two previous seasons are each one-eighth, 12.5%.

For illustration, suppose that a team won 100 games last year, 90 games the year before that, and 70 games the year before that. How many games would we expect them to win next year?

Last Year	100–62	Times 4	400–248
.500 Team	81–81	Times 2	162–162
Previous Year	90–72		90–72
Previous Year	70–92		70–92
Total			**722–574**
Percentage			**.557**
Projected to 162 Games			**90–72**

We would expect the team, given that history, to win 90 games this year.

This system establishes expected wins very accurately for groups of teams. If you take a group of teams which would be expected to win 90 games by this method, they will in fact win 90 games, on the average. If you take a group of teams which would be expected to win 70 games, they will win 70. If you can find a group of teams which would be expected to win 100, they will actually win 100, on the average. The method works in 1910, and it works in 1995.

So then, we can use this to evaluate the performance of the manager, by comparing how his teams *actually* performed to how they would have been expected to perform, based on previous seasons. Let's take the Texas Rangers in 1974, Billy Martin's first year there. The team had gone 63–96 in 1971 (in Washington), 54–100 in 1972, and 57–105 in 1973. Given that history, and given 160 games in 1974, we would expect them to finish 63–97. Figured as follows:

1973 Record	57–105	Times Four	228–420	
.500 Record	81–81	Times Two	162–162	
1972 Record	54–100		54–100	
1971 Record	63–96		63–96	
Total			499–778	.391
Projected to 160 games			63–97	

The team actually went 84–76, 21 games better than expected. This is very rare. Only a few managers will ever have a team finish 20 games ahead of where they could have been expected to finish. In 1996, two National League teams finished 10 games better than expected: San Diego at +15, and St. Louis at +12.

We figured win expectations for each season of the careers of a large number of managers. The resulting records are given in the chart (below):

Manager	Best Season	Good	Bad	Won–Lost	Pct	+/-
Felipe Alou	1994 Mon +12	4	1	392–315	.554	+19
Walt Alston	1965 LA +12	12	7	2,040–1,613	.558	+26
Joe Altobelli	1978 SF +12	2	2	437–407	.518	0

I should stop and explain what all of that means, in case any of it is unclear. Felipe Alou's best season, by this method, was 1994, when Montreal was 74–40, the best record in baseball at the time the season was stopped by the strike. This was 12 games better than the team could have been expected to play in 114 games, based on their performance in the previous seasons.

Alou has had four good seasons so far in his career, and only one bad season, with a good season being any season in which the manager's team outperforms expectations by three games or more, and a bad season being any season in which the team fails by three games or more to meet their expectations. From plus two to minus two, the season is neither good nor bad.

The next three columns are just the manager's career won–lost record and winning percentage, and the final column is his career plus or minus versus expectations. Alou's Expos were +11 in 1992, +7 in 1993, +12 in 1994, and +6 in 1996, but -17 in 1995, for a total of +19 games.

That's the beginning of the alphabetical chart; I'll switch now to putting managers in order of accomplishment.

Manager	Best Season	Good	Bad	Won–Lost	Pct	+/-
McCarthy, Joe	1932 NY +19	17	4	2,125–1,333	.615	+126
McGraw, John	1904 NY +27	17	9	2,784–1,959	.587	+116
Cox, Bobby	1991 Atl +26	9	1	1,201–1,028	.539	+115
Martin, Billy	1974 Tex +21	10	1	1,253–1,013	.553	+98
Williams, Dick	1979 Mon +21	11	5	1,571–1,451	.520	+92
Southworth, Billy	1942 StL +16	9	4	1,770–1,044	.597	+74
Clarke, Fred	1902 Pit +23	10	6	1,602–1,181	.576	+72
Huggins, Miller	1927 NY +25	9	5	1,413–1,134	.555	+68
Durocher, Leo	1954 NY +19	13	8	2,008–1,709	.540	+64
Richards, Paul	1951 Chi +17	7	2	923–901	.506	+63
Johnson, Davey	1984 NY +20	7	4	887–663	.572	+59
Harris, Bucky	1924 Was +16	13	11	2,157–2,218	.493	+52
McKechnie, Bill	1939 Cin +19	15	8	1,842–1,678	.523	+51
Griffith, Clark	1912 Was +27	9	8	1,491–1,367	.522	+45
Lopez, Al	1954 Cle +22	9	6	1,410–1,004	.584	+43
O'Neill, Steve	1952 Phi +13	7	2	1,040–821	.559	+43
Grimm, Charlie	1945 Chi +23	8	6	1,287–1,067	.547	+42
Chance, Frank	1906 Chi +28	6	3	,946–648	.593	+41
Weaver, Earl	1969 Bal +17	10	3	1,480–1,060	.583	+41
Murtaugh, Danny	1960 Pit +18	9	3	1,115–950	.540	+39
Anderson, Sparky	1984 Det +16	13	9	2,194–1,834	.545	+38
LaRussa, Tony	1988 Oak +24	12	6	1,408–1,257	.527	+35
Armour, Bill	1905 Det +12	4	1	382–347	.524	+33

Manager	Best Season	Good	Bad	Won–Lost	Pct	+/-
Ozark, Danny	1976 Phi +19	5	3	618–542	.533	+31
Moran, Pat	1919 Cin +26	6	3	748–586	.561	+30
Stallings, George	1914 Bos +28	6	5	879–898	.495	+30
Hodges, Gil	1969 NY +23	4	2	660–753	.467	+28
Lemon, Bob	1971 KC +17	3	3	430–403	.516	+28
Alston, Walt	1965 LA +12	12	7	2,040–1,613	.558	+26
Showalter, Bucky	1993 NY +12	3	0	313–268	.539	+26
Mele, Sam	1965 Min +19	3	3	524–436	.546	+25
Johnson, Walter	1930 Was +19	4	3	529–432	.550	+25
Piniella, Lou	1990 Cin +12	4	3	734–709	.522	+24
Cronin, Joe	1946 Bos +31	7	5	1,236–1,055	.540	+23
Gibson, George	1921 Pit +12	4	1	413–344	.546	+23
Rowland, Pants	1915 Chi +19	3	1	339–247	.578	+23
Jennings, Hughie	1915 Det +24	8	6	1,163–984	.542	+21
Herzog, Whitey	1985 StL +17	8	6	1,281–1,125	.532	+19
Cochrane, Mickey	1934 Det +27	2	2	366–266	.579	+19
Alou, Felipe	1994 Mon +12	4	1	352–315	.554	+19
Mauch, Gene	1982 Cal +16	10	8	1,902–2,037	.483	+18
Franks, Herman	1965 SF +6	3	0	605–521	.537	+18
Cobb, Ty	1923 Det +8	3	0	479–444	.519	+18
Rose, Pete	1985 Cin +17	3	1	412–373	.525	+18
Walker, Harry	1965 Pit +9	5	2	630–604	.511	+17
Howser, Dick	1980 NY +13	4	2	507–425	.544	+17
Bamberger, George	1978 Mil +21	2	4	458–478	.489	+17
Tebbetts, Birdie	1956 Cin +16	4	3	748–705	.515	+15
Dressen, Chuck	1953 Bkn +14	7	5	1,008–973	.509	+15
Vitt, Ossie	1938 Cle +6	3	0	262–198	.570	+15
Valentine, Bobby	1986 Tex +17	4	3	593–624	.487	+14
Sewell, Luke	1942 StL +15	3	3	606–644	.485	+14
Gordon, Joe	1959 Cle +10	2	0	305–308	.498	+14
Carrigan, Bill	1915 Bos +14	2	1	489–500	.494	+13
Virdon, Bill	1979 Hou +12	6	5	995–921	.519	+12
Craft, Harry	1958 KC +10	3	1	360–485	.426	+12
Hunter, Billy	1977 Tex +13	1	0	146–108	.575	+12
Craig, Roger	1986 SF +14	4	3	738–737	.500	+11
Fohl, Lee	1917 Cle +17	5	4	713–792	.474	+11
Frey, Jim	1984 Chi +24	2	3	323–287	.530	+11
Terry, Bill	1933 NY +15	5	4	823–661	.555	+10
Shotton, Burt	1929 Phi +17	5	3	697–764	.477	+10
Lefebvre, Jim	1991 Sea +7	1	0	395–415	.488	+9
Lasorda, Tommy	1988 LA +17	11	6	1,597–1,437	.526	+9

Manager	Best Season	Good	Bad	Won–Lost	Pct	+/-
Trebelhorn, Tom	1987 Mil +15	4	3	544–532	.506	+8
Scheffing, Bob	1961 Det +18	3	3	418–427	.495	+8
Speaker, Tris	1926 Cle +15	4	3	617–520	.543	+6
Garcia, Dave	1979 Cle +7	2	2	307–310	.498	+6
Hutchinson, Fred	1961 Cin +21	5	5	830–827	.501	+5
Leyland, Jim	1990 Pit +17	5	5	850–861	.497	+5
Rickey, Branch	1921 StL +16	4	5	597–664	.473	+4
Baker, Del	1940 Det +9	3	2	401–344	.538	+4
Kelly, Tom	1991 Min +16	5	4	785–791	.498	+4
Robinson, Wilbert	1920 Bkn +18	7	10	1,399–1,398	.500	+3
Haney, Fred	1940 StL +14	5	5	629–757	.454	+3
Zimmer, Don	1989 Chi +16	4	5	885–858	.508	+1
Dark, Alvin	1962 SF +10	6	4	994–954	.510	+1
Altobelli, Joe	1978 SF +12	2	2	437–407	.518	0
Gaston, Cito	1989 Tor +10	4	2	630–565	.527	-1
Bresnahan, Roger	1911 StL +13	2	2	328–432	.432	-1
Frisch, Frankie	1934 StL +13	7	6	1,138–1,078	.514	-2
Robinson, Frank	1989 Bal +22	5	5	680–751	.475	-2
Higgins, Pinky	1955 Bos +10	2	3	560–556	.502	-2
Dyer, Eddie	1949 StL +11	2	3	446–325	.578	-2
Rader, Doug	1989 Cal +12	2	3	388–417	.482	-2
Sawyer, Eddie	1950 Phi +15	2	5	390–423	.480	-3
Hornsby, Rogers	1926 StL +13	5	6	701–812	.463	-4
Rapp, Vern	1977 StL +6	1	2	140–160	.467	-4
Traynor, Pie	1935 Pit +8	3	2	457–406	.530	-4
Baker, Dusty	1993 SF +23	1	3	293–290	.503	-5
Gardner, Billy	1984 Min +11	1	2	330–417	.442	-5
Rodgers, Buck	1987 Mon +11	4	6	785–774	.504	-5
Quilici, Frank	1974 Min +2	0	1	280–287	.494	-5
Wathan, John	1989 KC +10	2	3	326–320	.505	-6
Houk, Ralph	1970 NY +12	7	10	1,619–1,531	.514	-7
Ott, Mel	1947 NY +13	3	2	464–530	.467	-7
Crandall, Del	1973 Mil +3	1	2	364–469	.437	-8
Berra, Yogi	1975 NY +4	1	1	484–444	.522	-9
Fox, Charlie	1973 SF +10	2	3	377–371	.504	-9
Stengel, Casey	1960 NY +15	9	11	1,905–1,842	.508	-9
Marion, Marty	1953 StL-11	1	2	356–372	.489	-11
Rigney, Bill	1962 Cal +17	9	8	1,239–1,321	.484	-11
Keane, Johnny	1964 StL +7	3	3	398–350	.532	-12
Johnson, Darrell	1975 Bos +12	3	4	472–590	.444	-12
Smith, Mayo	1968 Det +15	3	5	662–612	.520	-13

Manager	Best Season	Good	Bad	Won–Lost	Pct	+/-
Dykes, Jimmy	1934 Chi +14	9	10	1,406–1,541	.477	-14
Bragan, Bobby	1956 Pit +4	2	4	443–478	.481	-14
Schoendienst, Red	1967 StL +18	4	5	1,041–955	.522	-14
Bristol, Dave	1967 Cin +6	2	3	657–764	.462	-17
Stanky, Eddie	1952 StL +6	2	3	467–435	.518	-19
Torre, Joe	1982 Atl +12	5	8	986–1,073	.479	-19
Boudreau, Lou	1948 Cle +19	6	8	1,162–1,224	.487	-21
Corrales, Pat	1986 Cle +16	1	5	572–634	.474	-23
Williams, Ted	1969 Was +10	1	3	273–364	.429	-26
Fregosi, Jim	1993 Phi +19	4	6	861–938	.479	-26
McNamara, John	1986 Bos +14	6	7	1,168–1,247	.484	-27
Tanner, Chuck	1972 Chi +15	5	11	1,352–1,381	.495	-28
Mack, Connie	1909 Phi +20	26	22	3,731–3,948	.486	-49
Wilson, Jimmie	1943 Chi +3	1	6	493–735	.401	-55

I have about fifty notes of things I was supposed to explain about this chart; I'll try to keep them under control.

1) We didn't figure the records for the true nineteenth-century managers, for reasons you can figure out if you care.

2) This evaluation is careful, logical, and has a scientific basis, since the win expectation can be objectively verified by anyone who chooses to study the issue. Two teams win 63 games, 67 games, 66 games each, then hire new managers. One of those teams then wins 85 games, and the other wins 55. It is reasonable to conclude that one manager has had a better year than the other. This method is just a way of systematizing those type of comparisons. We can't compare each manager's season to a large field of teams coming off a string of identical seasons, of course, because there aren't that many identical strings of seasons. By using this method, we can establish what the field of teams coming off a string of identical seasons *would* do, if there were such a field.

3) At the same time, let's not overstate the value of the method. There could be a million reasons why a team could have a bad year or a good year, other than what the manager has done.

Walter Alston's teams were 427 games over .500 in his career, yet Walter scores at only +26. Why? Because his teams were always expected to do well. When his teams played well one year, they were expected to play well the next, so Walter got little credit for it. This may not be entirely fair to managers who stay in one job for a long period of time, as opposed to those who bounce from job to job, like Dick Williams (+92) and Billy Martin (+98).

4) In calculating expected wins, expansion years are a pain in the rear. For an expansion team, we just entered the "last year's record" at 54–108, and the previous year's records as the same. This creates an expected first-year winning percentage of .375, and the actual first-year winning percentage of all expansion teams is like .376 or something, so that's fine.

The problem is, it throws the league off-center. The "expected losses" for a league will outweigh the expected wins, by a large enough margin that it makes the data look funny. To prevent that from happening, you have to adjust upward the expected wins for all of the established teams, not only for the expansion year, but for the subsequent season, as well.

This is a petty detail, and I realize that 99% of you don't care, but the assumption of verifiable research is that someone else could duplicate your work, if they chose to, and reach the same conclusions. To make that viable, I have to explain the petty details.

5) The biggest surprise in the data is Bobby Cox. Bobby Cox, evaluated by comparing the performance of his teams to the expected performance of his teams, is closing in on the distinction of being the greatest manager of all time.

Will he make it? I wouldn't bet on it. It's a zero-sum game; an average team in any season is at zero. Cox is as likely to move *down* the list as he is to move up. Sparky Anderson, at one time, was +70. Cox, because of Atlanta's performance in recent years, has very high expectations to deal with. In 1996, Atlanta won 96 games. That's +0; they were expected to win 96.

Nonetheless, it's an impressive record. Cox has had nine good seasons as a manager, and he's never *really* had a bad one. His worst season as a manager was 1979, when he went 66–94 with a team that could have been expected to win 70. That qualifies as a bad season in the chart, but barely.

What makes Bobby win? The most obvious thing is that he has acquired Earl Weaver's uncanny ability to keep his starting pitchers healthy and productive. When Cox took over the Braves in 1978, they had posted the worst earned run average in major league baseball, 4.85. They cut that to 4.08 in 1978, to 3.77 in 1980, and 3.45 in 1981, better than the National League average.

He joined Toronto in 1982; they had been eleventh in the league in ERA. Their team ERA improved, under Cox, to fifth in the league in 1982, to third in 1984, and to first in 1985, his final year with the team. He inherited a team with three starting pitchers, Dave Stieb, Luis Leal, and Jim Clancy. Leal got hurt, but four years later Stieb and Clancy were still in the rotation, and both pitching better than they had when Cox arrived. They had been joined by Doyle Alexander and Jimmy Key, giving Cox the best starting rotation in the American League at that time.

In his second term in Atlanta, of course, he has done the same act, only better. John Smoltz, Tom Glavine, and Steve Avery were there when Cox returned in 1990. Five years later, they were still there, pitching better than they had in 1990, while the addition of Greg Maddux had created the most formidable starting rotation in many years.

6) Bobby Cox was +8 his first time in Atlanta, +49 in Toronto, and is +58 since returning to Atlanta (1990–1996).

Joe McCarthy was +36 in Chicago, +74 in New York, and +16 in Boston.

Casey Stengel was +55 with the Yankees, but -8 in Brooklyn, -25 in Boston, and -31 with the Mets.

Connie Mack was +1 with Pittsburgh in the 1890s, +69 from 1901 to 1914, -102 from 1915 to 1921, +92 from 1922 to 1931, and -109 from 1932 to the end of his career.

7) This book is not about how managers rate, and to the extent that I would rate managers, I would use the point system introduced earlier in this article, rather than the plus/minus system.

Nonetheless, I do believe there is some validity to the method. Let's look, for example, at the managers who had losing records in their careers, but who score on the plus side in this system.

That would include Bucky Harris (61 games under .500, but 52 games better than expectation), Gil Hodges (93 games under .500, but 28 games better than could have been expected), Gene Mauch

(135 games under .500, but 18 games better than expected), plus George Bamberger, Bobby Valentine, Luke Sewell, Bill Carrigan, Harry Craft, Burt Shotton, and several others.

I believe, in all cases except one (Fred Haney) that it would be fair to say that these men were successful managers, but just didn't have a lot to work with for most of their careers—thus, I believe that what the method is telling us is essentially correct.

On the other hand, we have managers who were over .500, but under expectation—Mayo Smith, Eddie Stanky, Red Schoendienst. In general, I would have to agree that an accurate assessment of these men's records is that they won, but given the teams that they had, they didn't win as often as might have been expected. It's a subjective judgment, but in general, I'll buy it.

Player/Managers

The 1930s was the last decade in which player/managers were common; between 1935 and 1955 they made a strong move toward extinction.

You may have heard it said that the player/managers were rarely effective after they stopped playing, and became just plain managers. Lou Boudreau, for example, managed three teams after he stopped playing, which was an unpleasant experience for all concerned. Frank Chance and Fred Clarke, the great player/managers of the first decade of the twentieth century, both developed a habit of getting the hell beat out of them as soon as they stopped playing, as did Bucky Harris and Rogers Hornsby and Frankie Frisch.

I have concluded that this belief is essentially false, for three reasons.

1) It's inherently inexplicable,

2) The statement attributes to one class of managers what is in fact generally true of *all* managers, and

3) The statement relies on a "false sorting" which makes the pattern seem stronger than it is.

First, why would player/managers become unable to manage after they became unable to play? You can make a *general* statement about player/managers having to adjust their approach to managing from the dugout, but when you try to make it specific, you realize it doesn't make any sense. What, specifically, are these managers going to forget how to do? Signal a bunt?

Second, *all* managers, as a group, are most effective in their early years on the job.

I did a study of 103 managers who managed at least 600 major league games, a group basically including all twentieth-century managers who had significant careers and are now retired. The study documented something which is apparent if you just look at the records. A huge percentage of managers have their best seasons

a) when they first get a chance to manage, and

b) in their first years on a new job.

This is almost a universal rule. There might be ten exceptions in the century—Casey Stengel, for example, and Gene Mauch. But the teams managed by these 103 managers outperformed expectations (see "Ranking Managers," page 139) by 221 games in their first seasons as major league managers (2.15 games per manager), and by a whopping 494 games (4.80 games per manager) in their second seasons, which in many cases was the first full season.

They continued to be enormously effective in their third seasons (+3.16 games, on average), and fourth (+2.37 games)—but after that, they went into idle. In seasons five through ten, these 103 managers improved their teams, on average, but by less than one game. In seasons eleven through fifteen, the teams managed by these men did not outperform expectations at all, and after year sixteen, they tended slightly to *under*-perform the natural expectation of the team.

I'll return to this theme in a moment, but what I am saying here is that since *all* managers have a strong tendency to lose effectiveness as they continue in the job, the fact that *player*/managers have the same tendency is not noteworthy.

And third, think about Miller Huggins. You may not even know that Miller Huggins began managing while he was still playing, and in fact was quite a successful player/manager. You may not know this, however, because everyone's image of Miller Huggins is formed by his most successful seasons, which were his years with the Yankees in the 1920s.

There are other examples like this, such as Leo Durocher. If a manager begins as a player/manager and has his best years as a player/manager, we think of him as a player/manager, like Lou

Boudreau. But if he has his best years as a dugout manager, we classify him as a dugout manager. This subconscious grouping tends to sharply reduce the post-career managerial success of player/managers, because if they *are* good, we tend not to think of them as player/managers at all.

The most interesting question here is why managers lose effectiveness as they remain in their job. I find myself discussing this constantly on talk shows, whenever a team changes managers. Some fan will always call, alleging that the fired manager was a scapegoat for the problems of the team. Mr. Wombat was a good manager two or three years ago, wasn't he? He won the league manager-of-the-year award just two years ago, didn't he? If he was a good manager then, why isn't he a good manager now?

Nonetheless, the most obvious fact about managers is that almost all managers become ineffective after two or three years in a position. I will cite a few examples of this, but I have misgivings about doing so, because citing examples tends to obscure the fact that *almost all* managers are "examples" of the same phenomenon:

Joe Altobelli improved the San Francisco Giants by 12 games his second year there, 1978. By the middle of the next summer, his clubhouse was in chaos.

He was hired to manage Baltimore in 1983 and won the World Series in his first season there. He was fired a year and a half later. The only seasons of his career in which his teams exceeded expectations were 1978 and 1983.

George Bamberger got the Milwaukee Brewers in 1978 and was phenomenally effective for two years, with his team exceeding expected wins by 21 games in 1978, and 12 more in 1979. He managed for five more seasons or parts of seasons after that, but all five of those teams failed to meet expectations.

Roger Craig took over San Diego in 1978 and had a great first year. The team collapsed in 1979.

Craig assumed command of the San Francisco Giants in late 1985 and the team exceeded expectations by 14 games in 1986, and 12 more in 1987. They were on target in 1988, and +9 in 1989, Craig's fourth year there. But the team failed to meet expectations in 1990, 1991, and again in 1992.

Jim Frey got his long-awaited opportunity to manage in Kansas City in 1980. He took the 1980 Royals to the World Series. By August of 1981, he was staggering around in a daze.

He managed the Chicago Cubs in 1984, and the team exceeded expectations by 24 games, moving from fifth to first in one season. But he managed them for two more years after that, during which they returned to the mediocrity from which they had sprung.

Clark Griffith managed the White Sox, Highlanders, Reds, and Senators from 1901 to 1920. All four of these teams improved dramatically in Griffith's first season as their manager, and two of them continued to improve in his second season. But all of them regressed after that.

The Senators are the most dramatic example. The Senators went 42–110 in 1909, 66–85 in 1910, and 64–90 in 1911. On this basis, they could have been expected to go 65–89 in 1912, the season in which Griffith arrived.

Under Griffith's management, they went 91–61, finishing second in the American League. They won 90 games again in 1913, and stayed over .500 in 1914 and 1915. They dropped under .500 in 1916 and 1917, and by 1919, they were back in seventh place.

Pinky Higgins's Boston Red Sox were +10 in 1955, his first season as a manager; they were expected to win 74, but won 84. The Red Sox remained in the plus category, by smaller margins, in 1956 and 1957—but Higgins managed them for parts of five more seasons, during all of which the Red Sox failed to win as many games as expected.

Bob Lemon was +17 his first full year in Kansas City, and +15 his first year in Chicago. He was +9 his first year in New York, when he took over in late July. The rest of his career, his teams consistently failed to meet their expectations.

Billy Martin, of course, improved every team he ever managed in his first season in control, usually by huge amounts. Within a year or two, all of those teams were ready to get rid of him.

Chuck Tanner, after two years on the job, was +28, his 1971–1972 White Sox having exceeded expectations by 13 and 15 games. He wound up his career -28.

Bobby Valentine improved the Rangers by 17 games in his first full season as their manager, 1986. He managed them until 1992, and they never had another season as good.

Ted Williams impressed the baseball world as a rookie manager in 1969, when he took the Senators to a record of 86–76. He managed them three more seasons, with records of 70–92, 63–96, and 54–100.

So managers have a strong tendency to lose effectiveness over time. The question now is, why?

I have probably thought more about that issue, over the years, than about any other issue discussed in this book. I have concluded that there are many reasons why this occurs, which unfortunately interact in ways that make them impossible to classify.

If a manager is successful, he changes the needs of the organization. By so doing, he often makes himself obsolete.

The most important question that a manager asks is "What needs to be changed around here?" Any manager, over time, loses the ability to see what needs to be changed.

Managers, and ball clubs, can be split A/B along many different axes—for example, high pressure/low pressure, platoon/nonplatoon, aggressive/patient, young/experienced. All of those categories are limiting. New managers are effective because they tend to pull their teams out of the rut created by overemphasizing any one category.

For example, a high-pressure manager will almost always, in time, find himself with an emotionally charged, uptight clubhouse in which no one feels at home. The more high-pressure a manager is, the more quickly that point will be reached. When that manager is replaced by a relaxed, low-pressure manager, almost everyone on the team will play better for some period of time.

Conversely, when a low-pressure manager remains in charge of a team for a period of time, the team will almost always lose focus. The players won't work as hard, and they won't concentrate on the things that the team needs them to work on. They'll lose their fear, and when they lose their fear, they'll lose their edge. When a high-pressure manager takes over, everyone plays harder, and the team plays better.

To sustain success over a period of time, a manager must avoid both of these traps: He must be neither too low-pressure nor too high-pressure. This is nearly impossible. Joe McCarthy was able to do it; Bobby Cox has been able to do it.

Thus, teams over time are whipsawed between high-pressure and low-pressure managers. The New York Yankees in the years of Billy Martin and Bob Lemon are the classic example, Martin being the highest of high-pressure managers, and Lemon the most casual of low-pressure managers. Each was effective because he replaced the other.

Similar things happen on all of the other axes. If a team *doesn't* use its bench, the bench will atrophy, and the team will become vulnerable to injuries. If a team overuses its bench, they'll have difficultly developing stars. The manager, to remain effective, must find exactly the right balance.

If the team uses too many veterans, within a couple of years age will catch up with them. In that case, they probably won't begin rebuilding until they go to another manager.

But if the team uses too many young players, they may have difficulty getting over the hump. In that case, they might not "arrive," as a team, until another manager comes along who brings in some veteran leadership.

This is not to say that all managerial styles are equal. I believe, rightly or wrongly, that low pressure is better than high pressure, young is better than old, and using the bench is better than not using the bench. My point is that there are many such orientations, and each of them creates pitfalls for the manager.

Even apart from those pitfalls, there are profound reasons why new managers tend to be more effective than established managers. There is the manager's loyalty to his players. A new manager owes nobody nothing. He can bench or release unproductive players without apology. An established manager can't do that—not only because of his own reluctance to break faith with players who have given him their best efforts, but because of what it means to the rest of the team. Good teams have the attitude that "we are all in this together." When a manager who has been a part of that "We" suddenly decides to toss Charlie out of the boat, it shakes the group identity of those who remain.

If a *new* manager throws Charlie out of the boat, everybody else says, "Uh oh. My job isn't safe here; I'd better bust my hump trying to impress this guy." If an *old* manager throws Charlie out of the boat, it's a betrayal. Everybody else says, "You can't trust that guy anymore. Charlie busted his butt for him, and look what happened to him."

Or ask this, "Why are first impressions lasting?" Because that's when you're paying the most attention. That fact gives a new manager a tremendous edge in trying to send a message to his team.

Even that is not the end of his advantage.

In the United States Army, the first sergeant is, in essence, the company's "manager." When I was in the army, it happened one time that I was assigned to one company for a longer period than the normal thirteen-month rotation, and for

this reason I was with the company when a new first sergeant came in, and still there a year later when the next new first sergeant arrived.

They were very different men, but both of them did many of the same type of things, which were intended to convey to the company this simple message: We care, and we're trying to make things better around here. One first sergeant, to demonstrate that he cared, took down some old, tawdry curtains which hung in the NCO club. The next first sergeant, to demonstrate the same point, put the same curtains back up.

One first sergeant, to show that he was interested in improving things, changed the seating in the mess hall. The next first sergeant shifted it again—more or less back to what it was.

One first sergeant shifted the exercise routine from the morning to the evening. The next first sergeant moved it back to the morning.

And both times, it worked. The attitude of the company, which was very negative as a starting point, improved tremendously when the first first sergeant took down the curtains in the NCO club, changed the seating in the mess hall, and moved the exercise period to 4:00. Over the course of the year the company grew stale, petty problems ground us down, and the attitude turned sour. When the other new first sergeant came in, he did exactly the opposite things—but had exactly the same effect.

Another thing . . . the game of baseball changes, over time, much more extensively than most people realize. The way the game is played now is very different from the way it was played ten years ago, and very, very different from the way it was played thirty years ago.

Newspaper and television commentators, driven by old ballplayers, almost always interpret those changes in a negative way, arguing that the game isn't as well played as it used to be. But in reality, new strategies and new ways of doing things sweep the game not because they *don't* work, but because they do.

I'll give you a simple example: catching a fly ball with two hands. Until about 1970, baseball players were taught to catch a fly ball with two hands. This was a universally accepted convention, notwithstanding the fact that it was a really stupid idea. You *don't* catch a fly ball with two hands, never did and never could. You catch the fly ball with the glove hand. The other hand was there to protect you if the ball popped out.

Well, the ball doesn't pop out that often, and if it does, you're not going to catch it with the other hand, anyway. What it does, when you try to catch a ball with two hands, is to change a natural, instinctive action to a forced, unnatural action. It throws your whole body out of alignment, and it limits your range of motion. It slows you down, and it causes a great many more errors than it prevents.

Nonetheless, that was how it was taught for many years, dating back to the time when gloves were small and awkward, fielding percentages were low, and it probably made sense to do it this way. When ballplayers started catching the ball one-handed, old ballplayers and old media guys criticized them for not doing things the "right" way, meaning the way that they were taught to do it when they were kids.

The younger managers of that time, like Earl Weaver and Whitey Herzog, accepted the change immediately. Just make sure you catch the ball; that's all we care about. The older managers continued to insist that outfielders make a show of catching the ball two-handed.

There are dozens of changes like that happening all the time. The older a manager is, the more likely he is to fight those changes. Older managers are trying to play the game the way it was played thirty years ago, usually without realizing it.

There are, of course, cases where old strategies work to the advantage of older managers. The most obvious example is Casey Stengel and platooning. Platooning was common when Casey was playing; by 1949, it was almost dead. Casey, an old manager, reached back for the old strategy, and it worked out great for him. But as a rule, I'm always going to bet on the younger manager.

There are long-term advantages to stability, of course. But few organizations can reach those long-term advantages, because few managers are able to do the job over a period of years. It's easy to say that if Dusty Baker was a great manager in 1993 he must be a good manager now, but it's just not true. It's not the way the world works.

It isn't *playing* managers who lose their ability when they stop playing. It's a universal curse, from which only great managers are exempt.

Johnny Neun

Johnny Neun had a short major league career, filled with oddities. In the space of forty-five days in the summer of 1927, Neun turned an unassisted triple play, stole five bases in a game, and stole home in both ends of a double header. By 1932 he was back in the minors, playing for Newark, at which time the Newark franchise was purchased by the Yankees.

By this good fortune Neun became a part of the Yankee system, and so he would remain for many years. A college man, he was hired to manage a low-level farm team in 1935. He succeeded at that, and in 1938, after Ossie Vitt got the Indians job, Neun was assigned to manage the Newark franchise, Double A. From 1938 to 1943 he traded jobs with Billy Meyer, one of them managing at Newark, and the other running the Yankees' other Double A powerhouse, the Kansas City Blues. In 1944 he returned to the major leagues as one of Joe McCarthy's coaches, and in 1946, after it became apparent that Bill Dickey was unsuited to the task, Neun managed the Yankees in the closing weeks of the 1946 season.

Bucky Harris got the Yankee job, but Neun was hired to manage the Cincinnati Reds in 1947. Several things went right for him. One of his pitchers, Ewell Blackwell, had a sensational season, 22–8 with a 2.47 ERA; he would have won the Cy Young Award had there been such an award at the time. He finished second in the MVP voting.

Neun also had the best shortstop in the National League that year, Eddie Miller, and one of the best third basemen, Grady Hatton. Those two guys hit 35 homers and drove in 164 runs, more than you expect from the left side of your infield. Unfortunately, he had absolutely nothing in the outfield. His only outfielder who hit more than six homers was Eddie Lukon, who homered 11 times in 200 at bats, but averaged just .205.

The irony is, Neun had one of the best power hitters in National League history available to him—but had sent him to Syracuse. Like Neun, Hank Sauer had seen the inner workings of the Yankee machine. Signed by New York in 1938, Sauer had spent three years as a Yankee prospect before being liberated in the midwinter draft by Cincinnati.

Sauer got into a few major league games in late 1941. He did well, hitting .303 with 4 doubles in 9 games, but nonetheless was sent back to the minors in 1942. He earned another late-season callup in 1942, and again succeeded, hitting 2 homers in 7 games, a .550 slugging percentage.

Bill McKechnie, however, was convinced that Sauer couldn't

play. Sauer was slow and a pretty awful outfielder, but looking backward, the Reds outfield at the time consisted of guys who couldn't field and couldn't hit, either, and the team was slipping further away from the pennant every year.

Anyway, Sauer went back to the minors for the 1943 season, then spent 1944 and most of 1945 in the navy. He got out of the service earlier than some of the other guys, which gave him 31 games in the majors in 1945.

Again, he was outstanding. He hit .293 with 5 homers, 20 RBI in the 31 games, including three homers in one game. He had now had three cups of coffee in the major leagues, and had played well all three times.

McKechnie sent him back to Syracuse for 1946. The Reds played Al Libke, Dain Clay, and Bob Usher in the outfield. Libke hit .253 with 5 homers in 431 at bats. Clay hit .228 with 2 homers in 435 at bats. Usher hit .204 with 1 homer in 92 games. The Reds finished 67–87 and were last in the major leagues in runs scored. Sauer drove in 90 runs and scored 99—for Syracuse.

So McKechnie got fired, and Johnny Neun got the job.

And sent Hank Sauer back to Syracuse.

Where, finally, Sauer could no longer be ignored. He hit 50 homers in 1947, drove in 141 runs. He was the minor league player of the year. Johnny Neun announced that winter that Hank Sauer would be his left fielder in 1948.

It was too late to save Neun's career. Blackwell was hurt, Miller was traded to Philadelphia for another outfielder, Hatton had an off season.

Hank Sauer had one of the most interesting careers of the 1950s. He was signed in 1938, remember. He got stuck in the Yankee system, got dumped on by McKechnie, had to go fight a war, got dumped on by Neun . . . by the time he got to play in the majors he was thirty-one years old.

He hit 288 major league homers, 281 of them after his thirty-first birthday. In his first season with the Reds he hit 35 homers, a Cincinnati record at the time. From his thirty-first birthday on he hit more home runs than Mike Schmidt or Jimmie Foxx or Frank Robinson or Reggie Jackson or Mickey Mantle or Ernie Banks or Harmon Killebrew. He won an MVP award at age thirty-five, driving in 121 runs for the Cubs. Two years after that he hit 41 homers, and three years after that, at age forty, he hit another 26 homers in 378 at bats.

Should Neun be faulted for failing to realize that Sauer could play?

Well, Sauer was a pretty bad outfielder. When he was young he had a good arm and near-average speed, but by the time he got to play in the majors the arm was gone and the speed was a problem.

There is a theory that managers will manage the way they played. Neun was a singles hitter, a lifetime .289 hitter and as fast as any infielder in baseball, but he couldn't hold a job because he had zero power. When he got to manage, he filled up his outfield with speedy singles hitters. And by so doing, he proved again what Lee Fohl, a 1920s manager, had established twenty years earlier: You cannot oppose a power-hitting offense with a run-at-a-time offense. You'll get beat.

Jolly Cholly

One of the biggest surprises to me, when I ranked the managers, was how high up the lists Charlie Grimm was. My impression of Grimm, to be honest, was that he was a well-liked guy who hung around and managed a long time, like Jimmy Dykes or Chuck Tanner, but that was about as much as you could say for him.

When you look carefully at his record, though, he ranks about even with Al Lopez, Whitey Herzog, Tony LaRussa, Frank Chance, those kind of guys. Not the ten greatest managers in history, but the class right behind them. Grimm:

1) Won the National League pennant in his first season (1932),

2) Kept the team about twenty games over .500 the next two years,

3) Won the pennant again in 1935, with 100 wins,

4) Kept the team twenty games over for two more seasons,

5) Was dismissed in the middle of the 1938 season, with the team still over .500,

6) Returned to the Cubs in midseason, 1944, at which point a losing team immediately began winning,

7) Won the National League pennant again in 1945,

8) Struggled for three and a half years after that, but

9) Got his next chance with the Braves in 1952, and won 85 to 92 games with them three straight years.

He had to go to the minors two or three times in midcareer to reestablish himself, but he did that very well, too, winning *The Sporting News* Minor League Manager of the Year Award in 1951.

I read his autobiography, *Jolly Cholly's Story*, which is a fun book but didn't do anything to alert me to the fact that he knew what he was doing as a manager. I gathered that, the nickname aside, he wasn't any jollier than any other manager when a player didn't run out a ground ball or missed the cutoff man, but his book doesn't impress upon you, as Leo Durocher would or Earl Weaver, that this was a man who was fully engaged with the issues of when you pull the infield in and when you play for the double play or how long you can afford to go with a first baseman who is hitting .180.

One of his pennants was registered during the war years, and there is a tendency to automatically discount whatever happened during the war because the game wasn't normal. While this discount is appropriate for players, a manager's job certainly didn't get easier during the war. If anything, wartime performance for managers probably should get extra credit, because wartime baseball was such a fluid situation, with players coming and going all the time, that it created opportunities for innovation and creativity. That kind of baseball is probably a truer test of the manager's skills than regular 1936- or 1976-style baseball, in which some teams just had the horses, and there wasn't much the other teams could do about it.

I can't tell you, in all honesty, what made Grimm a successful manager. I suspect that two key elements of his managerial style were

a) common sense, and

b) a positive outlook.

Decade Snapshot: 1950s

Most Successful Managers: 1. Casey Stengel
                                        2. Al Lopez
                                        3. Walt Alston

Casey Stengel was not only the most successful manager of the 1950s, but the most successful manager in history in any one decade.

Most Controversial Managers: Leo Durocher and Charlie Dressen

Others of Note: Fred Haney
                            Paul Richards

Stunts: August 24, 1951, Bill Veeck allowed 1,115 fans to help manage the St. Louis Browns. See "Popular Vote," page 170.

Typical Manager Was: Marty Marion. Much more than before, baseball managers began to rotate among teams. Only five men managed two different major league teams in the 1940s; fifteen men did so in the 1950s.

Percentage of Playing Managers: 7%

Most Second-Guessed Manager's Move: 1951, Charlie Dressen brought in Ralph Branca to face Bobby Thomson in the ninth inning of the third game of the National League playoff.

Clever Moves: Game Seven, 1955 World Series. The Dodgers led 2–0 going to the bottom of the sixth inning. Dodger manager Walt Alston moved his left fielder, Jim Gilliam, to second base and put Sandy Amoros in left field for defense. The Yankees got the first two men on, and Yogi Berra sliced a drive toward the left-field foul line, a ball that would unquestionably have been a two-run double had Gilliam remained in left field. Amoros's spectacular defensive play preserved the Dodgers' first World Series victory.

Player Rebellions: St. Louis, 1952, vs. Rogers Hornsby.

Evolutions in Strategy: To a 1930s baseball fan, "strategy" tended to mean things that the manager did with players already on the field—hit and run, steal, bunt, move the infield in, etc. By the 1950s, "strategy" had come to mean personnel moves—changing pitchers, changing lineups, making defensive moves. Platooning became common. The "clever move" above and Paul Richards maneuver with Harry Dorish (see page 183) are both examples of this.

The players of the 1920s and 1930s hated these changes and used them to explain, as old ballplayers always will, why baseball wasn't as good as it used to be. In the June 1956 edition of *Baseball Digest*, Pepper Martin said "They keep talkin' about what's wrong with baseball and that's a joke. Anybody that knows baseball, knows what's wrong. It's too routine and restricted. The rules cut down player individuality and the managers simply platoon and push the button and don't mix up the attack a-tall . . . I say throw the book away, because nobody ever wrote a decent book on how to play baseball and never will."

Rogers Hornsby, in *My War with Baseball*, complained that "too many managers are overmanaging. Games are won in the seventh, eighth, and ninth innings, so I'll grant you there is some excuse for managers switching all around in the late innings."

If a modern baseball fan could see an actual game from 1925 or 1935, I think the one thing that he would be most surprised about is how shallow the outfielders played. The infielders played ten feet closer to the plate in 1925 than they do now; the outfielders, probably thirty feet closer. They moved back gradually from 1920 to 1950, and probably reached their present depth about 1950 or 1955.

Evolution in the Role of the Manager: At the outset of this decade, it was still common for a manager to criticize his players in the press, and not uncommon for managers to yell at their players on the field in full view of the press and fans. Over the next fifteen years, 1950–1965, these practices were curtailed. Walter Alston and Ralph Houk were among those who set the standard of decorum which players came to expect.

Front offices in the 1950s made a concerted effort to convert managers into company men. In *Life* magazine on September 27, 1954, Hank Greenberg explained the firing three years earlier of Lou Boudreau:

> To my mind, Boudreau was not the ideal manager for a big league organization operating under the new methods.
>
> Each new player delivered in the spring to a big league manager under this farm system method represents upward of $100,000 of corporate spending . . . most of (which) is spent before the manager sees the boy under big league pressure. Extension of the front office operation, then, comes as the manager tests the new player under big league conditions. A single look, a few innings of competition in a game already lost will not suffice. . . .
>
> If a big league manager's pride and ego thrive upon his unique ability to detect talent or lack of it when others can't, he'll never get along with the front office.

This effort to convert managers into company men was an almost complete failure. With the Dodgers, it took; Walt Alston went along

Casey Stengel
(As he would be remembered today if he hadn't gotten the Yankees job)

with the front office's plan, Tommy Lasorda did, and it seems Bill Russell will, in exchange for job security and a steady commitment of resources. It worked in Cleveland, for a while, with Al Lopez. But major league managers, on the whole, have never accepted the right of the front office to make binding decisions about who should play and who shouldn't, and are no closer to doing so now than they were in 1954.

Tracers

The man Yankee fans knew as Moose vividly recalls an incident that underscored Stengel's desire to use the whole team. "I got taken out in one game in the first inning for a pinch hitter and I was batting clean-up. I came back to the bench and Eddie Robinson came in to pinch hit. Eddie got a bases-loaded double and we won 3–0. I was angry as heck because I had never been pinch-hit for before."
—Harvey Frommer,
Baseball's Greatest Managers

The game recalled by Skowron occured on June 10, 1954, at Yankee Stadium. Skowron is wrong on three details:

1) Skowron was hitting sixth, not cleanup.

2) Robinson hit a two-run single to make the score 3–0, not a bases-loaded double, and

3) The Yankees won the game 9–5, not 3–0.

This has to be the game, however, because it's the only time Stengel ever pinch-hit for Skowron in the first inning, and it generally accommodates what Skowron remembers.

The story as Skowron remembers it doesn't make any sense, because it implies that Robinson pinch-hit for Skowron with the score 0–0

CASEY STENGEL IN A BOX

Year of Birth: 1890. Stengel was only seventeen years younger than John McGraw. Stengel was hired to manage the Yankees at about the same age that John McGraw retired.

Years Managed: 1934–1936, 1938–1943, 1949–1960, 1962-65

Record as a Manager: 1,905–1,842, .508

Managers for Whom He Played: Bill Dahlen, Wilbert Robinson, Hugo Bezdek, Gavy Cravath, John McGraw, Dave Bancroft

Others by Whom He Was Influenced: Zack Wheat, a Hall of Fame outfielder with the Dodgers when Stengel came up, had lived in the Kansas City area, where Stengel was from. Wheat took Stengel under his wing, got him a locker next to his, and worked with him in the outfield.

Characteristics As a Player: Left-handed hitting and throwing outfielder, a decent ballplayer but lacked any one outstanding skill. Above average speed, good arm, some power, lifetime .284 hitter.

WHAT HE BROUGHT TO A BALL CLUB

Was He an Intense Manager or More of an Easy-to-Get-Along-With Type? Inside the locker room, he was intense. Stengel was friendly with the press, but distant and occasionally harsh with his players.

Was He More of an Emotional Leader or a Decision Maker? More of a decision maker.

Was He More of an Optimist or More of a Problem Solver? He was the ultimate problem solver. He never waited for things to break before he started to fix them.

HOW HE USED HIS PERSONNEL

Did He Favor a Set Lineup or a Rotation System? He rotated players with mad abandon. Stengel really was the first manager who made up a new lineup every day. We don't have counts, but he probably used 70 to 100 lineups every year with the Yankees, at a time when a lot of managers were using 15 or 20.

Did He Like to Platoon? He loved to platoon, and he loved to talk about why he platooned.

Did He Try to Solve His Problems with Proven Players or with Youngsters Who Still May Have Had Something to Learn? In midseason, he'd always prefer to bring in a veteran. He always wanted to spend a lot of time with a youngster in spring training before he put him in the lineup.

How Many Players Did He Make Regulars Who Had Not Been Regulars Before, and Who Were They? Stengel wouldn't make a man a regular unless the guy was really good; otherwise, he'd make him a platoon player. He did make a regular or near-regular out of Mantle, Hank Bauer, Gene Woodling, Whitey Ford, Billy Martin, Tony Kubek, Bobby Richardson, Bill Skowron, Gil McDougald, Ron Hunt, Lonny Frey, Len Koenecke, Max West, Eddie Miller, and a few others. Berra was sort of a three-quarters regular before Stengel got to New York.

Did He Prefer to Go with Good Offensive Players or Did He Like the Glove Men? Glove men. He wouldn't risk his defense by trying to play a hitter in the middle infield, for example.

Did He Like an Offense Based on Power, Speed, or High Averages? Not speed; none of Stengel's teams ever led the league in stolen bases. Five of his teams led in batting average, five in home runs. Stengel's Yankees had nowhere near as much power (relative to the era) as McCarthy's Yankees.

Did He Use the Entire Roster or Did He Keep People Sitting on the Bench? He used everybody.

Did He Build His Bench Around Young Players Who Could Step into the Breach If Need Be, or Around Veteran Role-Players Who Had Their Own Functions Within a Game? Some of each. Stengel always had on his bench two or three veteran players who had been outstanding regulars, but had slipped to part-time status, such as Enos Slaughter and Eddie Robinson. But he also had his platoon players—Bauer, Woodling, Cerv, Cliff Mapes—and he also had young players

in the first. This means that either:

1) The opposing manager took out his starting pitcher with the score 0–0, or

2) Stengel listed Skowron as his first baseman/cleanup hitter, then took him out of a scoreless game in the first inning even though the same pitcher was still on the mound.

Neither of these seems very likely. What actually happened makes much more sense. The Tigers started a lefty (Al Aber), who gave up two hits and two walks to the first five hitters. It's only 1–0, but the bases are loaded with one out. This is the Yankees; they're hard enough to beat if you start out even. Tiger manager Fred Hutchinson reasons, very sensibly, that if he leaves Aber out there for about two more hitters he can kiss this game good-bye, so he replaces Aber with a right-hander, Ralph Branca. Now Skowron, a right-handed hitting platoon player, is facing a right-hander. Casey Stengel, like Hutchinson, realizes that even though it is the first inning this is a game situation, and he uses his left-handed first baseman, Eddie Robinson. Robinson singles, and the Yankees have a 3–0 lead.

Popular Vote

Zack Taylor was an old catcher, played several years for Wilbert Robinson, parts of two years for Joe McCarthy, one season for Casey Stengel. In the early 1950s three American League teams were managed by Wilbert Robinson's old catchers—Taylor, Al Lopez, and Paul Richards. Taylor had attended Rollins College before entering baseball, and after his playing career was on the staff of the Joe Stripp baseball school, which tutored young players from all over the country.

He got the opportunity to manage, following Fred Haney into the Toledo job, then on to a job as a coach with the Browns. From 1948 to 1951 he was the Browns manager, losing about 100 games a year. He was the Browns manager at the time that Eddie Gaedel batted.

A few days after that, on August 24, 1951, Taylor took the field in civilian clothes and bedroom slippers, smoking a curved-stem pipe. He seated himself in a rocking chair near the dugout, picked up a newspapers and read leisurely as the game proceeded. It was Bill Veeck's latest stunt. Veeck had arranged a promotion in which two fans would would win the right to manage the team for a day.

that he was taking a look at, seeing if they could earn more playing time. Occasionally, like Elston Howard and Bobby Richardson, these players would emerge as regulars. More often, like Norm Siebern and Jackie Jensen and Jerry Lumpe, they would wind up with some other team.

All managers become burdened by their success, a heavy portion of which is their loyalty to a group of players. Stengel was different. With a few exceptions (Yogi Berra, Billy Martin) he made no emotional commitment to his players. He instructed them, corrected them, yelled at them, and if they didn't respond he traded them, but he kept them at arm's length.

In Stengel's years with the Yankees, there were an extraordinary number of times when a pitcher would give him a big season, then would disappear from the rotation by June of the following season. Bob Grim in 1954 (20–6), Tommy Byrne in 1955 (16–5), Johnny Kucks in 1956 (18–9), Tom Sturdivant in 1957 (16–8)—all of them dropped suddenly from the rotation the following summer. Don Larsen, despite pitching well as a spot starter for several seasons, was never able to break *into* the rotation.

This is unusual. Almost any manager, when a pitcher gives him a big season, will make a commitment to that pitcher. If he has a couple of bad starts, the manager will say "It's just a couple of bad starts; he'll get it turned around." If he has another bad start, the manager will say, "Well, we need him to pitch well if we're going to contend." Then he'll have a good start or two, and the first thing you know, he's 5–13, and you're out of the race.

Stengel didn't do that. With Stengel, unless you were Vic Raschi or Whitey Ford, you were only as good as your last start. And that was a large part of why he was able to stay on top, year after year, in a way that few other managers ever have. It's not that he wasn't "loyal" to his players, but his idea of loyalty wasn't "Joe helped me win the pennant last year, so I owe it to him to let him work through his problems." It was "These boys are trying to win. I owe it to them to do everything possible to help them win."

Stengel got started this way with the Yankees, I think, because he took over an old team, with repairs that just had to be made—but he won. He won in 1949 with a team that simply couldn't be forced through 1950, and he won in 1950 with a team that just wasn't going to make it through 1951. He got in the habit of looking to replace players, even though the team was doing well, and that habit served him very well.

GAME MANAGING AND USE OF STRATEGIES

Did He Go for the Big-Inning Offense, or Did He Like to Use the One-Run Strategies? Not one more than the other.

Did He Pinch-Hit Much, and If So, When? In 1954 the New York Yankees used 262 pinch hitters. The 1955 *Baseball Guide* reported that "the New York Yankees used more pinch hitters than any club in American League history in 1954 as Casey Stengel juggled his lineup constantly in a desperate attempt to overhaul the pennant-bound Cleveland Indians." The 262 pinch hitters were extremely successful, hitting .292 with a record-tying seven pinch-hit home runs.

Stengel was famous, at the time, for using pinch hitters in odd ways, particularly early in the game. There is a tracer in this book (see page 168) which concerns a Moose Skowron story about being pinch-hit for in the first inning. A famous Stengel quote occurred when Casey was asked by a reporter why he had used three pinch hitters in the first three innings of one game. "Whaddaya want me to do," he asked. "Sit there and lose?"

However, Stengel's pinch-hitting totals were *not* uniformly high—in fact, in many seasons he was at or near the bottom of the league in the number of pinch hitters used. In 1958 the Yankees used only 159 pinch hitters, while every other American League team used at least 189. This may be somewhat misleading, because remember, the Yankees were usually *ahead* in the game. Normal pinch-hitting situations occur when the team is *behind*, when they need runs.

The Yankee pinch hitters were almost always good. Pinch-hitting batting averages are normally low. Yankee pinch hitters hit .292 in 1954, when only one other American League team got a pinch-hitting average higher than .218. In 1958, when the Yankees were last in the league in pinch hitters used, they were again first in pinch-hitting average, at .275.

Was There Anything Unusual About His Lineup Selection? Everything about it was unusual. He rotated infielders around, one day at second, one day at short, the next day at third; I have never been able to understand how he was able to do this without undermining his defense.

Stengel never had a regular leadoff man and often used players who had below average speed or no speed at all in the leadoff spot. Look at his leadoff men in World Series games. In the 1951 World Series: Mantle, Mantle, Woodling, Bauer,

American League president Will Harridge had vetoed that idea, however, and Veeck decided instead to make everybody who had entered the contest a winner. 1,115 fans got placards, on which were printed "bunt," "steal," "yes," "no," etc. As the game progressed, these fans (one of whom was Connie Mack) held up their placards, voting on what the Browns should do.

The Browns won the game, 3–2. The fans voted on the starting lineup and opted to replace Taylor's choice at catcher, Matt Batts, with Sherm Lollar. What strikes me about this is that the fans were obviously smarter than Taylor was, at least in this respect. The Browns had acquired Lollar three years earlier, for nothing, and he had played about half the time, although he was one of the better hitters on the team. After the season the Browns traded him on to Chicago, where he played for Paul Richards. Richards made Lollar a regular catcher, and he was the second-best catcher in the American League during the 1950s.

Harry Craft

Harry Craft had a slow, languid walk, rolling gently from side to front, that fit perfectly with his mesmerizing Mississippi drawl. He had a habit of swallowing about three times before he said anything, the combination of which tended to reduce the number of questions in a press interview by roughly 80%. He was slow to anger, slow to criticize, careful to say nothing that he might come to regret.

Craft played baseball and football at Mississippi College in Jackson. He was a better football player than baseball player, but baseball got the best athletes at that time, and Craft signed with the Cincinnati Reds. Bill McKechnie brought him to the majors in 1938, and as a rookie he was probably the best all-around center fielder in the National League.

That was his best season. By 1942 he was a player/coach for Billy Meyer at Kansas City, the American Association team in the Yankee system. Craft always said that Meyer was the best manager he ever knew. His own chance to manage came at Independence in the Kansas-Oklahoma-Missouri League in 1949, still in the Yankee system. He had a seventeen-year-old Oklahoma

Woodling, Rizzuto. In the 1952 World Series: Bauer, Bauer, Rizzuto, McDougald, McDougald, McDougald, McDougald. In the 1953 World Series: McDougald, Woodling, McDougald, Woodling, Woodling. In the 1955 World Series: Bauer, Bauer, Cerv (!), Noren, Howard (!), Rizzuto, Rizzuto.

Did He Use the Sac Bunt Often? In Brooklyn and Boston, Stengel was a nonbunter, as one would expect from a John McGraw disciple. His Dodger and Brave teams were last in the league in bunts several times.

With the Yankees, this was no longer true. Stengel's Yankees never led the league in sacrifice bunts, but they were never last, either. They were always in the middle.

I looked at the game logs from Stengel's 63 World Series games to see *when* he would bunt. The most striking thing is that Stengel very often bunted with one out. Of his 23 World Series bunts, eight, or 35%, came with one out. In 1990s baseball, the one-out bunt is essentially extinct except for the squeeze play, but Stengel used it quite often. Also, Stengel bunted when his team was behind only four times in 63 games, which explains the low sac hit totals with Brooklyn and Boston.

Did He Like to Use the Running Game? Stengel's teams didn't steal many bases.

In What Circumstances Would He Issue an Intentional Walk? Most commonly to set up a double play.

Did He Hit and Run Very Often? My belief is that Stengel probably used the hit and run more often than any manager in baseball now (1996).

Were There Any Unique or Idiosyncratic Strategies That He Particularly Favored? One thing that stands out about Stengel's great teams in New York is their tremendous advantage in the double play categories.

To consolidate what you may already know, good teams do *not*, as a rule, have outstanding double play totals. A team with good pitching will normally not have large numbers of opposing baserunners, which limits the double play opportunities for their defense. Conversely, a team with a strong batting lineup will have many more runners on base than a team with a weak offense, and for that reason will tend to ground into more double plays. Thus, while double play skills may well be very important, there is not, in general, a strong correlation between double plays and wins.

The Yankees are an exception. In Stengel's first ten years in New York (1949–1958), the Yankees turned at least 180 double plays every year. They led the American League in double plays, as a team, in 1952, 1954, 1955, 1956, 1957, and 1958. Four of Stengel's teams in Brooklyn and Boston also led the league in double plays.

What makes this particularly notable is the tremendous instability in the middle of the Yankee infield in those same years. The Pirates led the league in double plays every year, too, but they had Mazeroski. The Yankees had no regular second baseman and no regular shortstop from 1954 to 1958—yet they led the league in double plays every season. At second base they used Gil McDougald, Jerry Coleman, Bobby Richardson, and Billy Martin 150 to 385 games each during those years, rotating more or less randomly among them, and sprinkling in a few games from Willie Miranda, Tony Kubek, Fritz Brickell, Phil Rizzuto, Mickey Mantle, and Bill Skowron. At shortstop the picture was even murkier, with no one playing more than 235 games at short for the Yankees over the five-year period.

How is this possible? How can you lead the league in double plays every year, without a regular shortstop or a regular second baseman? A few points:

1) Stengel did not use control pitchers. Unlike most successful managers, Stengel was perfectly willing to let a pitcher go out there and walk 150 batters a year. The Yankees had more opposition runners on base than one would assume, given the quality of the team.

2) The Yankees had lots of left-handed pitching. Left-handed pitchers force the opposition to use right-handed hitters, which means a few more double plays.

3) Stengel stressed that his middle infielders should cheat toward second in double play situations. I believe, although I can't prove it, that he probably stressed this more than almost any other manager.

4) He used ground ball pitchers. His pitching coach, Jim Turner, was a ground ball pitcher himself.

While the Yankee defense turned a great many double plays, the Yankee hitters grounded into very few. Yankee hitters were last in the league in grounding into double plays in 1950, 1952, 1953, 1954, 1955, 1956, 1958, 1959, and 1960. In the twelve years that Stengel managed the Yankees, the Yankees turned 2,233 double plays, while

kid named Mantle on his roster that summer, beginning his own minor league career, which made Craft's assignment easier. He moved up to Joplin the next year, and took Mickey with him. Mickey hit .383 and drove in 136 runs. This got Mantle to the majors quicker than it did Craft, but Craft arrived in 1957, in Kansas City.

Craft managed Kansas City from 1957–1959, and Houston from 1962 to 1964. His record is interesting because, on a simple level, it looks so awful—360 wins, 485 losses, a .426 winning percentage. His best full season was 1958, when he went 73–81 with the A's.

But compared to the expectations of his teams, Craft's record is actually quite good, scoring at +12. The A's had lost 102 games in 1956, and were headed for another 100-loss season in August 1957, when Craft was hired. They played .460 ball the rest of that season, averting 100 losses, and then outperformed expectations by 10 games in 1958; the A's 73–81 record that season was by far their best in their thirteen seasons in Kansas City. His other assignment was with an expansion team.

grounding into only 1,342. Even allowing that not all double plays are ground ball double plays, the Yankees in Stengel's years had an advantage of more than 40 double plays per season over their opponents—despite the fact that the Yankees, of course, always had more men on base than did the opposition.

How did Stengel's teams *avoid* grounding into double plays? His teams were not slow, to begin with; they didn't steal bases, but guys like Mantle, Bauer, Andy Carey, and Gil McDougald ran quite well.

He had many left-handed hitters, of course, and left-handed batters ground into double plays about 10% less often than right-handed hitters.

I suspect that the biggest part of this is simply that Stengel was *aware* of the double play, thought about it, and tried to make it work for him. I believe, although I can't prove it, that Stengel probably used the hit and run more often than any manager of the 1990s, and that he used it most often to avoid the double play.

In his autobiography, *Casey at the Bat*, with Harry Paxton, Stengel wrote about double plays, in passing, many times. Writing about his Boston team, he said that "we had some pitchers that could keep the ball low—Jim Turner, Lou Fette, Danny MacFayden, Milt Shoffner."

"Some managers have one special way they want double plays to be made," wrote Stengel (through Paxton). "My system was, make it any way you can. But be sure you find some way to make it, or I can't play you. I told the infielders that, and had my coaches telling them, and it ended up that we generally had good double-play men on the Yankees, except maybe in 1959." The 1959 Yankees fell to third in the league in double plays.

"In the middle of your order," he wrote later, "you should never have two slow-footed, right-handed sluggers batting one after the other, because the double plays will murder you." Stengel's *awareness* of the double play, and his ability to get an advantage in this area, was a critical part of the success of his 1950s teams.

How Did He Change the Game? His largest effect on strategy was his role in resurrecting platooning.

Stengel became such a giant character that you can't really talk about him in the past. He became an enduring part of the game.

HANDLING THE PITCHING STAFF

Did He Like Power Pitchers, or Did He Prefer to Go with the People Who Put the Ball in Play? Power pitchers. None of Casey Stengel's teams ever led the league in fewest walks.

Did He Stay with His Starters, or Go to the Bullpen Quickly? The bullpen. He was the quickest hook in baseball.

Did He Use a Four-Man Rotation? Never.

Did He Use the Entire Staff, or Did He Try to Get Five or Six People to Do Most of the Work? You couldn't even find the top five pitchers on Stengel's staff. He'd use his number-seven starter to start a World Series game.

How Long Would He Stay with a Starting Pitcher Who Was Struggling? Only one Stengel team, the 1938 Braves, led the league in complete games. Nine of Stengel's teams led the league in saves.

Was There Anything Unique About His Handling of His Pitchers? Again, everything about it is unique. To cite just four things:

1) He had nothing resembling a regular rotation.

2) He would get the starting pitcher out lightning quick if he showed any signs of faltering, unless that pitcher was one of his key men like Vic Raschi or Whitey Ford.

3) He would dump a pitcher who was successful for him last year if he lost confidence in him.

4) He was unusually patient with pitchers who had poor control.

What Was His Strongest Point As a Manager? In five words, what Stengel did differently from any other manager of his time was: *He used his entire roster.* Casey Stengel did for major league baseball what Dean Smith did for college basketball. This is an overstatement, but Casey Stengel changed baseball in this respect: that before Stengel, the good teams were simply those teams which had the best players. Everybody tended to put their eight best players on the field 150 games a year. That's not quite true, because there were always injuries, catchers needed a day off, people lost their jobs in midseason, and there was always the odd

Luke Appling

Luke Appling was a Hall of Fame shortstop and a successful minor league manager, whose failure to get a decent opportunity to manage in the majors is somewhat inexplicable.

When Appling retired as a player in 1950, he almost got the job as the White Sox manager, the job that went to Paul Richards. The general manager told him he preferred someone with managerial experience, so Appling went to the minors and was quite good as a minor league manager. He won pennants at Memphis in 1952 and 1953, and in 1952 was named the Minor League manager of the Year by *The Sporting News.*

Appling was outspoken about his desire to manage in the majors. He was well liked in baseball, and he was extremely famous. For some reason, the chance never came. He may have been regarded as too nice to manage, plus he was a chatterbox, a personality which may have been seen as unsuitable to the managerial seat. He finally did get to manage the Kansas City A's in late 1967, after Alvin Dark was fired, but managing a terrible team for 40 games when you're sixty years old is not a real opportunity.

manager who platooned his left fielders or something. But the idea of giving *good* players one or two days off a week, platooning *good* players, star-quality players, platooning them with other good players, up and down the lineup—that was new with Stengel.

If There Was No Professional Baseball, What Would He Probably Have Done with His Life? He'd have gone into vaudeville. He'd have been Jimmy Durante.

CASEY STENGEL'S
All-Star Team

		G	AB	R	H	2B	3B	HR	RBI	BB	SO	SB	Avg	SPct
C	Yogi Berra, 1950	151	597	116	192	30	6	28	121	55	12	4	.322	.533
1B	Sam Leslie, 1934	146	546	75	181	29	6	9	102	69	34	5	.332	.456
2B	Jerry Coleman, 1950	153	522	69	150	19	6	6	66	67	38	3	.287	.381
3B	Gil McDougald, 1951	131	402	72	123	23	4	14	68	56	54	14	.306	.488
SS	Phil Rizzuto, 1950	155	617	125	200	36	7	7	65	61	38	12	.324	.439
LF	Joe DiMaggio, 1950	139	525	91	127	33	10	32	122	80	33	0	.301	.585
CF	Mickey Mantle, 1956	150	533	132	188	22	5	52	130	112	99	10	.353	.705
RF	Roger Maris, 1960	136	499	98	141	18	7	39	112	70	65	2	.283	.581

		G	IP	W–L	Pct.	H	SO	BB	ERA	GS	CG	ShO	Sv
SP	Allie Reynolds, 1952	35	244	20–8	.714	194	160	97	2.07	29	24	6	6
SP	Bob Turley, 1958	33	245	21–7	.750	178	168	128	2.97	31	19	6	1
SP	Ed Lopat, 1951	31	235	21–9	.700	209	93	71	2.91	31	20	4	0
SP	Whitey Ford, 1956	31	226	19–6	.760	187	141	87	2.47	30	18	2	1
RA	Ryne Duren, 1958	44	76	6–4	.600	40	87	43	2.01	1	0	0	20

AL LOPEZ'S
All-Star Team

		G	AB	R	H	2B	3B	HR	RBI	BB	SO	SB	Avg	SPct
C	Sherm Lollar, 1959	140	505	63	134	22	3	22	84	55	49	4	.265	.451
1B	Vic Wertz, 1956	136	481	65	127	22	0	32	106	75	87	0	.264	.509
2B	Bobby Avila, 1954	143	555	112	188	27	2	15	67	58	31	9	.341	.477
3B	Al Rosen, 1953	155	599	115	201	27	5	43	145	85	48	8	.336	.613
SS	Luis Aparicio, 1959	152	612	98	157	18	5	6	51	52	40	56	.257	.332
LF	Minnie Minoso, 1960	154	591	89	184	32	4	20	105	52	63	17	.311	.481
CF	Larry Doby, 1954	153	577	94	157	18	4	32	126	85	94	3	.272	.484
RF	Al Smith, 1955	154	607	123	186	27	4	22	77	93	77	11	.306	.473

		G	IP	W–L	Pct.	H	SO	BB	ERA	GS	CG	ShO	Sv
SP	Bob Lemon, 1954	36	258	23–7	.767	228	110	92	2.72	33	21	2	0
SP	Early Wynn, 1954	40	271	23–11	.676	225	155	83	2.72	36	20	3	2
SP	Mike Garcia, 1952	46	292	22–11	.667	284	143	87	2.37	36	19	6	4
SP	Herb Score, 1956	35	249	20–9	.690	162	263	129	2.53	33	16	5	0
RA	Hoyt Wilhelm, 1965	66	144	7–7	.500	88	106	32	1.81	0	0	0	20

PAUL RICHARDS'S
All-Star Team

		G	AB	R	H	2B	3B	HR	RBI	BB	SO	SB	Avg	SPct
C	Gus Triandos, 1956	131	452	47	126	18	1	21	88	48	73	0	.279	.462
1B	Jim Gentile, 1961	148	486	96	147	25	2	46	141	96	106	1	.302	.546
2B	Nellie Fox, 1954	155	631	111	201	24	8	2	47	51	12	16	.319	.391
3B	Brooks Robinson, '60	152	595	74	175	27	9	14	88	35	49	2	.294	.440
SS	Chico Carrasquel, '54	155	620	106	158	28	3	12	62	85	67	7	.255	.368
LF	Minnie Minoso, 1954	153	568	119	182	29	16	19	116	77	46	18	.320	.535
CF	Jackie Brandt, 1961	139	516	93	163	18	5	16	72	62	51	10	.297	.444
RF	Bob Nieman, 1959	118	360	49	105	18	2	21	60	42	55	1	.292	.528

		G	IP	W–L	Pct.	H	SO	BB	ERA	GS	CG	ShO	Sv
SP	Virgil Trucks, 1954	40	265	19–12	.613	224	152	95	2.78	33	16	5	3
SP	Steve Barber, 1961	37	248	18–12	.600	194	150	130	3.34	34	14	8	1
SP	Billy Pierce, 1953	40	271	18–12	.600	216	186	102	2.72	33	19	7	3
SP	Chuck Estrada, 1960	36	209	18–11	.621	162	144	101	3.57	25	12	1	2
RA	Hoyt Wilhelm, 1961	51	110	9–7	.563	89	87	41	2.29	1	0	0	18

Stengel's Fans

It has been casually asserted by many baseball writers that Casey Stengel's greatest value to his teams was in attendance, or in publicity which could result in attendance.

Unfortunately for Topping and Weiss, Casey would surface again, with the neophyte New York Mets, and proceed to attract more fans to the ball park than all the stars he left behind.

—Peter Golenbock, *Dynasty*

The new Mets could not compete with (the Yankees) for the ticket dollar in New York with talent. They needed an attraction. There was only one attraction, only one man who could handle the press and win the public, Casey Stengel.

—Maury Allen, *You Could Look It Up*

How many fans a year was Casey Stengel worth? Let's say that a team was going to draw a million fans a year without Casey Stengel. How many would they draw with him?

There's no way of knowing *exactly*, but I thought maybe it wouldn't hurt to look. The obvious way to look at the issue is to compare the attendance of Stengel's teams in the years Stengel was the manager with the attendance of the same teams in the years just before and just after Stengel was the manager.

Casey's first major league team was the Brooklyn Dodgers, whom he managed from 1934 to 1936. In the three years that Stengel was the manager, the Dodgers drew an average of 464,774 fans—in fact, they were near that figure all three years. This figure was 5% above the National League average for the time:

		NL Avg	
Brooklyn, 1934–1936	464,744	443,487	+5%

Both of these figures were markedly higher in the period just before Stengel was hired, the three years 1931–1933:

Team	Avg Attendanc	League Norm	Difference
Brooklyn, 1931–1933	653,925	482,374	+36%
Brooklyn, 1934–1936	464,744	443,487	+5%

After Stengel was let go, Dodger attendance went back up:

Team	Avg Attendance	League Norm	Difference
Brooklyn, 1931–1933	653,925	482,374	+36%
Under Stengel	464,744	443,487	+5%
Brooklyn, 1937–1939	700,412	567,078	+24%

Charts such as this leave out many details, of course, so let's fill in a little bit. The Dodgers from 1914 to 1931 were managed by Wilbert Robinson, and their attendance was generally very good. In 1930, with a contending team, they drew a million-plus fans. From 1931 to 1933 the depression was settling in, and baseball attendance was declining everywhere. The Dodgers remained a pretty good team in 1931–1932, over .500 both seasons, but fell near to the basement in 1933, the year before they hired Stengel. Their attendance was in a sharp decline before Stengel was hired, and it hit rock-bottom under Stengel. Thus, such comparisons may be unfair to Casey.

By 1938 the depression was easing. In 1939 Leo Durocher took over, the team improved dramatically, and attendance jumped back near the million level. Again, this is not necessarily a fair basis for comparison to Stengel.

Stengel's second major league job was in Boston, where he managed the Braves for six seasons, 1938–1943. In the three seasons prior to Stengel's arrival (1935–1937), the Braves averaged 319,559 fans per seasons, which was 35% below the league norm:

Team	Avg Attendance	League Norm	Difference
Boston, 1935–1937	319,559	490,828	-35%

This period includes the 1935 season, when the Braves won only 38 games in a full season.

Stengel was hired in 1938. The Braves' attendance declined by 44,000 in 1938, despite the fact that the performance of the team was essentially the same as in 1937, and despite gains in attendance throughout most of the baseball world. It continued down from there—down another 55,000 in 1939, down another 44,000 in 1940. For the six years that Stengel was in Boston, the Braves averaged 281,510 fans per season:

Team	Avg Attendance	League Norm	Difference
Boston, 1935–1937	319,559	490,828	-35%
Boston, 1938–1943	281,510	550,823	-49%

Boston attendance dropped even lower in 1944, the first year post-Stengel, but recovered strongly in 1945 and 1946:

Team	Avg Attendance	League Norm	Difference
Boston, 1935–1937	319,559	490,828	-35%
The Stengel years	281,510	550,823	-49%
Boston, 1944–1946	517,514	834,487	-38%

Of course, there was a tremendous boom in baseball attendance after the war, so it is hardly fair to compare 1946 attendance figures to those from 1942. But on the other hand, that's why we look at both figures—the team's attendance, and their attendance compared to league norms. In 1946, Billy Southworth's first year in Boston, the Braves attendance was 87% of the league norm. In Stengel's years, it was consistently near 50% of the league norm.

In 1949, of course, Stengel was hired to manage the Yankees. By now the attendance boom had passed its peak, which was 1948.

In the last three years pre-Stengel, the Yankees drew an average of 2,272,783 fans—81% above the league norm:

Team	Avg Attendance	League Norm	Difference
New York, 1946–1948	2,272,783	1,256,933	+81%

In 1949 their raw attendance figure was almost exactly the same—2,281,676. This was 70% above the league norm.

In the following years, attendance both for the Yankees and for the American League went into a sharp decline. This decline is usually blamed on television, which came to dominate the nation's attention for a few years. For the twelve years that Stengel managed the Yankees, the team averaged 1,670,223 fans per season:

Team	Avg Attendance	League Norm	Difference
New York, 1946–1948	2,272,783	1,256,933	+81%
New York, 1949–1960	1,670,223	1,069,097	+56%

Attendance in New York declined somewhat more rapidly than throughout the rest of baseball. This continued to be true, however, after Stengel left the team:

Team	Avg Attendance	League Norm	Difference
New York, 1946–1948	2,272,783	1,256,933	+81%
New York, 1949–1960	1,670,223	1,069,097	+56%
New York, 1961–1963	1,516,743	978,486	+55%

The famous '61 Yankees drew 1.75 million fans, 72% above the American League average, but the team drew poorly in '62 and '63, when they were competing for attendance with the new New York Mets.

Which brings us to the final Casey Stengel experience, the Mets from 1962 through 1965, actually the first half of 1965. The Mets attendance started slowly, but exploded into a kind of phenomenon in 1964, when 1.7 million fans turned out to watch the lovable losers. There is, of course, no "before" data in this case:

Team	Avg Attendance	League Norm	Difference
New York, 1962–1965	1,375,861	1,222,617	+13%

Attendance continued to increase after Stengel had departed:

Team	Avg Attendance	League Norm	Difference
New York, 1962–1965	1,375,861	1,222,617	+13%
New York, 1966–1968	1,759,947	1,316,919	+34%

As I've said, there are innumerable factors which explain movements in attendance, and we should be cautious in rushing to any conclusions. I'm sure there are other ways you could arrange the data, which might create very different results.

In the case of the Yankees, for example . . . the relationship between the Yankees attendance and the league norms has flattened out constantly since about 1920. In the early 1920s the Yankees drew twice as many fans as the average American League team; now, they're about average. Each era, judged by the standards of the previous era, might tend to look flat.

Nonetheless, the data *is* curious. Just looking at the numbers, one would swear that Casey Stengel was working twenty-four hours a day to scare away the customers:

> After drawing 922,530 persons to the Polo Grounds the first year, the Mets vaulted over the million mark in attendance, toward two million, and stayed there.
>
> As Branch Rickey diagnosed the situation, the "perfect link" between the ball club and the public was Stengel.

—Joseph Durso, Casey

It is, in retrospect, not at all apparent that the Mets attendance in 1962 was especially good. The Mets drew 922,350 fans in their first season—fewer than the Seattle Mariners (1.3 million), the Toronto Blue Jays (1.7 million), or the Montreal Expos (1.2 million). They drew fewer than their expansion mates, the Houston Astros (924,456).

Those cities, of course, were new to baseball, and were excited to have a team. The Mets, on the other hand, came into a city accustomed to major league baseball. Like the Kansas City Royals, who drew 902,414 in their first season. In Kansas City.

The Mets attendance edged over the million mark in 1963 (1.08 million), and exploded toward two million in 1964, when

a) Shea Stadium opened, and

b) there was a World's Fair going on across the street.

At the time, New York sportswriters *thought* that the Mets were drawing huge crowds, and that Casey Stengel was the cause of this. Neither of these perceptions is self-evidently accurate. The crowds *weren't* all that large, and Casey Stengel probably wasn't responsible for their being as large as they were. Taking the whole package, the New York Mets in their first four seasons drew fewer fans than the Blue Jays in their first four seasons (1977–1980), and fewer than the Braves in their first four years in Milwaukee (1953–1956) *or* their first four years in Atlanta (1966–1969). Is 5.5 million fans in four seasons a good total, for a New York City expansion team with a new park, or a bad total? I don't know the answer, but it is at best a debatable proposition.

Could Casey Stengel in fact have had a negative impact on attendance, as the data seems to demonstrate? Let me throw out an argument, strictly on a for-what-it's-worth basis. Nobody goes to a ballpark to watch the manager. What does the manager do? He hides in the dugout. Hell, you can't even see him most of the time. Even when you can see him, you're not *watching* him. You're there to watch the players.

It wasn't the *fans* who loved Casey Stengel, it was the *writers*. The writers loved him because him because he was the greatest day-in, day-out baseball story since Babe Ruth. There was *always* something to say about him.

But if you focus on the slightly bigger picture, how does this change the publicity of the team? Does it result in more newspaper coverage? Is the sports editor going to say, "Oh, Casey Stengel's in town; we'd better add another reporter to cover the team." Is the publisher going to say, "Oh, we've got Casey Stengel to write about; we'd better add two pages to the sports section."

Of course not; that's not the way the world works. What happens is, Casey Stengel gets written about, *rather than the players*.

From the standpoint of the player, this may be a good thing. Many teams, and in particular many New York teams, have allowed the newspaper coverage to become an obstacle to the success of the team. The pressure for immediate success which can be generated by the New York media is enormous and has led directly to midcareer crises for many athletes. Stengel brought all that pressure upon himself.

But from the standpoint of selling tickets, it might not be a good thing, at all. If one buys the proposition that the fans pay to watch the players, not the manager, then it isn't a long reach to argue that any publicity which flows away from the players and toward the manager will be counterproductive in terms of attendance. The fact is, in any case, that all of Stengel's teams did poorly at the box office, with the arguable exception of the New York Mets.

Tracers

(Paul Richards) once used this same trick when he was managing the White Sox. Harry Dorish was pitching well for the Chicagoans in a tight game with the Red Sox. To bat went Ted Williams . . . Richards ambled to the mound, beckoning to Billy Pierce, a left-hander, in the bull pen.

"Don't leave, Harry" said Paul to Dorish. "I want you to play third base while Pierce pitches to Williams." Pierce retired Williams on a pop-up while Dorish stood uncomfortably at third base with his fingers crossed. Then the right-hander resumed his duties and won the game in the 13th.

—Arthur Daley,
The New York Times, June 14, 1965

The incident described by Daley occurred on May 15, 1951, in Fenway Park. Paul Richards also wrote about this incident in his 1955 book, *Modern Baseball Strategy.* Daley's account of it is exactly correct except for one detail: The White Sox won the game in eleven innings, not thirteen. It was a rather remarkable game. It was old-timers day in Fenway, so the game was attended by Cy Young and twenty-eight other players who had played in the American League in 1901. Nellie Fox hit his first major league home run, and Ted Williams hit his 300th. Fox's home run won the game.

Richards wrote that this strategy was "familiar to all of us on the sandlots," and Daley also wrote that the move was "strictly of sandlot derivation." The sandlots these gentlemen played on must have been considerably different than the sandlots in my neighborhood. I have to confess that in my neighborhood, we never really worried too much about the lefty/righty percentages.

Anyway, whatever its ancestry, this was apparently the first time this maneuver had been used in a major league game. It is still done once in a while. Whitey Herzog used this trick at least five times in the late 1980s, usually with Todd Worrell.

It has, however, never become a common strategy. What I was wondering is, why? If it's a good strategy, why isn't it used more often? Let's think about it.

The essential trade-off of the maneuver is that it gives the team in the field the platoon advantage for one hitter, at the cost of having a misaligned defense for that one hitter. The value of the platoon edge for one hitter is about .025 hits. Ted Williams would probably hit about .350 against a right-handed pitcher, but more like .325 against a lefty. The difference is the gain.

Of course, the left-handed pitcher could be a better pitcher than the right-hander, but that has really nothing to do with the subject. If you wanted the left-hander in the game because he was a better pitcher, you wouldn't distort your defense to bring him in for one hitter. You'd leave him in there to pitch.

What is the cost of having an out-of-position fielder, for one hitter? That's much harder to gauge, but my best guess is that it is in the same range. Richards put Dorish at third base. A key here is that it's Ted Williams at bat. Williams, of course, rarely hit the ball to third base; he was famous for pulling everything to the right side. Thus, one might argue, there is minimal defensive cost, because the third baseman is effectively out of the action with Williams at the plate.

Williams, however, *might* hit the ball to third. Did Ted Williams *ever* hit hard smashes to third base? Of course he did. Second, remember Murphy's Law. Third, remember that there was a runner on first base. In generalizing the situation, there would *always* be a runner on base, because you would probably never do something like this with the bases empty.

And if there's a runner on first base, and Williams rips a single to right field, what happens? There's a play at third base. The pitcher, playing third base, might have to make the catch and apply a tag to an oncoming runner—a routine play for an experienced third baseman, but far from an easy thing to do. What is the chance that an error will occur?

I don't know, but it seems to me that it's pretty good. Let's assume there is a one-in-eight chance that the pitcher will have to make a play of some kind during his stint at third base. A good major league third baseman normally fields about .950. A bad one may field about .900. This is worse than a bad third baseman; this is an experiment. He's going to field, let us guess, about .850.

If there is a one-in-eight chance that the pitcher will have to make a play at third base, and a 15% chance that he'll make an error if he does, then the chance that the out-of-position fielder will make an error on any one hitter is probably between .015 and .020. You're not gaining an awful lot by making the switch.

There is, however, something else which has happened here. You've taken your third baseman out of the game. In the original game, the Paul Richards maneuver, he had Minnie Minoso play-ing third base. When Dorish went back to the mound, Minoso couldn't go back to third base. Floyd Baker took his place.

Minnie Minoso was a .326 hitter. Floyd Baker was a .263 hitter.

So in order to gain 25 points on Ted Williams, Richards replaced a .326 hit-ter with a .263 hitter. The game went 11 innings, and Baker went to bat twice.

Um . . . I think we've figured out why this move never became common.

CHARLIE DRESSEN
and an Unidentified Dodgers Fan.

Dressen and Stengel

Charlie Dressen got a reputation as a smart guy due to an incident which occurred in the fourth game of the 1933 World Series. A young left-handed hitter named Cliff Bolton had come up to the Senators midway in the 1933 season and had made quite a reputation for himself as a pinch hitter, hitting .410 for the season (16-for-39), mostly as a pinch hitter.

The Giants, already up two games to one, scored in the top of the eleventh inning of Game Four, grabbing a 2–1 lead. With the bases loaded and one out, Washington sent Bolton up to pinch-hit. Bill Terry convened a meeting on the mound and decided that they had no option but to pull the infield in.

Dressen bolted from the bench, uninvited, and joined the conference. "No," he told Terry. "Don't bring them in. I know this guy from the Southern League. He's slow as hell, and if you throw him a fastball on the outside corner, he'll hit a ground ball to short. You can get out of this with a double play."

Terry stared hard at Dressen. Terry was the same age as Dressen, and he knew that Dressen had been managing in the Southern League most of the season. An injury to Johnny Vergez had left Terry short a third baseman down the stretch, and he had opted for a veteran, Dressen, who was hitting .332 at Nashville. Terry decided that Dressen knew what he was talking about. "Okay," he told the gathering. "Pitch him outside and play for two."

Cliff Bolton hit a ground ball to short, and the Giants were up three games to one. This incident became famous, and Dressen was hired to manage the Cincinnati Reds midway through the next season.

Charlie Dressen was born and raised in Decatur, Illinois. As a youth, he played quarterback on the team organized by George Halas, the Decatur Staleys, who later became the Chicago Bears. He would have liked to continue in football, and he would have liked to be a jockey, but he was at that awkward size: 5-5½, 146 pounds. A little too big to be a jockey, way too small to be a football player. He settled on baseball.

He was a consistent .300 hitter in the minor leagues and made the majors after a big season at St. Paul (American Association) in 1924, where he hit .347 with 18 homers and 151 RBI. He was purchased by Cincinnati that winter, played regularly for four years, hit okay, and was regarded as the best defensive third baseman in the National League other than Pie Traynor.

His bat betrayed him, and he bombed out of the National League by 1930, and then out of the top minor leagues (the International League and the American Association) by 1931. From his home in Decatur he ran around the Midwest all winter, trying to catch on as a minor league manager, but didn't find anything. By midsummer 1932 he had signed up to join the Decatur police force.

But then he heard that Fay Murray, owner of the Nashville team in the Southern Association, was considering a change of managers. Dressen borrowed money from a friend to get train fare to Nashville.

"Listen," he told Murray. "If I don't win more games than I lose here, you won't owe me a cent. I'll manage this team for the meal money until the end of the year, and then if we win more than we lose you can pay me my salary then."

Murray agreed to the deal. As Dressen told the story, they came down to the last day of the season with a .500 record under Dressen, so his whole salary for those two months was riding on the last game. They won the game, and Dressen got his money. Murray always said that he would have paid Dressen off anyway, but he wouldn't have rehired him for 1933.

Dressen's bat came back to life in 1933, and he wound up back in the major leagues, filling in for the World Championship team. Larry MacPhail was in the stands when the Cliff Bolton episode occurred, and hired him to manage the Reds a few months later.

MacPhail would be his biggest booster for many years. Dressen and MacPhail did a good job in Cincinnati. The Reds, who had finished last in 1931, last in 1932, last in 1933, and last in 1934, edged up to sixth place in 1935, their first full year under Charlie, and to fifth place in 1936. Larry MacPhail left the Reds after the 1936 season, and the Reds relapsed in 1937. Dressen was fired afer the season.

MacPhail landed the job as general manager in Brooklyn in 1938. He fired his manager after the 1938 season and hired Leo Durocher. A few days later, apparently without asking Leo, he hired Dressen as a coach.

Dressen became Leo Durocher's right-hand man, third base coach, drinking buddy, card-playing companion, researcher, horse race handicapper, and occasional rival. "Some doubt existed as to which of them was the true brains of the team," John Lardner wrote. "It depended on which of them you asked—Dressen or Durocher." Dressen had a fatal flaw: He couldn't shut up. This sometimes caused people to overlook the fact that he was, in truth, an extremely smart man. Durocher said that Dressen "could find out anything about anybody." Whenever there was a new player in the league who was causing the Dodgers some grief, Dressen was assigned to find out everything about him, most particularly what his weaknesses were. Dressen would check the new guy's record to see where he had played, figure out who he knew that could help him, get on the phone, and by the next day he'd give Durocher a full report.

He could steal signs, and he could call the pitches when the pitcher was in middelivery. There is a story told that later, when he was coaching with the Yankees, he worked out a set of signs to tip off the hitters about what the pitcher was throwing. Joe DiMaggio said that he didn't want to know, but Dressen said, well, he might as well give the signal, and DiMaggio could ignore it if he wanted to.

DiMaggio tried to ignore it, but one time Dressen signaled a curve, and DiMaggio picked up the signal. A fastball almost skulled him. "That's it," DiMaggio barked. "Knock it off before you get me killed."

Dressen relented. His chance to manage again was a long time coming, and before it came he was put out of baseball twice, by two different commissioners, both of whom were of the opinion that Charlie spent entirely too much time and too much money at the racetrack. After the 1942 season the aging Judge Landis leaned on Branch Rickey, the new power in Brooklyn, to break up "that nest of horse players and card sharks." He meant Durocher and Dressen and their show business buddies, many of whom circled like flies around the Dodgers clubhouse. Rickey fired Dressen to appease Landis, but when the team stumbled out of the gate in 1943, Durocher begged to have him back. Rickey relented, and rehired Dressen with a pledge to Landis that he would monitor their behavior.

MacPhail moved to the Yankees in 1945 and in 1947 offered Dressen $20,000 a year to come coach for the Yankees. It was an unheard salary for a coach, almost double what Dressen was making with Brooklyn, and he had been the highest-paid coach in the history of baseball with Brooklyn. Dressen accepted the assignment to coach third base for Bucky Harris. It wasn't the job he wanted, but the salary was right. He second-guessed Harris, as he had for years second-guessed Durocher, but Durocher had been his friend; Harris was not, and Dressen's late-arriving advice was not always well received. In 1947, when the new commissioner kicked Durocher out of baseball for a year, he also suspended Dressen for a month, for no apparent reason except that he was Durocher's friend and spent a lot of time at the racetrack.

By the late 1940s Dressen had been coaching in the New York area for a full decade. He was a New York personality—a raconteur, as they used to say. A storyteller and an urban adventurer, a friend to the barkeepers and the restaurateurs. He was tremendously popular with the older New York writers, and when Bucky Harris failed to solidify his grip on the managerial reigns, Dressen appeared to be the number-one candidate for the job.

Why he didn't get it is still a subject of some discussion. What it came down to was Charlie's ego. Dressen just couldn't resist telling you, pretty much on a daily basis, how smart he was. Walker Cooper once said that Charlie Dressen wrote a book on managing; on every page it just said "I." There is a story told, probably true, that one time in Cincinnati, when the Reds were dropping behind in the early innings, Charlie clapped his hands as his team took the field. "Hang in there, boys," he yelled to the departing players. "I'll think of something." Charlie was one of the few managers in baseball history who truly believed that *he* was the key to his team's success.

By the end of the 1948 season, Larry MacPhail was out of baseball. The Yankees were in the hands of George Weiss, a protégé of Ed Barrow, who had built the Yankees into the Gray Matron of the sports world. Barrow and Weiss loved players like Lou Gehrig, Tony Lazzeri, and Joe DiMaggio, who simply did their job and kept their mouths shut.

And so, in the famous fall of 1948, Dressen and Stengel traded jobs. Stengel came east to manage the Yankees, the job about which Dressen had dreamed for many years. Dressen went to Oakland, taking over for Casey as the manager of the Oakland Oaks.

Stengel and Dressen had as much in common

as Stengel and Billy Southworth, maybe more. Stengel was born in Kansas City in 1890; Southworth, in Nebraska in 1893; Dressen, in Illinois in 1898. Both Stengel and Dressen listed their ancestry as "Irish-German." Dressen was smaller than Stengel and Southworth and he was an infielder, while they were outfielders, but he had the same kind of playing career—a serviceable National League player, a regular for a few years, but certainly not a star. His first major league managerial opportunity came to him in the National League in 1934, exactly as it did for Stengel, and both of them took over down-and-out National League teams. Dressen was a little more successful than Stengel in that first opportunity, and lasted a half-season longer.

Dressen was, in Oakland, as successful as Casey had been. The team, which had gone 111–72, 96–90, and 114–74 in three years under Stengel (1946–1948), was 104–83 and 118–82 under Dressen in 1949–1950. It was not a Yankee farm team, but Billy Martin was there under Casey in 1948, and under Dressen in 1949. Until the mid-1950s, when Billy Martin was asked about managers he had played for, he would discuss Dressen and Stengel more or less on the same level. Dressen treated him well, and Martin for many years always talked about how much he had learned from Charlie Dressen.

The Leo Durocher era had run its course in Brooklyn. Burt Shotton, although winning the pennant in 1949, had failed to replace Durocher just as Bucky Harris had failed to replace Joe McCarthy despite winning the pennant in 1947. The parallel is precise. Joe McCarthy left the Yankees in June 1946. The team struggled through the rest of the season, but won the pennant in 1947 and finished just 2 games back in 1948.

Leo Durocher left the Dodgers in July 1948. The team struggled through the rest of the 1948 season, won the pennant in 1949, and lost by 2 games in 1950. That wasn't good enough, and, in both cases, the new manager was perceived as being too nice, too soft. Both teams (the Yankees in 1948, the Dodgers in 1950) then fired their manager and brought back to the majors the colorful skipper of the Oakland Oaks. In October 1950, Charlie Dressen was hired to manage the Brooklyn Dodgers.

Oh, what a team it was, Jackie Robinson's Dodgers. Between 1947 and 1956 they would win six pennants, for three different managers. In 1951, Dressen's first year in Brooklyn, his team won 97 games, and, as you all know, finished second, blowing a 13½ game lead over the last seven weeks. Walter O'Malley, amazingly enough, didn't fire Dressen, took responsibility for the defeat within the organization, and the Dodgers won the pennant in 1952.

In 1953 they won 105 games. The 1953 Dodgers, immortalized in Roger Kahn's classic *The Boys of Summer*, were one of the greatest teams of all time, despite falling to the Yankees in a six-game World Series tainted by an umpire's blown call. Four regulars are in the Hall of Fame (Roy Campanella, Jackie Robinson, Pee Wee Reese, and Duke Snider) and three others were of almost the same quality (Gil Hodges, Junior Gilliam, and Carl Furillo).

Charlie Dressen, at that moment, had one foot in the Hall of Fame, and the other on a banana peel. Unfortunately, all of his weight went on the banana peel.

Like Stengel, Dressen was enormously popular with the press, but not universally liked by his players. Casey's players, because the team enjoyed *so much* success, eventually had no choice but to buy into the lovable old coot image. Dressen bailed out before his success reached a comparable standard, which allowed his ex-players to cut him to ribbons with barbed wit. This, in turn, undermined his popularity with the press—but in 1953, the New York press coverage of Dressen and Stengel was more or less on a par.

For many years, it had been traditional to express one's appreciation for a successful season by giving the manager a multiyear contract. If things didn't go well you could fire the manager and pay off his contract. Walter O'Malley had, for some reason, developed a strong dislike for this policy and was determined that he would never again find himself in the position of paying somebody *not* to manage his ballclub.

Perhaps, on his own, Charlie Dressen could have lived with this. His wife was not prepared to. There were managers all around baseball who were getting three-year and four-year contracts, and Ruth Dressen was certain that her husband was every bit as good as any of them. She wrote a letter to the team expressing this opinion and absolutely demanding a multiyear contract. O'Malley refused. The Dressens insisted, refusing to sign a one-year agreement. O'Malley fired him.

The sudden firing of Charlie Dressen was among the biggest baseball stories of the 1950s. For many years, sportswriters liked to tell the "inside" story of the event, what was *really* going on in this small comic passion play. In retrospect, it seems obvious that what was "really" going on was exactly what O'Malley and Dressen *said* was going on. The Dodgers announced first that they wanted to rehire Charlie Dressen if they could. When they couldn't agree on a contract and gave the job to Walter Alston, they said publicly that the door was still open for Dressen to return, if he would agree to accept a one-year deal. For two months after that, almost until the beginning of spring training, they continued to insist that Dressen was welcome to return, if he would agree to the terms which had been offered.

Now, you cannot announce publicly that your ex-manager is welcome to return, and say privately something else. Suppose that Dressen then called a press conference and said, "Okay. I don't want to be stubborn about this; I'll come back." What could they have done, except to take him back?

What I'm saying is, there was a ton of newsprint invested at that time in why the

Dodgers *really* wanted to get rid of him, what the subtext was. The reporters just couldn't relate to the explanation that O'Malley gave, so they started making up stories as to why O'Malley wanted to get rid of Dressen. What the Dodgers wanted was for Dressen to return.

Dressen went back to Oakland for a year, won another pennant out there, then signed a multi-year contract to manage the Washington Senators. Did Dressen sincerely believe that he could make a winner out of the Senators? I think he did. He said he did; I believe him. The Senators—you probably don't remember this—had finished at or over .500 in 1952 and 1953, for Bucky Harris. They had slipped to sixth in 1954, but this was Chuck Dressen's chance to prove that *he* could do what Harris could not: win with the Washington Senators.

He lost 196 games in two seasons, started out 5–16 in 1957, and the team decided it was time to let somebody else finish out his contract.

Dressen was a nomad after that. He returned to the Dodgers for a year, as a coach. The reporters were sure he would soon replace Alston at the Dodger helm, but then, the reporters never did understand what O'Malley was doing. He got the Milwaukee job, after Fred Haney screwed it up in 1959, but Dressen wasn't much better, and the team's moment had passed. He moved on to Detroit, where he took on another underachieving team, which continued to underachieve.

There is little doubt that, had he just been able to swallow his pride, Charlie Dressen would be in the Hall of Fame today. Dressen had already won two pennants with the Dodgers. The team, under Walt Alston, would win two more pennants in the next three years, and would win six more pennants before Dressen died in 1966, a seventh within a couple of months.

At three key points in his career, Charlie's ego overwhelmed him. First, when he was in line for the Yankee job in 1949, his mouth cost him the opportunity. Second, when he had the best job in the National League, he gave it away in a fit of pride. Third, when his reputation would have gotten him almost any job, he chose one of the worst jobs in baseball, the Washington Senators assignment, because he failed to recognize the limits of what a manager could do.

I use the story of Charlie Dressen to teach my children the difference between security and self-confidence. Dressen was unquestionably a smart man, and a fine manager at least until 1953. On the surface, he boiled with self-confidence. He thought he knew more about baseball than anybody else in the world, and he couldn't resist telling you this. Had he not been quite so insecure, he could have resisted. I suppose one could say the same about Billy Martin or about Richard Nixon, but had he not been so insecure, he could have resisted the self-destructive excesses which gradually destroyed him.

Larsen and Turley

One of the fundamental questions of baseball is "What percentage of baseball is pitching?" Connie Mack made the argument that baseball is 75% pitching; other people have said 90%, 60%, 30%, whatever.

I used to make a living, sort of, by trying to devise ways to work these things out mathematically. In that line I once had the idea that one could solve this problem by studying pitchers who were traded or sold from very bad teams to very good teams, or who made similar moves as a free agent. Whenever a pitcher goes 9–16 or 11–17 or 8–13 for a bad team, announcers will say that he could turn that record around if he pitched for a better team. Whether this is true or not, there are always people ready to find out. The St. Louis Cardinals, one of the best teams in the National League in the 1960s, used to trade annually for a starting pitcher from the New York Mets, the league's worst team. Roger Craig, after going 10–24 and 5–22 for the Mets in their first two seasons (1962–1963), was traded to the Cardinals, where he went 7–9. Tracy Stallard, after going 6–17 and 10–20 with the Mets (1963–1964), was traded to St. Louis, where he went 11–8. Al Jackson, after going 8–20, 13–17, 11–16, and 8–20 with the Mets (1962–1965), was traded to the Cardinals, where he went 13–15. I think we've discovered a pattern here.

Anyway, it seemed to me, thinking about this, that one should be able to use these cases to figure out what "percentage" of a pitcher's record is controlled by his own pitching. If baseball were 100% pitching, then the pitcher's won–lost record should not depend at all on the team that he pitches for. His winning percentage should be 100% determined by his own performance. In this case, we should expect that a pitcher's winning percentage should not improve *at all* when he moved from a bad team to a good team.

If, on the other hand, baseball was zero percent pitching, then one would expect that a pitcher's winning percentage would improve by as much as the difference between the winning percentage of the teams. If baseball was zero percent pitching, then we would expect that a pitcher who moved from a .350 team to a .650 team would tend to improve his winning percentage from .350 to .650.

So if baseball is 75% pitching—that is, if a pitcher's winning percentage is 75% determined by his own performance—then we should expect that a pitcher's winning percentage should change, in moving teams, by only 25% of the difference between the teams. If baseball is 50% pitching— that is, if the pitcher's winning percentage is one-half determined by his own performance—then we should expect that a pitcher's winning percentage, when he changes teams, should improve by one-half of the difference between the teams. This, at least, was the theory.

I was never able to make the study work, for various reasons which can be summarized as "it was a naive study designed to test a naive assertion." There are many roadblocks to making the study work, two of which are just not going to be moved. Those two are:

1) A pitcher's won–lost record often isn't a good indication of how well he has pitched, and

2) A pitcher's performance level is not a constant. A pitcher who pitches well one year often will not pitch well again the next year, whether he changes teams or not.

Anyway, in 1953 the St. Louis Browns came up with two rookie pitchers with great arms, great stuff. The two were Don Larsen and Bob Turley. In 1953, the Browns' last year in St. Louis, Larsen went 7–12, and Turley, getting out of the army in midseason, went 2–6 but with a good 3.30 ERA.

In 1954, in Baltimore, Turley led the league in strikeouts (185) and kept his ERA at 3.46, but also led the league in walks (181), and wound up 14–15. Larsen was 3–21. This is not a misprint; three-and-twenty-one. He led the major leagues in losses, and posted one of the ugliest won–lost records in modern history.

After the 1954 season Turley and Larsen were traded to New York for a collection of players including Gus Triandos and Gene Woodling; actually, it turned out to be a pretty good trade for both teams. Both Larsen and Turley, in their first four years with the Yankees, had overall winning percentages in Whitey Ford territory. Larsen from 1955 to 1958 went 39–17 (.696), while Turley was 59–30 (.663). The success of these two pitchers was a key part of Casey Stengel's second four-pennant string, as they accounted for more than one-fourth of the Yankee wins in those years. In 1959 both men pitched poorly, and this was a key to bringing the four-year pennant run to an end.

Anyway, what I wanted to direct your attention to was that while Larsen and Turley were with St. Louis and Baltimore, their winning percentage was *worse* than that of the team they pitched for.

Year	Team	Team Won–Lost	Pct	Turley & Larsen	Pct	Difference
1953	St. Louis	54–100	.351	9–18	.333	-.018
1954	Baltimore	54–100	.351	17–36	.321	-.030

But when they moved to the Yankees, Turley and Larsen were better than the rest of the Yankee team:

Year	Team	Team Won–Lost	Pct	Turley & Larsen	Pct	Difference
1955	New York	96–58	.623	26–15	.634	+.011
1956	New York	97–57	.630	19–9	.679	+.049
1957	New York	98–56	.636	23–10	.697	+.061
1958	New York	92–62	.597	30–13	.698	+.101

How is this possible? How can two pitchers who are so bad that they drag down the performance of the league's worst team move to the Yankees, and be better than the rest of the Yankees? It's counterintuitive. From the standpoint of the issue raised before, it seems to indicate that the percentage of baseball success attributable to the pitcher is *less than zero*.

We know, instinctively, that this can't be right—but how do we explain it? You can write it off as a fluke, but then, what about Tommy Byrne? Tommy Byrne was a wild, hard-throwing lefty who had been with the Yankees earlier, but was traded to the Browns in 1951. With the Browns in 1951–1952 he went 11–24, a .314 winning percentage, essentially the same as Brown and Turley. Returning to the Yankees in 1954, he went 26–10 in his first three seasons back in New York, a .722 winning percentage. Like Turley and Larsen, he was worse than the Browns when he was with the Browns—but better than the Yankees when he was with the Yankees.

Part of the explanation for this is relatively simple: the Yankees had better coaching than the other teams. From Dom Forker's *Sweet Seasons*, the interview with Bob Turley:

> The Browns were a party-time club. Boy, they were bad . . . I went to the no wind-up delivery toward the end of the 1956 season. One night we were warming up down in the bullpen. Don Larsen was with

me . . . Jim Turner, the pitching coach, talked to Larsen and me. He got Larsen to go to the no wind-up because the other teams were stealing his signs. He was tipping his pitches. He got me to go to it to improve my control. I didn't sacrifice speed for control. But I gained rhythm.

The Yankees got better effort from many players than did other teams, because their players expected to win. Better effort and better coaching led to better performance.

A second part of the explanation is that the won–lost records of these pitchers are, in a sense, misleading, because of the way that Casey Stengel manipulated his pitching staff. Stengel liked to pitch certain pitchers against certain teams. In the years 1953–1960, for example, Whitey Ford had 40 decisions against the Chicago White Sox (he was 23–17), but only 15 decisions against Detroit (he was 8–7). The Tigers had a right-handed hitting lineup led by Al Kaline, Harvey Kuenn, Ray Boone, and Frank Bolling, and weren't a particularly good team. Casey preferred to go after them with somebody like Larsen, Turley, or Johny Kucks, and save Ford to pitch against Chicago. The White Sox and Indians were by far the best "other" teams in the American League over those years, accounting, between them, for nine of the ten best non-Yankee records of those years. Stengel pitched Ford a good bit against the Indians, but the Indians did have many right-handed hitters (Al Rosen, Rocky Colavito, Bobby Avila, and Al Smith). While the White Sox had both more left-handed hitters and more speed.

If Ford had simply pitched in rotation, taking his spot whenever it came up, he would have had as many decisions against one team as he did against another. He had more than twice as many decisions against Chicago as he did against Detroit, close to three times as many.

In the eight years 1953–1960, Ford had 37 decisions against the best non-Yankee team in the league, usually Chicago or Cleveland. He had 31 decisions against the second-best non-Yankee team, and 26 decisions against the third-best. He had 25 decisions or less against the fourth-best, fifth-best, sixth-best, and seventh-best teams.

Ford's record in those eight years is impressive enough on the surface; he was 124–58, a .681 winning percentage. But as good as that is, Ford (with the Yankees behind him) was really better than that. His winning percentage was depressed by the fact that he was pitching a disproportionate share of his games against the best teams in the league, probably to a greater extent than any other pitcher in baseball history.

Larsen, on the other hand, never beat the Cleveland Indians in his five years as a Yankee; he was 0–4 against them. He was just 4–4 against the White Sox. He was 12–3 against Baltimore, the team from which he had been acquired, and accounted for more than 70% of his wins against just three teams: Baltimore, Boston, and Kansas City.

It's not that Larsen *never* pitched against good teams; he did, after all, pitch in the World Series. He pitched against Brooklyn because Brooklyn balanced the percentages: They were a good team, but they were all right-handed except for the Duke.

After the Yankees fired Stengel, Ralph Houk put Whitey Ford in a straight four-man rotation, and let him take his turn on the schedule against whoever was due up next. Ford, who had never won twenty games for Stengel, went 25–4 in 1961, then 24–7 in 1963.

Red Rolfe

Red Rolfe was the third baseman for Joe McCarthy's Yankees in the late 1930s, a good ballplayer. He was a left-handed hitter, a four-time .300 hitter, and he scored an average of 138 runs a year over a three-year stretch, 1937–1939. Until Graig Nettles he was regarded as the best third baseman in Yankee history, and I suppose some people would argue that he still is.

Rolfe had finished his education before he entered baseball; he was a 1931 graduate of Dartmouth University, where he played for Jeff Tesreau, who had played for John McGraw. After his playing career Rolfe was head baseball coach at Yale, replacing Smokey Joe Wood. He coached a year with the Yankees, under Bucky Harris, and worked a year as the director of farm clubs for the Detroit Tigers.

In 1949 Rolfe was assigned to manage the Tigers. For two seasons he was tremendously successful. Taking over a .500 team, he went 87–67 in 1949 and 95–59 in 1950, missing Stengel's men by only 3 games. He made only a few personnel moves in those two years, but they were good ones. He replaced an unproductive first baseman with a productive platoon. The Tigers traded a marginal pitching prospect and $100,000 to the Browns for Gerry Priddy, who had an outstanding season at second base in 1950.

His young players seemed to be coming around. A pitcher named Art Houtteman, who had gone 2–16 in 1948, won 19 games in 1950. Houtteman was only twenty-two years old, threw very hard, and was at the time regarded as a superstar of the future.

In 1948 a twenty-one-year-old center fielder named Johnny Groth had a spectacular season at Buffalo, hitting .340 with 30 homers, 97 RBI, and leading the International League in hits (199), runs scored (124), doubles (37) and triples (16). Rolfe put him in center field, scooting Hoot Evers, who had been in center, over to left, and sending Vic Wertz, who had been in left, to right.

Groth was good in 1949, and in 1950 he was great. He hit .306 with 85 RBI, but what really gets your attention is his strikeout/walk ratio: 95 walks, only 27 strikeouts. He wasn't quite Joe DiMaggio, but projected from that point in his career, he looked very much like a Hall of Fame center fielder. The emergence of Groth gave the 1950 Tigers one of the best outfields in American League history:

Pos	Player	G	AB	R	H	2B	3B	HR	RBI	BB	SO	SB	Avg	SPct
LF	Hoot Evers	143	526	100	170	35	11	21	103	71	40	5	.323	.551
CF	Johnny Groth	157	566	95	173	30	8	12	85	95	27	1	.306	.451
RF	Vic Wertz	149	559	99	172	37	4	27	123	91	55	0	.308	.533

Red Rolfe was named the American League Manager of the Year in 1950. In a preseason poll in 1951, several sportswriters picked the Tigers to win the American League.

Even more quickly than things had come together for Red Rolfe, they fell apart on him. Art Houtteman was drafted by the United States Army. Hal Newhouser came up with a sore arm. Johnny Groth never had another season as good. Billy Evans, the Detroit general manager who had hired Rolfe, retired and was replaced by Charlie Gehringer.

Spiking Rolfe's rapid descent was a curious choice: He decided to make Vic Wertz a platoon player.

Vic Wertz in 1951 was only twenty-six years old. A slow-moving left-handed slugger, Wertz had come to the Tigers in 1947, and by 1949 had established himself as the cleanup hitter. He drove in 133 runs in 1949, 123 more in 1950. Rolfe's decision to convert him to a platoon player can perhaps best be explained by the old aphorism that a little learning is a dangerous thing.

Platooning, you will remember, had fallen into disuse from 1925 to 1945, but in the late 1940s underwent a strong revival. Stengel talked a lot about platooning and about how it helped him, so in the early 1950s platooning was a hot topic. There were no published stats at that time on how players hit against left-handed and right-handed pitchers, so Rolfe decided to start keeping his own stats.

And his own stats showed, guess what, that Vic Wertz didn't hit much against left-handed pitchers. This isn't terribly surprising. The exact statistics have, as far as I know, never been published, but Wertz probably batted 150 times against left-handers in 1950. If he hit .190 in those 150 at bats, that wouldn't be noteworthy. When you look at 150 at bats, you'll get numbers like that. My impression is that Rolfe may not have been maintaining the stats for a full season before he decided to platoon Wertz; it may have been only a couple of months.

Anyway, the Tigers stumbled out of the gate in 1951. Rolfe, searching for more offense, started platooning Vic Wertz with Steve Souchock, a veteran outfielder rescued from the Pacific Coast League. Wertz was not pleased, and blasted Rolfe in the newspaper. The Tigers fell to fifth place in 1951 (73–81), and in June, 1952, were mired in the basement with a record of 23–49, 7 games behind the St. Louis Browns. Rolfe was fired. He had lasted only a year and a half after being named the major league manager of the year.

The Tigers, cleaning house, traded Vic Wertz to the Browns; despite contracting polio in mid-career, Wertz would drive in 100 runs three more times for other teams. Red Rolfe returned to his native New Hampshire and would never manage again.

Platooning? Hey, platooning is a wonderful strategy. I'm all for it. Common sense dictates that you don't platoon guys who can drive in 125 runs a year.

Richards and Lopez

Paul Richards and Al Lopez were both born in 1908 in the South, Lopez in Florida, Richards in Texas. Both were catchers, and both reached the major leagues with Brooklyn, under Wilbert Robinson.

Richards was a better hitter in the minor leagues than Lopez, but converted to catching late, and did not have the innate defensive skills, the quickness and throwing arm, with which Lopez was gifted. Lopez got to Brooklyn first and had firm command of the job before Richards arrived. Richards was traded to New York and was a part of the 1933 Giants, along with Charlie Dressen and several other future managers.

Both Richards and Lopez played until the late 1940s. Lopez was a far better player than Richards, but Richards did receive one honor that eluded Lopez. In 1945, playing only 83 games, batting only 234 times, and hitting only .256, Paul Richards was honored by *The Sporting News* as the outstanding catcher in the major leagues, as recognized by his inclusion on the major league postseason All-Star team. He was probably the weakest player ever to win a place on that team.

Both received their chance to manage in the American League in 1951, Lopez with Cleveland, Richards with Chicago. Lopez took over a strong team; Richards, a young team which was acquiring talent.

Lopez managed 15 full seasons, parts of 17 seasons, retiring after the 1965 season, coming out of retirement briefly and unsuccessfully in 1968. Richards managed for almost 11 full seasons, stepping down in 1961 to become general manager of the expansion Houston Astros, then making an unsuccessful comeback, as a manager, in 1976.

Both managers had outstanding records. Lopez had a career winning percentage of .581 and managed the only two teams to take the American League championship away from Casey Stengel's Yankees. Richards's record is superficially bland, a .506 winning percentage and no titles, but his teams were 63 games better than they could have been expected to be based on their peformance in previous seasons. This would rank him as the tenth most successful manager of all time by that method.

He took over two down-and-out teams and systematically built them both into contenders. He took over the White Sox in 1951, after they had three straight seasons of 90+ losses. His team improved by 21 games in his first season; for that reason it might be worth a look at what happened on that team.

Richards used essentially the same team that the White Sox had the year before—catcher Phil Masi, first baseman Eddie Robinson, second baseman Nellie Fox, shortstop Chico Carrasquel, number-one starter Billy Pierce. The Sox did make a couple of trades, including a three-cornered trade in which they gave up their starting center fielder, Dave Philley, and their cleanup hitter, Gus Zernial, in exchange for a collection of young, unproven players including Minnie Minoso, who took Zernial's spot in left field. Jim Busby, up from the minors, went into center, which improved the team's defense, but the largest improvement was at second base, where Nellie Fox, a .250 hitter prior to Richards's arrival, blossomed suddenly into the Nellie Fox we remember today.

His team got steadily better from then on, winning 81 again in 1952, 89 in 1953, and 94 in 1954. He resigned late in the 1954 season, accepting the challenge of building a contender out of the hapless Baltimore Orioles.

Al Lopez in 1951 took over a Cleveland Indians team which had been winning 90 games a year like clockwork, and continued to win 90+ games a year. He had the big season in 1954, of course, and then began to feel unappreciated by the Indians' front office.

According to the 1957 *Baseball Guide:*

Despite leading Cleveland to another second-place finish, Al Lopez disclosed on September 29 that he would step down from his $40,000-a-year job following the Indians' closing game. The reported dissatisfaction of General Manager Hank Greenberg with the club's showing was said to have led Lopez to his decision . . . (On October 29) the White Sox signed Lopez as skipper at approximately the same salary he drew with Cleveland.

We have a habit of dating the thirty-five-year dead spot in the history of the Cleveland Indians from 1959, the Indians' last good season before the exile. In retrospect, it might be more accurate to date the collapse of the Indians from the departure of Al Lopez. The Indians, still winning 90 games a year under Lopez, played .500 ball in 1957–1958, under a series of different managers.

Anyway, Lopez moved on to Chicago, meaning he took over the team that Richards had so carefully constructed. Between the two had been a two-year stint for Marty Marion. The team played well for him, but, like Bucky Harris in New York and Burt Shotton in Brooklyn, Marion somehow never could step out of the shadow of his predecessor.

The Cleveland and Chicago franchises in the 1950s are intertwined like one big hillbilly family. Frank Lane was the general manager of both teams, Lopez managed both, and a seemingly endless list of players *played* for both teams— Minnie Minoso, who played for Cleveland, then Chicago, then Cleveland, then Chicago, but also Al Smith, Chico Carrasquel, Early Wynn, Eddie Robinson, Dick Donovan. The teams employed, at different times, many of the same scouts. Luis Aparicio, the defining White Sox player of the Al Lopez era, had actually made a handshake agreement to sign with the Indians for $10,000, but Hank Greenberg balked at paying the bonus, offended Aparicio during the subsequent negoti-

ations, and Aparicio signed with the White Sox for $6,000; from that moment, too, the decline of the Indians' franchise could be dated.

Since 1920, the Cleveland Indians had always been a solid franchise—not the Yankees, but one of the better teams in the American League. The White Sox had always been an also-ran organization—not the Senators, but one of the weaker teams. Somehow, out of this "melding" of the two franchises, the life force transferred from Cleveland to Chicago. The White Sox became what the Indians had been; the Indians became what the White Sox had been. Although the Paul Richards era prepared the way for what was to come, the movement of Al Lopez in October 1956 would have to be cited as the precise moment at which this transfer occurred.

Meanwhile, Paul Richards was doing in Baltimore exactly what he had done in Chicago, although it took a little longer. First, as he had done in Chicago, he traded a couple of his established talents for a package of unproven players—Willie Miranda, Gus Triandos. He began putting young players in the lineup to see what they could do. Tito Francona, Brooks Robinson, Wayne Causey, Bob Boyd, Billy Gardner. Some of them panned out; most of them didn't. He gave major league opportunities to minor league veterans and second chances to struggling stars, and by so doing came up with Jim Gentile and Hoyt Wilhelm. The Orioles, losers of 100 games in each of the two previous seasons, edged up to 57–97 in 1955, to 69 wins in 1956, to 76 wins in 1957, to 89 wins in 1960, and to 95 wins in 1961. (Actually, the 1961 Orioles were on target for 100+ wins until Richards resigned suddenly on September 1.)

As he had done in Chicago, Richards prepared the way for a highly successful era which did not actually arrive until he had moved on. Meanwhile, Lopez managed the White Sox for nine good years. Both Richards and Lopez were "defense first" managers. Lopez once said that all a team really needed was pitching and defense, because if you didn't allow the other team to score, eventually they would give you a run, and you'd win the game. Richards was less extreme in this regard.

Both Richards and Lopez were reluctant to give up on a player, even if they were not 100% satisfied with his performance. Both men followed a principle which seems to me self-evident, but which an astonishing number of managers do not recognize: never give up on a player until you know whom you're going to replace him with. Most major league managers, in my experience, will sometimes decide that a player can't play, bench him or release him, and then start looking around for somebody else to put into the slot. Both Richards and Lopez were careful to know what Plan B was before they dropped Plan A.

Lopez was a man of dignity and composure, a nice-looking man with brilliant white hair and sun-reddened skin. Richards was a tall, gaunt man with a caved-in mouth, a weak chin, shifty eyes, and salt-and-pepper hair that stuck out sideways although he tried to lay it flat across the top of his head. Lopez was a great admirer of Casey Stengel; Richards, of Leo Durocher. Paul Richards's luck, in any area of his life, was never as good as Al Lopez's. He wasn't as handsome or as athletic. He didn't get to the majors as quickly. Lopez took over two good teams; Richards took on building projects.

Both men managed many of the same players. Paul Richards's favorite player was Nellie Fox. When he was general manager at Houston in the 1960s and Nellie was about done, he traded to get him back. Lopez reportedly didn't much like Fox, who won an MVP award for him, and thought he was overrated.

Both Richards and Lopez had the reputation of being outstanding at working with pitchers, in part because they were ex-catchers, and ex-catchers get that reputation, but in large part because they were both "defense first" managers. Both men were able many times to take on pitchers who had been unsuccessful with other teams and turn them around—not because they were bril-

liant with pitchers, in my opinion, but because they put strong defenses behind the pitchers, which made the pitcher's stats look a whole lot better. Among the most amazing stats in baseball history: In 1954 Mike Garcia led the American League in ERA, at 2.64. The Cleveland Indians' *staff* ERA was 2.78.

In working on the managers' all-star teams, I noticed something that surprised me. Al Lopez managed sixteen 20-game winners in his fifteen full seasons as a manager. Paul Richards never managed a 20-game winner. None. He had a reputation as a great handler of pitchers, but he never had a twenty-game winner.

Even if you excluded the 20-game winners, Al Lopez could still pick a brilliant staff from seasons like Mike Garcia, 1954 (19–8, led the league in ERA) Bob Lemon, 1955 (18–10), Herb Score, 1955 (16–10, 245 strikeouts), Bob Shaw, 1959 (18–6), Gary Peters, 1963 (19–8, 2.33), and Juan Pizarro, 1964 (19–9, 2.56). Paul Richards just never had a starting pitcher who had that kind of a season. His best pitchers were all guys who were like 18–11 or 19–12.

This is not to detract from his record with pitchers. The White Sox team ERA improved from 4.41 to 3.50 the year that Paul Richards took over, and the White Sox had the second-best team ERA in the league from 1952 through 1954. In Baltimore he took over a team with little pitching, traded away his only established starter, but had the team about the league average in ERA in two years (1956), better than league the year after that, second in the league in team ERA for three straight years after that, and finally, in his last year there, with the best team ERA in baseball.

Paul Richards wrote a book, *Modern Baseball Strategy* (Prentice-Hall, 1955, with a foreword by Leo Durocher). The book is quite intelligent. He writes about managing, about the day-to-day details of how to manage a baseball team, rather than writing funny stories about silly stuff that happened twenty years ago. In many ways,

Richards was ahead of the other managers of his own time, and would be ahead of many of the managers of today. Al Lopez is a Hall of Famer and deserves to be; Paul Richards was a brilliant and talented manager.

But I wouldn't hire him. Richards was devious, a man who always had his own agenda. He was the kind of man who answered every question thoughtfully. What he was thinking about was what he wanted you to believe. I would want a manager who, like Paul Richards, was intelligent, was patient with young players, and who always had a plan three innings ahead and three years down the road. I would want a man who emulated Paul Richards in these respects. I wouldn't want the genuine article.

PAUL RICHARDS

Typecast

For most of Al Lopez's career, his first-base spot was occupied by old left-handed power hitters who had almost interchangeable records:

Year	G	AB	R	H	2B	3B	HR	RBI	BB	SO	SB	Avg	SPct
1951	128	486	65	131	12	5	27	103	37	71	0	.270	.481
1952	127	437	63	115	10	3	31	97	44	84	1	.263	.513
1956	136	481	65	127	22	0	32	106	75	87	0	.264	.509
1960	127	444	87	131	22	0	28	93	74	69	1	.295	.534
1961	141	492	76	145	26	6	27	92	61	62	1	.295	.537

These five records were compiled by Luke Easter (1951–1952), Vic Wertz (1956), and Roy Sievers (1960–1961); Sievers actually was a right-handed hitter. In addition to their almost identical records, these batters had a couple of obvious things in common. They were all thirty-three years old or older, and none of them could get out of his own way.

Lopez had numerous other old first basemen who *would* have compiled almost the same records, were it not for injuries. His 1959 team, American League champions, didn't have one of these guys. They had Earl Torgeson, an old left-handed power-hitting first baseman who couldn't get out of his own way, but Torgeson didn't hit, so they replaced him in midseason with Ted Kluszewski, another old left-handed hitting first baseman who couldn't . . . you get my drift.

One time when he got away from the mold was in the early 1960s, when the White Sox traded for Joe Cunningham. Cunningham was younger, faster, and wasn't a power hitter. Lopez tried him for a couple of years and decided to bo back to Bill Skowron.

Skowron by this time was in his mid-thirties. He had been a part of Stengel's Yankees for many years and had then been traded to the Dodgers in one of the strangest trades of all time, a trade which hurt both teams. Skowron never did hit 27 homers and drive in 96 runs for Lopez, but we know what Lopez had in mind.

Face Off

I once wrote an article discussing the greatest seasons ever by relief pitchers. I got a letter from a reader, in response, saying that Elroy Face, 1959, should not have been included in the discussion. Face won 18 games in 1959, a relief record; his 18–1 record is still the best one-season won–lost percentage ever, but the reader felt he didn't have a great season because "a relief pitcher's job isn't to *win* the game, but to close out somebody else's victory. A relief pitcher gets a win," he explained, "when he *doesn't* do his job. Face had only ten saves in 1959. That's what you judge a reliever by."

"No, no," I wrote back (or if I didn't write back, at least I intended to). "You're projecting the present onto the past. You're reading Face's record as if he was a modern reliever. Face wasn't used that way. Face wasn't used to 'save' games; he was simply used to pitch in close games whenever the starter was gone."

But years later, on a pregame show, I heard one of Face's teammates from the 1959 team talking about Elroy's big season. He remembered it pretty much the way the reader assumed it was—Face would come in with a 4–3 lead, give up a run, and become the winning pitcher when the Pirates scored in the ninth. So then I got to wondering, what are the facts here? How many of Face's wins *were* vultured? How many times did Face come into a game with the Pirates ahead, give up the tying run, but then get credited with a win when the Pirates came back to retake the lead?

I sent John Sickels to the library, to make a log of Elroy Face's performance in 1959. Here's what we found:

1. *Only three of Face's wins were vultured from other pitchers.* On April 24, May 14, and August 9, Face did enter the game with Pittsburgh ahead (in all three cases ahead by a single run), did allow the other team to score, and then was credited with a win that had originally belonged to some other pitcher.

2. *Two of Face's wins came after he entered the game with the Pirates behind.* On May 13 and June 11, Face entered the game with the Pirates trailing (in both cases trailing by a single run), and became the winning pitcher when the Pirates rallied.

3. *The great majority of Face's 1959 wins (13 of the 18) came after Face entered a tie game.*

We found that Face in 1959 had 10 saves, using a modern definition of a save. He is credited with 10 saves in the encyclopedias, but this was figured in the late 1960s, using a very broad definition of a save. A save was credited whenever a pitcher finished a game won by his team and was not the winning pitcher, regardless of the score. I mentioned this in another book, but Ernie Shore pitched a game in 1912 in which he entered the ninth inning with a 21–2 lead and surrendered ten runs, but held on to win, 21–12. Under the rules used to compile the encyclopedia, he should have been credited with a save, and he was. All of Face's saves were legitimate. Almost all of them were one-run games in which he pitched a full ninth inning or more to protect the lead.

What I am really investigating here, of course, is *how managers used their relief aces at that time*. Face is a case in point. His record is unusual, but not all that unusual; many relievers, from 1950 to 1966, had lopsided won–lost records, including the rookie troika of Hoyt Wilhelm, Joe Black, and Eddie Yuhas in 1952 (15–3, 15–4, and 12–2) and others such as Ron Perranoski, 1963 (16–3) and Phil Regan, 1966 (14–1). A 1990s relief ace would never compile such a record, because of the way relievers are used now. So how *was* Face used?

1. *Face never entered a game earlier than the seventh inning.* In this respect he was much like a modern reliever. He pitched 57 games, 93 innings. He entered the game 13 times in the seventh inning, 19 times in the eighth inning, 21 times in the ninth inning, and 4 times in the tenth inning. A modern relief ace normally makes about 80% of his entrances in the ninth inning.

2. *Face was used exclusively in close games.* In 41 of the 57 games in which he appeared, either the score was tied when he entered, or it was a one-run game. Most of the other games were two-run games. In this respect, Face was like a modern relief ace.

3. *Face was used utterly without respect to whether the Pirates were ahead or behind.* Face was brought into the game 16 times when the Pirates were ahead, 18 times when the score was tied, and 23 times when the Pirates were behind. In this respect, he was completely different from a modern relief ace.

4. *Face normally was brought in to start an inning.* Over 70% of the time, Face entered the game at the start of an inning, after a pinch hitter had been used in the previous half-inning.

In short, Elroy Face was used in the late innings of any close game whenever the starting pitcher was gone, regardless of whether the Pirates were ahead or behind.

Fred Haney

For most of his career, Fred Haney was no doubt a fine manager. In 1959, Fred Haney had the worst season of any major league manager in baseball history.

Haney's first major league manager was Ty Cobb. Unlike most people, Haney liked Cobb and felt that Cobb treated him well. Haney hit .352 in 81 games as a rookie in 1922, but his average sank like a bowling ball after that, and his career was short. He was a feisty little infielder with a quick wit, the very picture of a manager. Beginning in 1935 he was player/manager at Toledo, what had been Casey Stengel's job, and then Steve O'Neill's; the job was a springboard to the majors.

In Haney's first five seasons managing in the majors he finished eighth, sixth, eighth, eighth, and eighth. One season he didn't finish; he was fired at 15–29. This record isn't as bad as it sounds; he managed first the Browns and then the Pirates. Both teams had grown accustomed to mildew on the ceiling long before Haney took over, and the general perception was that Haney in St. Louis and Pittsburgh was like Casey in Brooklyn and Boston— a good manager, but nothing to work with.

His chance to work with good material finally came in Milwaukee in midseason, 1956. Milwaukee, a perennial contender, started slowly in 1956, and Charlie Grimm met the reaper in mid-June. The team went on a tear as soon as Haney was hired, seized first place within three weeks, and held a 5½ game lead in late July.

And a 3½ game lead on Labor Day.

And a one-game lead going into the final series of the year. The interesting question about the '56 Braves is how they avoided becoming infamous. If you ask any baseball fan to list teams which "blew" the pennant race, he'll list a few teams which had essentially the same type of record as Milwaukee— three or 4 games in front in early September, but a game short at the wire. The Braves avoided notoriety, I would guess, because:

1) They weren't a preseason favorite, and thus weren't expected to win, and

2) They got hot after Haney took over, creating the (justifiable) feeling that it would be unfair to load the failure on Haney.

Anyway, in 1957 they won the World Series. In 1958 they repeated as National League champions, and in 1959 Fred Haney walked around with his head so far in a gopher hole he couldn't wiggle his elbows. This is, of course, a subjective judgment; the Braves went 86–68, and stumbled into a playoff with the Dodgers, which left them 86–70. My assertion that Haney screwed up the pennant race is based on five things.

First, the talent on the 1959 Braves and Dodgers is an incredible mismatch. Without any exaggeration, the 1959 Dodgers shouldn't have been within 20 games of the Braves.

And second, third, fourth, and fifth, Haney made a string of obvious mistakes.

1) He rode his two best pitchers, Lew Burdette and Warren Spahn, into the ground, although he had many other talented pitchers.

2) He platooned Joe Adcock, one of the best power hitters in baseball, with Frank Torre and Mickey Vernon, who were hopeless.

3) Lacking an established second baseman after Red Schoendienst went down with tuberculosis, he refused to decide who he wanted to play second base. He ran second basemen in and out all year, getting worse performance from all of them than he could possibly have gotten from any of them.

4) He loaded up his bench with so many over-the-hill veterans, grumbling about the fact that they couldn't play anymore, that it was almost inevitable that the clubhouse atmosphere would turn sour.

Let's deal with the specific allegations first, and then we'll talk about the talent.

1) Warren Spahn won 21 games every year— had for years before Haney came, and would for years after Haney left. He went 21–12 in 1954,

20–11 in 1956, 21–11 in 1957, 22–11 in 1958, 21–10 in 1960, and 21–13 in 1961. Occasionally he would go 23–7 for variety.

In 1959, however, he pitched more innings than usual, leading the majors with 292—so he went 21–15. Lew Burdette was the same; after going 19–10, 17–9, and 20–10, he also pitched 290 innings (second in the majors), and had the same record as Spahn, 21–15.

It seems obvious, in retrospect, that loading an extra 40 innings each on his top two pitchers didn't get any extra wins out of them; it just got him three or four extra losses.

This would be excusable, perhaps, if Haney had been short of options. In fact, however, he had an excellent third starter, Bob Buhl, and a raft of hard-throwing youngsters. He tried to work Buhl harder than usual, too, but Buhl pulled up with a sore arm, so he had to back off. That still left him with Juan Pizzaro, Joey Jay, Carlton Willey, and Don Nottebart. Pizzaro, who may have had the best fastball in baseball at that time, went 6–2 in 1959, in limited action. When he got a chance to pitch regularly, with the White Sox in 1961, he immediately became one of the best pitchers in the American League. Joey Jay, a bonus baby pushed into service in 1958, went 7–5 (in 1958) with an ERA of 2.13. In 1961, when he got a chance to start regularly for Cincinnati, he won 42 games in two seasons. In 1959, used sporadically, he was not effective.

Carlton Willey had won 21 games for Wichita in 1957, and had gone 9–7 with a 2.70 ERA for Milwaukee in 1958, leading the National League in shutouts, with four. Still in the minors was Don Nottebart, who won 18 games that summer—and had won 18 in 1955, 18 in 1956, and 18 in 1957. When finally given a chance to work, he, too, turned out to be quite a competent pitcher. Haney didn't want to use any of them. He jerked them all in and out of the rotation, getting nothing much out of any of them.

Quite simply, Haney was afraid to let the young-

sters pitch. He knew that he had an outstanding veteran ball club, and he was afraid that if he allowed the youngsters to pitch, they'd lose it. He was back on his heels, playing defensively, playing not to lose. He did exactly what Casey Stengel never did with Whitey Ford: He tried to force his best pitchers to win it all on their own.

2) Joe Adcock was one of the best power hitters in the National League at that time. He had belted 38 homers in 454 at bats in 1956, as well as 15 in 288 at bats (1955), 12 in 209 at bats (1957) and 19 in 320 at bats (1958). Over a four-year period, that comes to 40 home runs per 600 at bats.

Adcock, however, was not much of a first baseman, and he and Haney never got along. Adcock had an injury in 1956, which enabled Frank Torre, a better defensive player, to slide into a platoon role with him.

Torre, however, didn't hit like a first baseman. He hit .258 with no homers in 111 games in 1956, and .272 with five homers in 1957. He did hit .309 in 1958, but in 1959 he fell into an intractable slump.

Joe Adcock was unhappy when he didn't play, and Adcock was not a man to suffer in silence. To try to keep Adcock happy, Haney played him some in the outfield, and if you thought Adcock was a bad first baseman, you should have seen him play the outfield.

It was one of those things. It was obvious to everybody (except Haney) that this just wasn't working, but once people began to question him about it, Haney couldn't admit that it wasn't working. He kept doing it, and it kept getting worse. Facing Don Drysdale in the one hundred fifty-sixth and deciding game of a 154-game season, Haney chose as his cleanup hitter not Henry Aaron (.355 with 39 homers), or Eddie Mathews (.306 with 46 homers), or Joe Adcock (.292 with 25 homers in 404 at bats), or Wes Covington or Del Crandall, both of whom were pretty good hitters. He chose Frank Torre, who had hit .228 with 1 homer in 115 games.

3) In spring training, 1959, Braves' second

baseman Red Schoendienst developed tuberculosis. Schoendienst was a tremendous player, and many people felt that the acquisition of Schoendienst in an early-season trade had propelled the Braves to the 1957–1958 pennants.

Lacking a second baseman, Haney decided to use fifty of them. Actually, he used eight—Bobby Avila (51 games), Chuck Cottier (10 games), Felix Mantilla (60), Joe M. Morgan (7), Johnny O'Brien (37), Mel Roach (8), Red Schoendienst (4 games, late in the season), and Casey Wise (20 games). The results, offensively and defensively, were gruesome. Whereas a typical National League team in 1959 got 100 double plays from their second basemen and 19 errors, the Braves got 88 double plays and 28 errors. Offensively, only one of the eight second basemen hit higher than .217, that being Bobby Avila, who hit .238.

None of those players, left alone, would have played as badly as all of them, playing a few days at a time in unfamiliar circumstances and under performance pressure.

4) On the Braves bench in 1959, in addition to whichever three second basemen weren't playing today, were Stan Lopata (thirty-three years old), Del Rice (thirty-six), Andy Pafko (thirty-eight), and Mickey Vernon (forty-one). In his bullpen was Bob Rush (thirty-three). All of these men had been fine performers in their day. Mickey Vernon, for example, had led the American League in batting in 1946, and Andy Pafko had driven in 110 runs for the Cubs in 1945. By 1959, they were done.

As anyone who has been around athletes ought to know, the most difficult years of an athlete's life are the years when he is coming to grips with the fact that his skills have gotten away from him. By loading his roster with players at that stage of their careers, Haney virtually guaranteed an unhappy clubhouse.

None of this would bother me, I suppose, if the Milwaukee Braves had accomplished some reasonable portion of what they should have accomplished between 1955 and 1965. Now, this is a dangerous argument, and it is a type of argument that I normally reject. There are people who would argue, for example, that Sparky Anderson gets no credit for the Reds of the 1970s, because the talent on that team was so tremendous they could have won for J. Henry Waugh. Joe McCarthy, of course, was called the "Push Button Manager," because his talent was such that it made winning seem automatic.

I reject that argument in those two cases, and in almost all others, for two reasons. First, the manager (usually) plays a huge role in *shaping* the talent available to him. Second, when the team wins, everybody deserves to participate in the credit. If the team loses, if they underperform, the manager will take the lion's share of the blame for that. If they win, he's got to get his share of the credit.

But there is an exception to every rule, and this is the exception to the rule that talent should not be held against the manager. The New York Yankees in the thirteen years beginning in 1949 won eleven pennants and eight World Series. The Braves, in their thirteen years in Milwaukee, won two pennants and one World Series. I would argue that if you compare the talent on those two teams, the Braves have the better of it. Both teams had three superstars who span most of that era—a left-handed starting pitcher (Warren Spahn and Whitey Ford), a power-hitting outfielder (Mickey Mantle and Henry Aaron), and one more, in both cases a left-handed slugger (Yogi Berra and Eddie Matthews). The Braves are not behind in this comparison. Spahn won about 50% more games in his career than did Ford, and Aaron and Matthews hit almost 50% more home runs than Mantle and Berra.

If you get beyond that point, you have a lot of players who match up well—but the Braves have *more* good players, beyond those front three, than do the Yankees. Both teams have right-handed power-hitting first basemen who platooned most of their careers, Adcock and Skowron. Advantage, Adcock. The Braves, throughout that era but in 1959 in particular, had a great number-two starter, Lew Burdette, and a fine number-three starter, Bob Buhl. They had one of the best relief aces of that era, Don McMahon. They had at least four other outstanding players—catcher Del Crandall, shortstop Johnny Logan, center fielder Bill Bruton, and left fielder Wes Covington.

Lots of teams had talent, but this team had Talent. They had talent like the Big Red Machine, talent like the Boys of Summer, talent like the 1936 Yankees.

And then you look at the 1959 Dodgers, who are one of the two or three weakest championship teams in the history of the National League. The '59 Dodgers had three or four leftover pieces of their glory days in Brooklyn (Gil Hodges, Duke Snider, Junior Gilliam), but, with the exception of Gilliam, they were half the players they once had been. They had several pieces of the great team that would emerge in the 1960s (Sandy Koufax, Maury Wills, John Roseboro), but those were immature players, their best years still on the horizon. They had Don Drysdale, who was 17–13, and who won only two of his last eleven starts. The only players they had who were in their prime were Charlie Neal, Wally Moon, Johnny Podres, and Roger Craig—none of whom was a star, let alone a superstar. It is astonishing that this patchwork collection, this team in the very center of a five-year transition, could somehow manage to beat a team like the 1959 Braves.

But how much of this was Fred Haney? Let's look more carefully at Haney's first two managerial opportunities, in St. Louis and Pittsburgh. It is true that the Browns had been bad for many years before Haney was hired. It is also true that they were worse under Haney than before or after. The Browns record under Haney, 125–227 (.355), was their worst under anyone who managed

them after 1913, except interim managers. Their record in 1939 (43–111) was the worst in their history. They had a better year in 1940, but Haney was fired early in 1941, with the team at 15–29. They played .500 ball the rest of that season, and were 13 games *over* .500 the next season.

Pittsburgh was very bad in 1952, the year before Haney was hired, but on the other hand, that was their first 100-loss season since the days of Honus Wagner. While Haney was there, they gave him Dale Long, Dick Groat, Roberto Clemente, Frank Thomas, Vern Law, Elroy Face, and Bob Friend. He gave them three last-place finishes, losing 100+ games the first two. I mentioned that Milwaukee took first place in late June 1956, shortly after Haney was hired. I didn't mention whom they took it away from: Pittsburgh. The same team that Haney had lost 94 games with the season before.

Of course, the Braves did *not* improve after they fired Haney; they continued to flounder. 1960 was a different race; the 1960 Pirates were a better team than the 1959 Dodgers, although not a whole lot better.

As I see it, the National League had one great team and some other good teams up until 1955. By 1962 the National League really had three championship teams—the Dodgers, the Giants, and the Reds. Between 1956 and 1961, they had the Braves, and that's it. The Braves should have been winning 100 games a year.

Was Fred Haney the worst major league manager ever? Well, he was better at the job than all of us who never did it. The question of who was the worst manager is like the question of who was the worst player: They're all better players than those of us who couldn't play. The *very* worst manager was probably somebody who kept the job only a few games, or somebody who kept the job only a half-season, like Maury Wills.

Haney had some good years. But when he had a bad one, it was a beauty.

The Information Bizness

Tony Kubek, the shortstop-turned-broadcaster, credits Casey Stengel with inventing the advance scout. Stengel introduced the pioneer in a Baltimore hotel meeting room. The Yankees were going to face Connie Johnson, a black pitcher. Stengel had sent to Baltimore, in advance of the team, Rudy York, the former slugger for the Tigers. York was famous for his ability to read pitchers. . . .

From such a humble beginning (if it really was the beginning . . .) the advance scout has grown into an important institution.

—George Will, *Men at Work*

It is common for people to believe that something begins at the time that they first become aware of it; this is one of the limitations of oral history. I should hasten to add that I hold both Mr. Kubek and Mr. Will in high esteem, and am loath to offend either man, but the idea that advance scouting began in 1957 is so misguided as to be comical.

References to advance scouting in baseball history go back almost a hundred years, if not more, and are commonplace throughout the century. Christy Mathewson, in *Pitching in a Pinch* (1912; actually written by Jack Wheeler) blamed the defeat of the Giants in the 1911 World Series on poor advance scouting:

Baker, of the Athletics, is one of the most dangerous hitters I have ever faced, and we were not warned to look out for him before the 1911 world's series, either. Certain friends of the Giants gave us some "inside" information on the Athletics' hitters . . . but no one spread the Baker alarm.

Frank Baker hit two crucial home runs in the series, one off of Matty, to become "Home Run" Baker.

Babe Ruth's Own Book of Baseball (1928; actually written by Ford Frick) contains several references to what would now be called advance scouting. In 1929, when Howard Ehmke stayed behind to watch the Cubs play in Brooklyn, New York, and Philadelphia, what was he doing? Advance scouting.

I have a copy of a book-length series of reports filed by Wid Mathews, scout for the Dodgers, during the 1947 season. It contains pages and pages of stuff like this:

HEINTZELMAN, L.H.P. - Hits R. : The outfield played him over to right field. 3B. a shade back. Stands up in the batters box and guards the plate.

Suggest breaking stuff and low all the way.

Pitched a nice game against the Cardinals and beat them. Never comes down the middle with the pitch at any time. Even behind the hitter he is still a pitcher pitching to spots that he thinks that he can get you out. Not too much stuff, but had good control. Changes up, pitches in on the handles, tight, here and there. He certainly wants to beat you.

I don't know what you'd call it, other than advance scouting.

Advance scouts, in fact, probably predate coaches as a part of baseball. As I explained somewhere in this book, up until about 1925, managers were largely responsible for bringing young players to the team. The top managers (Mack, McGraw, Clark Griffith, Pat Moran, and others) used scouts to help do this. Those guys had a cadre of old buddies that hung around the team, retired players like Rudy York, not quite employees, but picking up a little extra money doing odd jobs.

Managers were besieged by reports of young ballplayers. When they had some reason to believe that maybe a kid could be a good one, the manager would sometimes send a scout out to watch him for a couple of days, and see what he thought. This practice goes back at least to the turn of the century. Those scouts were also used sometimes to gather information about new players coming into the league.

There is a related practice here, however, which ends (or seems to end) at about the same time Kubek thought advance scouting was beginning. Kubek tells another famous story—you've probably heard it—about the Yankees hiring a private detective to shadow Kubek and his roommate, Bobby Richardson. It was the shortest such report in history: Kubek and Richardson had milk shakes, and were in bed by 9:00.

When did teams begin using private detectives to make reports on their players? Probably sometime in the 1890s. From 1900 to 1940, the practice was quite common. These men were hired by the manager, and reported to the manager. Joe McCarthy, for example, used a private detective to keep track of his drinking men, from Hack Wilson to Vern Stephens. He was effective with it. When the man started to drink too much and stay out too late, McCarthy knew it was time to have a talk with him.

McGraw and McCarthy weren't ashamed of using detectives, and they weren't particularly secretive about it. The detective would hang out in the hotel bar or in other night spots favored by the ballplayers, and check his watch when players came and went. The players often or usually knew who the detective was. Sometimes the detective was assigned to shadow a player. Babe Ruth reportedly spent some seasons under almost constant surveillance.

By 1950 this practice had acquired a bad odor, and it appears to have been on the way out well before 1960. The private detective who trailed Kubek and Richardson almost certainly did not report to Stengel, but to someone in the front office. In its time, though, it was just part of the culture. Before World War II, every "good" hotel hired a hotel dick. His job was to walk the halls, chase away anybody who didn't belong there, tell people who were making too much noise to quiet down, and, perhaps most importantly, to prevent unmarried couples from using the hotel rooms.

Banks hired bank dicks; trains used detectives, much like hotel detectives, to supervise the behavior of people riding the trains. It was intended to protect the patrons of the train or the hotel from thieves or from obnoxious behavior. The practice assumed, when you stop to think about it, that private businesses may have a right to police the behavior of private citizens. After the war, the culture became uncomfortable with this idea.

Of course, private detectives make a living by keeping secrets, and I wouldn't be shocked if I were to learn that baseball teams sometimes hire private detectives to watch their players, even now. But if they do, they sure as hell don't report to the manager.

The Mother Lode

The Dodgers of Branch Rickey's era were an incredible organization, with a tremendous impact even today. They had two Triple-A teams, Montreal in the International League and St. Paul in the American Association, and they used Ft. Worth in the Texas League, although technically Double-A, almost in the same way as the other two teams.

There were sixteen major league teams then and twenty-four Triple-A teams, plus the Senators didn't have their farm system organized yet, and didn't have a Triple-A team. The Dodger farm system was so strong that if the Dodger team plane had crashed, the Dodgers could have put together a contending team from the players trapped at Triple-A.

Not *some* or *many*, but *most* of the dominant field managers in baseball since 1960 were products of that extraordinary St. Paul–Montreal–Brooklyn–Fort Worth axis.

•Tommy Lasorda, of course, played for Walt Alston at Montreal and in Brooklyn, and coached for him for years.

•Don Zimmer played for St. Paul in 1953 and 1954 and came to the majors under Walt Alston in 1954.

•Dick Williams played years for Fort Worth, and played for St. Paul and Montreal, although he missed Alston in the minors (he played for him in the majors).

•Sparky Anderson came from the Dodger farms in the 1950s.

•Gene Mauch played for Brooklyn, Montreal, and St. Paul in the 1940s.

•Preston Gomez, who managed three teams in the National League, was an Alston lieutenant.

•Clyde King, who managed the Giants, Braves, and Yankees, spent almost his entire playing career in the Dodger system and played for Alston at Montreal.

•Danny Ozark, who managed the Phillies' first divisional champion, played for Alston at St. Paul and coached for him for years.

•Larry Shepard, in the majors forever as a pitching coach and manager of the Pirates for two seasons, pitched for Alston in the low minors in 1946 and 1947.

•Roger Craig came out of the Dodger farm system in 1955.

•Gil Hodges, of course, became the master of the Miracle Mets.

•Frank Howard managed a couple of teams; Dodger system, 1959.

•Roy Hartsfield, first manager of Toronto, had been Alston's coach.

•Bobby Bragan and Cookie Lavagetto were Dodgers of the 1940s, long-term Dodgers.

All of those guys, when they managed, brought their coaches with them. Who do you think their coaches were? Dodger-system instruction has pervaded the major leagues.

Branch Rickey took instruction seriously. He had a strong belief in education, in keeping with his generation, a generation which gave America a marvelous educational system. Rickey thought there was a right way and a wrong way to do everything. He wanted intelligent people in his system, top to bottom. The minor leagues were baseball education.

Decade Snapshot: 1960s

Most Successful Managers: 1. Walt Alston
                                2. Ralph Houk
                                3. Red Schoendienst

Most Controversial Manager: Dick Williams

Others of Note: Hank Bauer
                      Alvin Dark
                      Johnny Keane
                      Sam Mele
                      Mayo Smith

Stunts: On August 10, 1960, the Cleveland Indians and Detroit Tigers traded managers, Jimmy Dykes for Joe Gordon, the only such trade in baseball history.

The trade had no impact on the performance of either team. Gordon was fired by Detroit after the season; Dykes managed Cleveland one more year.

The Chicago Cubs in 1961–1962 used not one manager, but a rotating "college of coaches," each running the team for a few days at a time. This experiment has not been repeated.

Typical Manager Was: Sheriff Andy Taylor. The three most successful managers of the 1960s, Walt Alston, Ralph Houk, and Red Schoendienst, were all "understated" managers. World Series winners Hank Bauer (1966) and Gil Hodges (1969) were similar— big, strong, bull-necked men who underreacted to everything.

Percentage of Playing Managers: Less than 1%

Most Second-Guessed Manager's Move: September 1964, Gene Mauch dropped Dennis Bennett from his starting rotation, electing to use (or being forced to use) Jim Bunning and Chris Short on short rest. Bunning, 19–4 in early September, lost his last four decisions, and the Phillies blew a 6½ game lead with two weeks to play.

Clever Moves: In 1968 Al Kaline was hurt a good part of the season. When he got healthy late in the year and started playing well, the Tigers had four outfielders.

Detroit's number-one shortstop that year was Ray Oyler. He was a great glove man, but he hit .135. Oyler was backed up by Dick Tracewski, who wasn't quite as sharp with the glove, but who hit .156. Behind him was Tom Matchick, who wasn't a real good defensive player, but who hit .203.

So the Tigers had four outfielders and no shortstop. In the closing days of the season, manager Mayo Smith took his best defensive outfielder, Mickey Stanley, and put him at shortstop. Stanley had never played shortstop before, even in the minors.

Whether this move was clever or lucky, no one will ever know, but it worked out. The Tigers won the World Series with Mickey Stanley playing shortstop.

Player Rebellions: Harry the Hat Walker became unpopular with his players in his last year in Pittsburgh, 1967, although it didn't quite reach the point of open rebellion.

Evolutions in Strategy: The stolen base, after forty years of decline, came back into the game with a vengeance.

Relief aces, typically working 75 games and 120 innings, became an important part of almost every team.

Bobby Bragan had a theory that the traditional batting order was wrongly constructed. Bragan argued that every spot in the batting order was worth eighteen extra at bats over the course of the season, which, of course, is mathematically true. If you moved Henry Aaron from the cleanup spot to the leadoff spot, then, Aaron would gain fifty-plus at bats over the course of the season—more than offsetting, in Bragan's view, the loss in RBI opportunities.

Bragan talked about this for years, but he wasn't brave enough to actually do it until 1966, when his Atlanta team had so many cleanup hitters that he had no real option but to bat one of them leadoff. He led off with Felipe Alou.

Alou had a great year, leading the league in hits (218) and hitting 31 homers. The Braves led the league in runs scored, but his pitchers didn't hold up their end, and Bragan was fired in August.

Evolution in the Role of the Manager: Toward the end of the decade, more college men began breaking into the profession. Looking at the managers of 1969, for example, you have Walt Alston (B.S., Miami of Ohio), Dave Bristol (B.S., Western Carolina), Alvin Dark (attended LSU), Preston Gomez (attended Belen College), Joe Gordon (attended University of Oregon), Don Gutteridge (attended Kansas State College in Pittsburg, Kansas), Gil Hodges (attended St. Joseph's College in Rensselaer, Indiana), Clyde King (attended North Carolina), and Joe Schultz (attended St. Louis University).

LEO DUROCHER AND JOCKO CONLAN

WALTER ALSTON IN A BOX

Year of Birth: 1911

Years Managed: 1954–1976

Record As a Manager: 2,040–1,613, .558

Managers for Whom He Played: Alston had only one major league at bat, for the 1936 Cardinals (Frankie Frisch), and had played only a few years in the minor leagues before he became a minor league manager.

Others by Whom He Was Influenced: Alston was a Branch Rickey protégé.

Characteristics As a Player: Alston was a good minor league power hitter. He had bad knees, which prevented him from playing third base and probably prevented him from having a major league career.

WHAT HE BROUGHT TO A BALL CLUB

Was He an Intense Manager or More of an Easy-to-Get-Along-With Type? Easy to get along with.

Was He More of an Emotional Leader or a Decision Maker? A decision maker.

Was He More of an Optimist or More of a Problem Solver? An optimist. Alston waited for six and a half years for Sandy Koufax to find home plate. I doubt that any other manager in baseball history would have, except perhaps Connie Mack.

HOW HE USED HIS PERSONNEL

Did He Favor a Set Lineup or a Rotation System? He preferred to use a regular lineup.

Did He Like to Platoon? He often platooned at one outfield position, occasionally at one infield spot as well. The Dodgers in much of Alston's era fairly waded in switch hitters. If you've got three or four switch hitters in the lineup, you don't need to platoon.

Did He Try to Solve His Problems with Proven Players or with Youngsters Who Still May Have Had Something to Learn? The Dodgers had a wonderful farm system in Alston's era. It was always the first option to use a kid from the farm system. The second option was to trade two or three kids from the farm system to get a proven player.

How Many Players Did He Make Regulars Who Had Not Been Regulars Before, and Who Were They? Almost all of the Dodgers' key players from 1960 to 1980 broke in under Alston. The key names include Drysdale, Koufax, Wills, Roseboro, Perranoski, Garvey, Lopes, Russell, Cey, Tommy and Willie Davis, and Frank Howard.

Did He Prefer to Go with Good Offensive Players or Did He Like the Glove Men? Glove men.

Did He Like an Offense Based on Power, Speed, or High Averages? Speed. Ten of Alston's twenty-three teams led the league in stolen bases, as opposed to three in home runs, and only one in batting average.

Did He Use the Entire Roster or Did He Keep People Sitting on the Bench? He found work for everybody.

Alston pulled every lever frequently. His teams regularly led the league in stolen bases. They also led in sacrifice bunts; he bunted more often than Gene Mauch. He used an above-average number of pinch hitters. He made frequent defensive changes in the late innings. He went to his bullpen early, often leading the league in saves and being comparatively low in complete games, even with Koufax and Drysdale on the team. For most of his career, he made liberal use of the intentional walk (although he changed suddenly in this regard in 1969). He used the hit and run often, probably as often as anyone in the league at that time. He loved switch hitters, giving him the platoon advantage at least in theory a huge percentage of the time.

Some of this strategy may have been useless, excessive or even counterproductive—but it accomplished two things:

1) It got the entire roster involved in the game, and

2) It gave the Dodgers, and particularly Alston, control of the flow of the action.

Did He Build His Bench Around Young Players Who Could Step into the Breach If Need Be, or Around

Veteran Role-Players Who Had Their Own Functions Within a Game? Fifty/fifty. He had old, one-time regulars to pinch-hit, young kids with good legs to pinch-run and play defense. In fact, you can pick almost any year of Alston's career, and that's exactly what you'll find on his bench—two old pinch hitters, two to four young guys to run and play defense. It was a Dodger formula.

GAME MANAGING AND USE OF STRATEGIES

Did He Go for the Big-Inning Offense, or Did He Like to Use the One-Run Strategies? He used one-run strategies a great deal, even when he had a good offense. He used one-run strategies as much or more than any other manager in baseball history.

Did He Pinch-Hit Much, and If So, When? Pinch-hitting data is spotty, but Alston's teams were normally above average in pinch hitters used, and led the league at least once (1968).

Alston almost always had at least one weak hitter in his everyday lineup, sometimes as many as three. He used a lot of good field/no hit players like John Roseboro and Nate Oliver, so he had more opportunities than a typical manager would to pinch-hit for everyday starters.

Was There Anything Unusual About His Lineup Selection? A Dodger fan once pointed out to me that Alston, whether by chance or choice, had extremely good defensive first basemen, but was tolerant of less than outstanding defensive players in the middle of the infield. Alston's first basemen were Gil Hodges, who was outstanding defensively as well as at bat, Ron Fairly, who was more notably successful with his glove than his bat, Wes Parker, who was mostly a glove man, and Steve Garvey, who was a good defensive player although his arm was pathetic.

By contrast, his shortstops included Pee Wee Reese, Maury Wills, and Bill Russell. Reese had been a good shortstop, but he continued to play the position until he was pushing forty. Wills did win two Gold Gloves (1961–1962), but that was an odd situation, where there were only three or four regular shortstops in the league, and you couldn't give a Gold Glove to Dick Groat. Wills certainly was regarded as more of an offensive shortstop than a glove man. And Bill Russell was put at shortstop in desperation, when Bobby Valentine got hurt and other people failed. Russell, a minor

league outfielder, learned to play the position at the major league level and was competent enough, but not Ozzie Smith.

Did He Use the Sac Bunt Often? A lot. The Dodgers led the National League in sacrifice bunts in 1959 (100), 1960 (102), 1962 (83), 1964 (120), and 1965 (103). No National League team has bunted 120 times in a season since the Dodgers did in 1964.

Did He Like to Use the Running Game? Loved it.

In What Circumstances Would He Issue an Intentional Walk? As I mentioned, Alston made liberal use of the intentional walk until 1969. He used intentional walks
1) To avoid a good hitter,
2) To get a platoon edge, and
3) To set up a double play.
The most notable of those three points is the first one: He used the IBB to avoid a good hitter.

I don't know if you're aware of this, but a high percentage of intentional walks are not given to good hitters, but to number eight hitters. Eighth-place hitters are often walked to force the pitcher to the plate in a key situation, thus (perhaps) forcing the other team to change pitchers. In 1967, for example, Adolfo Phillips was intentionally walked 29 times, leading the National League (in fact, it was the second-highest total in the major leagues during the 1960s), and that same year a light-hitting catcher named Jerry May was intentionally walked 19 times in 365 plate appearances. In 1960 Hal Smith, a catcher who hit .228 for St. Louis, was third in the National League in intentional walks, with 13 (in 369 plate appearances).

Alston, to his credit, apparently did not use this stupid strategy. Look at the seven intentional walks that he issued during the 1956 and 1959 World Series:

> Walked Enos Slaughter to pitch to Billy Martin
> Walked Slaughter to pitch to Billy Martin
> Walked Mantle to pitch to Yogi Berra
> Walked Berra to pitch to Moose Skowron
> Walked Berra to pitch to Moose Skowron
> Walked Kluszewski to pitch to Sherm Lollar
> Walked Kluszewski to pitch to Sherm Lollar

He was always getting rid of good, veteran hitters.

Tracer

On October 4, 1962, Tom Tresh singled with one out in the ninth inning of the first game of the World Series. San Francisco manager Alvin Dark brought in a relief pitcher, Stu Miller, and at the same time switched catchers, with Johnny Orsino replacing Ed Bailey. It was a tie game, and the pitcher was scheduled to bat second in the ninth inning. Dark wanted to clear the way to keep Stu Miller in the game if the tie held into extra innings.

Noteworthy? It was the first time that the double switch was used in a World Series game.

Miller allowed Tresh to score, and Orsino grounded into a double play.

In 1969, Alston suddenly turned against the intentional walk, and decided to stop using it. His 1967 team led the National League in Intentional Walks with 101, which is the eighth-highest total of all time. In 1968 he issued 79 IBB, third-highest in the National League.

But in 1969 his total dropped to 41, *lowest* in the National League. In 1971 his team issued only 25 intentional walks, fewest in the National League by far, and the lowest total in the National League since 1964. In 1972 he was near the bottom of the National League in IBB, and in 1973 he was last.

His 1974 Dodger team issued only 9 intentional walks. This is an eye-popping statistic. Every other National League team in 1974 issued at least 52 intentional walks. Alston's team was about one-sixth of the next-lowest total. The 9 intentional walks issued by the Dodgers that season is six fewer than the next-lowest total since IBB were first counted in 1955, whether in the National League or the American, even including the strike-shortened seasons of 1981 and 1993.

In 1975 the Dodgers issued only 20 intentional walks, which is the third-lowest total ever issued by a National League team in a full season.

Did He Hit and Run Very Often? Yes.

How Did He Change the Game? I mentioned this somewhere else, but Alston made a point of treating his players with respect, at least in public. Players came to expect this.

Alston played a key role in the integration drama, having been selected by Branch Rickey to manage the Nashua team to which Roy Campanella and Don Newcombe were assigned.

In the 1970s, Alston and the Dodgers led the movement away from the four-man and toward the five-man starting rotation.

HANDLING THE PITCHING STAFF

Did He Like Power Pitchers, or Did He Prefer to Go with the People Who Put the Ball in Play? Power pitchers, more so than any other manager in history. Alston's teams led the league in strikeouts twelve times, including every year between 1954 and 1963.

Did He Stay with His Starters, or Go to the Bullpen Quickly? Early in his career, Alston's teams normally led the league in saves (1954, '55, '56, '57, '59, '62). As happened to many other managers, Alston stayed the same (in the way he used the bullpen), and the league passed him by. By the end of his career, he went with his starters longer than most other managers.

Did He Use a Four-Man Rotation? Most of his career he did, yes. The Dodgers switched to a five-man rotation in midseason, 1971, and used a five-man rotation all year in 1972, making them among the first teams to make the switch. They then returned to the four-man rotation from 1973 through 1975, but went back to a five-man rotation in 1976, his last year.

Did He Use the Entire Staff, or Did He Try to Get Five or Six People to Do Most of the Work? He used the entire staff.

How Long Would He Stay with A Starting Pitcher Who Was Struggling? If it was Koufax or Drysdale, he'd let them go. Otherwise, he tended to go to the bullpen.

Was There Anything Unique About His Handling of His Pitchers? Alston managed Mike Marshall when Marshall pitched 106 games, 208 innings in 1974. That was pretty unique.

What Was His Strongest Point As a Manager? His balance, and the sense of strength that it imparted. It was impossible to throw Alston off his game plan.

If There Was No Professional Baseball, What Would He Have Done with His Life? He would have been a schoolteacher.

WALTER ALSTON'S
All-Star Team

		G	AB	R	H	2B	3B	HR	RBI	BB	SO	SB	Avg	SPct
C	Roy Campanella, '55	123	446	81	142	20	1	32	107	56	41	2	.318	.583
1B	Gil Hodges, 1954	154	579	106	176	23	5	42	130	74	84	3	.304	.575
2B	Jim Gilliam, 1954	146	607	107	171	28	8	13	52	76	30	8	.282	.418
3B	Ron Cey, 1975	158	566	72	160	29	2	25	101	78	74	5	.283	.473
SS	Maury Wills, 1962	165	695	130	208	13	10	6	48	51	57	104	.299	.373
LF	Frank Howard, 1962	141	493	80	146	25	6	31	119	39	108	1	.296	.580
CF	Duke Snider, 1954	149	584	120	199	39	10	40	130	84	96	6	.341	.647
RF	Tommy Davis, 1962	163	665	120	230	27	8	27	153	33	65	18	.346	.535

		G	IP	W–L	Pct.	H	SO	BB	ERA	GS	CG	ShO	Sv
SP	Sandy Koufax, 1965	43	336	26–8	.765	216	382	71	2.04	41	27	8	2
SP	Don Drysdale, 1962	43	314	25–9	.735	272	232	78	2.84	41	19	2	1
SP	Don Newcombe, 1956	38	268	27–7	.794	219	139	46	3.06	36	18	5	0
SP	A Messersmith, 1974	39	292	20–6	.769	227	221	94	2.59	39	13	3	0
RA	Ron Perranoski, 1963	69	129	16–3	.842	112	75	43	1.67	0	0	0	21

AL DARK'S
All-Star Team

		G	AB	R	H	2B	3B	HR	RBI	BB	SO	SB	Avg	SPct
C	Gene Tenace, 1975	158	498	83	127	17	0	29	87	106	127	7	.255	.464
1B	Orlando Cepeda, '61	152	585	105	182	28	4	46	142	39	91	12	.311	.609
2B	Chuck Hiller, 1962	161	602	94	166	22	2	3	48	55	49	5	.276	.334
3B	Jim Ray Hart, 1964	153	566	71	162	15	6	31	81	47	94	5	.286	.498
SS	Bert Campaneris, '74	134	527	77	153	18	8	2	41	47	81	34	.290	.366
LF	Willie McCovey, 1963	152	564	103	158	19	5	44	102	50	119	1	.280	.566
CF	Willie Mays, 1962	162	621	130	189	36	5	49	141	78	85	18	.304	.615
RF	Reggie Jackson, '74	148	506	90	146	25	1	29	93	86	105	25	.289	.514

		G	IP	W–L	Pct.	H	SO	BB	ERA	GS	CG	ShO	Sv
SP	Juan Marichal, 1963	41	321	25–8	.758	259	248	61	2.41	40	18	5	0
SP	Jack Sanford, 1962	39	265	24–7	.774	233	147	92	3.43	38	13	2	0
SP	Catfish Hunter, 1974	41	318	25–12	.676	268	143	46	2.49	41	23	6	0
SP	Luis Tiant, 1968	34	258	21–9	.700	152	264	73	1.60	32	19	9	0
RA	Stu Miller, 1961	63	122	14–5	.737	95	89	37	2.66	0	0	0	17

1962

It may be that no manager in baseball history was ever more second-guessed for losing a pennant race than was Walter Alston in 1962. The Dodgers were heavy favorites to win the pennant before the season opened, being picked by almost 50% of sportswriters surveyed in the spring by *The Sporting News.*

They played marvelous baseball for four-plus months. Maury Wills stole 104 bases, breaking Ty Cobb's record. Tommy Davis won the batting title at .346 and drove in 153 runs, the most of any major league player since 1950. Don Drysdale was 21–4 in early August, on pace for thirty wins. On August 10 they were 80–36, 5½ games in front.

John Leonard, writing about the team almost twenty years later in *The Ultimate Baseball Book,* wrote that "the Giants caught the Dodgers on the last day of the season and beat them, of course, in a three game play-off, because Alston wouldn't use Drysdale and Stan Williams couldn't get my grandmother out." Leonard described Alston as a "dour ex-farm boy."

One of Alston's coaches, Leo Durocher, was overheard in a restaurant, saying that the team would never have collapsed if he had been managing. A National League umpire, Chris Pelekoudas, said that Maury Wills had cost the Dodgers the pennant by his effort to break Cobb's record. Junior Gilliam, he said, had taken a lot of hittable fastballs to allow Wills to steal.

What strikes me about this, in retrospect, is that no one should have to apologize for losing to the 1962 San Francisco Giants. Who were those guys? Look at this team:

Willie Mays had one of his best seasons, driving in a career high 141 RBI.

Orlando Cepeda at first base hit .306 with 35 homers, 114 RBI.

Felipe Alou in right field hit .316 with 25 homers, 98 RBI.

Jim Davenport was at third base, hitting .297 with 14 homers and a shortstop's range.

Willie McCovey couldn't break the lineup because of Cepeda, but he hit .293 off the bench with a .593 slugging percentage, 20 homers in 229 at bats.

Juan Marichal was the third starter, 18–11 with a 3.35 ERA.

Jack Sanford won 16 straight games, and finished 24–7.

Billy O'Dell won 19 games.

Billy Pierce was old, but he went 16–6.

The catchers were **Tom Haller** and **Ed Bailey,** who had the disadvantage of both being left-handed hitters, so they couldn't platoon. On the other hand, they were probably the two best catchers in the National League at that time. Between them they hit 35 homers in 526 at bats, drove in 100 runs, drew 93 walks. And they were both good defensive catchers.

The third catcher was **Johnny Orsino,** who hardly ever got to play, but he was a good player, too.

Harvey Kuenn was in left field; he was the same age as Willie Mays (thirty-one) and hit for the same average (.304). He'd been the American League batting champion in 1959 (.353), and was a career .303 hitter, with 2,000-plus hits.

This is an amazing team. The fourth and fifth outfielders were **Willie McCovey** and **Matty Alou.** Matty was a career .307 hitter, hit .292 that year. The fifth and sixth starting pitchers were **Mike McCormick** and **Gaylord Perry.** Between them they won 448 major league games, and three Cy Young Awards. **Stu Miller** was the top reliever; he was one of the best relievers of his era. The number-two reliever was **Don Larsen.**

This team scored fifty runs more than the 1961

☞

Yankees. They scored more runs than any other major league team between 1950 and 1982. Their starting rotation was far better than the '61 Yanks, although their defense was nowhere near as good. **Manny Mota,** another career .300 hitter, was buried on the bench. **Bob Niemann** was the top right-handed pinch hitter; he was a career .295 hitter, with power. The team had four Hall of Famers (Mays, McCovey, Marichal, and Gaylord Perry), one other guy who probably should be in the Hall of Fame (Cepeda), and four other players who had what you might call near Hall of Fame careers (Harvey Kuenn, Billy Pierce, and the two Alous.) At least nine other players on the team were good major league players for a long time.

Their weaknesses? **Chuck Hiller** was at second base, and he couldn't really play second. On the other hand, he hit .276 and scored 94 runs. Shortstop **Jose Pagan** was just average. McCormick and Perry and Miller, although outstanding pitchers, didn't have outstanding years. The team didn't win the World Series.

The Dodgers got ahead, and then they lost. In the mind of the typical sportswriter, when you get ahead you're supposed to win. This is particularly true if you represent a media center, New York or Los Angeles, because to a large segment of the media, the story of any season is either going to be the story of how the Dodgers won, or the story of how the Dodgers lost.

The story in 1962 was about how the Dodgers lost. The 1962 Dodgers were also a great team, but the 1962 Dodgers didn't have five Hall of Famers. The Dodgers had two Hall of Famers (Koufax and Drysdale), and one other guy who might be a Hall of Famer (Wills). They had many outstanding players, but they had no third baseman, and the bench was full of guys like Tim Harkness and Larry Burright.

The Dodgers got them in '63. The Giants spent the rest of the decade 2 games out of first place. Their manager, Alvin Dark, got a reputation as a racist, and after 1962 the team never seemed to reach down deep enough to pull out a big game. But nobody should have to apologize for losing a split decision to Joe Louis or Muhammad Ali. And nobody should have to apologize for finishing one game behind the 1962 Giants.

Adcock and Adair

Bill Adair's real name was Marion, but, like John Wayne, he thought better of it. Adair was a minor league infielder who would have had a major league career had it not been for World War II. At Montgomery in 1940 he hit .329 with 20 homers and led the Southeastern League in runs scored and RBI. After a good season at Memphis in 1942 he went off to the war, and by the time the war was over he was too old to be a prospect.

As a minor league manager, Adair was almost phenomenally successful, laying claim to nine pennants in his first twelve seasons. As a rookie manager in 1949, Adair led Owensboro to the Kitty League championship with an 82–40 record, also hitting .356 and driving in 120 runs for that team. In the next few years he would win pennants or postseason series at Bluefield (with a record or 80–40), Eau Claire (77–44), El Dorado (79–39), Panama City (73–47), Valdosta (94–45), Augusta (98–56), and Charleston (89–62). It seemed as if he could take any collection of unknown players into almost any league, and win two-thirds of his games, but Charleston had an off year in 1959 (77–84), and, amazingly enough, Adair opened the 1960 season without a job.

He returned to the American Association in May 1960 as manager of Louisville, the Triple-A franchise of the Milwaukee Braves. He led them to a second-place finish, then won both rounds of the playoffs, his ninth championship in twelve years.

Adair was Henry Aaron's first minor league manager. Aaron wrote twenty years later that "a guy couldn't have asked to break in under a better manager than Bill Adair. He was from Montgomery, Alabama, and I think that because he was a Southerner he was even a little more understanding of the little black kid he had playing beside him. He was a lot more than a manager to me." Actually, Adair was born in Mobile, Alabama, as was Aaron.

Adair coached for the Braves in 1962, under Birdie Tebbetts, but went back to the minors when Birdie lost the job. He managed Triple-A franchises in various leagues over the next decade— Toronto in 1963, Denver in 1964, Atlanta in 1965, Richmond in 1966. All of these teams finished over .500, although none won the pennant.

In the winter of 1966–1967, Adair was reported to be a candidate for the managerial opening in Cleveland. This was old news; he had been a candidate for several positions by that time, and, as before, he didn't get the job. It went instead to Joe Adcock.

Adcock, like Adair, had spent many years in the Milwaukee Braves' organization. Both men could have used the same references—Henry Aaron, Birdie Tebbetts.

Joe Adcock at the end of 1966 was winding up a distinguished major league career. He hit 336 major league home runs, and he was a better hitter than that number would suggest. He reached the majors in Cincinnati two years after another outstanding first baseman, Ted Kluszewski, and had to battle for playing time for several seasons. He had at least six major injuries in his career, was recommitted to a platoon role for three seasons in midcareer by a manager with an overgrown stubborn streak, and he played almost his entire career in very poor home runs parks. He hit more home runs in road games than Mel Ott. Had his luck been as good as it was bad, he would have hit twice as many home runs as he did. In the nine years that Adcock was a teammate of Henry Aaron, Adcock homered 8% more often, per at bat, than did Henry Aaron.

But having said that, Cleveland's decision to hire Adcock, rather than Adair, is mind-boggling. Adcock had *no* managerial experience, not even a winter league team somewhere. Cleveland's general manager, Gabe Paul, had known Adcock for many years. He liked Adcock, and when Adcock was ready to retire, Gabe thought he was ready to manage.

Adcock was the strong, stable type of individual who commanded the respect of his teammates, and Paul no doubt saw him as being in the mold of Walt Alston. He was intelligent, he had worked hard to learn the game, he was well liked; what else was there? Alston, of course, was a schoolteacher who had spent ten years in the minor leagues learning how to manage.

Adcock knew what he thought and didn't hide it. In his relationships with his peers, Adcock's tendency to sound off when he was unhappy was kept in context; Adcock was a friendly, open, basically likable guy who would complain a bit when things didn't go his way. In the manager's chair, the trait affected people in an entirely different way: Adcock was never satisfied. Like Rogers Hornsby, with whom Adcock had quarreled as a player, Adcock expected his players to work as hard at the game as he himself had worked. "Joe loves to correct faults," said Leon Wagner, "and that left me out. I've been trying to find a flaw that Joe could work on so that I could play more."

Popular with the press as a player, Adcock was touchy when criticized, and was perceived by both the press and his players as a grump. He lasted only one year as a manager, winning 75 games with a team that was well over .500 in 1965–1966, under Birdie Tebbetts, and well over .500 in 1968, under Alvin Dark.

This is a story about the manifest unfairness of the world. Adair, who was cheated out of his chance to play in the majors by World War II, was cheated out of his chance to manage because he lacked connections in major league circles. Adcock was a major leaguer, known to the men who ran the teams. Adair was a bush leaguer. In a baseball world that was often run by the whims of half-educated little czars, this was a defining distinction.

Adair eventually did get to manage in the majors, 10 games as an interim manager with the Chicago White Sox in 1970, and thus, in an alphabetical register of all the men who have managed in the majors, the first two men listed are Bill Adair and Joe Adcock. Adair continued to work in baseball for more than twenty years. He coached with Atlanta in 1967, with the White Sox in 1970. In the early 1990s he was still listed as a scout for the Philadelphia Phillies. He would be in his eighties now, and I assume he has retired.

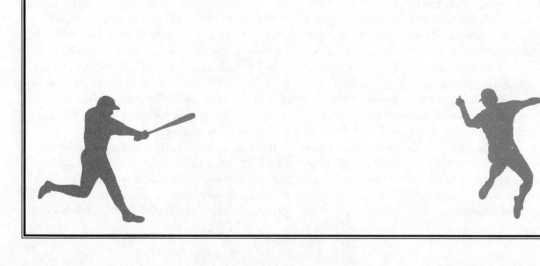

The Darrtown Farmer

By the method I established to measure these things, Walt Alston was the most successful manager of the 1960s, the third most successful manager of the 1950s, the sixth most successful manager of the 1970s, and the fifth most successful manager of all time.

It never got him a whole lot of respect.

Walter Emmons Alston was born in Venice, Ohio, in 1911. In grade school he was given the nickname "Smokey" after Smokey Joe Wood. Smokey started at Miami of Ohio in 1929, but quit after his freshman year to get married. The depression hit, and no good job could be found. The local Methodist church offered to help financially if he'd go back to college, so Alston returned to Miami, earned his degree, and wound up as the captain of both the college basketball team and the baseball team.

The day after he graduated in 1935, Alston was standing on a ladder helping his dad paint the house when a man drove up asking for him. The man was Frank Rickey, Branch Rickey's brother. He offered Walter no bonus, but a chance to play in the Cardinal farm system for $125 a month.

He was in the majors in less than two years. Alston hit .326 in the East Dixie league in 1935, fielding well enough at third base to earn a transfer across the infield, and hit exactly the same (.326) with a league-leading 35 homers in the Middle Atlantic League in 1936. The Cardinals had a rookie Hall of Famer at first base, Johnny Mize, but decided to call Alston up for a look. He pitched a lot of batting practice, and on the last day Mize was ejected after the other first baseman had been used as a pinch hitter. Alston got to play a few innings and bat once; he struck out. At the time, no one would have suspected that would be his only major league at bat.

Everything went wrong for him, as a player. Apart from being locked behind Mize, Alston was buried in the immense Cardinal system. Because he taught school in the off-season, he was unable to attend spring training. He began to have trouble with his knees. Although he had many good years left in the minors, by 1939 he was twenty-seven years old, and finished as a prospect.

In the spring of 1940 the Portsmouth team, for which Alston was laboring, started slowly. Mel Jones, Dodger road secretary, asked Alston if he had ever considered managing. Alston jumped at the chance; he knew, he said later, that managing was his only chance to stay in the game. He almost played himself out of his destiny. He managed in the Middle Atlantic League from 1940 to 1942 without much success, but as a hitter he led the league all three times in home runs and twice in RBI. When the war began to create shortages of talent, Alston was sent back to the International League—as a player. He didn't hit in the International League and was released early in the 1944 season.

Depressed, Alston went back to Ohio and tried to reconcile himself to life as a small-town school teacher. Alston's release, however, was noted by Branch Rickey, who was then building up the Dodger farm system. Rickey tried to call Alston, but the Alston farm had no phone. Rickey left messages with people all around town. Finally a grocer from Darrtown drove out to his farm to tell him, "Walt, there's this fellow named Rickey that's been trying to get in touch with you for about a week."

In 1946, when Rickey was ready for his great experiment, Alston was one of two managers chosen to lead the teams with black players. Managing in the New England League, Alston had Roy Campanella and Don Newcombe. "There was one guy, a manager, who used to ride me from the bench," recalled Alston in *The Man in the Dugout*, "asking me if I'm sleeping with

Campanella. One day I met him outside the clubhouse between games of a doubleheader and I stopped him.

"'Listen,' I said, 'You've been wondering if I sleep with Campanella. Well, the answer is no. The Dodgers go first class, we all get to sleep in separate rooms. But if you gave me my choice of sleeping with Campanella or with you, I'd sure as hell take Campanella.'" The team won the playoffs, his first championship as a manager, and Alston in 1947 moved up to the Western League. He won the playoffs there, too, and in 1948—Rickey was as methodical as he was creative—reached the Triple-A level, managing St. Paul.

The Dodgers at this time had two Triple-A teams, St. Paul in the American Association, and Montreal in the International League. Still laboring in perfect obscurity, Alston managed St. Paul for two years, Montreal for four. The Dodgers won the pennant in 1953 under Charlie Dressen, while Alston, with Montreal, won the Triple-A World Series. When Dressen shot his managerial career in the kneecap (see "Dressen and Stengel," page 185), Alston did not apply for the major league job. "I figured," Alston told Tom Meany in *The Artful Dodgers*, "that I had been in the organization long enough for them to know all about me and that if they felt I was qualified, they could get in touch."

To the absolute astonishment of the New York press, they did.

On November 23, 1953, Alston received a message from Buzzie Bavasi, instructing him to come to New York right away. The next day a New York paper had a front-page picture of a hand-lettered sign in a store window. The sign said "Walt Who?"

Alston was given a one-year contract, wrote Tom Meany, with no time off for good behavior. If it was surprising that Alston got the job, it was incredible that he kept it. With Casey Stengel managing the Yankees and Leo Durocher the Giants, reporters thought that a colorful personality was a necessity for a New York manager.

O'Malley's thinking was exactly the opposite: that it was time for a *professional* manager.

The newspapers treated him with barely disguised contempt. "If Alston doesn't win the pennant and beat the Yankees in the World Series," wrote John Lardner, "there's a clause in his contract which requires him to refund his entire salary and report immediately to the nearest Federal penitentiary."

Although most of the 1954 Dodgers accepted Alston's leadership because they had played for him in the minor leagues, Alston had serious conflicts with Jackie Robinson. Serving as his own third base coach exposed him to more criticism not only for taking on a tough job, but simply because he was *there* for the fans when they wanted to object to his strategy. Early in the season Duke Snider hit a ball into the left field stands and back out, the umpire ruling it a double. Jackie raced out of the dugout to argue—but Alston, coaching at third, didn't join in. Talking about the incident after the game, Alston referred to it as "Jackie's temper tantrum."

"The team might be moving somewhere," Robinson replied, "if Alston had not been standing at third base like a wooden Indian." Alston and Robinson had words several times. Alston's strategy came under fire. On May 1, 1954, Alston ordered Ted Kluszewski intentionally walked with the bases empty and the score tied in the bottom of the ninth. It didn't cost them the game, but led to predictable second-guessing.

Worse than arguing with your superstar is not winning, and the Dodgers didn't win, either. The Dodgers, winners of 105 games in 1953, came out in 1954 in a gang slump. Roy Campanella, MVP in two of the previous three seasons, had a hand injury, and hit .207. The 1954 Dodgers finished 5 games behind the Giants, their poorest season in six years.

Alston, against all odds, was given another chance. In the spring of 1955, Jackie Robinson found himself without a position; Alston's plans for him were vague. Robinson talked to the reporters, asking if any of them knew what Alston had in mind for him. Alston, thinking that Robinson was using the media to show him up, flew into a rage. There was a team meeting; Alston denounced "players who went to the press with questions about the team." He claimed that those players were cowards and detrimental to the club's spirit. Robinson erupted, saying that if Alston would talk to the players they wouldn't need to try to ask the reporters those things. The two headed for each other; Gil Hodges stepped between them.

On May 5, 1955, Don Newcombe refused to pitch batting practice. Alston told him to turn in his uniform. The two met the next day and made peace.

Charlie Dressen, like most managers of his generation, would light into a player in public. If a player pulled a rock on the bases, for example, Dressen would scream at him across the field in full view of the fans and the press. Alston never did that, and in time his players came to appreciate the courtesy.

Jackie Robinson came around. "Maybe it wasn't fair to keep comparing Walt to Dressen," he told a reporter. "He had certain faults in my eyes. Of course, it could have been my eyesight."

The Dodgers won 98 games in 1955, taking the pennant by 13½ games. The Dodgers and Yankees met in the World Series; they had met five other times in the previous fifteen years, and the Yankees had won every time. The Yankees won the first game. The Yankees won the second game.

You could have gotten bets down, at that moment, at a billion to one. The Dodgers swept the three games in Ebbets Field, however, and so the series went seven. Alston decided to start Johnny Podres. Eleven pitchers started games for the Dodgers that summer, and Podres was the only one with a losing record, but the Dodgers held a 2–0 lead going to the bottom of the sixth.

Alston made a defensive switch, putting Sandy Amoros into left field. Amoros made a game-saving catch, Podres finished the shutout, and the Dodgers, for the first time ever, were champions of the world.

For the first time in his life, Walter Alston was a star.

The Dodgers won the National again in 1956, but lost the series. They had an off season in 1957 as the team grew old and was disrupted by the impending move to LA. By 1958 the need to rebuild was obvious, but the Dodgers, perhaps wanting to keep marquee names for their new fans, stayed with the veterans. Roy Campanella was paralyzed in a car wreck before the season.

Charlie Dressen returned to the Dodgers as a coach, leading to speculation that he would soon be back in the manager's chair. The Dodgers endured their worst year in memory, finishing seventh. The pressure on Alston grew more intense; Alston signed another one-year contract.

And in 1959, with a team that had every right to finish fifth, Walter Alston won the World Championship. Maury Wills and Larry Sherry came up in midseason; Sherry was the immediate star. In the World Series Sherry won two games and saved two, Charlie Neal played great, and a journeyman outfielder named Chuck Essegian hit two pinch-hit home runs. They were, in my opinion, the weakest World Championship team of all time.

Managing in the largest city in the nation and then in the glitziest, Alston began to earn a grudging respect. He never backed away from an unhappy player. He was very deliberate. John Roseboro described him as "slow-witted," and Roseboro thought the world of him. For reporters, he had an extensive list of noncommittal responses . . . "It could be," "It's too early to tell," "Let's wait until we have a few more workouts." He never gushed about a rookie, or even a superstar. To Alston, hyping a player and criticizing him in public were two sides of the same coin and could only cause a manager problems. He never took credit for a win. He never blamed a player or an umpire for a defeat.

Alston didn't drink or play cards. He was, however, a big, powerful man, and tough. Once, managing St. Paul, he offered to take on a group of players who were cutting up on a train one at a time. In the spring of 1961 he caught Sandy Koufax and Larry Sherry out past curfew, and followed them to their room. When they locked him out, he splintered the door with his fist. In 1963, confronted by a busload of complaining players, Alston stopped the bus and told the entire team to stop bitching or step outside.

He was an amazing pool player, a better pool player than Leo Durocher, who virtually lived in pool halls. In college, Alston had a job racking balls at a pool hall. A carpenter, he built a pool room onto his house, and had his own table. He had a quiet wit and was a notorious practical joker. When the gargantuan Frank Howard came up, Alston told Pee Wee Reese, according to *The Man in the Dugout*, "Hey, I'd sure like to try some more of those kids out. Why don't you get on that Howard and agitate him a little bit and see if I can't get him back into the lineup." Howard had been nursing a minor injury. Then he told Howard, "Frank, goddamn, you don't have to take that from them." Next thing you know, Howard had Reese in the air like a rag doll, instructing him on how to treat a 260-pound rookie.

"Fun?" asked Reese. "I think you're trying to get me killed."

In the off seasons he went back to Darrtown and spent three months with his many hobbies. He made furniture and cabinets. He was a photographer and had a darkroom built in his house. He kept horses and of course hunted and fished. He was, in short, awfully sane, able to deal with pressure better than almost anybody who ever managed.

And it was a good thing, because he had to.

Leo Durocher was a Los Angeles resident, a celebrity, and widely expected to become the manager of the expansion Los Angeles Angels in 1961. He didn't, and in December 1960, Durocher alleged that he had been blackballed from baseball. Walter O'Malley offered Durocher a job as Alston's coach. Alston, to create the illusion of control, was flown to LA to make the announcement.

Alston and Durocher were diametric opposites. Walter bought his suits off the rack; Durocher owned six handmade tuxedoes. The two men hated one another. Durocher, even more than Dressen had been, was a superstar coach, and was seen by the public as a manager-in-waiting.

"We have to face facts," said Alston. "Leo is a colorful figure and a bold and amusing talker. I would be a damn fool if I tried to outdo him."

"Walt's idea is to carry over a beef until the next day, when heads are clear," said Durocher. "As a manager, I never did this."

The Dodgers of 1962 were a great team, locked in a breakneck race with another team just as good. In early August, during a long winning streak, a Dodger player missed a sign, and another ran into his own bunt for an automatic out. Durocher, in the dugout, said that fines should be levied. Alston turned on Durocher angrily and informed him that levying fines was the manager's job, and that he didn't believe in it. There followed a heated exchange.

A newspaper criticized Alston, saying he should not have berated his coach in front of the players. "You're pretty sensitive about Durocher's feeling," Alston told the reporter, "but you don't seem to care much about mine. What about the times he has shown *me* up in front of the players?"

The Dodgers were 4 games ahead with 7 to play, but 1962 was the revenge of 1959; by 1962 the Dodgers had a great team, but everything broke wrong at the end. The loss was devastating to the organization. The players locked themselves in the dressing room; Alston said that he doubted that any team in history was ever so shaken by a defeat. O'Malley and general manager Buzzy Bavasi were nowhere to be found. Alston walked calmly to the San Francisco clubhouse to congratulate Alvin Dark and then answered questions politely for an hour.

Durocher criticized Alston in the newspapers, blaming him for the collapse of the team. Charlie Dressen was hired back as a special assistant to the general manager; he let it be known that he wasn't too old, at sixty-four, to manage. The only thing certain was that Alston and Durocher couldn't *both* return—and yet, they did.

Alston had never been allowed to pick his own coaches. "We don't want bridge partners or cronies for assistants," explained O'Malley. "It is our job to get the most knowledgeable men, and it is the manager's place to solicit their advice and accept it or reject it. I admit that, in Durocher's case, he sometimes gives advice that isn't solicited, but that's Leo. We knew the nature of the man when we hired him."

In June 1963, with the team in Chicago, a newspaper reported that several players had complained to the front office about Alston's management. Buzzy Bavasi flew to Chicago to speak privately to the players. "If the Dodgers lose today," said Cub head coach Bob Kennedy, "Durocher will be manager tommorrow."

And the Dodgers won the World Championship once again.

Three times in his career, in 1955, 1959, and 1963, Walt Alston's managerial tenure had been put in extreme jeopardy—and three times, his team had responded with a World Championship. Alston had survived an incredible year of speculation and second-guessing.

After the third championship, O'Malley was committed to Alston, one year at a time forever if Walter chose. He signed a blank contract every fall, and O'Malley would fill in the figure. Baseball in 1963 entered a pitcher's era, and that was perfect for Alston. In a big-hitting era, with a slugging team, Alston's strategy tended to get in the way of his team; he would wind up ordering Duke Snider to bunt. In a pitching-dominated game, Walter's bunting, base stealing, and hitting and running helped the Dodgers scratch out a run or two. Koufax came into his own; he was half a pennant by himself. The Dodgers won the World Championship again in 1965, making Alston the first NL manager since John McGraw to win four World Championships. They won the National League in 1966.

Koufax retired after the 1966 season. Maury Wills was traded to Pittsburgh. There was a long coda to Alston's career; he managed another ten years after that, years during which little of any interest occured. He won one more National League championship, in 1974. On September 29, 1976, forty years to the day after his one major league at bat, Alston announced his resignation. He had won 2,040 major league games, more than any major league manager except Connie Mack, John McGraw, Sparky Anderson, Bucky Harris, or Joe McCarthy.

Alston returned to Darrtown. In theory he remained with the Dodgers as an advisor, went to the winter meetings with the group at least. He pursued all of his hobbies and added a new one, riding trail bikes. He built a lot of furniture. In April 1983 he suffered a heart attack, and on October 1, 1984, died at the age of seventy-two.

(Note: this an edited version of an article first printed in the 1989 edition of *The Baseball Book*. The original article was twice as long, but does contain much of the same material.)

Decade Snapshot: 1970s

Most Successful Managers: 1. Sparky Anderson
2. Earl Weaver
3. Billy Martin

Most Controversial Manager: Billy Martin

Others of Note: Danny Murtaugh
Danny Ozark
Chuck Tanner
Bill Virdon
Dick Williams
Tommy Lasorda

Stunts: 1977, Ted Turner took over as manager of the Atlanta Braves for one game.

In 1973, Billy Martin's Detroit Tigers team fell into a team batting slump. Martin, feeling that his players were trying too hard, decided to shake everybody up. He put the names of his starting players in a hat and wrote down the lineup in the order they came out. Norm Cash, a thirty-eight-year-old first baseman, became the leadoff man, and Eddie Brinkman, a career .224 hitter with no power, got the cleanup spot.

Sure enough, Norm Cash drew a leadoff walk late in the game, went to second on a ground ball, and came home on a two-out single by Eddie Brinkman. The Tigers won the game, 2–1.

In late 1973, Dick Williams (Oakland) was in a pennant race with a collection of weak-hitting second basemen. Since it was September and he had lots of players around, he started pinch-hitting for his second baseman, whoever it was, every time he came up, then putting another second baseman in the field. He did this the last three weeks of the season, using four second basemen every game. The A's held on to win the pennant.

Typical Manager Was: A pepperpot. Barney Fife staged a rebellion and took over the courthouse.

Whereas the top managers of the 1960s were the strong, silent types, the top managers of the 1970s (Anderson, Weaver, and Martin) were all little noisy guys in the Leo Durocher tradition. There was an article in *Sport* magazine in the mid-1950s on "Baseball's Best Bench Jockeys." Almost all of the people cited by the magazine as the most annoying bench players in baseball, including Chuck Tanner, Dick Williams, Billy Martin, Don Zimmer, and Gene Mauch, went on to become 1970s managers.

The top two managers of the 1970s, Sparky Anderson and Earl Weaver, were both minor league players (Sparky had one year in the majors) who quit playing early, managed in the minors, and made the majors (as managers) before they were forty. Joe McCarthy had done that, and Gene Mauch, but until 1970 it was uncommon.

Percentage of Playing Managers: 2%

Most Second-Guessed Manager's Moves:
1. Don Zimmer's decision to keep using Butch Hobson at third base in late 1978. Hobson's sore elbow impaired his throwing, and he became the first major league regular in sixty years to field below .900. The Red Sox, 14½ games ahead of the Yankees on July 18, eventually lost to the Yankees on Bucky Dent's home run.
2. 1977, Whitey Herzog of Kansas City ran through five pitchers in the eighth and ninth innings of the deciding game of the American League playoffs. The Royals, leading 3–1 after seven innings, lost 5–3.
3. 1977, Danny Ozark of Philadelphia failed to put in a defensive replacement for Greg Luzinski in the fourth game of the National League Championship Series, leading 5–3 going into the ninth. With two out in the ninth inning, Manny Mota hit a drive that bounced off of Luzinski's glove as he slammed into the wall, setting up a Dodger rally.

Clever Moves: In August 1978, Tommy Lasorda rescued the forty-year-old Vic Davalillo from the Mexican League. With two out in the fourth game of the NLCS, the Dodgers trailing 5–3 with nobody on, Lasorda sent Davalillo up to pinch-hit for his catcher. Davalillo beat out a drag bunt, sparking a three-run rally.

Player Rebellions: St. Louis, 1977, vs. Vern Rapp; Washington, 1971, vs. Ted Williams
A group of Ted Williams's players, led by Bernie Allen, formed what they called the Underminer's Club, dedicated to bringing about the firing of Williams.
After winning the World Series in 1972 and 1973, Dick Williams resigned as manager of the Oakland A's due to conflicts with the team owner. The veteran ball club did not at first accept the leadership of his replacement, Alvin Dark, and sometimes ignored directions from the bench. Team captain Sal Bando, going up the tunnel after a frustrating loss, shouted that Alvin Dark couldn't manage to a bleeping meat market.
To the credit of both Dark and the ball club, they pulled themselves together and won their third consecutive World Championship.

Evolutions in Strategy: The designated hitter rule took about 40% of the bunts and nearly 50% of the pinch-hitting opportunities out of the American League game, and elicited howls from purists which can still be heard echoing in the canyons of the West.

Evolution in the Role of the Manager: I don't have any data on the subject, but the number of coaches used increased dramatically throughout the 1960s and 1970s, while the specific roles assigned to the coaches became much better defined. In 1960, many major league teams did not employ a batting coach. The specific roles assigned to coaches—first base coach, third base coach, hitting coach, pitching coach, strength and conditioning coach, bench coach—certainly did not exist in 1960, and certainly did in 1980.

In 1970, many managers were in a precarious positon vis-à-vis the issue of the player's union. The "manager," by definition, is a member of management, yet unlike management he wears a uniform, and is on the field with the players. Some of the older managers of 1970, like Leo Durocher, got themselves into trouble with their teams by aligning themselves with management positions in the ongoing labor/management dispute. By 1975 they had mostly learned to stay out of it.

Sparky Anderson

SPARKY ANDERSON IN A BOX

Year of Birth: 1934

Years Managed: 1970–1995

Record As a Manager: 2,194–1,834, .545

Managers for Whom He Played: The only manager Sparky played for in the major leagues was Eddie Sawyer, the Phillies manager in 1959. Those for whom he played in the minor leagues include George Scherger, Tommy Holmes, Greg Mulleavy, Clay Bryant, and Mel McGaha. His first act as a Reds manager was to name Scherger, his first minor league manager, as a coach.

Others by Whom He Was Influenced: Sparky was close to Lefty Phillips, California manager from 1969–1971, and regarded Lefty as a mentor. Lefty was fifteen years older than Anderson and signed Sparky to his first minor-league contract.

As a youth, Sparky was a batboy for Rod Dedeaux, legendary coach at USC, who sent dozens of players to the major leagues. Also, since he was in the Dodger system from 1954 to 1958, he was essentially in the hands of Walt Alston, although he never got to play for the Dodgers in the regular season.

Characteristics As a Player: Anderson was a good minor league second baseman. His glovework was terrific, he was durable, and he was a decent singles hitter. He was a good bunter, and he wasn't slow. He played hard. He was second in the MVP voting in the International League in 1958.

He played only one year in the majors and then disappeared, but it has never been clear to me that the Phillies made a good decision to dump him after the 1959 season. He hit .218, but given another year, he might have hit .250 or .260. With his defense and peripheral skills, that would have been enough to make him a useful player. Anderson in 1959 was about the same as Glenn Beckert in 1965.

WHAT HE BROUGHT TO A BALL CLUB

Was He an Intense Manager or More of an Easy-to-

Get-Along-With Type? Early in his career, very intense. When he managed in the minors, in fact, his intensity bordered on self-destructiveness. With the Reds from 1970–1975, he was still an intense manager. As time passed, he grew more detached.

Was He More of an Emotional Leader or a Decision Maker? I would say more of an emotional leader.

Was He More of an Optimist or More of a Problem Solver? He was an optimist. He always believed that a player would get straightened out as long as it was reasonable to believe that.

In 1969–1970, Bobby Tolan was a great player. He missed 1971 due to a ruptured Achilles tendon suffered in an off-season basketball game, and was just pretty good in 1972. In 1973 everyone expected him to be back at full strength, but he hit .206. Anderson kept playing him all year, expecting him to get his bat going eventually.

In 1995 Mike Moore had an ERA of 7.53 and was giving up an opposition batting average .323, but Anderson just kept running him out there every fifth day, expecting him to turn it around.

HOW HE USED HIS PERSONNEL

Did He Favor a Set Lineup or a Rotation System? Basically, a set lineup.

Did He Like to Platoon? He platooned some. In 1970–1971, he platooned Bernie Carbo and Hal McRae in left field. In 1973 he platooned Denis Menke and Dan Driessen at third base. In 1980 he platooned Richie Hebner and John Wockenfuss at first base. At the end of his career, he made a platoon player out of Lou Whitaker. He never platooned a lot.

In 1995, his last year as a manager, Sparky started 97% right-handed hitters against left-handed pitchers, but also used 70% right-handed hitters against right-handed pitchers.

Did He Try to Solve His Problems with Proven Players or with Youngsters Who Still May Have Had Something to Learn? In the first decade of his career, Anderson was always eager to find young players of ability and get them into the lineup.

But late in his career, Anderson became almost entirely

dependent on established players, even when they weren't any good. From 1991 to 1994, with his team in a steep decline, he used hardly any everyday players who were under the age of thirty.

How Many Players Did He Make Regulars Who Had Not Been Regulars Before, and Who Were They? The list from the first ten years would include Ken Griffey, George Foster, Dave Concepcion, Dan Driessen, Cesar Geronimo, Kirk Gibson, and others. The list of players he brought along since 1990 is basically just Travis Fryman. In between, he had Cecil Fielder, Matt Nokes, Milt Cuyler, and a few others.

The turning point, in this regard, was Howard Johnson. Although Johnson was a player who had ability and who always gave a good effort, Sparky for some reason decided that he just didn't want him. From then on, he never seemed eager to make room for a young player. One could attribute this to the talent available to him, but I don't see that. In 1995 he had Franklin Stubbs, a thirty-four-year-old first baseman with a career average of .232, and he had Tony Clark, a twenty-four-year-old prospect of similar skills. He decided to use Franklin Stubbs.

Did He Prefer to Go with Good Offensive Players or Did He Like the Glove Men? Early in his career, he showed some fondness for glove men. He made a regular out of Cesar Geronimo, a strong defensive player with a short bat, and used Darrel Chaney in a support role for six years, although Chaney struggled to break the Mendoza Line. Tony Perez was a great hitter but a poor third baseman. Anderson moved him across the infield to first base, reducing his exposure in the field.

But late in his career, he moved strongly in the other direction. His early '90s Detroit Tigers teams were good hitting teams but were composed largely of designated hitters.

Did He Like an Offense Based on Power, Speed, or High Averages? Power, if you have to choose—power and walks. The 1975–1976 Reds were probably the most diverse, broad-based offense in the history of baseball. The 1976 Reds led the league in batting average (.280), in home runs (141), in doubles (271), triples (63), stolen bases (210), walks (681), and fewest grounded into double play (103). In most of these areas, they led the league by wide margins.

Only one team in the league was within 145 of them in runs scored, and that team was still more than 75 runs behind.

This is historically unique. The 1961 Yankees were below average in almost everything, as a team, except home runs and runs scored. The 1927 Yankees led in home runs and in batting average, but not in doubles, and certainly not in stolen bases. Even Joe McCarthy's great teams didn't lead the league in *everything*.

The World Champion Tigers of 1984 were similar, although less extreme: They had a good, broad-based offense.

The Tigers of 1993–1994 also had outstanding offenses, but all they did was draw walks and hit homers. In sum, nine of Anderson's teams led the league in home runs, four in stolen bases, two in batting average. Ten of his teams led the league in walks drawn, more than in any other category.

Did He Use the Entire Roster or Did He Keep People Sitting on the Bench? He had well-defined roles for the players on the bench.

Did He Build His Bench Around Young Players Who Could Step into the Breach If Need Be, or Around Veteran Role-Players Who Had Their Own Functions Within a Game? A good mix.

GAME MANAGING AND USE OF STRATEGIES

Did He Go for the Big-Inning Offense, or Did He Like to Use the One-Run Strategies? The big inning. His teams were below average in sacrifice bunts almost all of his career. His early Reds teams were high in stolen bases but ran at comparatively little cost, since their stolen base percentages were unusually good.

Did He Pinch-Hit Much, and If So, When? Almost all of his teams were near the league average in the number of pinch hitters used.

In his early years in Cincinnati, before Dave Concepcion took control of the shortstop job, he often pinch-hit for his shortstops (Woodward, Chaney, and Concepcion). Otherwise, in Cincinnati, 95% of his pinch hitting was for pitchers.

When he first came to the American League he seemed a little lost as to how to use his bench, but within a few years he developed a practice of rotating three or four players through one position where he didn't have a star, so as to get some playing time for his bench players. He also used the

DH rule the same way. The 1984 Tigers, for example, used seventeen players in the designated hitter slot.

Was There Anything Unusual About His Lineup Selection? It was standard. This reflects available talent, rather than choice, but of the 29 catchers in baseball history who had hit 30 home runs by the time Sparky retired in 1995, ten had done so for Sparky. He had gotten 30-homer seasons from Bench, Parrish, Nokes, and Tettleton.

Did He Use the Sac Bunt Often? No.

Did He Like to Use the Running Game? His Reds teams led the league in stolen bases in 1972, '73, '75 and '76. In Detroit, Ron LeFlore left after Sparky's first partial season there, and he never had a base-stealing team with the Tigers.

As I suspect most of you know, stolen base percentages are markedly higher on artificial turf than they are on grass—thus, Anderson adapted to the parks he was given in moving away from the running offense.

In What Circumstances Would He Issue an Intentional Walk? Like most of the Dodger-system managers from the 1950s, Anderson was very loose with the intentional walk. The 1993 Detroit Tigers issued 92 intentional walks, almost an American League record (the 1980 Mariners had issued 94). The 1989 Tigers also issued 91 IBB, the 1973 Reds issued 90, the 1991 and 1992 Tigers issued 88, the 1990 Tigers issued 86 . . . the list of American League teams issuing the most intentional walks since the DH rule was adopted is almost entirely composed of Sparky's teams.

In the first game of the 1975 World Series, Sparky intentionally walked Rick Burleson to pitch to Cecil Cooper. It worked, too; Cooper hit a fly to center, and the runner from third was thrown out trying to score.

These intentional walks never made any sense to me, but that's the way the Dodgers were taught to play the game in the mid-1950s, and that's the way all of those guys managed.

Did He Hit and Run Very Often? In the years since we have good data on the number of hit-and-run attempts, since STATS Inc. began keeping records in the late 1980s, Sparky's teams used the hit and run about as little as any team in baseball. Of course, they were low-average, power offenses, so that could be misleading. I think Anderson certainly used the hit and run more often with the Reds, when he had more speed, but

1) even there, he did not have a "bat control" offense. The Reds had power hitters who struck out a lot. Are you going to hit and run with George Foster? I don't think so.

2) I remember that Joe Morgan never liked to have the runner in motion when he was hitting. He thought it was distracting.

3) Nine of Sparky Anderson's teams led the league in strikeouts by hitters. You wouldn't think that would suggest a hit-and-run manager.

How Did He Change the Game? I don't know. I suspect that he did, but I can't say how.

HANDLING THE PITCHING STAFF

Did He Like Power Pitchers, or Did He Prefer to Go with the People Who Put the Ball in Play? No Sparky Anderson team ever led the league in (pitcher's) strikeouts. He did have some good power pitchers (Don Gullett, Tom Seaver briefly, Jack Morris), but he always rounded out the staff with guys who threw strikes and relied on the defense.

Did He Stay with His Starters, or Go to the Bullpen Quickly? In Cincinnati Sparky got the nickname "Captain Hook" because he would go to his bullpen so quickly. His teams led the league in saves in 1970, '72, '74, '75, and '76.

As happened to Alston and Durocher, however, he stayed about where he was, and the league passed him by in this respect. By the late 1980s, he was one of the *slowest* hooks in the majors. As the younger managers came into the game, they went to the bullpen earlier and earlier.

Did He Use a Four-Man Rotation? He tried to in 1970–1971, but he had so many injuries in his pitching staff that he was never able to establish the rotation that he wanted. The 1972 Reds won 95 games although they didn't have any pitcher with more than 15 wins, and the 1975–1976 Reds won 108 and 102 games although they, too, didn't have anyone with more than 15 wins.

In those years he switched back and forth between a four-man and five-man rotation, never getting either one entirely established. In this area—and perhaps *only* in this area—he

was more successful with the Tigers than he was with the Reds, keeping Jack Morris in essentially a four-and-a-half man rotation for many years.

Did He Use the Entire Staff, or Did He Try to Get Five or Six People to Do Most of the Work? He used everybody.

How Long Would He Stay with a Starting Pitcher Who Was Struggling? Early in his career, not long. Late in his career, a long time.

Was There Anything Unique About His Handling of His Pitchers? I said somewhere in this book that the Herman Franks strategy of using his relief ace *only* in save situations was universally adopted within a few years of its inception in 1978. Well, actually, this is not true. Sparky was the exception. Anderson never did adopt the practice of using his closer only in save situations, for which reason Mike Henneman, his closer from mid-1987 to late 1995, never had more than 24 saves.

Sparky did not have success with his pitching staffs equal to what he had with his everyday lineups. Seven of his teams led the league in runs scored; only two led in fewest runs allowed.

In the 1970s, when his pitching coach was Larry Shephard, Anderson's pitching staff had constant injuries, for which reason he had no stars. Very rarely, in those years, did he have a pitcher make it through two seasons without a major injury—yet his pitching was never bad. The Reds' team ERAs in those years were good. As soon as one pitcher went down, another would step in, they threw strikes, they played great defense, and they got the job done one way or the other.

With the Tigers, and with Roger Craig as his pitching coach, he had more luck at keeping the rotation together, and his overall results continued to be good through the mid-1980s.

Toward the end of his career, and with Billy Muffett as his pitching coach, Sparky seemed to give up on the idea of fixing his defense or his pitching staff. No Sparky Anderson team ever led the league in hits allowed or walks allowed until the 1990s. In 1990 they led in walks allowed; in '91, '92, and '95, in hits allowed. In part this was the fault of the defense, which was composed of thirty-two-year-old castoffs from other teams, and in part it may be attributed to a shortage of talent coming from the farm system—but Sparky dealt with those conditions magnificently as far as the offense was concerned. The Tigers had John Smoltz; they traded him. They had a young pitcher named John DeSilva, but they just wouldn't let him pitch. His teams continued to score runs in bunches, even though he didn't have a lot of talent coming along. But his pitching and defense were falling apart, and he didn't seem to have any idea how to fix them.

What Was His Strongest Point As a Manager? Loyalty and caring.

Leo Durocher, Billy Martin, Earl Weaver, and Sparky Anderson were all scrappy middle infielders. All were intense managers, not easygoing.

Durocher was intense, and Durocher had remarkable ability to get the most out of his players, but Durocher's problem was that most people thought he was a scoundrel. Those that didn't, you had to wonder about their judgment. Durocher used people. His success was in that he was good at it.

Billy Martin was a little different; he was more of a jerk, as opposed to a creep. Billy was more direct than Leo, less devious in his manipulation, and for this reason, he could wear out his welcome even more rapidly. Both men were clever, charming, and almost entirely amoral.

Earl Weaver was as intense as either of them, but Weaver was cold, distant. Weaver did not believe in making an emotional commitment to his players. Dick Williams could be put in the group, although Williams wasn't a major league middle infielder. Williams was intense, and Williams was a strong disciplinarian, but Williams would get grouchy.

One thing I think most people don't know about Dick Williams was that about half of Williams's players were quite fond of him, thought he treated them well. He wasn't a *bad* person; he wasn't obscenely self-centered, like Durocher and Martin, and he knew the meaning of the term "loyalty." But his attitude turned sour under stress, and he didn't know how to get beyond it.

Sparky was as intense as any of these men, and he was as much a disciplinarian as Williams. But he had something else: He cared about the people who played for him.

Obviously, Sparky was blessed with more talent than were most other managers. He took over a team with two all-time

greats (Rose and Bench), and two other players who were among the twenty-five best ever at their positions (Perez and Concepcion). Within two years, the Reds had traded for Joe Morgan and George Foster. He had almost as much talent in Detroit.

But you know, sometimes teams have talent and *don't* win. Look at the Twins in the 1960s—Harmon Killebrew, Bob Allison, Zoilo Versalles, Rod Carew, Tony Oliva, Camilo Pascual, Mudcat Grant, Jim Kaat, two more outstanding rookies in 1962 (Bernie Allen and Rich Rollins), and one more in 1963 (Jimmie Hall). That team had talent, too, but what did they do with it? Not much.

"Baseball is a simple game," Sparky once said. "If you have good players, and if you keep them in the right frame of mind, then the manager is a success. The players make the manager; it's never the other way." Sparky's combination of intensity and loyalty kept his team "in the right frame of mind" throughout a turbulent era. Many of his players got better in his hands. Dave Concepcion, when he came up, looked like any other twenty-two-year-old shortstop. George Foster didn't look like a player his first couple of years. Sparky believed in them, communicated to them that he expected them to work hard, and he expected them to get better.

Don't get me wrong; Sparky had a doghouse, too. Sparky was often accused of playing favorites. If he decided a young player couldn't play, it could be nearly impossible for that player to change Sparky's mind.

But when a player started going bad, Leo Durocher thought it was time to try somebody else. When one of his regulars started to struggle, Sparky thought it was his responsibility to figure out why and to figure out what could be done about it.

If There Was No Professional Baseball, What Would He Have Done with His Life? According to his own description, he'd have been a house painter.

SPARKY ANDERSON'S
All-Star Team

		G	AB	R	H	2B	3B	HR	RBI	BB	SO	SB	Avg	SPct
C	Johnny Bench, 1970	158	605	97	177	35	4	45	148	54	102	5	.293	.587
1B	Cecil Fielder, 1990	159	573	104	159	25	1	51	132	90	182	0	.277	.592
2B	Joe Morgan, 1976	141	472	113	151	30	5	27	111	114	41	60	.320	.576
3B	Tony Perez, 1970	158	587	107	186	28	6	40	129	83	134	8	.317	.589
SS	Alan Trammell, 1987	151	597	109	205	34	3	28	105	60	47	21	.343	.551
LF	George Foster, 1977	158	615	124	197	31	2	52	149	61	107	6	.320	.631
CF	Bobby Tolan, 1970	152	589	112	186	34	6	16	80	62	84	57	.316	.475
RF	Pete Rose, 1970	159	649	120	205	37	9	15	52	73	64	12	.316	.470

		G	IP	W–L	Pct.	H	SO	BB	ERA	GS	CG	ShO	Sv
SP	Jim Merritt, 1970	35	234	20–12	.625	248	136	53	4.08	35	12	1	0
SP	Gary Nolan, 1970	37	251	18–7	.720	226	181	96	3.26	37	4	2	0
SP	Jack Billingham, '73	40	293	19–10	.655	257	155	95	3.04	40	16	7	0
SP	Jack Morris, 1986	35	267	21–8	.724	229	223	82	3.27	35	15	6	0
RA	G. Hernandez, '84	80	140	9–3	.750	96	112	36	1.92	0	0	0	32

PHOENIX

In the early 1980s, just after Pete Vuckovich had won the American League Cy Young Award for Milwaukee, somebody said something to him about Paul Richards's wizardry with pitchers. "Yeah," said Vuckovich. "He's the guy who made a reliever out of me, and a starter out of Goose Gossage."

Richards, out of the managerial racket for years, had come back to manage the Chicago White Sox in 1976. Richards by then was a sour sixty-seven-year-old, out of tune with the players. He didn't understand how anything he did would be perceived. One time, during a rain delay, he went up to the chow line in the press box to have something to eat—an ordinary enough thing to do, but the press jumped all over him about it, for the simple reason that the other managers at that time wouldn't have done it.

Among the innovations which ruined his season was, as Vuckovich remembered, moving Goose Gossage to a starting role. Gossage had 26 saves and a 1.84 ERA in 1975, striking out 130 batters in 143 innings of relief. He was a big, strong guy, with the best fastball in the American League. In Paul Richards's time, relievers

EARL WEAVER IN A BOX

Year of Birth: 1930

Years Managed: 1968–1982, 1985–1986

Record As a Manager: 1,480–1,060, .583

Managers for Whom He Played: Weaver never played in the major leagues. Minor league managers for whom he played included Hal Contini, George Kissell, and Dick Bartell.

Others by Whom He Was Influenced: As a youth, he was influenced by Leo Durocher and Billy Southworth. As a young manager, he sought advice from Barney Lutz and George Staller, who were other managers in the Baltimore system.

Characteristics As a Player: A hustling second baseman, usually hit around .260 with no power and not much speed, good defense. He walked 100 times a year, and would have been a major league shortstop if he had an arm.

WHAT HE BROUGHT TO A BALL CLUB

Was He an Intense Manager or More of an Easy-to-Get-Along-With Type? Very intense.

Was He More of an Emotional Leader or a Decision Maker? A decision maker.

Was He More of an Optimist or More of a Problem Solver? Neither, exactly, but Weaver would give his established players every possible opportunity to work their way through a slump.

HOW HE USED HIS PERSONNEL

Did He Favor a Set Lineup or a Rotation System? His first team, the 1969–1971 Orioles, had essentially a settled lineup. In later years he used a bewildering rotation system which involved not only platooning at four or more positions, but also three-man and four-man platoons, offensive and defensive specialists, and curveball/fastball platoons.

Did He Like to Platoon? Boy, did he.

Did He Try to Solve His Problems with Proven Players or with Youngsters Who Still May Have Had Something to Learn? What he liked to do was take two or three veteran minor leaguers, each of whom was one tool or two tools short of a whole package, and try to find some way to use them that would hide their weaknesses and make maximum use of what they did well. He had great success with guys like Pat Kelly, Larry Harlow, Andres Mora, Terry Crowley, John Lowenstein, and Benny Ayala, who for the most part would never have gotten more than a cup of coffee with other teams.

He also did a good job of developing some young players, and he did look several years down the road, but only when he had a player with ability. He brought along Bobby Grich, Doug DeCinces, Don Baylor, and Eddie Murray. In 1982 he was the only man in the world who thought that Cal Ripken could be a major league shortstop.

How Many Players Did He Make Regulars Who Had Not Been Regulars Before, and Who Were They? The five best were the five I mentioned before—Grich, DeCinces, Baylor, Murray, and Ripken. He broke in many other rookies or first-time regulars, including Al Bumbry, Rich Dauer, Rick Dempsey, Elrod Hendricks, and Merv Rettenmund.

In the mid-1970s, at the beginning of the free agent era, the Orioles refused or were unable to pay top-flight salaries, for which reason the Orioles from 1975 to 1978 were hemorrhaging talent, losing many big-name free agents. Earl Weaver just kept reloading, filling in the blanks with the best available talent. His team, rather than fading, kept winning 90 to 100 games every year. Although that team wasn't as good as the 1969–1971 Orioles, this is the most impressive part of his record, when he kept the team in contention for several years with constantly changing and often unproven players.

Did He Prefer to Go with Good Offensive Players or Did He Like the Glove Men? Most of his players were clearly one or the other. There were many defensive specialists who played regularly for him for years, including Dempsey, Belanger, Larry Harlow, Etchebarren, Hendricks, Dauer, Paul Blair, and the aging Brooks Robinson. His teams always played outstanding defense. He also found room for

were veteran junk-ballers and pitchers with second-line stuff. Richards thought, naturally enough for a man of his generation, that a pitcher with Gossage's stuff would be more valuable in the starting rotation than he would in relief. Incidentally, this forced Pete Vuckovich, a rookie who had been a starter in the minors, to the bullpen. Gossage, in the middle of a string of eye-popping seasons as a reliever, went 9–17.

some players who were slow and *didn't* play great defense, including Boog Powell, Ken Singleton, and a boatload of pinch-hitting outfielders.

What Weaver *never* used were the guys who didn't do anything specific, but looked good in the uniform, the .260 hitters with 10 to 15 homers, a little speed and and so-so defense.

Did He Like an Offense Based on Power, Speed, or High Averages? Power. Oddly enough, only one Earl Weaver team led the league in home runs—but most of his teams were near the league home run lead.

Did He Use the Entire Roster or Did He Keep People Sitting on the Bench? He used everybody. Probably more than any other manager in history, Weaver had carefully defined roles for every player on his roster—not because he cared about the players, but because he cared about the games. It was important to Weaver to have a player matched up in his mind with every possible game situation. If I'm two runs down in the eighth inning and the other guy switches from a left-handed starter to a right-handed middle reliever and back to a left-hander, will I have a pinch hitter to hit for my second baseman? If the pinch hitter hits a three-run homer, will I have somebody who can go in at second base?

To Weaver, it was all but impossible to get every situation covered with just 25 men on the roster. It wasn't a question of having 25 players and only 18 of them playing; if he'd had 30 men, he'd have started pinch-hitting in the fourth inning, and he'd have used all 30.

Did Hhe Build His Bench Around Young Players Who Could Step into the Breach If Need Be, or Around Veteran Role-Players Who Had Their Own Functions Within a Game? Veteran role players.

GAME MANAGING AND USE OF STRATEGIES

Did He Go for the Big-Inning Offense, or Did He Like to Use the One-Run Strategies? He is the most outspoken advocate of the big inning in baseball history.

Did He Pinch-Hit Much, and If So, When? As you no doubt know, in baseball there is a considerable difference between what left fielders and first basemen hit, and what middle infielders hit. This difference is such that players who might not hit enough to be major league left fielders or first basemen, particularly if their defense is poor, will still hit more than some middle infielders.

Weaver exploited that differential by putting three or even four defensive specialists in the lineup, then pinch hitting for them with outfielders who were considered rejects by other teams. Of course, managers have done this for a hundred years, but Weaver did more of it than any other manager of his time, maybe more of it than any other manager of all time. Many managers simply put their eight best hitters in the field, or structure their roster in such a way that they have few opportunities to pinch-hit for the frontline players.

When the designated hitter rule was adopted in 1973, and Weaver no longer had to pinch-hit for his pitchers, he realized immediately that this in effect had expanded his roster, giving him more maneuverability with the bench. With the passage of time, the effect of the DH rule has been to allow managers to carry more pitchers, thus making more pitching changes. Weaver didn't do that. Weaver used nine pitchers, which meant that he had room for eight starters and eight bench players, one of whom would be the DH. He needed to have two catchers, and he liked to have a third catcher who could actually hit. He needed a defensive backup for the outfield and a defensive backup for the infield. That left room for four extra outfielders and first basemen, all of whom could reach the seats. He used them to pinch-hit for the guys, like Mark Belanger, Rick Dempsey, Rich Dauer, and Larry Harlow, whose job it was to catch everything and keep the starting pitcher in the game for the first seven innings.

Was There Anything Unusual About His Lineup Selection? His use of multiple defensive specialists was unusual.

Did He Use the Sac Bunt Often? He hated the bunt. In his early years he bunted 60 to 85 times a season, normal totals. As he got more settled into the job he began to bunt less and less. By the end of his career he was down to about 30 bunts a season.

Did He Like to Use the Running Game? He did not.

In What Circumstances Would He Issue an Intentional Walk? Whenever there was a blizzard in hell.

Frank Lucchesi

Anger, said Albert Einstein, is man's natural reaction to being lied to. Lenny Randle was making $80,000 a year, and on the verge of losing his job. In his third year as a regular Randle's average skidded to .224. He wasn't the kind of defensive player who could get by with that, and the Rangers had a hot prospect who was set to take his job.

Randle was an intense, highly motivated player. He went to Venezuela that winter, worked hard on his defense. He reported early to spring training and asked for a meeting with the manager. "If I'm not going to play here," he said, "trade me."

The manager was Frank Lucchesi. He was only fifty at the time this happened, but he looked sixty, and if you'd had to manage the kind of teams he had, you'd look old, too. Lucchesi assured Randle that the second base job was still up for grabs, notwithstanding what the newspapers had to say.

Randle, according to Lucchesi, was by far the hardest worker in camp that spring. The rookie, Bump Wills, reported a week late—but when the spring schedule began, Wills was in the lineup almost every game.

Randle was furious. He

Weaver's teams were usually last in the league in IBB, or very close to it. One of the most memorable games in Kansas City Royals history was a game in which George Brett came to the plate representing the winning run, runners on first and second, two out, Tim Stoddard on the mound. Weaver ordered Stoddard to walk Brett, unconventional strategy with the open base being third. It didn't work; Amos Otis worked Stoddard for a game-winning walk.

Did He Hit and Run Very Often? No.

How Did He Change the Game? Weaver was an outspoken advocate of the big inning, and an outspoken opponent of the bunt. His willingness to challenge orthodoxy on this subject, combined with his success, helped push the sacrifice bunt toward extinction.

Weaver was somewhat out of step with the baseball of the 1970s, which featured new stolen base records every year, but might be considered one of the architects of the baseball of the 1990s, which involves a lot of crowding the plate and trying to line the outside pitch into the opposite-field seats.

HANDLING THE PITCHING STAFF

Did He Like Power Pitchers, or Did He Prefer to Go with the People Who Put the Ball in Play? He liked veteran pitchers who threw strikes. None of his teams ever led the league in strikeouts or in walks allowed. Four of his teams led the league in fewest walks allowed.

Did He Stay with His Starters, or Go to the Bullpen Quickly? He stayed with his starters. In 1979, for example, he used only 167 relievers in 159 games, the fewest of any team in baseball. The other American League teams averaged 219.

Did He Use a Four-Man Rotation? He did, all his career. He was also an outspoken advocate of the four-man rotation, arguing that "it's easier to find four guys who can pitch than it is five." In this area, history ignored him.

Did He Use the Entire Staff, or Did He Try to Get Five or Six People to Do Most of the Work? He always had a small staff and tried to get as many innings as he reasonably could out of his front four.

How Long Would He Stay with a Starting Pitcher Who Was Struggling? A long time. In 1976 Mike Cuellar complained about not being given a chance to work through his troubles. Weaver said, "I gave Mike Cuellar more chances than I gave my first wife."

Was There Anything Unique About His Handling of His Pitchers? The most amazing thing about Earl Weaver's record is his phenomenal ability to keep his starting pitchers healthy, while pitching them 260 innings a year.

I have always believed that *most* major league pitchers would be outstanding, if they could stay healthy. *Most* pitchers, if they could stay in the rotation for two or three years without breaking down, would figure out some way to get the job done.

But most of the time, most pitchers are either a) inexperienced, b) injured, or c) working their way back from an injury. What was *most* unusual about Earl Weaver was his ability to keep his starting pitchers on the mound and in the groove year after year.

And I honestly have no idea how he did this. I've read his books; nothing in there explains it. I can understand part of it. His defense was outstanding; that reduced the pressure on his starting pitchers. I know that Weaver believed in simplifying the work. He didn't want pitchers out there trying to throw five or six pitches; he wanted them to find their best stuff and use it. That, no doubt, was a help.

I know that he was religious about not pushing his pitchers to do too much early in the season, and that, no doubt, was part of the explanation. I know the meaning of the term "Baltimore draft." For many years the Baltimore Orioles were well stocked with pitchers who had good fastballs and absolutely refused to throw them to you. But having said all of that, I cannot explain why Weaver was able to get 270 good innings a year out of Mike Cuellar, when all of his previous managers had found that he would break down after about 180.

What Were His Strongest Points As a Manager? Intelligence, intensity, patience. Understanding of how an offense works.

There is a cliché in sports about "playing within yourself," which means doing the things that God has given you the ability to do, rather than trying to make plays that just aren't there to be made. Weaver managed within himself. Weaver

went back to the clubhouse one day, packed his bags, and said he was heading out. Gaylord Perry and Mike Hargrove talked him out of leaving, but Randle made no effort to hide his anger. "If I had wanted to be a reserve," he said, "I would have joined the National Guard. I've been lied to and I've been misled. There was never an attempt made to let me win the second base job. It was decided last December, or earlier, who would play second base. Why couldn't these people be truthful?"

Lucchesi chose his words a little less carefully. "I wish they'd have let him go," Lucchesi told the reporters. "If he thinks I'm going to beg him to stay on this team, he's wrong. I'm sick and tired of punks making $80,000 a year moaning and groaning about their situation."

Surveys show that 99.6% of all employees resent being called "punks" in the newspaper, and in this respect, Randle was clearly in the majority. Lucchesi's subsequent apology did something to reduce the tension. On March 26, 1977, Lucchesi was on the field in street clothes as the players began batting practice. Randle approached Lucchesi, and the men began a quiet conversation. There was no evidence of anger.

Suddenly, Randle lashed out with his fists, striking Lucchesi in the face again, and again, and again, then kicking him as he went down. It wasn't a fight; it was an assault. Lucchesi was rushed to the hospital. He had a concussion, a triple fracture of his cheekbone, a split lip, and a back injury. The cheekbone required surgery.

Randle's reputation, in many ways, survived the assault better than Lucchesi's did. Randle was suspended and fined and faced civil action, but he hit .304 that summer, for the New York Mets. He played regularly for several more seasons, not bad for a marginal talent with a major scandal in midcareer. Lucchesi had pretty well proven that he couldn't manage a major league team anyway, and this incident confirmed that impression.

Each generation of sportswriters has its own list of examples of how far sports have fallen. For five years, this incident was part of the repertoire. The assault, unprecedented in sports history, was a shock to all who knew Lenny Randle. He was well liked. He was polite,

believed that if you understood and you respected the limitations of the athlete, then you could focus on the things that the man *could* do.

Do you all know the story of Steve Dalkowski? Steve Dalkowski is the original Nuke LaLoosh, the most famous wild, hard-throwing left-hander in the history of minor league baseball. No one knows for sure how fast his fastball was, but it was certainly over a hundred. At Kingsport in 1957, Dalkowski struck out 121 men in 62 innings. Unfortunately, he walked 129, and threw 39 wild pitches. He gave up only 22 hits—but allowed 68 runs. He allowed three hits but almost 19 walks per nine innings pitched.

He did this kind of stuff for years. At Stockton in 1960 he struck out 262 men in 170 innings, but also walked 262, finishing 7–15. This part of the story is well known, but what fewer people know is that Earl Weaver eventually managed Steve Dalkowski, at Elmira in 1964. Weaver, at his own instigation, gave all his players IQ tests. He discovered that Dalkowski's IQ was about 60. When he saw that, Weaver realized immediately what the problem was: Dalkowski simply could not process the information that he was being given. The Orioles had coaches out there trying to teach him to throw a change, trying to teach him pick-off plays, trying to teach him how to hold the runners, how to pitch off the stretch. "The more you talked to Dalkowski," Weaver said, "the more confused he became."

So Weaver simplified the routine, stripped down what Dalkowski was being taught. He told him to forget about the curve and changeup, and to throw the two pitches he had, a fastball and a slider. And he told him, again and again and again, to throw strikes. Don't worry about anything else; just throw strikes.

And it worked. Dalkowski, who had a career record of 28–69 in the minor leagues before that season, walked only 62 men in 108 innings for Weaver, struck out 141 and finished 8–4 with a 2.83 ERA. In his last 57 innings at Elmira, according to Weaver, he struck out 110 batters, walked 11, and had an ERA of 0.16.

The next year in spring training, some coach took him aside to work on his curve, Dalkowski hurt his arm, and his career was over, but the story illustrates something essential about Earl Weaver as a manager. Weaver found out what Dalkowski *could* do.

See, managers spend a lot of time talking about what some player *can't* do. Weaver wasn't interested in what a player *couldn't* do. He was interested in what the player *could* do. If he can't hit a breaking pitch, you don't play him against Bert Blyleven. If he can't run, you pinch-run for him—but you don't let that stop you from developing what the player *can* do. It's the things that players *can* do that will win games for you.

If There Was No Professional Baseball, What Would He Have Done with His Life? He'd have been a bouncer at a midget bar.

articulate, approachable. He had tried his hand at standup comedy. His version of the incident was that he lost control when Lucchesi again called him a punk. Lucchesi denied this, and either way, there's no justification for a twenty-eight-year-old athlete beating up an old man.

EARL WEAVER'S
All-Star Team

		G	AB	R	H	2B	3B	HR	RBI	BB	SO	SB	Avg	SPct
C	Earl Williams, 1973	132	459	58	109	18	1	22	83	66	107	0	.237	.425
1B	Eddie Murray, 1982	151	550	87	174	30	1	32	110	70	82	7	.316	.549
2B	Bobby Grich, 1974	160	582	92	153	29	6	19	92	90	117	17	.263	.431
3B	Brooks Robinson,'70	158	608	84	168	31	4	18	94	53	53	1	.276	.429
SS	Cal Ripken, 1985	161	642	116	181	32	5	26	110	67	68	2	.282	.469
LF	Ken Singleton, 1977	152	536	90	176	24	0	24	99	107	101	0	.328	.507
CF	Al Bumbry, 1980	160	645	118	205	29	9	9	53	78	75	44	.318	.433
RF	Frank Robinson, '69	149	539	111	166	19	5	32	100	88	62	9	.308	.540

		G	IP	W–L	Pct.	H	SO	BB	ERA	GS	CG	ShO	Sv
SP	Mike Cuellar, 1969	39	291	23–11	.676	213	182	79	2.38	39	18	5	0
SP	Dave McNally, 1970	40	296	24–9	.727	277	185	78	3.22	40	16	1	0
SP	Jim Palmer, 1975	39	323	23–11	.676	253	193	80	2.09	38	25	10	1
SP	Steve Stone, 1980	37	251	25–7	.781	224	149	101	3.23	37	5	1	0
RA	Eddie Watt, 1969	56	71	5–2	.714	49	48	26	1.65	0	0	0	16

DICK WILLIAMS'S
All-Star Team

		G	AB	R	H	2B	3B	HR	RBI	BB	SO	SB	Avg	SPct
C	Gary Carter, 1980	154	549	76	145	25	5	29	101	58	78	3	.264	.486
1B	Alvin Davis, 1987	157	580	86	171	37	2	29	100	72	84	0	.295	.516
2B	Alan Wiggins, 1984	158	596	106	154	19	7	3	34	75	57	70	.258	.329
3B	Sal Bando, 1973	162	592	87	170	32	3	29	98	82	84	4	.280	.498
SS	Rico Petrocelli, 1969	154	535	92	159	32	2	40	97	98	68	3	.297	.589
LF	Carl Yastrzemski, '67	161	579	112	189	31	4	44	121	91	69	10	.326	.622
CF	Andre Dawson, 1980	151	577	86	178	41	7	17	87	44	69	34	.308	.492
RF	Reggie Jackson, '73	151	539	99	158	26	2	32	117	76	111	22	.293	.531

		G	IP	W–L	Pct.	H	SO	BB	ERA	GS	CG	ShO	Sv
SP	Jim Lonborg, 1967	39	273	22–9	.710	228	246	83	3.16	39	15	2	0
SP	Vida Blue, 1971	39	312	24–8	.750	209	301	88	1.82	39	24	8	0
SP	Catfish Hunter, 1972	38	295	21–7	.750	200	191	70	2.04	37	16	5	0
SP	Ken Holtzman, 1973	40	297	21–13	.618	275	157	66	2.97	40	16	4	0
RA	Rollie Fingers, 1973	62	127	7–8	.467	107	110	39	1.91	2	0	0	22

The Highway Man

I haven't counted, but I'm fairly sure that more major league managers were born in St. Louis than in any other city. Dave Garcia was born in St. Louis in 1920, as was Dick Sisler. Hank Bauer was born in St. Louis in 1922. Red Schoendienst was born in a small town just outside St. Louis in 1923, and Yogi Berra was born in St. Louis in 1925.

Vernon Rapp was born in St. Louis in 1928; Dick Williams was born there in 1929, and Earl Weaver was born in St. Louis in 1930. Whitey Herzog was born in a small town just south of St. Louis in 1931.

What do we learn from the managerial experience of Vernon Rapp? Out of this distinguished line of managers, none came to a major league opportunity with better credentials than Vern Rapp. Rapp was a catcher, like Yogi Berra and Joe Garagiola. Well, not *too much* like them. He started well, hitting .315 with 89 RBI in the Ohio State League in 1946, but as he moved up the line, he stopped hitting and started to think about managing.

In 1955 he was playing for Charleston in the American Association, for Danny Murtaugh. Charleston had a miserable team, and Murtaugh was fired in July, with a record of 31–64. Rapp moved into the hot seat, but had no better luck, going 19–40 the rest of the way.

He was a player/coach for several years after that and began his managerial career in earnest in the early 1960s. From 1965 to 1968 he managed in the Cardinal system, with great success, and in 1969 joined the Cincinnati Reds, at Indianapolis. Managers do not announce that they have applied for a job and not gotten it, but rumors were that Rapp almost had the Cincinnati Reds' managerial assignment in 1970, the job that went instead to Sparky Anderson. Rapp had managed in the Cardinal system with Sparky, but above him. Rapp, anyway, returned to Indianapolis.

His teams often finished first but lost the playoff. He finished first but lost the playoff at Tulsa in 1965, did the same at Arkansas in 1966 and again in 1968, finished first but lost the playoff with Indianapolis in 1971 and again in 1974.

In the winter of 1975 Rapp thought he had landed a job as a coach for the Reds, under Sparky. The job went to Russ Nixon instead. Crushed, Rapp told his family he would give himself one more year to get to the majors. If he didn't make it, he'd call off the dogs and go home.

He took a job as manager of the Denver Bears, the Triple-A franchise of the Montreal Expos. The Bears won their division by 13½ games, and crushed Omaha in the playoffs. *The Sporting News* named him the 1976 Minor League Manager of the Year, officially christening him the top managerial candidate in the minors.

He was flooded with major league offers. Two teams wanted him to be a major league coach. He accepted one job, from the Blue Jays, before his hometown team, the Cardinals, called about a job as a manager. The Giants called; they wanted to talk to him about managing, too, and then a third team, after he had already accepted the job with the Cardinals. After thirty years, Vern Rapp was going home to manage the Cardinals.

Rapp had strong ideas about what he wanted to do. As Dick Williams had done in Boston ten years earlier, he came on like a house afire. "Shave!" he told his players. "Lose some weight! Practice that rundown play! Get a haircut! Bunt! Tote that barge! Lift that bale! Get to bed by midnight, 1 AM after a night game!" This is a paraphrase, not a direct quote. My point is that none of this is new. Sparky Anderson and Dick Williams were among the major league managers in the mid-1970s who successfully enforced rules not much different from those propounded by Rapp. He prohibited long hair, mustaches, blue jeans, and drinking in the hotel bar (although, since Rapp himself did not drink, his enforcement of the latter rule was sporadic. And the hair policy, it was eventually revealed, was initiated by the owner).

The Cardinals, in any case, rolled gradually toward open revolt. With the retirement of Bob Gibson, the biggest stars on the Cardinals were Lou Brock, Ted Simmons, and Al Hrabosky. Rapp initially appointed Brock, the veteran superstar, a player/coach, but soon found himself at odds with Simmons and Hrabosky—with Simmons, about his weight, and with Hrabosky, about his hair.

Ted Simmons was not Cecil Fielder; he may have been a little soft, but to look at him, you wouldn't have automatically registered that he needed to visit Duke University in the off-season. Rapp suggested that he lose ten pounds, he did, and he had a great year.

Al Hrabosky had been the best reliever in baseball in 1975, when he was 13–3 with 22 saves and a 1.97 ERA. Hrabosky was a small man, very ordinary looking, but he wore a Fu Manchu and long hair that stuck out of the bottom of his cap like crisp, angry straw. He would go behind the mound and bury his head in his chest as if in a trance, then explode from his reverie with the force of a small tornado. Heaving forward his chest, he would stalk to the mound, seize the ball, glare briefly at the batter, and rip through his motion as if he had just received a divine commandment to strike out this hitter. The fans loved it. "The Mad Hungarian" he was called, and while batters would never admit to being intimidated by the schtick, they had to admit that it did tend to put you off your game. You were thinking about whether he was *really* crazy, and it interfered with your ability to concentrate on the pitch.

Well, here comes Vern Rapp, and he tells Hrabosky to shave and get a haircut. Now, a Mad Hungarian with a shave and a haircut is quite a bit like a crocodile with dentures, so Rapp and

Hrabosky soon found themselves at loggerheads. Hrabosky, during spring training, refused to shave or cut his hair, and said in comments to the media that there was considerable dissension on the team. Many players, he said, were unhappy. No one came forward to support him, and Hrabosky apologized to the team. "Maybe I was a little selfish and a little childish about the matter," he said. "I accept (the hair code) now." This statement, *The Sporting News* reported with a straight face, "put to rest the hint of dissension on the club."

In late May, with the Cardinals near first place, Rapp sent a message through a coach, asking Hrabosky to come to his office after a game. Hrabosky did not report. Rapp suspended him for two days.

A few days later a starting pitcher, John Denny, was reported unhappy over being taken out of games, not allowed to finish his starts.

A young outfielder, Bake McBride, had had, in previous seasons, bushy, muttonchop sideburns. Rapp had ordered him to get rid of them, which he did, with a little quiet grumbling. By June 1, they seemed to be gradually returning. McBride was traded to Philadelphia.

One time Rapp sent Lou Brock up to pinch-hit. (Brock had apparently decided to pass on the player/coach responsibility and concentrate on playing.) Anyway, the opposition switched to a left-handed pitcher, and Rapp switched to a right-handed hitter, Mike Anderson, even though Anderson couldn't hit his hat size. Anderson grounded into a double play. The fans were livid, and the erstwhile player/coach joined the ranks of those uncertain about Rapp's leadership.

Bastille Day is not widely celebrated in St. Louis, but on July 14, 1977, the Cardinals were in Philadelphia. It was a hot, sultry afternoon and nobody was in a good mood. Vern Rapp called a "motivational meeting"—his term. He started by making some friendly comments, apparently intended to motivate a few of the guys to shave a little closer. He mentioned the players' high salaries—four or five men on the team were making $100,000 at that time—and suggested that they weren't all earning their money. Lou Brock smiled politely, spoke softly, and tried to explain to Rapp that the team would go along with him on the big things if he would just bend a little on some petty rules. Rapp stared a moment at Brock and then snapped, "I'm not going to change."

And he walked out.

The team sat a moment in stunned silence. A few men snorted and headed for the field.

Roger Freed was a thirty-one-year-old outfielder who had played for Rapp in the minors. He believed in what Rapp was trying to do, or at least believed that Rapp was the manager, right or wrong, and deserving of the team's best efforts. Sensing disaster, Freed hurriedly reorganized the meeting. He spoke up for Rapp, asking the team to hang together. A few other players offered less supportive comments. Hrabosky announced in a postgame radio interview that he wanted out.

"I've said it before," Rapp told a reporter. "I didn't come here to be liked. I'm not trying to treat them like little kids. It's just that they haven't been accustomed to discipline. Today it's do your own thing, be a free soul, live today because tomorrow may never come. But reality has got to come some time."

Cardinal broadcaster Jack Buck, attempting to defend Vern Rapp, ripped Hrabosky, but conceded that Rapp was "a one-dimensional man."

Hrabosky suggested he might file a union grievance over the hair policy. Marvin Miller said that Hrabosky would unquestionably win the grievance.

When the team got back to St. Louis Rapp had a meeting with the general manager, Bing Devine, and the owner. Several announcements were made in an effort to stabilize the situation:

• The hair code was suspended for the balance of the season.

• Vern Rapp's contract was extended.

• The Cardinals announced that they would comply with Hrabosky's desire to be traded at the earliest opportunity. "I intend to call your bluff," Busch said in a prepared statement directed at Hrabosky. "You said in the newspaper that you can only get batters out by being psyched up with your mustache and beard. Then go ahead and grow it. But boy, are you going to look like a fool if you don't get the batters out." Hrabosky pitched a little better the rest of the season, and was traded that winter.

The smoke from this conflagration blotted out all other news about the Cardinals' season, creating the widespread impression that the team was in chaos. In objective terms, the 1977 Cardinals had a pretty decent campaign. After losing 90 games under Red Schoendienst in 1976, the '77 Cards finished 83–79, an eleven-game improvement. Bob Forsch won 20 games. On August 25 they were 71–55, just a few games behind the Phillies. They faded badly after the Phillies pulled away.

You would have had to read the papers carefully to detect the positive elements in this. The *story* about the Cardinals that year was "Rapp fighting with his team."

Rapp opened the 1978 season as the Cardinals' manager, but the problems didn't go away. In early April he had a jaw-to-jaw discussion with Garry Templeton, his young shortstop, after Templeton criticized the third base coach. Once he went out to get his pitcher, Buddy Schultz. As Schultz left the mound, Rapp made a sarcastic comment. Schultz turned and screamed at him.

At least twice in early 1978, Rapp had temper tantrums during postgame interviews.

Finally, in mid-May, Ted Simmons cranked up the clubhouse stereo after a tough loss. Rapp yelled at Simmons and called him a loser. He apologized, but Cardinal broadcaster Jack Buck heard about the comment. Rapp, scheduled to do a radio interview, begged off. Buck filled in and reported that Rapp had called the local legend a loser.

Vern Rapp was fired the next day. He blamed his dismissal on Jack Buck.

What do we learn from the dismal baseball life of Vern Rapp? Nobody really *liked* the man; he said, after all, that he didn't come here to be liked, and he certainly succeeded in that. Baseball is full of unwritten novels. Here is a man who worked thirty years to get to the majors, and then had a major league career with the approximate duration and enjoyment of a proctologist appointment. You have to feel something for him, I think.

Lou Brock said it was just the Peter Principle. Rapp had the skills to get to the job, but not the skills to do the job. I talked to Al Hrabosky about it once, in 1978. He said that Rapp was very insecure, and very negative. He'd give you the ball and say "Don't walk anybody." Every expression of individuality was a personal threat to him.

We know this already, but it is worth noting: In hiring a manager, look for someone who is *secure* and *positive*.

Some people thought Rapp was lost in time, a 1950s manager unable to deal with a different generation of players—but his story, in broad elements, is the same as the story of Ozzie Vitt, 1940. Sarcasm and autocracy make an unpalatable mix to any generation of players.

His story teaches us, as the world often does, that nothing is more "real" than appearances. Rapp succeeded, in a very narrow sense. He did better with the team than they had done the year before, and far better than they would do for the popular manager who followed him, Ken Boyer. If there had been a perception that he was succeeding in 1977, he would have been able to build on that in 1978. He was perceived as having failed, and that perception ultimately washed the success from under his feet.

But to me, the most striking fact here is this: that Rapp had no experience on a major league roster. I believe that was among the things that defeated him.

Rapp had very strong ideas about how his players should behave, and that's good. He had no clear understanding of how those ideas would play out in a major league setting. "It's my way or the highway," Rapp told his players. There was no give in him after the rules were laid down, and for that reason, it was critical for the rules to be aligned with real-world expectations *before* they were announced. If he had gotten past that, I believe that he might have been a good manager. If he had just one year to sit on a major league bench, to bend his ideas to what he saw around him before anybody took a position on them, he might have been great. Sparky Anderson had that one year. Earl Weaver had a half-year. I think it's a prerequisite for the job.

National Intentions

The major league record for intentional walks issued in a season is 116, by the San Diego Padres in 1974 (John McNamara). The top ten, if you are curious, are as follows:

Team, Year	IBB	Manager
1. San Diego, 1974	116	John McNamara
2. San Diego, 1980	113	Jerry Coleman
3. New York Mets, 1979	107	Joe Torre
4. San Diego, 1977	106	McNamara and Al Dark
5. Cincinnati, 1989	105	Pete Rose
6. Pittsburgh, 1975	102	Danny Murtaugh
7 St. Louis, 1970	102	Red Schoendienst
8. Chicago Cubs, 1977	101	Herman Franks
9 Los Angeles, 1967	101	Walt Alston
10. St. Louis, 1974	99	Red Schoendienst

The top fifteen teams on that list are all National League teams, and you might assume that this was because of the DH rule.

Actually, it isn't, at least not entirely. Probably because of the influence of the Dodger organization, the intentional walk has always been much more popular in the National League than in the American League.

The intentional walk became an official stat in 1955. I asked my computer to draw up a list of the teams issuing the most intentional walks in the years 1955–1960, the preexpansion era. The 1959 Pittsburgh Pirates (Danny Murtaugh) issued the most, 84, but the top sixteen teams on that list are all National League teams.

I drew up the same list for the next era, the 1961–1972 era (postexpansion, pre-DH). In that era there were twenty-two teams which issued 80 or more intentional walks. Twenty-one of the twenty-two were National League teams, the exception being the 1972 Cleveland Indians.

Decade Snapshot: 1980s

Most Successful Managers: 1. Tommy Lasorda
                                    2. Whitey Herzog
                                    3. Tony LaRussa

The "success scores" for Lasorda, Herzog, LaRussa, and Sparky Anderson are all almost the same, all 16 to 18. There was no one manager who was tremendously successful during the 1980s.

Most Controversial Manager: Pete Rose

Others of Note: Roger Craig
                     Dick Howser
                     Davey Johnson
                     Gene Mauch
                     John McNamara

Typical Manager Was: Hal Lanier or Gene Michael—a light-hitting utility infielder from the 1960s. Don Zimmer, Lee Elia, Steve Boros, Chuck Cottier. Doc Edwards and Pat Corrales are the same, except they were catchers. The percentage of managers who never played in the majors began to increase in the early 1970s. By the mid-1980s, about one-fourth of major league managers had never played in the majors.

Percentage of Playing Managers: 1%

Most Second-Guessed Manager's Moves:
1. In 1986, Boston manager John McNamara always put in Dave Stapleton for Bill Buckner at first base when he had a lead in the late innings. In Game Six of the 1986 World Series the Red Sox scored twice in the top of the tenth inning, grabbing a 5–3 lead. McNamara forgot to put Stapleton in the game. A two-out ground ball went between Buckner's legs, scoring two runs for a 6–5 New York victory.
2. With two out in the ninth inning of the fifth (and deciding) game of the 1985 National League Playoff, the Dodgers led St. Louis 5–4. They were one out away from going to the World Series. Runners were on second and third, first base empty, and the Cardinals' best hitter, Jack Clark, was at the plate.

Most people assumed that Tommy Lasorda would walk Clark and pitch to the on-deck hitter, Andy Van Slyke. He didn't. Clark hit a home run, and the Cardinals went to the Series.

Everybody in the world second-guessed Lasorda for pitching to Clark, including Cardinal manager Whitey Herzog, who said, "I've always figured that if I can pitch to a guy making $1.3 million a year or a guy making $100,000 a year, I pitch to the guy making $100,000."

As I've written elsewhere, the percentage calculations which drive strategic decisions in baseball are normally so close and so complicated that it is categorically impossible to state with any assurance what the correct course of action would be. This case is an exception: Lasorda's decision, although it didn't work out, was unquestionably the correct one. To load the bases with a one-run lead to let a right-hander pitch to a left-handed hitter (Van Slyke) would have been lunacy.

3. In the 1981 All-Star Game, Jim Frey used all of his players, and had to allow his pitcher (Dave Stieb) to bat in the ninth inning, with his team trailing by one run.

Clever Moves: Al Oliver was a left-handed line-drive hitter who hit the ball hard on the nose more often than any other hitter of his era. He wasn't the *best* hitter, because there's more to the game than that, but if you bought the theory that the hitter succeeds when he hits the ball hard, then Al Oliver was the best hitter in baseball.

He was old by 1985, DHing or coming off the bench to pinch-hit for Toronto, but late in the season, he was on a tear. The Blue Jays also had a very strong right-handed DH, Cliff Johnson, and they also platooned at several other positions. The Kansas City relief ace was Dan Quisenberry, a right-handed submariner who, like most right-handed submariners, had trouble getting out left-handed hitters. To make things worse, Oliver was a low-ball hitter.

In Game Two of the American League Championship Series, Al Oliver beat Quisenberry with a tenth-inning single. In Game Four, he beat him again, with a ninth-inning double. Oliver's swing was a perfect match for Quisenberry's pitches. One didn't get the feeling, frankly, that Quisenberry would ever get Oliver out—and that fact essentially took the Royals relief ace out of the series.

Down three games to one, Dick Howser had to figure a way to get Dan Quisenberry back in the series. He got a shutout in Game Five, from a lefty, which made it three games to two.

In Game Six, Howser started a right-handed pitcher, which got Oliver in the starting lineup. He switched to a left-handed pitcher, ordinarily a starter, in the sixth inning. Al Oliver sat down—and Quisenberry came in to get the save, knotting the series at three.

In Game Seven, Howser started his best pitcher, Bret Saberhagen. Bobby Cox, gambling that Howser wouldn't use Saberhagen as a decoy, started his left-handed hitters, including Oliver. Howser pulled Saberhagen after three shutout innings, bringing in another left-handed starter. This left Bobby Cox with an impossible quandary: leave his left-handers in the game, possibly letting them bat three times each against a lefty, or take Oliver and the others out, and let Quisenberry back in the game?

Cox took Oliver out. Quisenberry finished up, and the Royals were on to the World Series.

Bobby Cox is a great manager, and Dick Howser, in all honesty, was not. But at exactly the wrong moment, Cox let Howser get one step ahead of him.

The most *important* smart move of a manager in the 1980s was Tony LaRussa's decision to make a relief ace out of Dennis Eckersley. Eckersley was a player known to carry around a huge ego, and he had won 150-plus games as a major league starter. By 1987 he seemed to be washed up. LaRussa, somehow, was able to convince Eckersley that he should accept the challenge of being a relief ace—and for the next six years, he was probably the most effective closer in the history of baseball.

Evolutions in Strategy: The sacrifice bunt, early in the decade, reached its all-time nadir in popularity as a strategic weapon.

The stolen base, which made a comeback in the 1960s after decades of obsolescence, reached its plateau in 1976, and has remained at essentially the 1976 level ever since.

Evolution in the Role of the Manager: Free agency fundamentally reshaped the role of the manager, probably to a greater extent than anything which had happened since the coming of general managers in the 1920s. Free agency—the right of a player to pick up and move once the season was over—transferred power from the manager to the player, and thus forced managers to become salesmen, rather than autocrats. With long-term contracts, a manager could no longer tell a player "Do this my way or get out."

The most common way of looking at this is to say that the managers at that point lost all control of the players. A more accurate way to look at it, I think, is to say that the managers

a) lost *some* control over the players, and

b) were forced to become more resourceful in finding ways to maintain their authority.

An example of what *can* happen to a manager in this environment is Sparky Anderson with Mike Moore in Detroit, 1993–1995. Moore signed a long-term contract with the Tigers in 1993, but posted earned run averages of 5.22 in 1993, 5.42 in 1994, and 7.53 in 1995, despite which Anderson continued to run him out to the mound every fifth day until late 1995. Sparky's view of the situation was, "We paid him a lot of money to pitch; I've got no choice but to pitch him."

I don't really understand the logic of this. I mean, you're going to have to pay Mike Moore the money one way or the other, right? If you've got better pitchers, why do you have to keep pitching Mike Moore? What do you gain from it?

But in a more general way, there is no question that this does very often create a quandary for managers. If a player signs a five-year, $25-million-dollar contract, the manager, as a practical matter, *has* to play him until it becomes extremely clear that he's worse than a replacement-level player.

WHITEY HERZOG IN A BOX

Year of Birth: 1931

Herzog is within a few weeks of the same age as Mickey Mantle. Both were signed by the Yankees when they graduated from high school in 1949. Herzog got a bigger bonus.

Years Managed: 1973, 1975–1990

Record as a Manager: 1,281–1,125 .532

Managers for Whom He Played: He began and ended his major league career playing for Charlie Dressen. In between, he also played for Cookie Lavagetto, Harry Craft, Bob Elliott, Paul Richards, Luman Harris, Billy Hitchcock, and Bob Scheffing. He also played for Ralph Houk in the minor leagues.

Others by Whom He Was Influenced: Although he never played for the Yankees in the major leagues, Herzog was in the Yankee system from 1949 until April 1956, and was more influenced by Casey Stengel than by anyone else.

Characteristics As a Player: Left-handed hitting outfielder, solidly built line-drive hitter, ran well until a leg injury in 1959 took most of his speed. Selective hitter, drew a lot of walks. Couldn't hit left-handers, and had trouble with the breaking ball.

Herzog hit only .257 in an eight-year major league career, but with better luck he could easily have had a 1,500-game career. Three things prevented that from happening:

1) He was with the Yankees, who weren't short of players. When Herzog hit .351 with McAlester in 1950, no one really got too excited.

2) He had reached Triple-A by age twenty (September 1952), but was drafted after the 1952 season and spent two crucial years in the United States Army.

3) On returning, he had a big year with Denver (1955) and was traded to the Senators, who parked his butt on the bench after he didn't play too well in his rookie season. He got a chance to play again in 1959 and was playing extremely well for Kansas City, posting a .446 on-base percentage, when a combination of two quick leg injuries ended

his season in early June. He was never a regular again, although he had some decent years off the bench.

WHAT HE BROUGHT TO A BALL CLUB

Was He an Intense Manager or More of an Easy-to-Get-Along-With Type? He was fairly intense. He wasn't grouchy, and he wasn't a bitch-bitch-bitch type, but he established clear expectations for his players.

Was He More of an Emotional Leader or a Decision Maker? Both, but I would say more of a decision maker.

Was He More of an Optimist or More of a Problem Solver? He was a problem solver. You've seen the drawing of the two buzzards on a limb, and one of them says, "Patience, my ass. I say let's kill something." That's Herzog; he didn't believe in waiting around for something good to happen. He always wanted to *make* it happen.

He was like Casey in this respect, that what a guy did last year didn't mean anything to him. He didn't read the stats and say, "Well, this is what this guy can do and this is what that guy can do, so I'll play this guy." That's what 90% of the managers will do. Herzog looked at it more like "What are this guy's skills, and what kind of effort is he giving, and what are this other guy's skills, and what kind of effort is he giving?" He was going to play the guy who had more to offer.

HOW HE USED HIS PERSONNEL

Did He Favor a Set Lineup or a Rotation System? He never used a set lineup. He moved people in and out of the lineup and up and down the batting order on a daily basis.

Did He Like to Platoon? He did platoon, yes. Herzog knew that he himself couldn't hit a left-hander, and looked for that in other players. Sometimes he saw it even when it wasn't there. He platooned Andy Van Slyke, when he might have been better off to put Van Slyke in the lineup and let him play.

Because he had many switch-hitters in addition to his platoon tendencies, Herzog's "Platoon percentages" (see "The Manager's Record," page 295) were extraordinarily high, probably over .85, possibly over .9, meaning that in some seasons 85 to 90% of his lineup would have had the platoon edge on a given day. The switch-hitters who were regulars for him included Vic Harris, Willie Wilson, U. L. Washington,

Garry Templeton, Ozzie Smith, Willie McGee, Terry Pendleton, Vince Coleman, and Jose Oquendo.

Did He Try to Solve His Problems with Proven Players or with Youngsters Who Still May Have Had Something to Learn? Youngsters, 90% of the time. Almost the first thing he said after he was hired to manage the Kansas City Royals was "Frank White is now a regular." An exception would be the bullpen problem in St. Louis, when he went after Bruce Sutter because he didn't want to put an an inexperienced pitcher into the closer role.

How Many Players Did He Make Regulars Who Had Not Been Regulars Before, and Who Were They? In Texas, Vic Harris and Jeff Burroughs. In Kansas City, Frank White, Al Cowens, Willie Wilson, and U.L. Washington, plus pitchers Larry Gura, Rich Gale, and Mark Littell. In St. Louis, David Green, Willie McGee, Lonnie Smith, Terry Pendleton, Mike LaValliere, Vince Coleman, and Jose Oquendo, plus pitchers Joaquin Andujar (sort of; see below), Gary Mathews, Joe Magrane, John Stuper, Dave LaPoint, and Todd Worrell.

Many of these were unexpected promotions to regular status—for example, the Royals before Herzog were dubious about Frank White's bat. The Yankees, who had Willie McGee, didn't think he was regular material. Vince Coleman landed in the 1985 opening-day lineup after hitting .257 at Louisville in 1984, and Larry Gura was regarded as potentially a pretty decent middle reliever until Herzog agreed to give him a couple of starts and see what he could do.

The moves that best define Herzog, however, were the acquisitions of Lonnie Smith and Joaquin Andujar. Lonnie Smith was fast and a perpetual .320 hitter in the Phillies' minor league system, but had led American Association outfielders in errors in 1976, 1977, 1978, and 1979. The actual errors were just the tip of the iceberg; you really had to see him play. Lonnie had very small hands and feet. The small hands often allowed the ball to slip away as he was attempting to throw, and the small feet caused him to fall down in the outfield at least once every game. It wasn't as damaging as it looked, because, since Smith fell down chasing the ball all the time, he knew that you couldn't lie there and look embarrassed, you had to hop right back up and start chasing that ball again, and he did. His defensive effort was very good, and his arm was pretty good if he could get a grip on the ball. He threw out an awful lot of base runners who

would try to take advantage of him. A single would bounce away from him, Lonnie would fall down, the runner would try to take second, and Lonnie would throw him out; this happened a lot, and he often led the league in assists as well as errors.

Anyway, Smith's career had been on hold for at least five years, because the Phillies had Greg Luzinski in left field, and they just couldn't feature this guy playing center or right, no matter what he might hit. Herzog said, in essence, "Okay, he's got some problems in the outfield, we're not going to worry about that." He traded a couple of washed-up pitchers for Lonnie and put him in left field; Smith stole 68 bases and scored 120 runs, and the Cardinals won the World Series.

Joaquin Andujar was a hell of a nice guy most of the time, but he was one of baseball's leading head cases. He spent six long years in the Cincinnati Reds system, because Sparky Anderson just couldn't stand him, then spent five-plus years tormenting the Houston Astros with flashes of brilliance. He made the All-Star team twice with early-season runs, but finished 9–10 for Houston as a rookie, then 11–8, 5–7, 12–12, and 3–8. He was 2–3 at the strike in the 1981. That's 42 wins and 48 losses, if you're counting, and Houston manager Bill Virdon was mighty tired of counting.

Herzog said, in essence, "So the guy is a little bit different; we're not going to worry about that." Andujar went 6–1 for the Cardinals when play resumed in 1981, then went 15–10 in 1982, 20–14 in 1984, and 21–12 in 1985.

Andujar's agent was David Hendricks; I knew David well in those days. David worked twelve hours a week, at least, trying to keep Joaquin focused. Herzog hated agents, but he understood that he and Hendricks had a common interest in keeping Andujar pointed at the goal line, and they worked at it together. Herzog understood something about Andujar that Bill Virdon had never been able to take in: The less he pitched, the crazier he acted. The worst thing you could do to Joaquin Andujar was to stop pitching him. For Houston, Joaquin would have a bad outing or two, then he would do something or say something inappropriate, and Virdon would send him to the bullpen to get straightened out. This remedy was 100% certain to make Joaquin do or say something even more inappropriate, and a cycle of frustration and failure was well established.

In St. Louis, Andujar would have a bad outing, and then he would do or say something kind of different, and Herzog would send him back to the mound and he would pitch a three-hit shutout. And people would slap their knees and say, "Boy, that Joaquin, he's a character, ain't he?" Whitey worked with Joaquin Andujar much the same way that Connie Mack had worked with Rube Waddell.

Did He Prefer to Go with Good Offensive Players or Did He Like the Glove Men? Herzog's offenses were always based around speed, which is more valuable on defense than it is on offense, so this dilemma never presented itself. The genius of Herzog's system was that he was able to find the *offensive* ability within players who were generally regarded as *defensive* players.

Eight of Herzog's teams led their league in fielding percentage. Despite Lonnie Smith, none led the league in errors.

Did He Like an Offense Based on Power, Speed, or High Averages? Speed, obviously. Nine of Herzog's teams led the league in stolen bases and eight led in triples, whereas none led the league in home runs or slugging percentage.

In the main, this was a reaction to the parks that he was given, which were large parks with artificial turf. Herzog wouldn't have tried to play what became known as "Whitey Ball" had he been hired to manage, let us say, the Tigers. But it was also a perfect accommodation to Herzog's philosophy, because what Herzog looked for were *athletes*, guys who could run and throw. Simply stated, the large parks tended to take the home runs out of the game and allow the best athletes to win.

Did He Use the Entire Roster or Did He Keep People Sitting on the Bench? Herzog said many times that if a guy was good enough to be on his roster, he was good enough to play. He wasn't going to have a guy on his bench that he was afraid to put in the lineup in a critical situation.

Thus, when September came and the rosters were expanded, Herzog would call up the fastest guy in his system, whoever that was, and start using him as a pinch runner, right in the middle of a pennant race. Everybody on his bench, for the most part, could count on 60 games and 125 at bats a year, with the exception maybe of a utility infielder, who might have 80 games but very few at bats, or a pure pinch hitter like Steve Braun, who might have 70 games but 70 plate appearances.

Did He Build His Bench Around Young Players Who Could Step into the Breach If Need Be, or Around Veteran Role-Players Who Had Their Own Functions Within a Game? Young players in the main, with two or three veterans in clearly defined roles. What Herzog absolutely *wouldn't* have on his bench was a twenty-eight-year-old guy who resented the fact that he wasn't playing every day. He thought those kind of guys were poison. He wanted the guys who were *hungry*, who appreciated the opportunity, or those who had accepted that this was the only way they were going to be able to stay in the major leagues.

Herzog had wonderful benches; this is one of the most important, but least recognized, features of his style. On his 1977 team in Kansas City, which won 102 games, he had Joe Zdeb and Tom Poquette, who platooned in left field, Pete LaCock, a left-handed hitting first baseman, and John Wathan, a right-handed hitting catcher/first baseman/out-fielder who was always one step faster than you thought he was. All of these guys hit .290 or better, and they understood that their opportunities were limited, so if they wanted to stay in the majors they had better get in there and figure out some way to make something happen. On his best team in St. Louis he had Tito Landrum, Art Howe, Steve Braun, Mike Jorgensen—the same kind of guys.

GAME MANAGING AND USE OF STRATEGIES

Did He Go for the Big-Inning Offense, or Did He Like to Use the One-Run Strategies? He liked speed, as opposed to one-run strategies. His best teams were mostly below the league average in sacrifice bunts, although his 1986 team, which finished under .500, led the league in sac bunts.

Herzog's teams, in addition to being fast, were enormously aggressive on the bases, thus ran themselves out of many innings. Hal McRae, one of Herzog's favorite players, used to run into 25 outs a year, at least. If a ball might be a single or a double, Herzog expected you to leave the batter's box thinking "Double." Another manager might yell at you for getting thrown out. Herzog would get on you if you didn't get a base that you could have gotten.

Did He Pinch-Hit Much, and If So, When? He pinch-hit a good deal. His best teams all led the league or were near the league lead in pinch hitters' batting average, in large part because he gave his bench players enough at bats to keep them sharp.

Was There Anything Unusual About His Lineup Selection? One of his teams had a lineup of Jack Clark and seven leadoff men. That was a little unusual.

Herzog's lineups were dominated by a certain *kind* of player—a thin, fast guy, often a switch-hitter, who might not have been valued by many organizations. It's not just that Herzog let these guys play, but that they played *better* for him than they did for anybody else. Dave Nelson played one year for Whitey Herzog, and hit .286 with 43 stolen bases. The rest of his career, he was a .230 hitter. Herzog communicated to these players what he wanted them to do: slap the ball over the infield and run like hell.

Willie Wilson never hit higher than .281 in the minor leagues. As a rookie, Herzog used him as a pinch runner/ defensive sub, and he hit .217. So Herzog put him in the lineup every day, and he hit .315.

Herzog was fired, but Wilson hit .300 for several years following that, even won a batting championship. Then the Royals hired a batting coach, Lee May, who taught Willie to "drive" the ball. After that, Willie hit the ball much, much harder. The ball would hang in the air, the outfielder would catch it, and Wilson was a .260 hitter the rest of his career.

Herzog would never have stood for it. Herzog would have hit the problem dead-on within a matter of weeks, and gotten a resolution one way or another. The resolution might have been that Wilson would have to go. The resolution might have been that Wilson would go back to slapping singles. The resolution might have been that Lee May would resign. But one way or another, Herzog would have gotten something done.

Did He Use the Sac Bunt Often? Below average in most seasons.

Did He Like to Use the Running Game? More than any other manager in the last fifty years.

Did He Draw the Infield in Much? More than I would have liked, as a Royals fan. That was one thing I always disliked about his managing, that he often had his teams try to make the almost-impossible play. Runners on first and second, bunt near the mound. Herzog would teach his pitchers that if you took time to look at third and see if there was a play there, you'd lost the play—therefore, if you think you can make the play, just grab the ball and fire to third.

He got burned by this play many times, because pitchers would throw to third and lose the out, thus setting up big innings. But it just wasn't in his nature to do it the other way. Herzog hated complacency. He understood that complacency was anathema to competition—therefore, he couldn't teach his players to play it safe, to take the sure out at first. He always taught his players to "go for it."

In What Circumstances Would He Issue an Intentional Walk? One of the countless controversies of Herzog's career occurred in the wake of the 1985 National League Playoffs, when Tommy Lasorda chose not to intentionally walk Jack Clark with a young player, Andy Van Slyke, on deck. Clark homered. Massive second-guessing followed. Somebody asked Herzog what he we would have done, and Herzog told them. "If I have a choice to pitch to a guy making $2 million a year or a guy making $100,000 a year," he said, "I always pitch to the guy making $100,000."

Most of Herzog's teams were above the league average in intentional walks. In 1985 he had issued 80 intentional walks, just missing the National League lead.

Did He Hit and Run Very Often? Quite often. His teams were fast, and he had many "contact" hitters, so the hit and run was always a viable option.

Were There Any Unique or Idiosyncratic Strategies That He Particularly Favored? He liked odd defenses. The Paul Richards trick, placing a pitcher in the field for one hitter, then putting him back on the mound—Herzog probably did that more times than any other manager in history.

Against Reggie Jackson, he'd use the Ted Williams shift. Against some right-handed sluggers, like Jim Rice, he would put three fielders on the left side of the infield. I've seen him use five infielders in a game situation; I've seen him use four outfielders. He was never afraid to try something.

How Did He Change the Game? In the 1970s and early '80s, when stolen base totals were booming, Whitey Herzog's success was one of the chief engines pulling the game. In the last ten years stolen bases have declined—but stolen bases per game even now, after years of the home run revolution, are still much higher than they were between 1920 and 1975. Were it not for Whitey Herzog's influence, I doubt that that would be true.

HANDLING THE PITCHING STAFF

Did He Like Power Pitchers, or Did He Prefer to Go with the People Who Put the Ball in Play? His number-one pitcher was normally a power pitcher—Dennis Leonard in Kansas City, Joaquin Andujar in St. Louis. The rest of his staff was mostly composed of finesse pitchers, like Larry Gura in Kansas City and John Tudor in St. Louis.

Herzog, in all honesty, did not have great success in developing pitchers. Unable to hit a curveball himself, he liked young pitchers with big curveballs, like Greg Mathews and Dave LaPoint. These guys didn't amount to much, and Herzog never played any real role in developing a Hall of Fame–type pitcher.

Did He Stay with His Starters, or Go to the Bullpen Quickly? He used his bullpen. In a game situation, Herzog would switch constantly from left-handers to right-handers and back to left-handers, in a way that was unusual twenty years ago.

Did He Use a Four-Man Rotation? Strictly a four-man rotation for most of his career, yes, with a fifth starter making 15 to 20 starts a year to take the pressure off the front four. Herzog normally had at least one starter pitching 260 or more innings. In this respect, he was very different from Casey Stengel.

Did He Use the Entire Staff, or Did He Try to Get Five or Six People to Do Most of the Work? Herzog wanted to get, and normally did get, about 900 innings a year from four pitchers. Once he got into the bullpen, though, everybody was in the game.

How Long Would He Stay with a Starting Pitcher Who Was Struggling? It would depend on the pitcher.

What Was His Strongest Point As a Manager? Attitude. Aggressiveness. Directness.

Whitey Herzog would not strike you as a sophisticated

man. He was plainspoken, a little overweight, red face, red nose, a mop of hair falling down over his forehead, eyes blinking constantly. Frumpish.

You could see him, if you chose, as crude—and, in fact, he *was* often crude. You could see him, if you chose, as down-to-earth, honest, straightforward, and guileless. You could see him as a man who understood sophistication and saw right through it.

Whitey Herzog's career was a long series of controversies, battles. Poorly chosen words. He spoke frankly. People would ask him what he thought, and he would tell them, and very often people hated him for that. Tick off the names—John Mayberry, Charlie Lau, Muriel Kaufmann, Garry Templeton, Ted Simmons, Keith Hernandez. Whitey had a serious run-in with each of these people, and in every case it meant that somebody had to get out of town. John Mayberry was a big hero in Kansas City. Whitey didn't care. Charlie Lau was the biggest name in coaching at the time. Whitey fired him. Ted Simmons was virtually an institution in St. Louis, a pillar of the community. Bigger than the ball club. Whitey asked him to play first base, for the good of the team. Simmons said he'd think about it. Whitey told him he could think about it in Milwaukee.

Garry Templeton was supposed to be a superstar, the best young shortstop St. Louis had seen since Rogers Hornsby. Whitey said, "I can't win a pennant with that boy playing shortstop. If we're in Cincinnati he doesn't want to play 'cause it's too hot. If we're in Montreal he doesn't want to play 'cause it's too cold. I've got to have a shortstop I can count on."

Later, when Keith Hernandez was the toast of New York, somebody asked Whitey why he had traded away this pearl of western civilization. Whitey told him. Went over like a lead balloon in New York, but he didn't back away, and he didn't lie.

See, Whitey understood something, which is that *sports are essentially conflict.* A manager who backs away from conflict is useless. A player who backs away from conflict is useless.

This directness, this willingness to do battle, enabled him to establish expectations for his players. Everybody had a weight limit. Everybody was expected to report to camp in shape.

Herzog had worked for several years in scouting and player development, and he was very, very good at it. He made his own decisions about who could play and who couldn't. This is extremely unusual. Few people in baseball are willing to look at a young man who hasn't yet played in the majors and who doesn't have the "hot prospect" label, and say, "Here's a guy who can play for me." Herzog was never dependent on established stars, because he was always willing to rest his fate on young, unproven players.

Whitey was the boldest man in baseball. He looked for an attitude, a willingness to get it done. When a player lost that edge, that fearlessness, that love of risk, he lost his value, and then his manager had a problem. If the manager faced that problem head-on, there would be conflict. If he didn't, there would be mediocrity.

If There Was No Professional Baseball, What Would He Probably Have Done with His Life? County sheriff.

TOMMY LASORDA IN A BOX

Year of Birth: 1927

Years Managed: 1977–1996

Record As a Manager: 1,599–1,439, .526

Managers for Whom He Played: In the majors, Lasorda played for Walt Alston (Brooklyn, 1954–1955) and Lou Boudreau (Kansas City, 1956). In the minors, he played four years for Alston (1950–1953), and also played five seasons for Clay Bryant (1949, 1957–1960). His first minor league manager, with Concord (North Carolina State League) in 1945, was John (Pappy) Lehman. He also played for Ralph Houk at Denver in 1956.

Others by Whom He Was Influenced: When he was in the army, 1946–1947, he worked with Bobby Bragan, and he and Bragan got along well. He also attended Dodger training camps for several years when Branch Rickey was running the camps. All of the members of the Dodger system from that era are, in essence, Branch Rickey disciples.

Characteristics As a Player: A small left-hander with a big curve, very poor control. Aggressive, cocky. Prone to get into fights. He was 0–4 with a 6.52 ERA in the major leagues, but had many good seasons with Montreal in the International League, where he won 107 games.

WHAT HE BROUGHT TO A BALL CLUB

Was He an Intense Manager or More of an Easy-to-Get-Along-With Type? Intense. A *positive* intense, perhaps, but not, by nature, easy to get along with.

Was He More of an Emotional Leader or a Decision Maker? An emotional leader.

Was He More of an Optimist or More of a Problem Solver? More of an optimist. I guess you could describe him as an impatient optimist.

HOW HE USED HIS PERSONNEL

Did He Favor a Set Lineup or a Rotation System? A set lineup.

Did He Like to Platoon? No.

Did He Try to Solve His Problems with Proven Players or with Youngsters Who Still May Have Had Something to Learn? Primarily with young players. However, the Dodgers would occasionally go after a talented player who had struggled for some other team, more so under Lasorda than Alston.

How Many Players Did He Make Regulars Who Had Not Been Regulars Before, and Who Were They? Many. Lasorda managed nine Rookies of the Year—Rick Sutcliffe, Steve Howe, Fernando Valenzuela, Steve Sax, Eric Karros, Mike Piazza, Raul Mondesi, Hideo Nomo, and Todd Hollandsworth. I doubt that any other manager managed half as many award-winning rookies. Among other players broken in by Lasorda: Pedro Guerrero, Greg Brock, Mike Marshall the outfielder, Jose Offerman, Mike Scioscia, Orel Hershiser, Tim Belcher, Ramon Martinez, Alejandro Pena, Mariano Duncan, Bob Welch, Dave Stewart, Chan Ho Park, and John Wetteland.

Did He Prefer to Go with Good Offensive Players or Did He Like the Glove Men? The Dodger defenses during much of Lasorda's tenure were notorious. They led the league in errors six times under Lasorda, and when they didn't lead they were close to the lead. Among the more notable fiascos: Jose Offerman at shortstop, Pedro Guerrero's long war with third base, and Steve Sax, his second baseman, developing a mental block about throwing the ball to first base.

In fairness to Lasorda, there is reason to believe that Lasorda, left to his own devices, would never have played Offerman at shortstop or Guerrero at third. The Dodgers sometimes make those decisions in the front office and tell the manager to live with them. But if Lasorda gets credit for the talent which came out of the Dodger farm system in the years he managed, he is equally responsible for the periodic failures to effectively deploy that talent.

Did He Like an Offense Based on Power, Speed, or High Averages? Dodger Stadium won't sustain an offense based on high averages. The Dodgers have to work with power and speed.

Did He Use the Entire Roster or Did He Keep People Sitting on the Bench? He had regulars and bench players. His players rarely moved from one class to the other.

Did He Build His Bench Around Young Players Who Could Step into the Breach If Need Be, or Around Veteran Role-Players Who Had Their Own Functions Within a Game? Eighty percent veterans. His 1981 bench, when he won the World Championship, featured two thirty-five-year-old left-handed hitting outfielders (Jay Johnstone and Rick Monday), a thirty-two-year-old backup catcher (Steve Yeager), a thirty-six-year-old pinch hitter (Reggie Smith), a thirty-year-old utilityman (Derrel Thomas), and a thirty-two-year-old backup infielder (Pepe Frias), with no significant roles for anyone under the age of thirty.

His 1985 bench did include a young Candy Maldonado, but also included a thirty-two-year-old left-handed hitting outfielder (Terry Whitfield), two thirty-six-year-old backup infielders (Bill Russell and Enos Cabell), a thirty-three-year-old infielder (Bob Bailor), and a thirty-eight-year-old pinch hitter (Al Oliver), plus Steve Yeager and Jay Johnstone, still hanging around. His last Dodger team had a bench including Tim Wallach, Wayne Kirby, and Tom Prince.

GAME MANAGING AND USE OF STRATEGIES

Did He Go for the Big-Inning Offense, or Did He Like to Use the One-Run Strategies? He used one-run strategies quite frequently.

Did He Pinch-Hit Much, and If So, When? He used an above-average number of pinch hitters. Many of his teams had at least one regular who didn't hit much, like Steve Yeager. His 1988 team, which also won the World Championship, had four regulars or quasi-regulars who didn't hit—Franklin Stubbs (.223), Alfredo Griffin (.199), Jeff Hamilton (.236), and Mike Davis (.196). He pinch-hit with Danny Heep, Mickey Hatcher, Tracy Woodson, Mike Devereaux, and Mike Sharperson, and was able to pull the team along.

Was There Anything Unusual About His Lineup Selection? Two things—the stretching of the defense, discussed above, and the unusual stability of the lineup. His first team, of course, kept their infield intact for many years. Even after that the Dodgers, because they make committee

decisions about who plays what position, will sometimes stick with a player longer than any other organization likely would. Franklin Stubbs is a good example. The Dodgers kept playing him from 1984 to 1989 because they were apparently convinced that he would eventually hit. It took them five years to decide that Jose Offerman was really going to keep making 35 errors a year, and there was nothing they could do about it.

Did He Use the Sac Bunt Often? Yes.

Did He Like to Use the Running Game? Yes.

In What Circumstances Would He Issue an Intentional Walk? To avoid a big hitter and get the platoon advantage, obviously, but also Lasorda would frequently walk the number-eight hitter to force the pitcher to the plate.

Did He Hit and Run Very Often? Yes.

Were There Any Unique or Idiosyncratic Strategies That He Particularly Favored? Not that I know of.

How Did He Change the Game? I don't know. If you're a Dodger fan and you know the answer to this question, I'd be interested to hear about it.

HANDLING THE PITCHING STAFF

Did He Like Power Pitchers, or Did He Prefer to Go with the People Who Put the Ball in Play? Power pitchers, but not as much as Alston. Lasorda had his share of power pitchers (Bob Welch, Hideo Nomo, Chan Ho Park, Rick Sutcliffe, Tom Niedenfuer, Ramon Martinez, Ismael Valdes, Fernando Valenzuela), but he also developed and/or worked with a good number of the other kind, including Orel Hershiser, Tommy John, Jerry Reuss, and Tom Candiotti.

Did He Stay with His Starters, or Go to the Bullpen Quickly? He was always inclined to go with his starting pitchers, even at the beginning of his career. He adjusted toward using more relievers as the game moved in that direction, but he was always behind the league, always going further with his starters than were most other managers. Eight of his teams led the league in complete games.

Joe Altobelli

In the early 1970s Altobelli managed the Rochester Red Wings to four pennants, led by players like Bobby Grich and Don Baylor, and was named the 1974 Minor League Manager of the Year.

He got a chance to manage the Giants, who had a good year in 1978. On a team flight in 1979, two players, under the influence, made indiscreet remarks about Altobelli. Altobelli banned alcohol from future flights. Players ignored the ban, which led to conflict. A religious revival swept the clubhouse and split the team. Altobelli, irritated with second-guessing by reporters, fired an obscene tirade, which was captured on tape. He was fired in September 1979.

He got a second chance when Earl Weaver retired in Baltimore. Getting good performance out of veteran role players, the Orioles won the World Championship in 1983. In 1984 the team began to fall apart. Peter Gammons wrote that Altobelli's "tendency to shyness and withdrawal— some players called him Foggy behind his back—had created a deadened atmosphere." Weaver was summoned from retirement in a messy transition, during

Did He Use a Four-Man Rotation? No. The Dodgers moved to a five-man rotation before he took over the team.

Did He Use the Entire Staff, or Did He Try to Get Five or Six People to Do Most of the Work? He relied heavily on his top pitchers.

How Long Would He Stay with a Starting Pitcher Who Was Struggling? Longer than most managers.

Was There Anything Unique About His Handling of His Pitchers? His staffs were always balanced, almost what one could see as "computer balanced" or "balanced on paper." He always had a couple of hard-throwers, a finesse pitcher and a sinker-ball specialist or a knuckleballer, one or two young pitchers, and one or two veterans. Until the 1990s he always had a mix of right-handed and left-handed starting pitchers. The famous "United Nations starting rotation" that he had at the end of his career is a fitting image for him, although it is an aberration in that he had no left-handed starter.

What Was His Strongest Point As a Manager? Lasorda is, by nature, a tough, aggressive, confrontational person, a street fighter. To avoid coming off as a vulgar martinet, he developed this warm, affectionate, hyper-positive persona, this give-me-a-hug-now, rah-rah, bleed-Dodger-blue gimmick, which eventually consumed his public image.

It is common for college coaches to do this kind of stuff. College coaches will often hug their players, tell them that they love them, and stress the importance of genuinely *caring* about one another within the team, turning the team into a family. It isn't common for a professional manager to attempt this, at least with the same intensity. Sure, managers will talk about the team as a family, and managers will talk about the importance of watching out for your teammates. All managers will talk about taking pride in the uniform. It goes on Page Three. Lasorda put it on Page One and put a banner over it. Lasorda made a ritual of forced enthusiasm and open displays of affection.

Much of this Hollywood affection no doubt seemed as superficial to members of the team as it did to a large segment of the public—yet it had an undeniable effect. It created and/or sustained a definite image for the Dodger organization, in a time when most of the other teams, even including the Yankees, were drifting toward a fuzzy sameness, a lack of clear identity due to the constant shuffling of personnel. "You wear the uniform of the Rangers or the Padres or the Indians," said one player, "you *join* the Dodgers. You're a part of something. You know it from the moment Tommy gives you his first hug."

If There Was No Professional Baseball, What Would He Probably Have Done with His Life? He'd have tried different things until something clicked. He'd have had a few prizefights, tried his hand at promoting fights, and maybe gone on to become Angelo Dundee. If that hadn't worked, he'd have gone to Hollywood, maybe wound up as a Norman Lear–type behind-the-scenes power. If that didn't work, he might have become a New Age television guru, a titan of late-night television, hawking kitchen utensils specially designed to improve your karma. One way or another, he was going to make a million dollars a year.

which Altobelli wandered through the Orioles' offices asking "Does anyone know if I've been fired?"

WHITEY HERZOG'S
All-Star Team

		G	AB	R	H	2B	3B	HR	RBI	BB	SO	SB	Avg	SPct
C	Darrell Porter, 1979	157	533	101	155	23	10	20	112	121	65	3	.291	.484
1B	Jack Clark, 1987	131	419	93	120	23	1	35	106	136	139	1	.266	.597
2B	Tommie Herr, 1985	159	596	97	180	38	3	8	110	80	55	31	.302	.416
3B	George Brett, 1979	154	645	119	212	42	20	23	107	51	36	17	.329	.563
SS	Ozzie Smith, 1987	158	600	104	182	40	4	0	75	89	36	43	.303	.383
LF	Lonnie Smith, 1982	156	592	120	182	35	8	8	69	64	74	68	.307	.434
CF	Willie McGee, 1985	152	612	114	216	26	18	10	82	34	86	56	.353	.503
RF	Al Cowens, 1977	162	606	98	189	32	14	23	112	41	64	16	.312	.526

		G	IP	W–L	Pct.	H	SO	BB	ERA	GS	CG	ShO	Sv
SP	Dennis Leonard, '77	38	293	20–12	.625	246	244	79	3.04	37	21	5	1
SP	Larry Gura, 1978	35	222	16–4	.800	183	81	60	2.72	28	8	2	0
SP	Joaquin Andujar, '85	38	270	21–12	.636	265	112	82	3.40	38	10	2	0
SP	John Tudor, 1985	36	275	21–8	.724	209	169	49	1.93	36	14	10	0
RA	Bruce Sutter, 1984	71	123	5–7	.417	109	77	23	1.54	0	0	0	45

TOMMY LASORDA'S
All-Star Team

		G	AB	R	H	2B	3B	HR	RBI	BB	SO	SB	Avg	SPct
C	Mike Piazza, 1995	112	434	82	150	17	0	32	93	39	80	1	.346	.606
1B	Steve Garvey, 1978	162	639	89	202	36	9	21	113	40	70	10	.316	.499
2B	Davey Lopes, 1979	153	582	109	154	20	6	28	73	97	88	44	.265	.464
3B	Ron Cey, 1977	153	564	77	138	22	3	30	110	93	106	3	.241	.450
SS	Bill Russell, 1978	155	625	72	179	32	4	3	46	30	34	10	.286	.365
LF	Kirk Gibson, 1988	150	542	106	157	28	1	25	76	73	120	31	.290	.483
CF	Reggie Smith, 1977	148	488	104	150	27	4	32	87	104	76	7	.307	.576
RF	Pedro Guerrero, '85	137	487	99	156	22	2	33	87	83	68	12	.320	.577

		G	IP	W–L	Pct.	H	SO	BB	ERA	GS	CG	ShO	Sv
SP	Orel Hershiser, 1988	35	267	23–8	.742	208	178	73	2.26	34	15	8	1
SP	Ramon Martinez, '90	33	234	20–6	.769	191	223	67	2.92	33	12	3	0
SP	Tommy John, 1977	31	220	20–7	.741	225	123	50	2.78	31	11	3	0
SP	F. Valenzuela, 1986	34	269	21–11	.676	226	242	85	3.14	34	20	3	0
RA	Todd Worrell, 1995	59	62	4–1	.800	50	61	19	2.02	0	0	0	32

Random Bites

In the process of researching this book, I gave John Sickels a list of managers and asked him to count the number of times each man had led the league in various categories. How many times did Whitey Herzog's teams lead the league in stolen bases?

I wanted this information to refer to in writing comments about the managers, and I used it often in that respect. But I thought the data was interesting in and of itself, so I thought maybe we should take a couple of pages to put it on record, as reference material. Alphabetically:

Walt Alston Categories in which his teams led the league most often: pitcher's strikeouts (12), ERA (11), stolen bases (10), shutouts (10), walks drawn (6), saves (6), control (6; fewest walks will be referred to in these charts as "control"). Alston's teams never led the league in hits, hits allowed, or batter's strikeouts.

Sparky Anderson most often: walks drawn (10), home runs (9), batter's strikeouts (9), runs scored (7), fielding percentage (7), saves (6). Teams never led in strikeouts, errors, or control.

Cap Anson most often: runs scored (8), doubles (7), home runs (7), slugging percentage (7), complete games (6), saves (5), double plays (5). None of his teams led the league in hits allowed, walks allowed, or control.

Frank Chance most often: Six of his teams led the league in shutouts, five in ERA. Despite the most famous DP combination in history, none of Chance's teams led the league in double plays. Also, none led in batter's strikeouts, walks allowed, or errors.

Fred Clarke most often: triples (8), control (7), hits (5), slugging percentage (5), runs scored (4), stolen bases (4). None of his teams led the league in errors, walks drawn, batter's strikeouts, saves, hits allowed, or walks allowed.

Charlie Comiskey most often: ERA (5), home runs (4). Teams never led the league in triples, hits allowed, walks allowed, or errors.

Joe Cronin most often: batting Average (8), hits (7), doubles (4), slugging percentage (4), fielding percentage (4). None of his teams led the league in home runs, batter's strikeouts, complete games, or ERA.

Leo Durocher most often: walks drawn (8), runs scored (5), triples (5), saves (5), control (5). Fewest: hits (1), hits allowed (1), errors (1), double plays (1).

Charlie Grimm most often: fielding percentage (6), complete games (5), errors (4). Teams never led the league in hits, triples, home runs, stolen bases, errors, or walks allowed.

Ned Hanlon most often: triples (7), stolen bases (5), batting average (5). Teams never led the league in batter's strikeouts, complete games, hits allowed, pitcher's strikeouts, or double plays.

Bucky Harris most often: triples (11), hits (6), double plays (6), stolen bases (5), walks allowed (5). Teams never led the league in walks drawn, led only once in doubles, home runs, batter's strikeouts, complete games, pitcher's strikeouts, fielding percentage, control.

Whitey Herzog most often: stolen bases (9), fielding percentage (8), triples (8). Teams never led the league in home runs, batter's strikeouts, slugging percentage, hits allowed, pitcher's strikeouts, shutouts, or errors.

Ralph Houk most often: slugging average (4), hits (3), triples (3), batting average (3), hits allowed (3). Teams never led the league in walks drawn, stolen bases, pitcher's strikeouts, walks allowed, or shutouts. The 1961 Yankees were the only team Houk managed that led the league in home runs.

Miller Huggins most often: home runs (10), batter's strikeouts (8), slugging percentage (7), ERA (6), runs scored (5). Teams never led the league in doubles, stolen bases, walks allowed, or errors.

Hughie Jennings most often: hits (7), runs scored (6), batting average (6), slugging percentage (5). None of Jennings's teams led the league in walks given, shutouts, or in any fielding category.

Tommy Lasorda most often: complete games (8), shutouts (6), errors (6), ERA (6), home runs (5). His teams never led the league in hits, doubles, triples, batting average, walks drawn, batter's strikeouts, stolen bases, hits allowed, or fielding percentage.

Al Lopez most often: complete games (6), ERA (6), stolen bases (5), fielding percentage (5), control (5), home runs (4), saves (4). Teams never led the league in hits, walks drawn, batter's strikeouts, hits allowed, walks allowed, or errors.

Connie Mack most often: pitcher's strikeouts (16), home runs (13), walks allowed (12), errors (12), fielding percentage (9), batter's strikeouts (9), slugging percentage (9), batting average (8). Least often: walks drawn (1), stolen bases (2), control (2), triples (3), saves (4).

Billy Martin most often: fielding percentage (4), saves (4), complete games (3). None of Martin's teams led the league in triples, hits allowed, double plays, or control.

Joe McCarthy His teams led the league in walks drawn 14 times, in home runs 13 times, in runs scored 13 times. Other high categories: slugging percentage (10), ERA (10). None of McCarthy's teams led the league in hits allowed, only two led the league in walks allowed, and only two led in control.

John McGraw most often: saves (17), runs scored (14), stolen bases (12), home runs (11), batting average (11), control (11). Only one of McGraw's teams led the league in hits allowed, only one led in triples, and only two led in complete games.

Bill McKechnie most often: complete games (9), fielding percentage (5), triples (4), stolen bases (4), saves (4), shutouts (4), ERA (4), double plays (4), control (4). None of his teams ever led the league in home runs, hits allowed, walks allowed, or errors.

Danny Murtaugh most often: double plays (7), triples (6), hits (5), batting average (4). None of his teams led the league in walks drawn, batter's or pitcher's strikeouts, stolen bases, hits or walks allowed, shutouts, errors, or fielding percentage.

Steve O'Neill most often: complete games (7), control (6), shutouts (6), doubles (4), pitcher's strikeouts (4). Teams never the league in home runs, batter's strikeouts, stolen bases, errors, double plays, or hits allowed.

Frank Selee most often: home runs (4), complete games (4), fielding percentage (4), control (4), walks drawn (3), shutouts (3). His teams never led the league in hits, triples, batting average, walks allowed, batter's or pitcher's strikeouts, errors, or double plays.

Billy Southworth most often: hits (6), complete games (6), shutouts (5), batting average (5), doubles (5), slugging percentage (4), pitcher's strikeouts (4), ERA (4). None of his teams led the league in saves, errors, or walks allowed.

Casey Stengel most often: double plays (10), saves (9), shutouts (7), runs scored (6), slugging percentage (6), pitcher's strikeouts (6), home runs (5), batting average (5). Teams never led the league in doubles, stolen bases, fielding percentage, or control.

Earl Weaver most often: ERA (8), fielding percentage (8), complete games (6), walks drawn (4), shutouts (4), control (4). Teams never led the league in hits, hits allowed, walks given, strikeouts, or errors.

Dick Williams most often: control (4), doubles (3), home runs (3), pitcher's strikeouts (3), shutouts (3). None of his teams led the league in errors or fielding percentage.

Harry Wright most often: shutouts (6), saves (5), home runs (5), doubles (5). His teams never led the league in batter's strikeouts, hits allowed, or errors.

Sacrifice Hits Data Chart

There are a couple of huge charts at the end of this article, and what are they doing there? The creation of data is a holy act; not really, but occasionally I need to feed my own caricatures.

This data is here because it isn't anywhere else. All discussions of the sacrifice bunt are starved for data. Baseball fans can discuss the theory of the sacrifice at great length, so long as the discussion does not require specific facts. When it does require specific facts, you're out of luck, because no baseball reference book contains any significant historical information on sacrifice hits.

These charts are intended to repair the oversight. The charts contain the number of sacrifice hits by each major league team in each season since 1893, whatever the sac hit was at that time. Therein lies a tale, a tale best told by John Schwartz in the 1981 *Baseball Research Journal*.

Sacrifice hits have been a part of baseball since 1889, but the definition of a sacrifice has changed more times than OJ's alibi. For the first four years of that period, 1889–1892, I have been unable to locate any systematic data on team sacrifice hit totals. The 1893 data is presented in the chart. According to Schwartz, in 1893 a player received credit for a sacrifice "for advancing baserunners on bunts, ground outs and fly balls," and a sacrifice was charged as an at bat, not exempted as it is now.

Since a sacrifice was credited essentially any time a baserunner moved up on an out, there is a simple relationship between "sacrifices" and team performance: The best teams have the most sacrifices. They have to, because they have the most baserunners. The Pirates, who led the league in team on-base percentage (.377), also led in sacrifices, 360, while St. Louis, a bad team with few baserunners, was last in the league in what could more accurately be called BABO, or "baserunners advanced by outs."

In 1894 the National League adopted the modern sacrifice hit rule—bunts only, no at bat charged. The average number of sacrifices per team dropped from 276 to 96—actually, not that far from a modern norm.

In the mid-1890s a huge number of runs were scored, which tended to argue against the use of the sacrifice bunt. Over the next few years the number of runs scored dropped steadily and in dramatic increments, from 7.36 runs per team per game in 1894 to 5.88 in 1897, to 4.96 in 1898, to 4.43 in 1902, and 3.52 in 1907. In twelve years, runs scored fell by 52%.

As runs scored fell, sacrifice bunts increased—from 83 per team per season in 1895, to 94 in 1897, to 112 in 1898, to 114 in 1902, to 161 in 1907. Sacrifice bunts per game nearly doubled, while the number of baserunners fell sharply.

At this point, our story is interrupted by a rules change. In 1908 both leagues decided to include what we would now call sacrifice flies in the "sacrifice hit" category. The number of sacrifices per team jumped from 161 in 1907 to 204 in 1908.

Sacrifice totals dropped somewhat after 1920, when the lively ball era pushed runs scored back up, and thus made the sacrifice bunt a less attractive option. In 1926 the sacrifice hit category was further expanded to include fly balls moving runners from second to third.

This creates so much noise in the data that in the era 1908–1930, and in particular 1926–1930, it is difficult to say what the record shows. It appears, for example, that Connie Mack bunted relatively little; this, at least, is the conclusion we would draw from studying the data of the years 1901–1908, 1931–1938, and the early 1940s, when we have clean data. (In fact, in the sacrifice hit data, you can almost "see" the date when Connie faded into the background and allowed his son Earle and then Al Simmons to run the team. As long as Connie was in charge, the team was below average in sacrifice bunts. The totals shot up when his assistants took over.)

Anyway, the A's were generally below average in sacrifice bunts—but led the league in sacrifice hits in 1926, 1929, and 1930, and were second in 1927. The conclusion I would draw from this is that Mack's teams, like Tom Kelley's teams today, must have been exceptionally good at moving up on fly balls.

In 1931 all fly balls were taken out of the sacrifice hit category, and the modern sacrifice hit rule, which had been in effect from 1894 to 1907, was essentially reinstated. It has been in effect ever since then, except for the 1939 season, when sacrifice flies were again counted as sacrifice hits.

At the turn of the century, the teams with the most sacrifice bunts were the best teams. The New York Giants led the National League in sac hits in 1903–1904, and the Cubs, Frank Chance's great Chicago Cub teams, led the league in sac hits in 1905, 1906, 1908, 1909, 1910, 1911, and 1912. The White Sox, a perennial contender, led the league in sac hits several times, and the other league leaders were generally pretty good teams.

This is the only era in which sacrifice hits are closely related to team wins. Sacrifice hits are statistically connected to wins and losses through at least twenty different bridges, the four most important of which are power, speed, strategy, and skill:

Power discourages a team from bunting. You don't bunt with Harmon Killebrew at bat or on deck.

Speed, in a similar way, discourages bunting.

Power and speed tend to create an inverse relationship between sacrifice hits and wins. The best teams have the most power, and therefore the least need to bunt in the early innings. **Strategy** and **bunting skill,** on the other hand, tend to create a positive correlation between sacrfice hits and wins—strategy, because a team is much more likely to bunt when they are two or three runs ahead than when they are two or three runs behind, and skill, because good teams in the aggregate tend to be good at everything, including bunting. Good teams tend to be good even at things which are clearly distant from wins and losses—for example, good teams commit 35% fewer balks than bad teams. The numbers involved are so small that the balks themselves are insignificant, but good teams commit fewer balks simply because good teams tend to be good at everything.

These various cross-correlations tend to cancel one another, so that in modern baseball there is essentially no overall relationship between sacrifice bunts and team wins. Good teams are neither more likely nor less likely to bunt, on the average, than bad teams.

But the baseball of 1900–1920 was different in two key respects—one, that there was virtually no power in the game, and two, that teams bunted a great deal more. Teams bunted, when they got a leadoff man on and weren't two or three runs behind, a very high percentage of the time. Everybody did; all teams, so the teams with the most sacrifice bunts tended to be simply the teams with the most baserunners. After 1920, however, this is never true.

This is not an article about the wisdom or advisability of bunting; that article, "Rolling in the Grass," is on page 130. This is just about who bunts how much. A list of managers who bunted a lot: Fielder Jones, Frank Chance, Jack Barry, Bill McKechnie, Charlie Grimm, Joe Cronin, Billy

Southworth, Paul Richards, Walter Alston, Gene Mauch, Dave Bristol, John McNamara, Dick Williams, Tommy Lasorda. Managers who bunted very little include John McGraw, Joe McCarthy, Bucky Harris, Frankie Frisch, Earl Weaver, Bob Lemon, Billy Gardner, Bill Virdon, and Danny Ozark. Some notes about those lists:

Fielder Jones played for the Brooklyn Bridegrooms for several years before Ned Hanlon came over to manage the team. He played for Hanlon for a couple of years, then for Clark Griffith for a couple of years, taking over the White Sox in 1904. His Sox teams were very successful, and became famous as the Hitless Wonders of 1906, a World Championship team which hit .230 for the season, with seven home runs. Most of Jones's teams led their league in sacrifice hits, including the White Sox in 1904, 1905, 1906, and 1908, and the St. Louis Terriers (Federal League) in 1915.

Frank Chance managed the Cubs from 1905 to 1912, leading the league in sacrifice hits every year but one. They missed the lead by two (197–195) in 1907.

Jack Barry was the shortstop on Connie Mack's $100,000 infield, an outstanding bunter himself. He managed for only one year, but that team, the 1917 Red Sox, recorded 310 sacrifice hits, a modern (post-1900) major league record. Less than 50 of these would have been sacrifice flies; probably more than 250 were actual bunts.

Bill McKechnie managed in the majors for twenty-five years. About twenty of his teams were over the league average in sacrifice hits, and his Cincinnati Reds led the league in 1938, 1939, 1940, and 1945.

Charlie Grimm managed the Cubs 1932–1938, during which time he successfully prevented McKechnie from leading the league in sacrifice bunts. Grimm took over the Cubs in midseason, 1932, and managed them until midseason, 1938. His first two pennant-winning teams, the 1932 and 1935 Cubs, both led the league in sac bunts, as did the 1936 and 1937 teams.

In Grimm's second managerial assignment, Chicago 1944–1949, he did *not* bunt very much, but with Milwaukee he led the league in sacrifice bunts in 1954 (110) and 1956 (142).

Actually, Grimm was replaced early in 1956 by Fred Haney, but the 142 bunts recorded by that team, under Grimm and Haney, were the most of any major league team in the 1950s, and are more remarkable because it was a power-hitting team with Henry Aaron, Eddie Mathews, Joe Adcock, Bobby Thomson, and Del Crandall in the everyday lineup. Joe Adcock, who hit 38 homers that year in 454 at bats, also laid down 11 sacrifice bunts. Johnny Logan bunted 31 times, Bill Bruton 18 times, Danny O'Connell 16, and Lew Burdette, a pitcher, 11.

Many times a first-year manager will have an atypically high bunt total, presumably because the new manager is checking out his personnel. Ordering bunts is a way to find out who can bunt.

Joe Cronin ranks with Frank Chance, Billy Southworth, Paul Richards, and Gene Mauch as the five most committed "bunters" in baseball history. He managed the Washington Senators 1933–1934; they led the league in sacrifice hits both years, by good margins. Moving to Boston in 1935, he led the league in sacrifice hits there in 1935, 1936, 1938, 1941, 1942, and 1946. This is notable in part because Cronin managed big-hitting teams in a hitter's park, Fenway Park.

Cronin himself, as a player, did not bunt a whole lot, and was not famous for his bunting skill. He bunted five to ten times a season.

Billy Southworth bunted more than any other manager of the 1940s, and more than any manager since.

Southworth's idea was to get the lead—get a man on base, bunt him over, get a run, put the pressure on the other team. He had teams with extremely high batting averages, and he usually had one or two players who drew an exceptional number of walks. His teams led the league in bunts in 1941, 1942, 1943, 1944, 1947, and 1948, and the 1943 St. Louis Cardinal total of 172 sac bunts is the highest team total since 1931, except the 1939 season when sacrifice fies were counted as sac hits. That team (the 1943 Cardinals) won 105 games.

Paul Richards bunted more than any other manager of the 1950s. He managed the White Sox 1951–1954; they led the league in sacrifice bunts the first three of those seasons. The Orioles, managed by Richards 1955–1961, also led the league in sac hits in 1957 and 1959.

Walter Alston did everything a lot—bunted a lot, stole a lot of bases, made a lot of pitching changes, used a high number of pinch hitters and pinch runners. The Dodgers led the league in sacrifice bunts almost every year in the Maury Wills era (1959, 1960, 1962, 1964, 1965), but even when Alston had the power-hitting team in Brooklyn in the mid-1950s, he was still consistently above the league average in the number of sacrifice hits.

Gene Mauch is, of course, famous for playing "Little Ball." He managed in the majors twenty-six seasons, with his teams leading the league in sacrifice bunts fifteen of those twenty-six years. All four of the teams that he managed (Philadelphia, Montreal, Minnesota, and California) led the league in sacrifice hits at least three times while Mauch was their manager. The Minnesota Twins in 1979 bunted 142 times, the most of any major league team since the schedule expanded to 162 games in 1961.

Dave Bristol was a journeyman manager who managed Cincinnati (1966–1969), Milwaukee (1970–1972), Atlanta (1976–1977), and San Francisco (1979–1980), with no particular success. His teams led the league in sacrifice bunts when he was with Cincinnati, Milwaukee, and San Francisco, and finished second his one full season in Atlanta.

John McNamara was another journeyman manager of the same era; he managed Oakland, San Diego, Cincinnati, California, Boston, and Cleveland, with very limited success. He led the league in sacrifice bunts with San Diego (three times) and California.

Dick Williams was also another revolving-door manager of the same era, although he was extremely successful. With Boston in 1967 he bunted 85 times, just missing the league lead (88). The Moutache Gang in '72 and '73 led the American League in sac bunts, as did California in '74 and '75, when Williams managed them.

Williams managed Montreal 1977–1981; they led the league in sac hits three times during that period (1977, 1979, 1981). Moving on to San Diego, he again led the league, in 1983.

Williams's first sixteen teams were all above the league average in the number of sacrifice bunts, but at the end of his career he either changed his mind about the value of the bunt or, more probably, just didn't have any good bunters. His last few teams didn't bunt much.

Tommy Lasorda's Dodgers led the league in sacrifice bunts six times. The 107 sac hits recorded by the Dodgers in 1993 are the highest total of the 1990s.

Among (younger) contemporary managers, the two most inclined to bunt are probably Bob Boone, a Gene Mauch disciple, and Jeff Torborg. Torborg led the American League in sac bunts, with Chicago, in 1989, '90, and '91.

On the other side, we have a list of managers who did not tend to use the bunt.

John McGraw bunted a lot in his first years as a manager, but suddenly lost enthusiasm for the bunt after 1908. The Giants were below the league average in sacrifice hits every single year between 1911 and the end of McGraw's career except 1930, when

a) there was a lot of garbage in the stats, and

b) the Giants exactly matched the league average.

The 95 sacrifice hits recorded by New York in 1925 were the lowest total by any major league team in the years 1908–1930, when sacrifice flies were included in the sacrifice hit category. The 49 sacrifice hits by the Giants in 1932 is the lowest total by a National League team in the first half of the century.

The Giants in 1911 stole 347 bases, which remains a modern major league record. What appears to have happened, in part, is that McGraw decided that, if you have the speed, the stolen base is a better gamble than the bunt.

Relative to the other managers of his time, McGraw may be the most notable nonbunter ever. The key words are, relative to the other managers of his time. In McGraw's time, teams bunted with tremendous frequency. In the game of 1907, when teams scored 3.52 runs per game, that may have made sense. Through most of the next twenty-five years, run frequencies went steadily up, and bunt totals, logically, should have dropped. It may be simply that what the data shows is that John McGraw was a faster learner than most of the other managers.

Joe McCarthy didn't bunt much, and if Gene Mauch had had his teams, I'm not sure Gene Mauch would have bunted much, either. Seven of McCarthy's Yankee teams were last in the league in sac hits, as were the Red Sox in 1948 and 1950. The 1941 Yankees bunted only 49 times, lowest total in the American League in the years 1901–1950.

Bucky Harris managed Detroit in 1929 and 1930, Boston in 1934, Washington in 1936, 1940, and 1942, and Detroit in 1956. All of those teams were last in their leagues in sacrifice hits.

Frankie Frisch was himself an outstanding bunter. Frisch played for John McGraw, and was, up to a point, a John McGraw disciple. Of course, Frisch and McGraw quarreled, which led to Frankie's departure from New York in midcareer, but Frisch later managed St. Louis, Pittsburgh, and the Cubs. All three teams were last in the league in sac bunts at least once while Frisch was there.

Ralph Houk managed the 1961 Yankees and nineteen other major league teams, most of which weren't terribly good. The '61 Yanks were last in the league in sacrifice bunts, from which we would not infer anything much, but Houk also had six other teams which were last in the league. In 1973 Houk managed the Yankees; they bunted only 27 times, which was then a major league record low. In 1974 Houk moved to Detroit, and in 1974 the Tigers were last in the major leagues in sac bunts.

Earl Weaver, of course, spoke freely of his dislike for the sacrifice bunt.

Bob Lemon managed the Kansas City Royals in 1971 (45 bunts, major league low), the White Sox in 1977 (33 bunts, major league low), and the Yankees in a long series of partial seasons.

Billy Gardner played for Paul Richards for several years and speaks highly of Richards, who made him a regular after he had spent years as a bench player. Nonetheless, Gardner was probably the most enthusiastic nonbunter in major league history. He managed for parts of six seasons, and usually bunted less than thirty times a year.

Bill Virdon was a dour man who managed the Astros for many years and also managed the Pirates, Yankees, and Expos for a year or two. In the early part of his career his team's sac hit totals are notably low, although later on this is not true.

Danny Ozark managed the Phillies in the 1970s, always finishing near the bottom of the league in sacrifice hits. He also managed the Giants part of the 1984 season, when they bunted only 39 times, lowest total for any National League team in the 1980s.

Tom Kelly, an admirer of Ralph Houk, has become the most notable nonbunter among contemporary managers. Kelly bunted an average amount early in his career, but has dropped to about twenty bunts a season.

SACRIFICE HITS
National League 1894–1995

Yr	Bos	Chi	Cin	Bkn	Phi	Pit	NY	Stl	Bal	Cle	Lou	Was	Avg
1893	313	332	245	243	301	**360**	255	175	275	323	283	207	276
1894	64	75	60	100	119	**163**	80	112	151	77	93	56	96
1895	**126**	80	56	66	120	106	38	64	125	87	58	68	83
1896	98	92	**127**	94	95	108	72	101	98	106	53	99	97
1897	114	103	**131**	115	97	98	45	80	72	98	101	72	94
1898	134	113	136	91	120	**141**	61	117	79	125	**141**	88	112
1899	133	148	133	75	117	143	61	108	94	57	**160**	90	110
1900	107	**130**	108	78	113	110	80	80					101
1901	**136**	68	113	80	124	115	73	122					104
1902	131	**153**	98	118	122	118	106	108					119
1903	99	118	96	124	155	109	**185**	103					124
1904	101	141	135	129	119	124	**166**	129					131
1905	85	**193**	174	136	174	159	138	109					146
1906	119	**231**	164	162	145	190	154	139					163
1907	133	195	195	**197**	130	178	165	156					168
1908	194	**270**	214	166	213	184	250	164					207
1909	189	**248**	212	173	239	211	151	119					193
1910	181	**234**	182	183	205	198	193	153					191
1911	152	**202**	185	157	186	193	160	181					177
1912	168	**182**	175	159	179	181	152	166					170
1913	169	158	162	147	**183**	152	112	156					155
1914	**221**	191	149	100	161	156	139	187					163
1915	**194**	182	192	175	181	162	122	175					173
1916	202	166	127	**203**	179	166	134	116					162
1917	182	**202**	131	162	186	174	151	160					169
1918	151	**190**	162	118	119	180	121	141					148
1919	156	167	**199**	153	123	144	128	143					152
1920	166	**220**	194	189	159	174	124	192					177
1921	198	**208**	195	164	112	203	166	195					180
1922	174	**205**	189	178	140	175	159	161					173

Year									Avg
1923	168	151	**185**	148	110	103	113	135	139
1924	104	**163**	159	143	131	151	127	145	140
1925	145	150	**173**	114	133	135	95	134	135
1926	199	199	**239**	158	153	190	139	212	186
1927	197	207	**219**	166	177	214	180	171	191
1928	191	210	**212**	160	159	202	173	187	187
1929	**197**	163	175	155	135	176	154	154	164
1930	154	148	174	147	148	**196**	165	185	165
1931	123	125	93	69	100	**130**	59	90	99
1932	105	**118**	100	99	125	96	49	69	95
1933	134	108	115	90	125	**147**	86	101	113
1934	81	93	78	77	79	59	**108**	76	81
1935	80	**150**	80	70	84	77	116	97	94
1936	99	**137**	67	79	103	82	123	71	95
1937	113	**119**	72	109	75	89	90	89	95
1938	78	88	**89**	80	86	81	88	83	84
1939	122	140	**193**	107	144	156	108	167	142
1940	62	70	**125**	77	87	63	86	88	82
1941	70	99	102	106	90	95	96	**126**	98
1942	90	104	94	119	99	87	77	**130**	100
1943	98	96	119	99	101	86	107	**172**	110
1944	112	105	100	118	109	80	115	**124**	108
1945	91	95	**150**	111	71	88	100	138	106
1946	135	116	122	**141**	103	101	86	97	113
1947	**129**	64	95	115	82	70	64	68	86
1948	**140**	70	79	100	82	56	65	76	84
1949	96	87	76	**102**	74	86	64	94	85
1950	74	54	72	**88**	66	54	75	73	70
1951	79	56	64	75	**103**	76	82	86	78
1952	92	63	53	104	**107**	70	88	65	80

	Mil	Chi	Cin	Bkn	Phi	Pit	NY	StL	Avg
1953	80	73	68	75	67	89	67	55	72
1954	**110**	56	101	79	84	99	84	44	82
1955	72	69	76	75	53	**93**	69	56	70
1956	**142**	87	90	86	52	95	59	41	82
1957	64	58	84	78	52	**97**	32	45	64

	Mil	Chi	Cin	LA	Phi	Pit	SF	StL	Avg
1958	**79**	42	76	68	70	68	68	44	64
1959	64	62	53	**100**	59	77	73	60	69
1960	59	64	60	**102**	66	69	60	52	67
1961	62	52	50	96	**108**	64	70	70	72

	Mil	Chi	Cin	LA	Phi	Pit	SF	StL	Hou	NY					Avg
1962	47	54	57	**83**	**83**	54	76	69	34	58					62
1963	82	64	62	85	**87**	63	72	85	86	46					73
1964	54	55	65	**120**	97	87	78	94	87	52					79
1965	58	48	73	**103**	75	67	80	72	57	76					71

	Atl	Chi	Cin	LA	Phi	Pit	SF	StL	Hou	NY					Avg
1966	72	80	69	84	78	73	70	59	**97**	63					75
1967	57	**93**	56	91	90	63	92	54	65	68					73
1968	86	74	64	79	64	96	92	67	**97**	75					79

	Atl	Chi	Cin	LA	Phi	Pit	SF	StL	Hou	NY	Mon	SD			Avg
1969	87	72	**100**	96	61	73	82	57	68	82	57	56			74
1970	54	75	58	72	62	53	66	52	63	74	**107**	83			68
1971	91	92	69	72	55	62	69	63	65	91	**102**	87			77
1972	55	67	65	89	69	52	64	58	62	86	**108**	90			72
1973	65	75	78	81	56	60	75	89	83	108	**115**	73			80
1974	**109**	80	68	86	84	54	75	68	83	87	106	83			82
1975	72	107	66	104	88	76	62	92	97	75	110	**133**			90
1976	107	75	67	91	59	61	80	86	57	92	75	**125**			81
1977	83	69	62	83	59	49	78	66	76	63	69	**90**			71
1978	61	84	84	111	61	64	**127**	55	76	71	62	114			81
1979	62	77	62	83	60	98	89	63	109	66	67	**113**			79
1980	69	69	78	96	77	75	**100**	73	89	73	76	92			81
1981	56	53	53	62	44	54	65	46	79	41	63	**72**			57
1982	96	76	88	**106**	85	78	59	87	68	64	85	86			82
1983	78	71	72	86	80	84	64	72	81	66	78	**89**			77
1984	64	59	71	**92**	39	81	51	68	87	59	74	64			67
1985	65	66	72	**104**	49	91	93	70	66	89	61	75			75
1986	79	54	65	81	66	68	101	**108**	53	75	53	66			72
1987	**86**	59	57	82	63	71	55	84	58	70	57	81			69
1988	74	57	69	95	67	66	91	105	77	65	66	**106**			78
1989	65	80	66	83	57	83	82	78	83	56	71	**95**			75
1990	49	61	88	71	59	**96**	76	77	79	54	88	79			73
1991	86	75	72	**94**	52	49	90	58	63	60	64	78			70
1992	93	78	66	**102**	64	89	**102**	68	88	74	82	78			82

	Atl	Chi	Cin	LA	Phi	Pit	SF	StL	Hou	NY	Mon	SD	Col	Flo	Avg
1993	73	67	63	**107**	84	76	102	59	82	89	100	80	70	58	79
1994	60	54	53	51	51	36	65	44	**73**	59	53	67	50	42	54
1995	56	71	62	68	77	51	79	48	78	**92**	58	56	82	69	68
1996	69	66	71	74	54	72	77	**88**	68	75	79	59	81	41	70

SACRIFICE HITS
American League 1901–1996

Yr	Mil	Bos	Chi	Cle	Det	Was	Bal	Phi	Avg
1901	122	105	127	75	**131**	80	97	78	102

Yr	StL	Bos	Chi	Cle	Det	Was	Bal	Phi	Avg
1902	104	100	154	118	83	81	115	118	109

Yr	StL	Bos	Chi	Cle	Det	Was	NY	Phi	Avg
190	111	147	142	151	**170**	81	129	101	129
1904	122	145	**197**	169	154	132	133	137	149
1905	151	137	**241**	148	181	165	158	165	168
1906	171	134	**227**	190	175	144	191	157	174
1907	121	135	181	**187**	162	141	125	176	154
1908	223	172	**236**	228	189	194	188	177	201
1909	130	174	232	124	226	193	208	**248**	192
1910	147	**227**	159	190	197	170	176	199	183
1911	141	212	221	160	181	149	184	**231**	185
1912	139	190	201	**208**	151	144	152	201	173
1913	136	168	194	**208**	156	111	138	174	161
1914	147	170	204	154	205	177	140	**217**	177
1915	173	265	**270**	177	202	187	169	137	198
1916	164	**238**	221	234	202	165	155	158	192
1917	167	**310**	232	262	193	176	188	203	216
1918	176	**193**	164	170	143	134	171	130	160
1919	201	190	**223**	221	209	168	165	121	187
1920	208	219	194	**256**	219	199	174	169	205
1921	205	186	186	**232**	230	188	189	135	194
1922	203	161	231	203	**244**	152	218	170	198
1923	209	161	249	199	**256**	232	145	170	203
1924	187	193	**232**	163	224	232	189	156	197
1925	143	135	**231**	180	221	208	174	187	185

Yr	StL	Bos	Chi	Cle	Det	Was	NY	Phi	Avg
1926	205	165	229	222	236	195	218	**239**	214
1927	191	191	**244**	212	202	199	203	217	207
1928	**214**	206	200	191	163	180	146	200	188
1929	191	177	154	202	122	185	145	**213**	174
1930	151	144	155	175	144	171	161	**182**	160
1931	61	68	**105**	91	63	96	87	79	81
1932	90	80	89	**110**	85	95	76	94	90
1933	87	117	108	101	93	**128**	78	80	99

											Avg
1934	101	85	111	87	101	**131**	89	99			101
1935	116	**137**	112	88	110	75	71	86			99
1936	72	**108**	107	77	88	61	67	74			82
1937	85	103	**111**	96	70	67	61	70			83
1938	106	**112**	78	78	75	93	61	78			85
1939	132	140	**154**	120	146	134	92	138			132
1940	63	91	**110**	61	77	61	76	69			76
1941	89	**115**	74	101	82	62	49	76			81
1942	96	**123**	90	90	73	54	84	74			86
1943	106	113	72	121	**123**	88	93	95			101
1944	107	110	67	107	111	108	102	**122**			104
1945	**124**	87	100	119	102	114	95	96			105
1946	84	**106**	78	96	104	86	80	105			92
1947	76	95	56	93	97	72	86	**144**			90

	StL	Bos	Chi	Cle	Det	Was	NY	Phi			Avg
1948	113	66	73	85	**130**	84	78	120			94
1949	83	78	84	113	107	63	84	**117**			91
1950	97	62	106	86	**110**	74	85	73			87
1951	92	59	**103**	63	86	64	91	61			77
1952	86	66	**121**	84	80	79	94	102			89

	Bal	Bos	Chi	Cle	Det	Was	NY	Phi			Avg
1953	89	99	**120**	90	63	82	77	51			84
1954	99	78	96	**107**	80	77	84	54			84

	Bal	Bos	Chi	Cle	Det	Was	NY	KC			Avg
1955	70	69	**111**	87	71	79	79	58			78
1956	84	68	**86**	81	58	75	82	67			75
1957	**110**	41	75	78	96	50	93	62			76
1958	62	60	72	69	**75**	57	72	64			66
1959	**88**	65	84	60	73	64	76	69			72
1960	72	70	95	**97**	85	86	81	75			83

	Bal	Bos	Chi	Cle	Det	Min	NY	KC	Cal	Was	Avg
1961	78	81	71	73	64	67	57	**89**	80	73	73
1962	75	59	**82**	52	56	71	79	78	**82**	71	71
1963	73	44	79	**88**	64	84	66	77	84	57	72
1964	69	35	**96**	63	71	74	68	53	78	66	67
1965	**95**	57	89	90	69	77	72	74	93	63	78
1966	82	65	**109**	56	67	49	58	71	69	84	71
1967	82	85	67	85	78	66	78	59	**88**	63	75

	Bal	Bos	Chi	Cle	Det	Min	NY	Oak	Cal	Was					Avg
1968	80	77	**90**	69	73	69	56	78	75	46					71

	Bal	Bos	Chi	Cle	Det	Min	NY	Oak	Cal	Was	KC	Sea			Avg
1969	74	67	70	47	63	65	63	74	**75**	51	57	72			65

	Bal	Bos	Chi	Cle	Det	Min	NY	Oak	Cal	Was	KC	Mil			Avg
1970	64	34	51	76	83	79	60	73	69	44	63	**115**			68
1971	85	75	81	67	62	64	77	80	83	58	45	**107**			74

	Bal	Bos	Chi	Cle	Det	Min	NY	Oak	Cal	Tex	KC	Mil			Avg
1972	65	56	68	83	74	73	74	**100**	66	84	72	78			74
1973	58	54	49	40	48	34	27	**67**	60	45	49	61			49
1974	72	64	70	56	41	64	49	60	**82**	81	56	56			63
1975	73	75	50	64	37	62	54	74	**97**	64	68	73			66
1976	57	55	79	67	46	**93**	50	58	92	72	71	78			68

	Bal	Bos	Chi	Cle	Det	Min	NY	Oak	Cal	Tex	KC	Mil	Sea	Tor	Avg
1977	48	45	33	94	45	81	46	64	74	**116**	49	60	81	81	66
1978	41	65	63	92	57	**109**	37	108	72	83	55	89	68	77	73
1979	42	42	58	70	56	**142**	50	75	79	78	57	72	61	65	68
1980	42	40	67	60	63	92	51	99	71	70	34	58	**106**	63	65
1981	26	37	48	46	50	36	40	46	**51**	36	28	35	41	44	40
1982	57	53	54	74	41	22	55	50	**114**	64	32	56	42	48	54
1983	46	49	53	48	48	29	37	55	**68**	38	32	61	40	36	46
1984	45	36	37	37	48	26	64	37	65	47	41	42	**66**	35	45
1985	31	50	59	38	40	39	48	63	**99**	34	44	54	28	21	46
1986	33	44	50	56	52	44	36	56	**91**	31	24	53	52	24	46
1987	31	52	54	44	39	47	38	50	**70**	42	34	63	38	30	45
1988	40	66	**67**	36	66	37	36	54	63	48	46	59	40	34	49
1989	63	52	**85**	72	35	51	58	36	54	63	42	51	35	30	52
1990	72	48	**75**	54	36	40	37	60	58	54	31	59	41	18	49
1991	47	50	**76**	62	38	44	37	41	63	59	53	52	55	56	52
1992	50	60	47	42	43	43	26	**70**	56	56	45	61	52	28	49
1993	49	**180**	72	39	33	27	22	46	50	69	48	57	63	46	50
1994	16	38	**51**	33	17	22	27	24	42	41	32	28	48	30	32
1995	40	45	46	31	35	18	20	32	33	49	**66**	41	52	33	39
1996	31	33	56	34	48	20	41	35	45	32	**66**	45	46	38	41

Leading Off

I wrote a couple of articles earlier about lineup selection, which argued that

1) it is impossible to evaluate all of the alternative batting lineups a manager could select, because the number of options is so astonishingly large, and

2) to the extent that we can study the subject, we find that it doesn't make any difference anyway.

Now I'm going to go in a different direction for just a moment. Even though I know, from studying the issue, that it makes virtually no difference what order you put the hitters in, there are two things that managers do with their batting orders which seem to me to be questionable. One is to waste the number-two spot in the batting order.

Almost any manager can recognize a good leadoff man if he has one, and all managers put their best hitters with some power in the three-four spots in the order. Those aren't variables. What varies is the use of the two spot. Some managers will fill the two spot with the best hitter available who isn't a leadoff hitter or a power hitter. Other managers, however, will put a little singles hitter there who hits about .260 with a .315 on-base percentage. I'm not sure why they do this; they'll talk about "bat control" and "moving the runner into scoring position," but the effect is to divide the leadoff man from the good hitters:

> Most of the time a manager will try to place a player in the lead-off position who has proved his ability to draw bases on balls—and one who has an overall aptitude for reaching first base. . . . In the second position, look for a player who bunts well and is a good right-field hitter, whether he bats left- or right-handed.
>
> —Paul Richards, *Modern Baseball Strategy*

Look, the number of runs you can generate by "moving runners" is essentially zero. If you ask a baseball fan how many times per season a runner would be on first base when a single is hit, he might very probably say, "I don't know. Two or three hundred?" It *seems*, in the absence of evidence, as if it might be common for this to happen.

But in fact, the answer is twenty to thirty-five for a typical player, maybe fifty once in a great while. And *any* runner will go from first to third on a single sometimes, no matter how slow he is, and any runner will be stopped at second sometimes, no matter how fast he is. So the potential for that play to make a difference in runs scored is just not as large as many people would imagine that it is.

The same with all of the other plays on which speed and bat control might interact—scoring from first on a double, for example, or moving up on a ground out. The actual number of times per season that these plays occur is not as large as many people would imagine that it is, and the num-

ber of additional runs that result from runners advancing on outs is very small. *The greatest difference in baseball is between a runner being on base and being out.* Everything else is trivial. If you get runners on base, you'll score runs. If you don't, you won't. Once in a while, of course, there is an out that results in a run—but even in those cases, a hit would have resulted in the same run. As a rule, there is no such thing as a "good out."

So what I say is, forget about getting "good outs" from the number-two spot in the order. Forget about bunting and forget about hitting to right field, and concentrate on getting somebody in there who gets on base. In the long run, you'll score more runs. The baseball leadoff hitter in baseball history is Rickey Henderson. The best number two hitter would be Rickey Henderson, too.

The other thing that bothers me about the way managers pick lineups is the use of the five-six spots in the order. Who is a typical number-five hitter, in modern baseball? It's the old power hitter, the guy who used to be a cleanup hitter but isn't anymore. The typical number-five hitter is a thirty-five-year-old right-handed hitter who hits .270 with 28 homers, but can't run. Cecil Fielder, Eddie Murray, Gary Gaetti, Tim Wallach. Moose Skowron batted fifth for the '61 Yankees; Gabby Hartnett batted fifth for the 1930 Cubs. These are prototypical number-five hitters.

To back off and run at this from a slightly different direction, a major league team will usually score more runs in the first inning than in any other inning, for obvious reasons. The first inning is the "structured" inning, the inning in which the leadoff hitter leads off, and the cleanup hitter cleans up.

But in which inning do teams score the *fewest* runs? The second inning, of course. The top of the order usually bats in the first, the bottom of the order usually bats in the second. After that, it drifts toward a random alignment; a team will score as many runs on average in one inning as they will in another.

Few people are aware of this, but if you combine the first inning and the second inning and compare it to the rest of the game, there is no net increase in runs scored. The second inning, in the aggregate, tends to be as far *below* average as the first inning is above average.

It seems to me that based on this one fact, one can make an argument that there is something seriously wrong with the traditional batting order. Managers, in structuring their lineup, are attempting to maximize runs scored in the first inning—but in effect, they are structuring not one inning, but two. And on balance, they're not gaining anything. Managers, given just one opportunity a game to "fix" an inning, contrive to do it in such a way that they are in general no better off than they would be if they simply started the lineup at some random point.

And if you think about it, who is most often leading off the second inning? Of course: those number-five hitters. The thirty-five-year-old right-handed power hitters who can't run.

I believe you're better off to put a line-drive hitter in the number-five spot and shift the aging right-handed power hitter down to number seven or number eight. There are two possibilities: either the number-five hitter does bat in the first inning, or he doesn't. If he does bat in the first inning, he is most likely going to be batting with a runner in scoring position, so then who do you want up there: the line-drive hitter, or the low-average power hitter?

If he *doesn't* bat in the first inning, then he's got to be batting first or second in the second inning. And if he leads off the second inning, who would you rather have up there: the line-drive hitter, or the low-average power hitter?

Either way, I would argue, you're better off with the line-drive hitter hitting fifth and the power hitter hitting seventh or eighth, given that the two hitters are of equal ability.

Of course, my studies show that it doesn't make any big difference one way or the other. In the 1990s, unlike any other period in baseball history, we have offenses which consist of just wall-to-wall power hitters; power hitters leading off, power hitters hitting eighth. The cleanup hitter is now just the best power hitter.

If there were such a thing as a manager who could "create" runs by maximizing his batting order, one would think that his team would score more runs than predicted by the runs-created formula. If there were managers who were losing runs by misaligning their batting orders, one would assume those teams would score fewer runs than predicted by the formula.

In fact, however, there are no teams which consistently outperform or consistently underperform their expected runs created. In any season, of course, there will be some team which has 750 "formula runs," but which actually scores 780 or even 800 runs. But if you look at the same teams the next season, you'll find that they don't score any more runs than expected.

Any real "trait" or "ability" of a team will tend to be at least somewhat predictable from season to season. The teams which hit lots of home runs in 1997 will tend to hit lots of home runs again in 1998. The teams which steal bases in 1997 or which have good pitching in 1997 will tend to be the same in 1998. Having an efficient offense or an inefficient offense is not a trait which can be predicted, or which persists from season to season; it's just a random occurrence.

If batting order *did* have a significant impact on the number of runs scored by the team, one would not expect this to be true.

The Manager's Record

The theory of this book, as you may remember from the introduction, was to ask very specific questions about baseball managers and generate specific, objective answers to those questions.

Some years ago, in writing a *Baseball Abstract*, I was struck by the fact that the discussion of baseball managers proceeds almost in a vacuum of organized information. Take two baseball players—let's say Jay Buhner and Steve Finley. If you ask a baseball fan a series of comparative questions about those two, like "Which one has more power?" "Which one runs faster?" and "Which one has a better throwing arm?" he will know the answers. Even if the difference between the two is very slight, like the difference between Cecil Fielder's speed and Harold Baines's, he will still know.

But if you ask parallel questions about two *managers*, he will *not* know the answers. Who is quicker to go to the bullpen: Don Baylor or Felipe Alou? Who platoons more: Bobby Cox or Tony LaRussa? Who uses the hit and run more: Bob Boone or Phil Garner? The average baseball fan, unless he has read this book, doesn't have a clue what the answers to these questions would be.

Think about it this way: What do you put on the back of a manager's baseball card? Take one and flip it over. We have hundreds of statistics about baseball hitters, but we know how to summarize a player's abilities into a simple chart which tells us what the hitter does well, and what he doesn't do so well. Same thing with a pitcher's card—we condense his performance into ten or twelve categories which tell you how much he pitched, how well he pitched, and a little bit about what type of pitcher he is. You look at the back of a manager's card, and it will tell you that he hit .238 at Pittsfield in 1971. It doesn't have anything to do with how he manages.

What, *specifically*, does one manager do that another manager might not do? Does he pinch-hit a lot, and if so, under what conditions? Does he like to platoon? Is he aggressive about using his bullpen? Does he hit and run much? Is he prone to bring the infield in? Does he favor the intentional walk? Simple, objective questions which have simple, objective answers.

I began addressing these subjects about ten years ago. We haven't made great progress in the last ten years, but the discussion has advanced a little bit. Old records have been compiled which will tell us, for example, how many relievers each manager used each season. The wizards of STATS Inc. have begun collecting specific information about many related issues, such as hit-and-run plays and attempted bunts. We have a good deal of information now that we did not have ten years ago.

But the discussion has not moved forward as much as perhaps it should have because that information has not yet reached the public. It hasn't reached the public because it has not yet been put into a *form* that the average fan can use.

That is the purpose of this article: *to construct what might become, with luck, a "standard form" of a manager's record.* How do we put this information into a form that the customer can use? In a record book we have a form for batters' records, a form for pitchers' records, a form for fielders' records. What is the form for managers' records?

All right, we've got about fifteen categories to work with here. There are some record books which use more. STATS' *Major League Handbook* has twenty-four categories of information for hitters and twenty-four for pitchers, not counting the year, team, or league. The *Sporting News Baseball Register*, on the other hand, has only sixteen, the weekly summaries in *USA Today* have seventeen, and the batting lists in the Sunday newspapers, for the most part, still have less than ten. That form, in many papers, hasn't been updated since the time of Ty Cobb.

Baseball cards can have anywhere from eight to eighteen categories in the back-of-the-card record. Media guides usually have fourteen to sixteen categories in the batting or pitching record. Anything above 15 is pushing our luck, plus, if we do this job right and people actually start to *use* the form that we establish, there will be pressure to add things. People will start to say, "Well, I think the record ought to have included this or that or the other." When they say that often enough we'll have to accommodate them.

As a starting point, we'll need to have "games managed." Enough managers are fired during the season that, if you don't have the games to establish context, you'll get confusing data, one guy with 128 games managed mixed in a chart with the other guys at 162 games. Also, off to the right, we'll need the won–lost record and the winning percentage—just the basic information which is in the Managers Register of the *Baseball Encyclopedia*. Let's do Tony LaRussa, since he's a great manager and I haven't said much about him in the book:

Year	Tm/Lg	G	W–L	Pct.
1979	Chi/A	54	27–27	.500
1980	Chi/A	162	70–90	.438
1981	Chi/A	106	54–52	.509
1982	Chi/A	162	87–75	.537
1983	Chi/A	162	99–63	.611
1984	Chi/A	162	74–88	.457
1985	Chi/A	163	85–77	.525
1986	Chi/A	64	26–38	.406
1986	Oak/A	79	45–34	.570
1987	Oak/A	162	81–81	.500
1988	Oak/A	162	104–58	.642
1989	Oak/A	162	99–63	.611
1990	Oak/A	162	103–59	.636
1991	Oak/A	162	84–78	.519
1992	Oak/A	162	96–66	.593
1993	Oak/A	162	68–94	.420
1994	Oak/A	114	51–63	.447
1995	Oak/A	144	67–77	.465
1996	StL/N	162	88–74	.543

LaRussa's career won–lost record is 1,408–1,257. I'm not going to run a totals line, because as this record develops we'll have many blank spaces for missing data.

There are a number of other things that we *could* put in here. The Macmillan *Baseball Encyclopedia* has a column for "ties" and a column for "no decision," which is obviously a waste of space, because you've got a whole lot of zeroes and ones there.

The *Baseball Encyclopedia* also has a column for "standing," for which one can make a better argument. This column says "3" if the team finished third in their league or division. If the manager was fired with the team in fifth place and they improved to finish fourth, there would be two numbers in the column, a "5" in boldface, and a "4" which is not in boldface.

If I was designing this chart thirty years ago, I would probably have gone with that, but I'm not going to include it here. In modern baseball the number of possible "positions" is not consistent. When you see a "4," you don't know whether that's fourth in a four-team division, or fourth in a five-team division. If it was a record from 1991, it could be fourth in a seven-team division. You wouldn't know instinctively, when you saw the number, what it meant. In modern baseball, a second-place team can win the World Series, so if you put in this category, you'd have to have a code saying "WC," for "wild card."

To some degree you can replace the information by using boldface. If a team finishes 91–71, the baseball fan knows automatically that that's a good record. If the team finishes first, you can put the "91" in boldface. That's what the reader needs to know. If the team finishes 75–87, the reader doesn't really care very much whether they finished third or fourth.

Let me suggest this. If the team finishes first in the division, we'll put the wins in boldface. If they finish with the best record in the *league*, we'll put both the wins and the winning percentage in boldface. Okay?

A couple of other things that we *could* do here. We could put in the performance of the team *against their expected wins*. Remember that formula—expected winning percentage equals:

> Last year's winning percentage times .5, plus
> The previous year's winning percentage times .125, plus
> The year before that's winning percentage times .125, plus
> A .500 record times .25.

We could figure the expected wins for each team, and thus highlight the good years in the manager's record by showing them as "+11" or whatever, while the weak seasons would be shown as minuses.

I'd like to do that, and I'd choose that over the "team standing" column, but I can't quite recommend it. First, it is different from the information which is traditionally included in a player's record. We don't have a category next to batting average which tells you what the player's expected batting average was. This *is* a different situation, so I could get beyond that argument, but there is also the matter of explaining it to the audience. A record is supposed to be automatically assimilated by the reader. Putting in "versus expected wins," or "VEW" for short, would raise a question in the reader's mind. Expected versus what? Who says St. Louis was expected to win 79 games in 1996?

Or, on the other hand, you could put "+12" there when the team *improved* by 12 games, and "-7" when the team declined by 7 games. This presents its own problems, however. Suppose that the team went 83–79 last year, started out 41–56 this, and that manager was fired. The team then went 30–35 under the new manager. What do you put there? They were better than they were under the previous manager, but still not as good as they were last year. Do they get a "+" or a "-"?

You could use "games behind"; that's kind of standard, too. But again, who cares? If the team finished 78–84, do you *care* whether they finished 12 games behind or 14 games behind? Perhaps, but we've got limited space.

So let's not do any of that. We've got wins, losses, and winning percentage; that's all we have room for. From now on, let's concentrate on describing the performance of the manager.

Well, what does the manager do?

The manager writes a lineup. There is a statistic which has become common in recent years, which is *the number of distinct lineups used by the manager during the season.* A few local newspapers are using it, and it does tell you something significant about the manager, which is whether he likes a settled lineup, or prefers to shuffle. Let's do that for Tony LaRussa. I won't do the back years, because I don't want to make up data, but we have the information (from STATS Inc.) for the years 1993–1996:

Year	Tm/Lg	G	LUp	W–L	Pct.
1993	Oak/A	162	**149**	68–94	.420
1994	Oak/A	114	97	51–63	.447
1995	Oak/A	144	120	67–77	.465
1996	StL/N	162	120	88–74	.543

The "149" is boldfaced for 1993 because that led the league.

Next to the number of lineups used in the STATS *Major League Handbook* are two categories entitled "% LHB vs. RHSP" and "% RHB vs. LHSP." For 1996, the start of this chart looks like this:

	% LHB vs. RHSP	% RHB vs. LHSP
Buddy Bell	36.6	96.9
Terry Bevington	64.5	82.5
Bob Boone	71.6	78.8
Phil Garner	47.6	90.1

This, to me, is a classic case where less information would be more. The problem with this chart, for me, is that it pushes my mind through a series of mental flip-flops before I can process it. Let's see now; would a "platoon" manager be a manager who has a large *total* in these two columns, or a manager who has a large *differential* between the two?

What we want to know, I think, is *the percentage of starting players who had the platoon advantage.* If you give us that, we've got information that can be readily understood. Bob Boone has a "Pl %" ("platoon percentage") of .741, meaning that *74.1% of the hitters in Bob Boone's starting lineup have the platoon advantage.*

If we give the reader just that, then standards and norms will develop rapidly. See, we are trying to develop information which everybody will understand, and everybody can use. If we put out the information in this form, then a TV announcer can say, in the first year, that "Phil Garner had the platoon advantage with 58.6% of the players in his lineup last year. That's a little below the league average, which is 62%, so he doesn't platoon a whole lot." Then in the second year, the ESPN guy can say, "Phil Garner's platoon percentage last was .586, while the league average was .621, so he's not really a platoon manager."

And then in the third year, the announcer can say, "Phil Garner's platoon percentage last year was only .586," and everybody will know what he means, because by that time the standard will be established in the viewer's mind. He can say, with emphasis, "Bob Boone had a platoon percentage of *.721* last year," and everybody will know immediately what that means. This is the data for Tony LaRussa, as best I know it:

Year	Tm/Lg	G	LUp	Pl%	W–L	Pct.
1993	Oak/A	162	149	.594	68–94	.420
1994	Oak/A	114	97	.602	51–63	.447
1995	Oak/A	144	120	.576	67–77	.465
1996	StL/N	162	120	.525	88–74	.543

LaRussa's platoon percentages are low, and the percentages tend to be higher in the American League than they are in the National; see, already we are learning something from doing this.

Another advantage of choosing these two pieces of information is that *this information can be re-created from box scores.* You could go back and figure, if you wanted to, how many lineups Casey Stengel used in 1955, and how many Paul Richards used, and how many Al Lopez used. You could figure out how many of those hitters had the platoon advantage, what the league norm was in 1955, and what it is now. In this way, you could get a better understanding of how the game has changed since then, as well as a better understanding of those managers.

Okay, we've got six categories of information in there now, leaving us nine to work with. Let's do something about the handling of the pitching staff.

An obvious variable among managers is their tendency to use the bullpen, as opposed to their preference for leaving the starting pitcher in the game. There are many ways to measure this. We could, for example, put "complete games" and "saves" in the manager's record.

There are a couple of reasons not to do this. Both complete games and saves reflect an element of ability, as opposed to managerial style. That isn't a big deal, because after all, what doesn't, but another reason not to include this information is that it is already in the record, in other places.

There is third reason, however, which is that *complete games are headed toward zero.* We're within a few years now of complete game norms, for a team/season, below ten. That's not going to be very helpful to the reader. Saves track wins, particularly if complete games are near zero, and we already have wins.

Another thing we could include would be "quick hooks" and "slow hooks", which are categories that I invented about fifteen years ago, and which STATS figures and prints in the annual *Handbook.*

That would be okay, but there are problems. You have to explain the categories to the audience. It's a simple concept, but we don't want to explain any more than we have to. A bigger problem is that the categories have tended to slip over the years, and will continue to do so in the future. I intended for them to "balance," as many quick hooks as slow hooks, and they did balance fifteen years ago. There are a lot more quick hooks than slow hooks now, and if we moved the standards, we'd probably be back where we are in another fifteen years. I don't think that's what we want to do.

We could do something *like* complete games or "slow hooks," which would be "long starts," meaning any start in which the pitcher threw more than 115 pitches. That would be all right, but the best thing we can do, I believe, is just "relief games." The information already exists, although you rarely see it. I think this is the one category here which best summarizes the tendency of the manager. Don Baylor in 1995 used 456 relievers; Dallas Green used only 298. Don Baylor used

449 relievers in 1996, leading the majors again, while the Mets under Dallas Green (for most of the season) once again used the fewest relievers of any National League team (325). That's clear, it's short, and it traces directly back to the manager. I think that's what we should use:

Tony LaRussa

Year	Tm/Lg	G	LUp	Pl%	Rel	W–L	Pct.
1993	Oak/A	162	**149**	.594	**424**	68–94	.420
1994	Oak/A	114	97	.602	**308**	51–63	.447
1995	Oak/A	144	120	.576	358	67–77	.465
1996	StL/N	162	120	.525	413	88–74	.543

LaRussa never led the league in relievers used until his team was in decline in 1991, but he has often been among the league leaders. Again, I think standards would develop in this area, so that a TV announcer within three or four years would be able to say "Bucky Showalter used only 302 relievers last year," and the audience would get it immediately.

STATS also prints games with three pitchers and two runs or less. The San Diego Padres in 1996 (under Bruce Bochy) had 32 games in which they used at least three pitchers, but gave up no more than two runs. That's kind of redundant, I think. STATS prints "first batter platoon percentage," meaning "When a reliever comes in the game, how often does he have the platoon advantage on the first batter?" This is an interesting concept, but the data are not as interesting as the idea behind them, since the answers tend to cluster between 58% and 64%. They also figure what we could call "long saves" or "LS," which is saves of more than one inning pitched. That's interesting data. On that chart, Lou Piniella and Felipe Alou stick out like an ex-wife at a family re-union, while some guys have almost no long saves . . . let's put that on the "B" list, and we'll work it in if we have room.

I think we have to try to describe, in this chart, *how the manager uses his bench*. Art Howe, in 1996, used 74 pinch runners. Jim Fregosi used only 12. That's a real difference. It says something about what the manager values. Tom Kelly used 207 pinch hitters that year; Davy Johnson used 85. Joe Torre used 55 defensive substitutes; Cito Gaston used only 11.

This chart would be more interesting if we showed different managers, rather than different years for one manager, so let's try that. We'll add three categories: "PH" ("pinch hitters used"), "PR" ("pinch runners used"), and "DS" ("defensive substitutes"):

1996 Managers
National League

MANAGER	G	LUp	Pl%	PH	PR	DS	Rel	W–L	Pct.
F ALOU	162	113	.523	240	31	30	433	88–74	.543
D BAKER	162	129	.517	250	17	15	425	68–94	.420
D BAYLOR	162	91	.483	288	31	16	**447**	83–79	.512
B BOCHY	162	114	.546	289	29	15	411	**91–71**	.562
J BOLES	75	50	.482	132	13	17	200	40–35	.571
T COLLINS	162	111	.363	257	30	**38**	371	82–80	.506
B COX	162	89	.617	254	32	27	408	96–66	.593
J FREGOSI	162	114	.581	239	12	6	387	67–95	.414

	G	LUp	Pl%	PH	PR	DS	Rel	W–L	Pct.
D GREEN	131	79	.513	213	43	21	260	59–72	.450
R KNIGHT	162	147	.565	313	17	27	425	81–81	.500
R LACHEMANN	86	47	.442	149	12	2	212	39–47	.453
T LaRUSSA	162	120	.525	246	25	13	413	88–74	.543
T LASORDA	76	44	.487	149	12	9	178	41–35	.539
J LEYLAND	162	117	.511	299	18	14	422	73–89	.451
J RIGGLEMAN	162	87	.496	326	34	21	439	76–86	.469
B RUSSELL	86	37	.470	154	33	12	205	49–37	.570
B VALENTINE	31	28	.571	88	7	12	75	12–19	.414

1996 Managers
American League

MANAGER	G	LUp	Pl%	PH	PR	DS	Rel	W–L	Pct.
B BELL	162	128	.500	123	29	17	**426**	53–109	.327
T BEVINGTON	162	109	.694	148	59	52	391	85–77	.525
B BOONE	161	**152**	**.741**	172	53	28	322	75–86	.466
P GARNER	162	114	.586	115	48	46	385	80–82	.494
C GASTON	162	87	.701	126	23	11	303	74–88	.457
M HARGROVE	161	96	.627	115	20	25	382	**99–62**	**.615**
A HOWE	162	124	.485	124	**74**	40	419	78–84	.481
D JOHNSON	163	100	.693	85	33	38	378	88–74	.543
T KELLY	162	120	.589	**207**	28	12	387	78–84	.481
K KENNEDY	162	124	.558	151	54	27	409	85–77	.525
M LACHEMANN	112	80	.613	101	11	14	272	52–60	.464
J McNAMARA	49	39	.624	45	11	10	113	18–31	.367
J OATES	163	73	.625	89	43	10	347	**90**–72	.556
L PINIELLA	161	99	.566	190	28	14	403	85–76	.528
J TORRE	162	131	.653	92	62	**55**	411	**92**–70	.568

Most of this information, if you're wondering, comes from the STATS *Handbook*.

There are some notes worth making about this chart. Bobby Cox, the hugely successful manager of the Atlanta Braves, uses a very settled lineup, and Mike Hargrove of Cleveland uses one of the most set lineups in the American League. There is a great danger here of confusing cause and effect, but let's move on. Jim Fregosi, who used defensive substitutes with great effect in his 1993 championship season, had lost confidence in his bench by 1996, and had more or less stopped making any in-game use of his reserves. Phil Garner rarely pinch-hits; he uses his bench for pinch runners and defensive substitutes. I did not know these things.

The National League, of course, uses more pinch hitters, because they don't have the DH rule. Platoon percentages are higher in the American League than they are in the National because STATS includes the starting pitcher in the counts of how many right-handed hitters are in the lineup against lefties and vice versa. This is an illogical decision, I know, but they didn't ask me. Even adjusting for that, there is somewhat more platooning in the American League, because the DH rule in effect expands the roster, since teams don't have to carry as many pinch hitters.

You might have guessed that the DH rule would mean *less* substitution on defense, because the rule allows you to play a bad fielder without putting him in the field. In fact, the opposite is true: The American League uses about 35% *more* defensive substitutes, every year.

We're going to have to pass up about fifty categories of information that we *could* add to the chart here. We could, for example, include pinch-hitting batting average, pinch-hitting home runs, and some code about whom the manager tends to pinch-hit *for*. We could include information about which position defensive substitutes are most often used at, who is pinch-run for, how many bases the pinch runners steal, how many runs the pinch runners score, how often a manager pinch-hits when he is ahead, and how often he pinch-hits when he is behind . . . we could make a monster chart out of how the manager uses his bench. The goal here is to focus on the most valuable information and reduce it to a cohesive table.

I want to develop a record here such that a general manager, reviewing the records of a half-dozen candidates to be his new field manager, could associate the tendencies of the manager with the attributes of his ball club. "Oh, I see," he might say, reviewing the record of Phil Garner. "His bench is speed and defense. Well, I don't know about that for our club, but he does vary the lineup quite a bit. That would be good for us, get some of the guys on the bench in the lineup a little more." How would Terry Collins fit our team? Is Sparky Anderson worth another look? These questions need information. The form would summarize the information.

We've used ten columns so far; we have five left. I'd like to do something which describes the offensive/defensive orientation of the manager, but I don't see how we can do it. Dallas Adams developed something called the "offensive fraction." If a team scores a lot of runs and allows a lot of runs, or has a tendency in that direction, their offensive fraction will be high, over .500. If they tend to score not too many runs and allow fewer, attempting to win games 2–1, that creates a low offensive fraction, under .500.

That would be a good thing to include, but I don't think I will. The offensive fraction is heavily indebted to the characteristics of the park. If a team plays in a hitter's park, like Fenway or Coors Field, they're going to have a high offensive fraction 90% of the time. If they play in Dodger Stadium, they're going to have a low offensive fraction 90% of the time. If we were to do that at all, we'd almost have to do a "park-adjusted" offensive fraction. Then you'd find just the opposite: the team that plays in Dodger Stadium would almost always have a high offensive fraction, and the team which plays in Fenway Park would normally have a low offensive fraction.

Besides that, I can just hear myself on a call-in show. "Bill, can you explain to us the concept of a park-adjusted offensive fraction?" Um . . . well, not really. We're trying to assemble *simple* information here, clearly understood. Idiot accessible, if you will.

STATS Inc. carries information on the number of starts by pitchers on three days' rest, which is an interesting thing to know, but I'm afraid that in ten years, we'd have columns of zeroes there.

Let's deal with some strategies. What the manager does, other than deploy his personnel, is to order strategies—intentional walks, sacrifice bunts, stolen bases, the hit and run. This is the main area that we should address next.

"Intentional walks" already appear on the pitcher's record, and in general I don't want to reproduce a lot of information that we already have access to. In this case, because of the importance and clear relevance of the statistic, I'll make an exception; IBB will be added to the chart. Going back to Tony LaRussa:

Year	Tm/Lg	G	LUp	Pl%	PH	PR	DS	Rel	IBB	W–L	Pct.
1979	Chi/A	54								27–27	.500
1980	Chi/A	162						236	44	70–90	.438
1981	Chi/A	106						173	17	54–52	.509
1982	Chi/A	162						258	30	87–75	.537
1983	Chi/A	162						243	32	99–63	.611
1984	Chi/A	162						238	26	74–88	.457
1985	Chi/A	163						305	35	85–77	.525
1986	Chi/A	64								26–38	.406
1986	Oak/A	79								45–34	.570
1987	Oak/A	162						328	21	81–81	.500
1988	Oak/A	162						290	27	**104–58**	**.642**
1989	Oak/A	162						317	23	**99–63**	**.611**
1990	Oak/A	162						303	19	**103–59**	**.636**
1991	Oak/A	162						**397**	30	84–78	.519
1992	Oak/A	162						**400**	46	**96–66**	**.593**
1993	Oak/A	162	**149**	.594	117	36	38	**424**	59	68–94	.420
1994	Oak/A	114	97	.602	89	28	14	**308**	30	51–63	.447
1995	Oak/A	144	120	.576	113	38	24	358	26	67–77	.465
1996	StL/N	162	120	.525	246	25	13	413	43	88–74	.543

LaRussa's teams issued the fewest intentional walks in the American League in 1988 and 1990, and he has been near the bottom of the league in every season of his career except 1993, when his team was somewhere in the middle. In 1996, the fewest intentional walks were issued by Minnesota (27) and Colorado (19); the most were issued by the New York Mets (73) and the Detroit Tigers (63). Bad teams tend to issue the most intentional walks, although this is not universally true.

The other "decision" categories which are top candidates to be included would be "hit-and-run attempts," "stolen bases" and/or "stolen base attempts," "sacrifice hits" and/or "sacrifice bunt attempts," and "pitchouts called."

That's six categories and we've only got five spaces left, so obviously we've got to do a little triage. "Stolen base attempts" obviously are better than "stolen bases"; the question is, do we want to combine "stolen base attempts" with "hit-and-run attempts," into something called "runners in motion" ("RIM")?

I don't think we have to do that. The hit-and-run data is interesting. Art Howe used the hit and run only 61 times in 1996; Bob Boone used it 172 times. That's a real difference, and we're not duplicating any other information.

A drawback is that this information can't be reconstructed for past managers. You can't go back to 1946 and figure out how many times Leo Durocher ordered the hit and run, but this is an argument *not* to combine the hit-and-run with the stolen base data, since the stolen base info does exist for many earlier years. If we combined them we would be losing some of the information that we *could* put into a managers record for Casey Stengel or Leo Durocher.

So we'll use "SBA" and "H&R" ("stolen base attempts" and "hit-and-run attempts"); this leaves us three categories. One should be used for "PO," "pitchouts called." This is the 1996 chart:

1996 Managers
National League

MANAGER	G	LUp	Pl%	PH	PR	DS	Rel	SBA	H&R	PO	IBB	W–L	Pct.
F ALOU	162	113	.523	240	31	30	433	142	79	25	33	88–74	.543
D BAKER	162	129	.517	250	17	15	425	166	125	**96**	60	68–94	.420
D BAYLOR	162	91	.483	288	31	16	**447**	**267**	126	89	19	83–79	.512
B BOCHY	162	114	.546	289	29	15	411	164	109	65	47	**91**–71	.562
J BOLES	75	50	.482	132	13	17	200	90	54	11	19	40–35	.571
T COLLINS	162	111	.363	257	30	**38**	371	243	131	35	60	82–80	.506
B COX	162	89	**.617**	254	32	27	408	126	66	34	64	**96–66**	**.593**
J FREGOSI	162	114	.581	239	12	6	387	158	80	5	49	67–95	.414
D GREEN	131	79	.513	213	**43**	21	260	125	83	34	59	59–72	.450
R KNIGHT	162	**147**	.565	313	17	27	425	234	113	36	66	81–81	.500
R LACHEMANN	86	47	.442	149	12	2	212	86	32	4	30	39–47	.453
T LaRUSSA	162	120	.525	246	25	13	413	207	**141**	41	43	88–74	.543
T LASORDA	76	44	.487	149	12	9	178	76	37	23	35	41–35	.539
J LEYLAND	162	117	.511	299	18	14	422	175	116	46	50	73–89	.451
J RIGGLEMAN	162	87	.496	**326**	34	21	439	158	102	65	55	76–86	.469
B RUSSELL	86	37	.470	154	33	12	205	84	61	26	31	49–37	.570
B VALENTINE	31	28	.571	88	7	12	75	20	19	3	14	12–19	.414

1996 Managers
American League

MANAGER	G	LUp	Pl%	PH	PR	DS	Rel	SBA	H&R	PO	IBB	W–L	Pct.
B BELL	162	128	.500	123	29	17	**426**	137	87	13	63	53–109	.327
T BEVINGTON	162	109	.694	148	59	52	391	146	88	57	60	85–77	.525
B BOONE	161	**152**	**.741**	172	53	28	322	**280**	172	38	32	75–86	.466
P GARNER	162	114	.586	115	48	46	385	149	73	32	33	80–82	.494
C GASTON	162	87	.701	126	23	11	303	154	69	34	37	74–88	.457
M HARGROVE	161	96	.627	115	20	25	382	210	80	41	42	**99–62**	**.615**
A HOWE	162	124	.485	124	**74**	40	419	93	61	37	61	78–84	.481
D JOHNSON	163	100	.693	85	33	38	378	116	65	13	35	88–74	.543
T KELLY	162	120	.589	**207**	28	12	387	196	94	12	27	78–84	.481
K KENNEDY	162	124	.558	151	54	27	409	135	75	24	41	85–77	.525
M LACHEMANN	112	80	.613	101	11	14	272	55	32	**60**	32	52–60	.464
J McNAMARA	49	39	.624	45	11	10	113	29	26	22	15	18–31	.367
J OATES	163	73	.625	89	43	10	347	109	88	8	44	**90**–72	.556
L PINIELLA	161	99	.566	190	28	14	403	129	65	40	52	85–76	.528
J TORRE	162	131	.653	92	62	**55**	411	142	70	19	35	**92**–70	.568

Johnny Oates, an ex-catcher, called only eight pitchouts all season, and incidentally only three in 1995; Dusty Baker called 96. Of course, Oates had Ivan Rodriguez; you don't *need* to call a pitchout for Ivan. Under Sparky Anderson in 1995, the Tigers called 77 pitchouts. Under Buddy Bell in 1996, they called 13.

"Sacrifice bunts," or "sacrifice bunt attempts"? I'd like to have both and the success percentage, too, but the number of attempts obviously seems like the better piece of information. American League "sacrifice attempts" ("SA") in 1996 ranged from 33 (Tom Kelly) up to 93 (Bob Boone). If you go back to 1995, you'll find that they ranged from 25 (Tom Kelly) to 98 (Bob Boone). Switching back to the Tony LaRussa form:

Year	Tm/Lg	G	LUp	Pl%	PH	PR	DS	Rel	SBA	H&R	PO	SA	IBB	W–L	Pct.
1993	Oak/A	162	**149**	.594	117	36	38	**424**	190	**186**	61	59	59	68–94	.420
1994	Oak/A	114	97	.602	89	28	14	**308**	130	73	32	31	30	51–63	.447
1995	Oak/A	144	120	.576	113	38	24	358	158	105	42	42	26	67–77	.465
1996	StL/N	162	120	.525	246	25	13	413	207	**141**	41	**117**	43	88–74	.543

That's fifteen categories. There is one other piece of information I think should be included, but on which I have no data. That would be *the percentage of runs scored in big innings*, a big inning being defined as three runs or more. I think it's a fundamental schism among managers: Play for one run, or go for the big inning? Some of the other categories here relate to that issue, but a column which addresses it directly should still be included in the chart, if the data is in fact interesting.

I wish there was some way to put something in the chart about the use of rookies. You could make up a category, "percentage of games started by rookie pitchers," I suppose; Earl Weaver would rank extremely low in this, Joe McCarthy very high. What would you call it? "POGSBRP"? We're looking for simplicity; if it takes a seven-letter acronym to make a title, that's a good indication that you're going down the wrong road.

I'd like to have something about the type of pitchers that a manager likes to use. I don't know how to put that in there, either. Something about the average age of the roster would be good. It isn't difficult to calculate—just multiply each player's plate appearances by his age and divide by the team plate appearances—and it is easy to understand. There just isn't room.

Does the manager's record that I have proposed leave out as much as it contains? Of course. So does a hitter's record; so does a pitcher's record. And, of course, the record revealed here would be heavily colored by the talents of the team. Mike Hargrove in 1993 used 80 defensive substitutes; in 1995 he used 21. A few changes in personnel dramatically changed the way he used his bench.

But all statistics are colored by circumstance. Would John Smoltz win 24 games if he was still with Detroit? Of course not. Would Andres Galarraga hit 47 home runs if he played for Florida? Of course not.

I am not blind to the limits of the chart, and I'm not suggesting that you should be. My goal, essentially, is *to feed information into the discussion*. This information exists anyway, but it exists like wheat. I am trying to make it into bread. If we develop this record, if we publish it, if we get it into the record books and onto the backs of baseball cards, the average fan will know more about managers than he does now.

The records of all 1995–1996 managers are given on the following pages, with some brief comments to help the reader take in the import of the record. There is an oversight in statistical history: We have somehow forgotten to construct a record which describes the tendencies of a manager. I am trying to repair that oversight.

FELIPE ALOU

Year	Tm/Lg	G	LUp	Pl%	PH	PR	DS	Rel	SBA	H&R	PO	SA	IBB	W–L	Pct.
1993	Mon/N	163	**137**	.538	254	30	58	385	*284*	156	44	120	38	94–68	.580
1994	Mon/N	114	72	.528	143	**33**	7	259	**173**	85	20	72	24	**74**–40	**.649**
1995	Mon/N	144	116	.532	200	36	10	396	169	104	22	74	20	66–78	.458
1996	Mon/N	162	113	.523	240	31	30	433	142	79	25	97	33	88–74	.543

Experimented with his lineup in 1993–1994; has had more settled lineup the last two years. Doesn't platoon much, pinch-hits less than average but uses a fair number of pinch runners and defensive subs. Was very aggressive at sending runners in 1993–1994, much less so the last two years.

SPARKY ANDERSON

Year	Tm/Lg	G	LUp	Pl%	PH	PR	DS	Rel	SBA	H&R	PO	SA	IBB	W–L	Pct.
1993	Det/A	162	112	.720	116	59	37	375	167	118	78	47	**92**	85–77	.525
1994	Det/A	115	75	.710	64	35	10	246	79	63	**69**	29	51	53–62	.461
1995	Det/A	144	103	.503	151	43	11	366	109	59	**77**	43	**63**	60–84	.417

Used intentional walk more than any other recent manager. Called many pitchouts.

DUSTY BAKER

Year	Tm/Lg	G	LUp	Pl%	PH	PR	DS	Rel	SBA	H&R	PO	SA	IBB	W–L	Pct.
1993	SF/N	162	83	.508	247	20	34	414	185	155	79	128	46	103–59	.636
1994	SF/N	115	76	.541	177	16	9	288	154	**133**	78	88	24	55–60	.478
1995	SF/N	144	96	.451	230	23	13	381	184	128	**77**	101	33	67–77	.465
1996	SF/N	162	129	.517	250	17	15	425	166	125	**96**	103	60	68–94	.420

Calls more pitchouts than any other contemporary manager. Doesn't platoon much; fairly aggressive about sending runners.

DON BAYLOR

Year	Tm/Lg	G	LUp	Pl%	PH	PR	DS	Rel	SBA	H&R	PO	SA	IBB	W–L	Pct.
1993	Col/N	162	136	.399	301	32	38	**453**	236	**166**	75	88	66	67–95	.414
1994	Col/N	117	76	.481	**224**	12	12	329	144	114	52	65	30	53–64	.453
1995	Col/N	144	87	.521	257	23	11	**456**	184	91	24	102	24	77–67	.535
1996	Col/N	162	91	.483	288	31	16	**447**	**267**	126	89	115	19	83–79	.512

Relatively settled lineup; doesn't platoon. Goes to the bullpen more often than any manager in history.

BUDDY BELL

Year	Tm/Lg	G	LUp	Pl%	PH	PR	DS	Rel	SBA	H&R	PO	SA	IBB	W–L	Pct.
1996	Det/A	162	128	.500	123	29	17	**426**	137	87	13	63	63	53–109	.327

Unable to draw any solid conclusions based on one year's data. Experimented with lineup much more than Anderson did, went to the bullpen more readily. Put runners in motion much more.

TERRY BEVINGTON

Year	Tm/Lg	G	LUp	Pl%	PH	PR	DS	Rel	SBA	H&R	PO	SA	IBB	W–L	Pct.
1995	Chi/A	114	87	.706	99	30	24	285	115	83	47	61	29	57–56	.504
1996	Chi/A	162	109	.694	148	59	52	391	146	88	57	75	60	85–77	.525

Middle-of-the-road manager, not at the top or bottom of any list. Uses a good number of pinch runners; calls a fairly large number of pitchouts.

BRUCE BOCHY

Year	Tm/Lg	G	LUp	Pl%	PH	PR	DS	Rel	SBA	H&R	PO	SA	IBB	W–L	Pct.
1995	SD/N	144	96	.602	262	30	23	337	170	108	38	68	26	70–74	.486
1996	SD/N	162	114	.546	289	29	15	411	164	109	65	73	47	**91**–71	.562

Pinch-hits more than average.

JOHN BOLES

Year	Tm/Lg	G	LUp	Pl%	PH	PR	DS	Rel	SBA	H&R	PO	SA	IBB	W–L	Pct.
1996	Fla/N	75	50	.482	132	13	17	200	90	54	11	26	19	40–35	.571

Too early to draw any solid conclusions. Experimented with the lineup more than Lachemann had with the same team, went to the bullpen more freely, bunted less.

BOB BOONE

Year	Tm/Lg	G	LUp	Pl%	PH	PR	DS	Rel	SBA	H&R	PO	SA	IBB	W–L	Pct.
1995	KC/A	144	127	.755	222	44	17	308	173	79	32	98	24	70–74	.486
1996	KC/A	161	152	.741	172	53	28	322	280	172	38	93	32	75–86	.466

Wide-open, aggressive manager who is near the top of almost every chart. Changes his lineup every day, many of the changes driven by platooning. Pinch-hits and pinch-runs frequently, puts runners in motion more than any other American League manager. Bunts more than any other AL manager. Relatively cautious in using his bullpen.

TERRY COLLINS

Year	Tm/Lg	G	LUp	Pl%	PH	PR	DS	Rel	SBA	H&R	PO	SA	IBB	W–L	Pct.
1994	Hou/N	115	74	.501	**224**	12	13	268	168	88	37	90	28	66–49	.574
1995	Hou/N	144	106	.482	**302**	38	11	384	**236**	**130**	44	97	39	76–68	.528
1996	Hou/N	162	111	.363	257	30	**38**	371	243	131	35	94	60	82–80	.506

Uses his bench freely. Likes to use the running game. Looks for "matchups" in his lineup; didn't have enough left-handed batters in Houston to platoon much, particularly after they traded Luis Gonzalez.

BOBBY COX

Year	Tm/Lg	G	LUp	Pl%	PH	PR	DS	Rel	SBA	H&R	PO	SA	IBB	W–L	Pct.
1993	Atl/N	162	47	.693	250	**58**	65	353	173	101	66	103	59	**104**–58	**.642**
1994	Atl/N	114	64	.641	163	30	**25**	244	79	60	44	83	39	68–46	.596
1995	Atl/N	144	59	.610	224	**48**	**40**	339	116	64	41	77	38	**90**–54	**.625**
1996	Atl/N	162	89	**.617**	254	32	27	408	126	66	34	90	64	**96**–66	**.593**

Platoons as much as any National League manager, but doesn't *experiment* with the lineup. Uses many pinch runners and defensive substitutes. Middle-of-the-road in using one-run strategies. Relatively low totals of relievers used.

JIM FREGOSI

Year	Tm/Lg	G	LUp	Pl%	PH	PR	DS	Rel	SBA	H&R	PO	SA	IBB	W–L	Pct.
1993	Phi/N	162	73	.695	231	20	**73**	350	123	56	30	116	33	**97**–65	.599
1994	Phi/N	115	85	.670	169	15	19	243	91	56	12	59	24	54–61	.470
1995	Phi/N	144	96	**.735**	245	6	9	341	97	49	33	92	26	69–75	.479
1996	Phi/N	162	114	.581	239	12	6	387	158	80	5	77	49	67–95	.414

Platooned very aggressively until 1996. Had a strong plan for his bench in 1993; no apparent plan in 1996. One of the older managers of 1996, had been pushed near the bottom of the list in relievers used.

PHIL GARNER

Year	Tm/Lg	G	LUp	Pl%	PH	PR	DS	Rel	SBA	H&R	PO	SA	IBB	W–L	Pct.
1993	Mil/A	162	134	.652	126	25	36	353	231	153	30	74	58	69–93	.425
1994	Mil/A	115	94	.597	53	33	24	252	96	77	23	46	16	53–62	.461
1995	Mil/A	144	120	.622	83	**67**	**52**	321	145	67	52	64	23	65–79	.451
1996	Mil/A	162	114	.586	115	48	46	385	149	73	32	72	33	80–82	.494

Liked to send his baserunners in his earlier years; hasn't done so as much since the home run explosion began in 1994. Rarely pinch-hits; uses his bench for pinch runners and defensive substitutes. Doesn't platoon much; limited use of the intentional walk.

CITO GASTON

Year	Tm/Lg	G	LUp	Pl%	PH	PR	DS	Rel	SBA	H&R	PO	SA	IBB	W–L	Pct.
1993	Tor/A	162	72	.580	30	33	42	344	219	84	67	61	38	95–67	.586
1994	Tor/A	112	59	.541	41	16	21	221	105	47	48	44	16	53–59	.473
1995	Tor/A	144	82	.649	85	24	7	265	91	20	57	47	26	56–88	.389
1996	Tor/A	162	87	.701	126	23	11	303	154	69	34	63	37	74–88	.457

Most conservative, virtually inert manager in baseball. Doesn't pinch-hit, pinch-run, or use defensive substitutes. Uses settled lineup; slow to go to the pen. Rarely orders intentional walk. Doesn't platoon; platoon percentage was high last year (.701) due to switch-hitters in his lineup.

DALLAS GREEN

Year	Tm/Lg	G	LUp	Pl%	PH	PR	DS	Rel	SBA	H&R	PO	SA	IBB	W–L	Pct.
1993	NY/N	124	75	**.742**	238	14	30	223	83	86	38	91	48	46–78	.371
1994	NY/N	113	77	**.690**	200	19	15	238	51	63	53	67	33	55–58	.487
1995	NY/N	144	94	.665	243	19	10	298	97	83	30	**123**	38	69–75	.479
1996	NY/N	131	79	.513	213	**43**	21	260	125	83	34	69	59	59–72	.450

Stayed with his starters longer than any other NL manager. Bunts freely. Platooned quite a bit in 1993–1994.

MIKE HARGROVE

Year	Tm/Lg	G	LUp	Pl%	PH	PR	DS	Rel	SBA	H&R	PO	SA	IBB	W–L	Pct.
1993	Cle/A	162	92	.669	**184**	22	**80**	410	214	138	77	56	53	76–86	.469
1994	Cle/A	113	53	.712	79	16	**31**	222	179	62	40	43	22	66–47	.584
1995	Cle/A	144	64	.626	101	34	21	335	**185**	50	22	40	12	**100**–44	**.694**
1996	Cle/A	161	96	.627	115	20	25	382	210	80	41	58	42	99–62	.615

Was aggressive in using his bench until his team developed; hasn't been the last two years. Lets his baserunners go. Settled lineup; platoon percentages driven up by switch-hitters.

ART HOWE

Year	Tm/Lg	G	LUp	Pl%	PH	PR	DS	Rel	SBA	H&R	PO	SA	IBB	W–L	Pct.
1993	Hou/N	162	92	.610	254	26	29	324	163	106	57	107	52	85–77	.525
1996	Oak/A	162	124	.485	124	**74**	40	419	93	61	37	49	61	78–84	.481

Platoon manager in Houston, but didn't have any left-handers to work with in Oakland. Used 74 pinch runners to try to minimize the effects of slow team.

DAVY JOHNSON

Year	Tm/Lg	G	LUp	Pl%	PH	PR	DS	Rel	SBA	H&R	PO	SA	IBB	W–L	Pct.
1993	Cin/N	118	93	.485	182	33	42	279	145	83	53	63	27	53–65	.449
1994	Cin/N	115	79	.544	195	22	12	261	170	94	47	74	22	66–48	.579
1995	Cin/N	144	106	.579	258	18	31	330	258	78	8	87	25	**85**–59	.590
1996	Bal/A	163	100	.693	85	33	38	378	116	65	13	46	35	88–74	.543

His 85 pinch hitters used was the fewest in baseball; totals were high in Cincinnati because he was using a seven-man outfield. Conservative, close-to-the-vest manager in most respects. Doesn't go to the bullpen quickly, doesn't tend to put his runners in motion.

MIKE JORGENSEN

Year	Tm/Lg	G	LUp	Pl%	PH	PR	DS	Rel	SBA	H&R	PO	SA	IBB	W–L	Pct.
1995	StL/N	96	84	.541	151	8	11	231	83	47	13	37	14	42–54	.438

Record too brief for any solid analysis.

TOM KELLY

Year	Tm/Lg	G	LUp	Pl%	PH	PR	DS	Rel	SBA	H&R	PO	SA	IBB	W–L	Pct.
1993	Min/A	162	138	.474	162	32	29	356	142	115	37	39	34	1–91	.438
1994	Min/A	113	86	.551	95	22	6	272	31	84	28	31	10	3–60	.469
1995	Min/A	144	118	.553	190	17	4	336	162	**109**	28	25	11	56–88	.389
1996	Min/A	162	120	.589	**207**	28	12	387	196	94	12	33	27	78–84	.481

Interesting manager; tends to be near the top or bottom of all lists. Switches his lineup quite a bit, but doesn't platoon. Fairly aggressive on the bases and led the league in pinch hitters used. Doesn't bunt, doesn't give intentional walks. Doesn't call pitchouts.

KEVIN KENNEDY

Year	Tm/Lg	G	LUp	Pl%	PH	PR	DS	Rel	SBA	H&R	PO	SA	IBB	W–L	Pct.
1993	Tex/A	162	118	.571	129	42	66	359	180	140	26	95	42	86–76	.531
1994	Tex/A	114	76	.574	61	17	14	301	117	62	9	61	17	52–62	.456
1995	Bos/A	144	107	.653	112	29	21	**370**	143	57	17	55	20	**86**–58	.597
1996	Bos/A	162	124	.558	151	54	27	409	135	75	24	39	41	85–77	.525

Experiments with his lineup. Doesn't platoon. Standard strategy in most respects.

RAY KNIGHT

Year	Tm/Lg	G	LUp	Pl%	PH	PR	DS	Rel	SBA	H&R	PO	SA	IBB	W–L	Pct.
1996	Cin/N	162	**147**	.565	313	17	27	425	234	113	36	96	**66**	81–81	.500

Used 147 lineups in 162 games, most in the National League. Very liberal use of pinch hitters, relievers, and one-run strategies.

MARCEL LACHEMAN

Year	Tm/Lg	G	LUp	Pl%	PH	PR	DS	Rel	SBA	H&R	PO	SA	IBB	W–L	Pct.
1994	Cal/A	74	53	.645	61	12	8	164	71	63	4	40	10	30–44	.405
1995	Cal/A	145	93	.687	141	16	13	368	97	77	34	51	16	78–67	.538
1996	Cal/A	112	80	.613	101	11	14	272	55	32	**60**	48	32	52–60	.464

Led the American League in pitchouts called despite being fired in early August.

RENE LACHEMANN

Year	Tm/Lg	G	LUp	Pl%	PH	PR	DS	Rel	SBA	H&R	PO	SA	IBB	W–L	Pct.
1993	Fla/N	162	102	.653	242	15	47	409	173	105	35	77	58	64–98	.395
1994	Fla/N	115	92	.562	183	11	6	300	91	44	21	63	33	51–64	.443
1995	Fla/N	143	104	.530	227	24	20	400	184	70	9	105	40	67–76	.469
1996	Fla/N	86	47	.442	149	12	2	212	86	32	4	42	30	39–47	.453

Standard strategy in most respects. Didn't need to call pitchouts because of his catcher, Charles Johnson.

GENE LAMONT

Year	Tm/Lg	G	LUp	Pl%	PH	PR	DS	Rel	SBA	H&R	PO	SA	IBB	W–L	Pct.
1993	Chi/A	162	92	.642	87	46	57	322	163	110	82	93	36	**94–68**	**.580**
1994	Chi/A	113	104	.654	102	15	16	239	104	70	56	**67**	16	67–46	.593
1995	Chi/A	31	23	.706	39	4	1	88	34	15	20	12	11	11–20	.355

Liked to bunt.

TONY LARUSSA

Year	Tm/Lg	G	LUp	Pl%	PH	PR	DS	Rel	SBA	H&R	PO	SA	IBB	W–L	Pct.
1993	Oak/A	162	**149**	.594	117	36	38	**424**	190	**186**	61	59	59	68–94	.420
1994	Oak/A	114	97	.602	89	28	14	**308**	130	73	32	31	30	51–63	.447
1995	Oak/A	144	120	.576	113	38	24	358	158	105	42	42	26	67–77	.465
1996	StL/N	162	120	.525	246	25	13	413	207	**141**	41	**117**	43	88–74	.543

Likes to use the hit and run. Obsessed with having left-handers in the bullpen.

TOMMY LASORDA

Year	Tm/Lg	G	LUp	Pl%	PH	PR	DS	Rel	SBA	H&R	PO	SA	IBB	W–L	Pct.
1993	LA/N	162	96	.486	298	48	39	346	187	161	39	**137**	68	81–81	.500
1994	LA/N	114	55	.514	209	25	14	239	111	64	13	66	21	58–56	.509
1995	LA/N	144	66	.512	270	42	22	355	172	77	18	100	29	**78**–66	.542
1996	LA/N	76	44	.487	149	12	9	178	76	37	23	44	35	41–35	.539

Tended to ride with his starting pitcher. Settled lineup; didn't platoon. Bunted whenever the opportunity presented itself; made frequent use of the intentional walk.

JIM LEYLAND

Year	Tm/Lg	G	LUp	Pl%	PH	PR	DS	Rel	SBA	H&R	PO	SA	IBB	W–L	Pct.
1993	Pit/N	162	107	.511	296	16	44	384	147	126	39	100	43	75–87	.463
1994	Pit/N	114	**94**	.542	170	16	13	285	78	65	38	48	31	53–61	.465
1995	Pit/N	144	**124**	.570	282	8	4	391	139	94	51	69	36	58–86	.403
1996	Pit/N	162	117	.511	299	18	14	422	175	116	46	101	50	73–89	.451

Would be interesting to have more data from his best teams. Has experimented with his lineup in recent years.

JOHN McNAMARA

Year	Tm/Lg	G	LUp	Pl%	PH	PR	DS	Rel	SBA	H&R	PO	SA	IBB	W–L	Pct.
1996	Cal/A	49	39	.624	45	11	10	113	29	26	22	18	15	18–31	.367

Not enough data.

JOHNNY OATES

Year	Tm/Lg	G	LUp	Pl%	PH	PR	DS	Rel	SBA	H&R	PO	SA	IBB	W–L	Pct.
1993	Bal/A	162	103	.606	70	51	36	329	127	90	30	65	50	85–77	.525
1994	Bal/A	112	67	.544	45	26	18	234	82	46	11	24	16	63–49	.563
1995	Tex/A	144	93	.682	108	30	25	310	137	74	3	63	28	74–70	.514
1996	Tex/A	163	73	.625	89	43	10	347	109	88	8	41	44	**90**–72	.556

Uses as few lineups in a season as any manager in baseball. Uses as few pinch hitters and as few relievers as anybody. Never calls pitchouts.

LOU PINIELLA

Year	Tm/Lg	G	LUp	Pl%	PH	PR	DS	Rel	SBA	H&R	PO	SA	IBB	W–L	Pct.
1993	Sea/A	162	117	.649	168	41	32	353	159	152	83	159	56	82–80	.506
1994	Sea/A	112	98	.506	**113**	24	28	252	69	55	37	54	28	49–63	.438
1995	Sea/A	145	98	.562	137	41	22	324	151	77	40	66	32	**79**–66	.545
1996	Sea/A	161	99	.566	190	28	14	403	129	65	40	65	52	85–76	.528

Led the American League in pinch hitters in 1994, and was second last year. Who would you pinch-hit for, in his lineup? Will order a pitchout.

PHIL REGAN

Year	Tm/Lg	G	LUp	Pl%	PH	PR	DS	Rel	SBA	H&R	PO	SA	IBB	W–L	Pct.
1995	Bal/A	144	104	.658	154	51	26	336	137	70	36	54	28	71–73	.493

The 1995 record was unremarkable.

JIM RIGGLEMAN

Year	Tm/Lg	G	LUp	Pl%	PH	PR	DS	Rel	SBA	H&R	PO	SA	IBB	W–L	Pct.
1993	SD/N	162	114	.496	317	36	51	397	133	104	67	110	**72**	61–101	.377
1994	SD/N	117	93	.580	184	28	19	273	116	73	52	80	**41**	47–70	.402
1995	Chi/N	144	92	.528	196	9	30	414	142	104	53	90	**51**	73–71	.507
1996	Chi/N	162	87	.496	**326**	34	21	439	158	102	65	79	55	76–86	.469

Fairly stable lineup, but manages as if he had a twenty-eight-man roster once the game begins. Uses many pinch hitters, many relievers. Never misses a chance to call a pitchout or order an intentional walk.

BILL RUSSELL

Year	Tm/Lg	G	LUp	Pl%	PH	PR	DS	Rel	SBA	H&R	PO	SA	IBB	W–L	Pct.
1996	LA/N	86	37	.470	154	33	12	205	84	61	26	44	31	49–37	.570

Too early to draw any firm conclusions. Experimented with his lineup less than Lasorda had, used three times as many pinch runners. Substantially reduced intentional walks (compared to Lasorda), although they remained fairly high.

BUCKY SHOWALTER

Year	Tm/Lg	G	LUp	Pl%	PH	PR	DS	Rel	SBA	H&R	PO	SA	IBB	W–L	Pct.
1993	NY/A	162	99	.688	150	40	38	332	74	51	24	35	58	88–74	.543
1994	NY/A	113	79	.632	95	31	3	241	95	41	22	34	18	**70**–43	**.619**
1995	NY/A	144	107	.738	124	30	20	302	80	47	29	27	15	79–65	.545

Relatively conservative manager, doesn't use large number of relievers or substitutes, except that he will pinch-run if the potential run is meaningful.

JOE TORRE

Year	Tm/Lg	G	LUp	Pl%	PH	PR	DS	Rel	SBA	H&R	PO	SA	IBB	W–L	Pct.
1993	StL/N	162	118	.646	264	33	52	423	225	162	52	81	50	87–75	.537
1995	StL/N	47	36	.543	99	6	4	146	42	18	14	26	11	20–27	.426
1996	NY/A	162	131	.653	92	62	**55**	411	142	70	19	53	35	**92**–70	.568

In 1994, when his team had no obvious defensive sore point, he used zero defensive subs; last year he led the majors, with 55, mostly getting Mariano Duncan and Wade Boggs out of the lineup in the late innings. Platoons some, uses his bullpen heavily, makes substantial use of one-run strategies.

BOBBY VALENTINE

Year	Tm/Lg	G	LUp	Pl%	PH	PR	DS	Rel	SBA	H&R	PO	SA	IBB	W–L	Pct.
1996	NY/N	31	28	.571	88	7	12	75	20	19	3	25	14	12–19	.414

This record doesn't go back far enough to establish what he usually did with Texas.

BOBBY COX

Decade Snapshot: 1990s

Most Successful Managers: 1. Bobby Cox
                                         2. Cito Gaston
                                         3. Lou Piniella
                                         4. Tony LaRussa

Most Controversial Manager: Dallas Green
Dallas Green was the last of the hard-ass managers, surviving from the pre–free agency era.

Others of Note: Felipe Alou
                            Mike Hargrove
                            Dave Johnson
                            Tom Kelly
                            Kevin Kennedy
                            Jim Leyland

Stunts: As you know, many pitchers are most effective when they are told to go out there and throw as hard as they can for as long as they can, without having to worry about pacing themselves. Baseball freethinkers, for that reason, have long discussed the possibility of abandoning the roles of "starter" and "reliever," and using all of the pitchers on a staff in two- or three-inning stints.

On July 24, 1993, the Oakland A's decided to try it. The A's formed three groups of pitchers, each of which would be assigned to pitch three innings every third day, with a bullpen of two or three pitchers to close out victories and cover any unexpected gaps.

This was Dave Duncan's idea, and Tony LaRussa's decision to put it into practice. Needless to say, the A's were struggling at the time, or the idea wouldn't have had much appeal. They continued to struggle, losing four out of five games before deciding to chuck the plan. The pitchers didn't like it, and it just didn't work.

Typical Manager Is: better educated than in previous generations. Over 80% of current managers have attended college (twenty-three of twenty-eight), and four of the five exceptions are among the oldest managers in baseball. About 40% are college graduates. Within twenty years, almost all major league managers will have degrees.

Percentage of Playing Managers: None.
The last playing manager was Pete Rose, who retired as a player after the 1986 season.

Most Second-Guessed Manager's Moves:
1. 1995, Bucky Showalter lost confidence in his bullpen during the American League Championship Series. David Cone started the fifth game on three days rest, threw 146 pitches,

and surrendered the lead in the eighth inning. In the ninth inning, Showalter turned the game over to Jack McDowell, who

a) was pitching on one day of rest,

b) was making his first major league relief appearance, and

c) had been hammered two days earlier.

McDowell lost the game in the eleventh.

2. On May 29, 1993, Texas manager Kevin Kennedy used Jose Canseco to pitch the final inning of a 15–1 blowout. Canseco seriously injured his arm, a "complete tear of the ulnar collateral ligament in his right elbow," and had to have the Tommy John surgery to repair the damage. He was out essentially the rest of the season.

Player Rebellions: 1992, Montreal against Tom Runnells.

Buck Rodgers was (or is) a relatively high-pressure manager. On June 3, 1982, a struggling Milwaukee team replaced Rodgers with a good ole boy named Harvey Kuenn. "Have fun," Kuenn ordered his new team. The Brewers relaxed and surged to the American League championship.

On June 2, 1991, the Montreal Expos also decided to replace Buck Rodgers, but they went the other direction. They opted for a more intense, higher-pressure manager named Tom Runnels. They coasted along the rest of the season, about the same as before.

At spring training, 1992, Runnells addressed his team in combat fatigues. The press talked about Runnells's running a boot camp; he was apparently trying to lighten the atmosphere, deliver the message, "Yes, it's a boot camp, but let's keep our sense of humor about it." The incident made Runnells look silly, and his team began to drift away from him. By mid-May, the thirty-seven-year-old manager was described by Peter Gammons as "a nervous wreck." He was fired on May 22.

Evolutions in Strategy: The most notable trend now in motion in the major leagues is the dramatic increase in the frequency of pitching changes. The number of pitchers used per game has increased more than 20% in the last five years, as roster spots traditionally reserved for pinch hitters, pinch runners, and defensive substitutes are now being used for extra relievers.

The number of complete games in the major leagues now is less than one-half of what it was in 1988.

As you no doubt know, we are in a high-scoring era. In mid-1990s baseball there are many walks, fairly high batting averages, and historic numbers of home runs. This tends to discourage the use of all one-run weapons—sacrifice bunts, stolen bases, intentional walks. They're all down some. Double plays are up.

The number of hit batsmen per game has increased by more than 60% since 1989.

Evolution in the Role of the Manager: As escalating salaries have made it more impossible to keep a core of talent together, the manager has come to represent the "center" of a team in a way that he did not twenty years ago. At the beginning of spring training, many teams are composed of strangers. The manager has increased responsibility, or if you prefer, increased opportunity, to establish the tenor of the team.

Right-Handed Sluggers

Of the seven teams in history which grounded into 169 or more double plays, six were the Boston Red Sox of 1949, 1951, 1980, 1982, 1983, and 1993.

When in Doubt

The plight of Davey Johnson in Cincinnati, forced out after winning his division with a third-rate team, is typical of the modern manager. Building for tommorrow? Forget it. The manager of the nineties has a three-year contract and a month-to-month lease on his condo. A manager's job is as solid as his last homestand. As one manager said recently, "It's always been 'What have you done for me lately?' But now, after what's happened to Bucky Showalter and Dave Johnson, even winning doesn't seem to be enough to keep the buzzards off your back."

—Made-up Quote by Imaginary Old Sportswriter

Okay; I made that quote up, because I forgot to save one, but if you listen carefully the next time a manager gets fired, you will hear somebody say how quick "they" are to fire the manager anymore. Of course, if you had listened carefully twenty-five years ago, when Dave Bristol was fired or Eddie Kasko or Ken Aspromonte, I'm sure you would have heard the same thing, so this isn't evidence, but it introduces the issue: Is managerial stability decreasing? Are teams today quicker to fire the manager than they were a generation ago? Are they slower? Has there been any change?

In 1945 the average major league manager had been employed in his current position for 8.37 seasons. Of course, averages are often misleading, as we all know from the example of the man with one foot in a fire and the other in a block of ice. (On average, he was comfortable.) By 1945 Connie Mack had been employed in his current position for forty-five years, which tends to infarcalate the average.

Taking Connie Mack out of it, however, the average for the other fifteen managers in 1945 was still almost six years. The other managers at that time included Joe McCarthy in New York, where he had been for fifteen years, Jimmie Dykes in Chicago (he had been there for a dozen years, with-

out winning anything), and Joe Cronin, winding up his eleventh year as a player/manager in Boston, where he had won absolutely nothing as yet. Several other managers had been occupying their current positions since the late 1930s.

In the first season of major league baseball (1876) the average major league manager had had his job, obviously, for only one season. From 1876 to the turn of the century this average worked its way slowly upward, peaking at 4.16 years per manager in 1897.

That average dipped a little in 1898, when Cap Anson was forced out in Chicago, and was driven under 2.00 by the startup of the American League, which, of course, had no established managers.

That effect was very temporary, and by 1908 the tenure average was back to 4.06 years. The average continued to ascend over the next two decades, partly because of Connie Mack and John McGraw, but partly for other reasons, as we shall see in a moment. By 1926 the average was up to 7.25 years per manager. Connie Mack was then in his twenty-sixth season with the A's, and John McGraw in his twenty-fifth season in New York, but the tenure average of the other fourteen managers was still 4.64 seasons. In 1926 only one major league manager took over a new team, that being Joe McCarthy in Chicago.

The winter of 1926–1927 was of great controversy in baseball, and two of the controversies sent a total of three managers moving on toward new challenges. Rogers Hornsby exhausted the patience of Sam Breadon and Branch Rickey in St. Louis, despite leading the Cardinals to their first World Championship, and was traded to New York. Speaker and Cobb were forced from their roosts in Cleveland and Detroit. Normal attrition caught up with other managers; altogether, eight of the sixteen teams had new managers in 1927, dropping the average to 6.18.

But then the average began to click back

upward. It went down, of course, when McGraw retired, but another decade of steady progress had pushed the tenure average, by 1945, to 8.37 years, an all-time record.

It is surely not a coincidence that this happened during the war. Baseball men hunkered down and waited for the war to be over. In a sense, the war years were the truest test of a manager's skills. With almost all of the established stars leaving the game, everybody was scrambling for players. The manager who could make a quick and accurate assessment about a player he didn't know, the manager who could form and execute Plan B quickly when Plan A went off to war, the manager who could find a use for a one-skill or two-skill talent—that manager never had a larger advantage than during the war.

But at the same time, everybody had an alibi. When a team performed badly, how could you blame the manager? After all, he had lost his cleanup hitter. He'd lost his starting catcher. He'd lost his best pitcher. Every manager had a ready excuse—and, in fact, few managers were fired during the war years.

After the war ended, managers started to drop like flies. By 1949 the tenure average was down to 5.25 seasons, which would have been 2.33 seasons if you didn't count Connie Mack. Connie retired, and the average dropped to 2.12 seasons in 1952—the lowest it had been since 1902. Thus, when average managerial tenure is plotted on a chart across time, the lowest point in modern history and the highest point are separated by only seven seasons—1952 and 1945.

Average tenure is one way to measure managerial stability, but probably a better way is by focusing on the percentage of teams which have *new* managers. In theory—that is, in a vast universe—these two measurements would be tied in an inverse knot. If one-fourth of all teams replace their manager in any season, then the average managerial tenure has to be 4.00 years. If one-

fifth of teams change managers, then the average manager's tenure has to be 5.00 years.

However, this would only be true if you had a very, very large number of teams. With a limited number of teams, probably the best way to make an estimate of managerial stability is to take a group of seasons and figure the percentage of teams which hired new managers.

In baseball's opening act, 1876–1979, 68% of all teams had new managers in any season. Of course, in the first season, when there were eight teams, all eight had new managers, so that starts us out at 100%.

Managerial stability increased steadily for more than a half-century after that. Teams became less and less inclined to fire the manager. In the 1880s, 52% of all teams had new managers. In the 1890s this figure declined to 48%, then to 36% in the first decade of the twentieth century, then to 33%, then 25%. Of the 160 major league teams in the 1940s, only 34 had first-year managers. That's 21%. This chart gives the data for each of major league baseball's first eight decades:

Years	Teams	Number with New Managers	Percentage
1876–79	28	19	68%
1880–89	150	78	52%
1890–99	128	62	48%
1900–09	152	55	36%
1910–19	160	52	33%
1920–29	160	40	25%
1930–39	160	43	27%
1940–49	160	34	21%

A word of explanation. We counted the number of *teams* with new managers, not the number of new managers—thus, if a team had four new managers in a season, that counts as one, not four. If a team changed managers in midseason, that counted as a season with a new manager, the same as if the change were made the previous winter. If a man managed a team for four years and was forced out in midseason, that counted as the first season for the new manager, rather than the fifth season of the old manager—with a couple of exceptions. We ignored interim managers, and we ignored people who managed only a few games. Joe McCarthy managed the Chicago Cubs until the closing days of the 1930 season, when he was replaced by Rogers Hornsby. That counts as the last season for Joe McCarthy, not the first season for Rogers Hornsby.

Also, for obvious reasons, we ignored the leagues which were only in existence for a year or two, the Federal League, the Player's League, and the Union Association. Including them would have given us misleading spikes in the data.

Anyway, it is clear that, within this time frame, a trend was in motion. Teams *were* becoming progressively more reluctant to fire the manager.

This ended at the end of World War II. From the 1940s through the late 1980s, the position of managers became more tenuous:

Years	Teams	Number with New Managers	Percentage
1940–49	160	34	21%
1950–59	160	49	31%
1960–69	198	74	37%
1970–79	245	81	33%
1980–89	260	94	36%

From the 1920s through the 1940s, about one team in four changed managers. From 1950 to 1990, it became one team in three. In this latter era, the tenure average for major league managers was always around 3.00 years. Discounting expansion teams, the percentage of teams with new managers was higher in the 1980s than in any decade since 1900–1909.

Why did the position of manager suddenly become less solid about 1950? The reasons are probably cultural. I came of age in the 1960s. As children of the '60s, we looked back on the 1950s as a quiet, sleepy period when nothing of much interest happened. I think it is fair to say that this remains the prevailing image of the Eisenhower era.

In retrospect, it is apparent that nothing could be further from the truth. Our country experienced more broad, fundamental changes in the 1950s, I believe, than in any other decade in American history. What we experienced in the 1960s was not underlying change, but something more like a cultural panic. When the aggressive, let's-do-it-now-and-ask-questions-later attitude which had characterized Americans for 150 years met up with postwar technology and a booming economy, the pace of change exploded. We all became a little quicker, a little more aggressive, a little more bloodless, and a little less committed. In the 1960s, we started to worry about that. The rate of firing managers increased in the 1950s for precisely the same reason that the divorce rate increased, and for precisely the same reason that baseball teams, after fifty years of standing still, began racing around the continent. We turned impatient.

In the 1990s, at least so far, the rate of changing managers has gone back to its pre-1950 levels:

Years	Teams	Number with New Managers	Percentage
1980–89	260	94	36%
1990–96	191	51	27%

At the start of September 1995, the average major league manager had been employed in his present position for 4.82 seasons. This is the highest average tenure since Connie Mack retired.

As to why this may have happened . . . I don't really know, but a few thoughts.

1) It may be that the 1994–95 strike had an effect similar to World War II: it provided every failing manager with a ready excuse.

2) It may be that, as players change teams more rapidly, management looks to managers to

provide some stability within the organization. Or, stated another way, it may be that since it is easier to move players, it is less necessary to move managers.

3) It may be, John Sickels suggests, that the large corporations which own most teams today are less impulsive than the independent operators of earlier days. Calvin Griffith would fire his manager because attendance was down.

4) The decade's not over. The data may change before it is.

One thing I notice is that, in modern baseball, a World Championship seems to inoculate a manager for a period of several years. In the 1960s and '70s (and before), managers of World Championship teams normally were fired or forced out within two or three years, unless they won another World Championship. From 1962 to 1980 the nineteen World Championships were won by sixteen different managers—only four of whom were still managing the same team three years after their last World Championship. Only Walt Alston, Red Schoendienst, Earl Weaver, and Chuck Tanner were able to hold their jobs for three solid years without winning another invitation to the White House.

But in recent years, winning a World Championship has seemed to guarantee the job. Opening 1996, the winners of the World Championship in 1981, 1987, 1988, 1991, 1992, and 1993 were still employed with the same teams, granted that that's only three managers. Tony LaRussa, who won the World Championship in Oakland in 1989, stayed there for six frustrating years afterward and left on his own terms. Perhaps Sparky Anderson illustrates the change best. With Cincinnati in the 1970s, nine years of brilliant success didn't save him; he was let go two years after winning the 1976 World Championship, and he won 180 games in those two years. But with Detroit, one World Series was enough to sustain him through eleven years of sometimes gruesome performance.

The bottom-line data are pretty clear. Modern teams do *not* hurry to fire the manager—in fact, quite the opposite is true. Managers today are not quite college professors, but they're not fruit flies, either.

Tolerance, Tolerance

This is ten degrees off the subject, but it is something I feel strongly about. Marge Schott is the owner of the Cincinnati Reds. In a report broadcast on ESPN on March 5, 1996, Ms. Schott was asked about an armband swastika that she reportedly had in her house. Yes, she said; she did have such an object. It was taken from a Nazi soldier in World War II, and given to her by her husband, a World War II veteran.

Sensing a minefield, she attempted to cover herself—by defending Adolf Hitler. Hitler, she said, "was good at the beginning, but he went too far."

Ms. Schott has a history of insensitive remarks, and so the media world landed on her shoulders and began to kick viciously at her teeth. Talk show hosts quickly revised their monologues to include Marge Schott jokes, Marge the Bigot. A tabloid television show had a poll question for the day, "Should Marge Schott be thrown out of baseball?"

Another ESPN reporter asked acting commissioner Bud Selig whether any disciplinary action was planned, implying that some such action was appropriate. Ms. Schott issued a quick apology, but on May 8, 1996, *USA Today* reported in a front-page story that "Bud Selig says (the apology) is inadequate and that disciplinary action could be expected."

Am I the only one here who is profoundly offended by the idea of punishing Marge Schott for what she says? To deal with the smallest issue first, I am mystified by how it is decided that we should take offense at these remarks. We live in a society in which offensive behavior is commonplace. I can walk two blocks from my office and find 500 things at which I could, if I chose, take offense—obscenities spray-painted on the sides of buildings, homeless people begging for money, posters of naked women hanging in the windows of music stores, tobacco ads, gay couples making out in the park, and people playing their car radios loud enough to wake Beethoven. Our culture dictates that we put up with these things. I'm okay with that, but how in the world, in such a society, do people choose to be offended by some essentially innocuous comments by a daffy old woman a thousand miles away?

It's a free country; you can choose Marge to be offended by, if you want to. But even so, when did historical ignorance become a punishable offense? To me, the idea of censuring Marge Schott because she doesn't have a firm grip on the history of the Third Reich is a great deal more offensive than anything she said.

Marge Schott, says a friend of mine, was acting as a representative of the Cincinnati Reds, and thus as a representative of major league baseball. Freedom of speech means that the law will not punish her for what she says—but major league baseball may.

This is not an argument about *how* we should punish people who express opinions that we disagree with. It is an argument about *whether* we should punish people who express opinions we disagree with. Voltaire said, "I may disaprove of what you say, but I will defend until death your right to say it." What are we saying here? I may disagree with what you have to say, but I will only punish you by civil sanctions, as opposed to criminal penalties?

I have learned, in middle age, that I have a far different concept of what it means to be liberal than does most of our society. Liberalism is not grounded in sensitivity, which is the determination to say or do nothing which might give offense; rather, it is grounded in *tolerance*, which is the determination not to *take* offense.

Taking offense is a cottage industry in this country. We have an antieverything defamation society, so that no matter what you say about anybody, it is somebody's job to take offense. Whenever someone who is vulnerable to this kind of attack says anything which can be contorted into an objectionable statement, fifty reporters will immediately check their Rolodexes to see whose job it is to be offended by this.

The people who do this are not going to stop as long as it keeps working. But, backing away from the immediate controversy, why are we doing this? Is that subsection of the media which generates these controversies serving us well, and should they be allowed to drive the national discussion in this way? Or should we, as a culture, start to nod politely and ignore them?

In the last twenty years TV networks, school districts, corporations, political candidates, and baseball teams have been forced to fire someone who made "insensitive" remarks. The time has come, I would suggest, to stop and ask ourselves whether we are doing the right thing. What if, the next time an owner (or a broadcaster) makes a statement which some people may find offensive, we first stop to ask ourselves a series of simple questions.

•Has this individual used a racist or otherwise objectional epithet?

•Has this person *intentionally* advocated policies we find reprehensible?

•Has this person made remarks which are derogatory to some group of citizens—not merely *offensive* to them, but actually insulting?

If an answer in there is yes, then there may be a legitimate cause of action against the offender. But if the answers are all no, then maybe his employer should, instead, release a prepared statement.

> This network in no way advocates, endorses, or agrees with the statements made by Mr. Bigmouth. However, we do believe in freedom of speech. We feel it would be inappropriate to punish Mr. Bigmouth for statements with which we do not agree.

This won't satisfy anybody, so three days later you're going to need to release another statement:

> This network is aware of the continuing controversy engendered by Jim Bigmouth's unfortunate remarks about lesbian cheerleaders. Our network in no way approves of those remarks, nor endorses the idea that lesbian cheerleaders need special underwear.
>
> However, we are firmly committed to the concept that free speech advances the nation's debate, and thus becomes an integral part of the process of reform. We feel it would be unwise to interfere with that process. Mr. Bigmouth will remain on the air.

That won't shut them up, either, so seven days later, you issue another statement. Don't say anything that isn't true—rather, say what *is* true: that freedom of speech is a higher value than pandemic sensitivity.

Tolerance for what other people say flows naturally from an understanding of why they say it. Adolf Hitler received positive press comment in this country up until 1939. Marge Schott is old enough to have been influenced by that.

One of the things that bothers me about these sensitivity lynchings is that almost all of the victims are older citizens, like Marge Schott, Al Campanis, and Jimmy the Greek. This is America; respect for our elders is strictly optional. But what this is, really, is Baby Boomers punishing members of the prewar generation for their inability to navigate the rapids of post-1960s political sensitivity.

Marge Schott's husband fought in World War II. Maybe it's just me, but I feel the generation that actually fought the war has earned the right to say whatever the hell they want to about Adolf Hitler. Al Campanis was a teammate and friend of Jackie Robinson, one of the people who actually *helped* when the bullets were flying in that war. He is entitled, by virtue of that, to try to tell us whatever he wants to about race relations.

Was he right? Of course not; he was expressing old ideas, and old ideas are often wise, and often foolish. *But we can listen.* We are not *required* to ram his comments back down his throat.

No one's speech is "too wrong" to be heard.

This would be a different argument if Ms. Schott had said something which was *truly* intolerant—if, for example, she had used an ethnic slur, or if she had advocated policies of racial injustice. When someone associated with the game crosses that line, we have a conflict between our desire to respect her freedom of speech, and our legitimate need to dissociate ourselves from what she says. Even in that case, I would argue that our efforts to dissociate ourselves from what she says must not trample on her right to say what she thinks.

But that's a harder case. Marge Schott in the ESPN interview did not *mention* Jews. The question here is, has baseball's compulsive fear of being accused of insensitivy so overwhelmed our respect for freedom of speech that *any* speech may be punished if anything "insensitive" may be inferred from it?

For many years, businesses discriminated against African Americans on the theory that their other customers demanded segregation. "We can't serve Negroes," a restaurant would argue, "because it would upset our white customers."

Well, this is a similar situation. Baseball teams and television networks are trampling on the free speech of their employees and associates, on the theory that the public demands them to. The public has no right to that demand. Let me suggest that the law could allow businesses to punish inappropriate political commentary by employees or associates only when they can demonstrate that

a) there have been actual negative consequences to the inappropriate speech, rather than merely the *fear* of repercussions, and

b) they have attempted other remedies to cure the problem.

Almost any enterprise could claim to have met that burden, including baseball in the case of Marge Schott, but the existence of such a law would enable a person accused of insensitivity to fight back. If a business fired someone or took some other action against them based on a careless remark, the ex-employee could sue, just as, under current law, the ex-employee would be able to claim sex discrimination, age discrimination, or whatever.

Businesses, being wary of lawsuits, would have to balance the fear of criticism with respect for the rights of their employees before they took action.

A book I would like to read—tell me if there is such a book— would be an account of the role of the media in lynchings. I would guess that if you studied lynchings, you would find, in more cases than not, that the local newspapers played a key role in whipping up hysteria against the victims.

Well, this is essentially a modern lynching. Why did people participate in lynchings, anyway? They participated to prove to themselves that they were better than those they attacked. What is gay bashing? It's an infantile effort to prove oneself morally superior to the person being attacked.

And that's what's happening here, too. We're beating up Marge Schott to prove to ourselves that we're better than she is. But are we, really? Which of us has no bigotry in our soul, no dark pockets of unvented anger? We may be more clever than Marge, more discreet in our bigotry, but I don't really believe that the Lord made any of us tolerant by nature.

We have an instinctive urge to band together and destroy invaders. Denied that urge by a society so compulsively open that no one may be targeted as an outsider, we act out our defensive aggression against those who deny our shared values. But this is a tragically closed circle, for what is dangerous about intolerance is the anger and self-righteousness that it occasions, and not merely that it is directed at "innocent" targets. Intolerance directed within the society is not *less* dangerous than intolerance directed at external targets, but *more* dangerous.

But, says my friend, what Marge Schott says may harm baseball. If you were Jewish and lived in Cincinnati, would you still go to Reds games? If a restaurant owner in your hometown made remarks offensive to you or those in your group, would you still patronize that restaurant?

If it was a good restaurant, absolutely.

There is much more to be said for forgiveness and tolerance than for self-righteousness and hypocrisy. The principle that citizens may be punished for "erroneous speech" is a short road to hell. The idea that we should punish people for expressing erroneous ideas is a million times more dangerous than the idea that Adolf Hitler was good in the beginning.

Give the lady a break. You'll need it yourself some day.

Revolving Door

Do players today jump from team to team more often than they did in previous eras? It is a commonplace of sports journalism to assume that they do. This is usually cited in a pejorative fashion, as in "How can the teams today expect fans to develop any strong loyalty, when they know the players they root for will be gone in a year or two?"

This is my third published study of the subject.

The first study, published in the late 1970s, looked at the issue by taking a fixed group of players from a base season (1910, 1920, 1930, 1940, etc.), and then checking to see how many of those players were still with the same team one year later, two years later, three years later, etc. The conclusion at that time: There was no such change. The percentage of players who were still with the team one year later or two years later or five years later was the same in 1975 as it had been in 1965, or 1955, or 1915.

The second study, published in the mid-1980s, showed the same thing: There was still no change in the rate of player retention, given a fixed set of players. I added a second study of the issue at that time, designed to answer essentially the same question in a different way. Suppose that you focus on all players as they play their 500th major league game, their 1,000th major league game, their 1,500th major league game, etc., and you ask for each player "Is he still with his original major league team?" This study also found no change. A given player playing his 1,500th major league game in 1985 was as likely to be with his first team as he would have been in 1975, or 1955, or 1935.

I used a slightly different method this time. This study focused on five-year intervals— 1990–1995, 1980–1985, etc. The exact question that I asked was this: Given all the major league players who were active in both 1990 and 1995, how many of them were still with the same team at the end of 1995 that they were with at the beginning of 1990? And how does this compare with earlier eras, 1980–1985, 1970–1975, etc.?

This study shows that what sportswriters have been saying for at least twenty years is now true: players today *do* change teams more often than they did in the past.

There were 268 players who played in the major leagues in both 1960 and 1965. Eighty-four of those 268, or 31%, played with only one team throughout that era.

The data from 1970 to 1975 were essentially the same, except that the major leagues had expanded. There were 344 players who played in the majors in both 1970 and 1975. Of those 344 players, 103, or 30%, were still with the same team.

From 1980 to 1985, despite the beginning of the free agent era, the percentage actually *increased* slightly, to 32%—128 of 406.

But when 1995 is compared to 1990, there are 444 players who played in both seasons. Only 100 of those 444 players, or 23%, were with the same team in both seasons. Lets put that in chart form:

Years	Players Who Played in Both Seasons	Number with Same Team	Percentage
1960–65	268	84	31%
1970–75	344	103	30%
1980–85	406	128	32%
1990–95	444	100	23%

The data from the earlier eras, 1950–1985, suggests that about 21% of all major league players changed teams each year, and 79% did not (79% to the fifth power is 31%.) The data from 1990 to 1995 suggests that the one-year moving percentage has increased from 21% to 26%—a substantial change.

The Modern Bullpen

In the 120-year history of major league baseball, the standard use of relievers has never arrived at a static equilibrium. The rules effectively governing the use of relief pitchers have been in constant motion—sometimes moving fast (like now), sometimes moving a little more slowly, but always moving. The bullpen of 1996 is radically different from the bullpen of 1986—as the bullpen of 1986 was different from that of 1976, 1976 was different from 1966, and 1966 was different from 1956.

As a starting point, we may assume that baseball began without relief pitching. This is not technically true. Even in 1876, the first season from which decent records may be reconstructed, Harry Wright's Boston Red Caps used 21 relief pitchers in 70 games. The rules originally allowed a pitcher (or other player) to be replaced when he was injured or with the consent of the other team.

So relievers do not start out at true zero, and Dan Quayle is not a complete idiot, but it's close enough for government work, and we'll mark it at zero. The rules were changed to allow substitutions without challenge in 1891, and the number of relievers used began to edge upward. For a hundred years since then, it has gone only upward:

Year	MLG	GIR	RePG
1880	680	76	.11
1890	3,213	349	.11
1900	1,136	221	.19
1910	2,497	1,217	.49
1920	2,468	1,531	.62
1930	2,468	2,232	.90
1940	2,472	2,391	.97
1950	2,476	2,770	1.12
1960	2,472	3,593	1.45
1970	3,888	6,468	1.66
1980	4,210	6,586	1.56
1990	4,210	8,484	2.02
1996	4,534	11,059	2.44

"GIR" stands for "games in relief," "MLG" is "major league games," and "RePG" stands for "relievers per game." The number of relievers used per game has gone down only in the 1970s, and that was simply an effect of the designated hitter rule. The use of relievers went up in the National League in the 1970s, but dipped by more than 20% in the American League in 1973, when the DH rule was adopted.

You will note that the number of relievers used per game is now surging upward more rapidly than at any other point in baseball's history, but the numbers are getting us ahead of the narrative. There were two strands in the early development of the bullpen, the "relief ace" strand and the "starter as closer" strand. The latter strand is best represented by Mordecai Brown and Albert Bender. Brown rivaled Christy Mathewson as the best pitcher in the National League in his time, compiling records of 26–6, 29–9, and 27–9 with ERAs, over a four-year period, never getting *higher* than 1.47. He also led the NL in saves, retrospectively figured, in 1908, 1909, 1910, and

1911. Bender was an American League contemporary, one of the best pitchers in the American League at that time. The two men shared the save record for many years, with 13 apiece, although neither pitcher was aware of this until he had been dead for a number of years.

Doc Crandall was the top reliever of the era, not counting the pitchers like Brown and Bender, who worked 80% of their innings as starters. As early as 1906, John McGraw had used a teenager named George Ferguson to close out some victories (six or seven saves, depending on the source). McGraw had visions of Ferguson becoming a great pitcher, but Ferguson developed bad habits, and the relief job passed to Doc Crandall. Crandall was a part-time infielder, a lifetime .285 hitter who was used by McGraw as a backup second baseman, shortstop, pinch hitter, and reliever. Christy Mathewson wrote about him in *Pitching in a Pinch:*

> Otis Crandall came to the New York club a few years ago a raw country boy from Indiana. I shall never forget how he looked the first spring I saw him in Texas. The club had a large number of recruits and was short of uniforms. He was among the last of the hopefuls to arrive and there was no suit for him, so, in a pair of regular trousers with his coat off, he began chasing flies in the outfield. His head hung down on his chest, and, when not playing, a cigarette dropped out of the corner of his mouth. But he turned out to be a very good fly chaser, and McGraw admired his persistency.
>
> "What are you?" McGraw asked him one day.
>
> "A pitcher," replied Crandall. Two words constitute an oration for him.
>
> Crandall warmed up, and he didn't have much of anything besides a sweeping outcurve and a good deal of speed. He looked less like a pitcher than any of the spring crop, but McGraw saw something in him and kept him. The result is he has turned out to be one of the most valuable men on the club, because he is there in a pinch. He couldn't be disturbed if the McNamaras tied a bomb to him, with a time fuse on it set for "at once." . . .
>
> His specialty (is) to enter a contest, after some other pitcher had gotten into trouble, with two or three men on the bases and scarcely any one out. After he came to the bench one day with the threatening inning behind him, he said to me:
>
> "Matty, I didn't feel at home out there to-day until a lot of people got on the bases. I'll be all right now." And he was. I believe that Crandall is the best pitcher in a pinch in the National League and one of the most valuable men to a team.

The McNamaras were the Tim McVeighs of their day, a pair of radical union leaders who left a bomb at the offices of the *Los Angeles Times*, killing twenty-one people. Damon Runyon wrote that Crandall was "without equal as an extinguisher of batting rallies" and "the greatest relief pitcher in baseball." These quotes are borrowed from *Pen Men*.

Crandall pitched 23 games in relief in 1909, a major league record at the time, then upped the record to 24 in 1910, to 26 in 1911, to 27 in 1912, to 32 in 1913. Other pitchers chased just behind him; by 1913, a half-dozen other pitchers were pitching as many games in relief as Crandall had in 1909.

While Crandall pitched 30 games a year out of the bullpen, he also started 10 to 20 games a season, not to mention pinch hitting and playing second base. As a reliever he went 7–1 in 1910, 7–0 in 1911. What does this tell you? *He was almost always used when his team was behind.* Unlike the modern relief ace, who is used only when his team is *ahead*, Crandall normally came in when the starter was ineffective, and thus, when the team was behind. Crandall had almost twice as many relief wins as saves.

Crandall was a good pitcher. He was not as good as his won–lost records suggest. He was 18–4 in 1910, 15–5 in 1911, but in addition to entering many games protected from a loss by the fact that his team was already behind, he started 33 games over those two seasons, most of them against bad teams. McGraw would use Mathewson and Marquard and Tesreau against the other contenders, figuring that Crandall could beat the Braves and the Cardinals.

Crandall was far from a pure reliever; still, he is the first career reliever of any significance. Crandall pitched in relief 168 times in his career, the most of any pitcher pre-1920. Just two games behind him was his longtime teammate, Red Ames. Ames was a better starter than Crandall; he started about twenty-five times a year, pitched in relief about ten times a season, and had a long career, adding up to 166 relief appearances, although he was basically a starting pitcher.

Sad Sam Jones pitched 39 games in relief in 1915, taking the record away from Crandall, and Dave Danforth pitched 41 games in relief in 1917. These were young pitchers who were trying to establish themselves as starters. When they had some success as relievers, they moved into a starting assignment. Bernie Boland pitched 37 relief games for Detroit in 1916, George Cunningham 36 games for the same team the next season. They were the same, young pitchers trying to get established. Thus, we should note, the cliché about relievers being old broken-down starters is distinctly *untrue* about the first generation of relievers. The bullpen started not as a refuge for old starters, but rather as a kind of try-out camp for young, unproven starters.

This article is not about relief pitchers. That story has been told, and very well, by John Thorn in *The Relief Pitcher* (E. P. Dutton, New York, 1979), and Bob Cairns in *Pen Men* (St. Martin's Press, New York, 1992). This article is about strategy, about how relief pitchers have been used by their managers over time.

In early August 1923, the Washington Senators purchased the contract of Fred Marberry, a twenty-four-year-old Texas right-hander. The press called him "Firpo" because he looked like a boxer of that name, but Marberry didn't like the name and was called Fred by those who knew him. Marberry had a fastball and nothing much else. The Little Rock team, from whom the Senators had purchased him, had been using him mostly in relief, and Senators manager Donie Bush continued in this way, giving Marberry four starts late in 1924 (all of which he won), but using him seven times in relief.

In the history of relief pitchers, Firpo Marberry is the dog that didn't bark. What is exceedingly curious about Firpo Marberry is that there *isn't* a Firpo II, a Firpo III, and a Firpo IV. In 1924 the Senators gave Bucky Harris, their young second baseman, the opportunity to manage the team. Harris used Marberry, in 1924, more or less as other young relief pitchers had been used—as a spot starter against weak teams and a patron of nearly lost causes.

As the season wore on, however, Harris gained confidence in Marberry and began using him to *save* games. The term "saves" was not used, but Marberry was the first pitcher aggressively used to protect leads, rather than being brought in when the starter was knocked out. Thus Marberry is, in my opinion, the first true reliever in baseball history. He pitched 55 times in 1925, always in relief, and saved 15 games. He saved 22 games in 1926, retrospectively figured. It would be many years before anyone would save more. He was a modern reliever—a hard-throwing young kid who worked strictly in relief, worked often, and was used to nail down victories.

And the Senators won. The Washington Senators, the most famous down-and-outers of their time, won their first American League pennant in 1924, and the World Series, and their second American League pennant in 1925. They had been sub-.500 in 1922 and 1923; they added Marberry, used him in relief, and won two pennants.

It should have sent shock waves through baseball. "Hey, this reliever stuff really works!" people should have said. This is what happens when someone uses a new and unique strategy, and wins two league championships with an also-ran team.

What happened here was, everybody got credit for the Senators' success except Marberry. Bucky Harris became one of the biggest stars in the game, the subject of a hero-worship biography. He would manage another twenty-five years on the coattails of his 1924–1925 success. Walter Johnson got credit for it. He was named the MVP in 1924. Roger Peckinpaugh got credit for it; he was named the MVP in 1925. (He then made six errors in the 1925 World Series, prompting a sportswriter to comment that he was not only the MVP of the American League, but of the National League as well.) Sam Rice and Goose Goslin and Joe Judge and Stan Coveleski got credit for it. Firpo Marberry? He was just a reliever.

Even Bucky Harris didn't follow through on Marberry's success. He didn't use Marberry in the seventh game of the 1925 World Series, and Marberry began to slide gradually out of the "closer" role. He started five times in 1926, ten times in 1927. Eventually Harris was replaced, and Marberry began to start more and more.

Marberry's success was reinterpreted as a failure. Muddy Ruel said about Marberry that "he couldn't keep the pace through a whole ball game. He was invincible for two or three innings, but he couldn't go the distance." This quote, which is borrowed from John Thorn's *The Relief Pitcher*, is patent nonsense. "Marberry pitched relief," people said, "because he *couldn't* start. He was an oddity—a good pitcher, but not able to start."

Firpo Marberry made 187 starts in his career, and won 94 of them. Marberry won a higher percentage of his career starts than many Hall of Famers, if not *most* Hall of Famers, including his contemporaries. He won a better percentage of his career starts than Don Drysdale, Waite Hoyt, Eppa Rixey, Ted Lyons, Steve Carlton, Tom Seaver, Red Faber, Jesse Haines, Catfish Hunter, Ferguson Jenkins, Robin Roberts, or Red Ruffing. This does not prove that he should be a Hall of Famer or that he would have been a Hall of Fame starter, but to suggest that he failed as a starting pitcher is absurd.

Baseball historians, looking backward, have tended to hang a line between Firpo Marberry and twenty-first-century relievers, and to say that this is the seminal experience of the modern reliever. In fact, the line that begins with Firpo Marberry, ends with Firpo Marberry. It ends, actually, in the middle of Marberry's career.

What happened is that conventional assumptions had, for the moment, proved stronger than the power of a successful innovation. The traditional way of thinking about pitchers was that

a) a starting pitcher should finish the game whenever possible. If he doesn't finish the game, he hasn't done his job.

b) the only pitchers on the staff who really count are the starters. The relievers are just substitutes, bench warmers.

These ideas were so deeply entrenched in the minds of baseball men that it was easier to re-interpret Marberry's accomplishments as a failure, or at best as a function of Marberry's "peculiar" limitations, than it would have been to deal with the message of Marberry's success. Marberry himself said that he much preferred to be a starting pitcher. Bucky Harris, who had made Marberry the first modern reliever, managed until 1956, during most of which time he backed steadily away from the use of relief aces. Managers simply were not ready to accept the idea that a relief pitcher could be as valuable as anyone on the staff.

As to where relief strategy *did* go, when it didn't go where Firpo Marberry had attempted to lead it, consider this fact. In 1927, every major league pitcher made at least one relief appearance. All of them, everybody appearing in more than six games. There are many seasons in that era, 1925–1940, for which this statement is *almost* true (that is, every pitcher pitched in relief except for one or two men).

You will remember that there were two strands in the early development of relief pitching. From 1925 to World War II, the strand which begins with Three Finger Brown and Chief Bender was the dominant model for the bullpen. There was, in that era, no such thing as a pure reliever, and no such thing as a pure starter. Everybody was a hybrid.

Bob Boone, short of pitching in 1995, tried using Kevin Appier on a four-man rotation. "Pitchers have been starting on a four-day rotation for a hundred years," Boone said. "Maybe we should go back to basics." This raises a deceptively difficult question: When did the four-man rotation really start?

That question has no answer. Certain *elements* of the four-man rotation, as Boone suggested, go back to the 1890s. But no major league manager, from 1925 to 1945, used a four-man rotation in the sense that we mean the term now. You couldn't. The schedule wouldn't allow it. Teams from 1925 to 1945

a) had many more off days and travel days in the schedule than we do now,

b) had many scheduled doubleheaders, and

c) had many more rainouts than modern teams.

The 1943 Chicago White Sox played 57% of their games in doubleheaders. That's the record, but teams in this era commonly played 40% or more of their games in doubleheaders. Five-game weekend series were not unusual. Six-game and seven-game series, resulting from rainouts earlier in the year, were not terribly unusual. You can't run a four-man rotation through a seven-game, four-day series.

I may be beating a dead horse here, but historians who write about the bullpen in the Lou Gehrig era normally focus on Mace Brown, Clint Brown, Jack Russell, and a few other pitchers, leading up to Johnny Murphy. My point is that that is *not* the bullpen of that era; those guys are anomalies. The bullpen of that era is Dizzy Dean, Carl Hubbell, and Lefty Grove. Dizzy Dean in 1934 won 30 games, but he also finished second in the league in saves—behind Carl Hubbell. Lefty Grove saved more games in his career than Mace Brown did.

Managers did not prefer to put their leads into the hands of marginal pitchers. And relievers, in this era, were essentially marginal pitchers. As Rogers Hornsby wrote in *My War with Baseball*:

> Pitchers in my day took more pride in their pitching. They didn't want to come out. Truthfully, we didn't have any relief specialists. If somebody did lose his stuff, we'd bring in the best guy we had available. We would, of course, use some judgment and not waste our star pitcher if we were behind 8–2 in the third inning.

Relief aces began to reappear in significant numbers during World War II. Necessity was the mother of acceptance. Most of the really good pitchers went off to war, and marginal pitchers became the rule, rather than the exception. Managerial thinking changed; the circumstances of the game changed. As to who led the way in changing the thinking of managers, I would cite three men: Joe McCarthy, Leo Durocher, and Bucky Harris.

Joe McCarthy persuaded Johnny Murphy to accept a place in the bullpen and promised him that he would be paid at the same level as a successful starter.

McCarthy, in the first ten years of his managerial career, used his staff the same way other managers of his time used theirs—everybody starts, everybody relieves. By 1935 McCarthy was under pressure to win in New York. The Yankees, accustomed to some success, won only one pennant in McCarthy's first five seasons there, 1931–1935. In midseason, 1935, McCarthy divided his staff into starters and relievers. Red Ruffing, from 1936 to the end of his career in 1947, never pitched in relief—the first pitcher in many years to be used in that way.

And at the same time Johnny Murphy became baseball's first *career* relief ace. He was the first pitcher moved to the bullpen even though he was pitching well.

Murphy was not alone in the Yankee pen; the 1935–1936 Yankee bullpen also was staffed by Pat Malone, Jumbo Brown, and Ted Kleinhans. The 1936 Yankee team is remembered as the first of a series of formidable teams, teams which for four years dominated baseball as no other team ever has. They could equally well be remembered as the first team in baseball history which had a starting staff and a relief corps, and minimal shifting between the roles.

Leo Durocher went to the bullpen as aggressively as any manager of the 1940s, using about 180 relievers a year in a time when most other managers used about 120. "Perhaps the manager who led the way in constant and frequent substitutions to take advantage of every break," reported *Baseball Magazine* in March 1948, "was—and again probably will be—Leo Durocher of the Brooklyn Dodgers. Leo always played percentage. If a left-handed hitter was coming up in a tight situation Leo never hesitated, regardless of how well a right-handed pitcher was working. Out came the right-hander and in went a southpaw, to get what slight edge there might be."

Leo also made a historically important decision when he moved Hugh Casey, a big, hard-throwing pitcher, to a full-time relief role. Casey was the first prominent hard-throwing reliever since Marberry. The fact that a superstar manager, Durocher, did this with a team that was always in contention was a factor in the "relief breakthrough" of the late 1940s.

And **Bucky Harris,** after twenty years of trying to act normal, converted Joe Page from a mediocre starter/swing man into a dominating closer.

Harris managed the Yankees in 1947–1948. He made Page a reliever. Casey Stengel inherited Page in the bullpen, and Page had a huge impact on the pennant races in 1947 and 1949. This event, more than any other one thing, brought about general acceptance of the concept of full-time relievers as a positive asset to a team.

Between 1949 and 1952, there was a great rush to the bullpen.

• In 1950 a bespectacled thirty-three-year-old career minor leaguer named Jim Konstanty pitched 74 times for the Philadelphia Phillies, winning 16 games and being named the Most Valuable Player in the National League.

• In 1951 the Boston Red Sox took Ellis Kinder, who had won 23 games for them in 1949, and moved him to the bullpen. Kinder went 11–2 with a 2.55 ERA.

•In 1952 a Negro League import named Joe Black went 15–4 with a 2.15 ERA, pitching relief for the National League champion Brooklyn Dodgers.

•Right behind the Dodgers were the New York Giants, featuring their own rookie relief ace, Hoyt Wilhelm. Wilhelm went 15–3 with a 2.43 ERA. Because Wilhelm pitched a few more innings than Black, he qualified for the NL ERA lead and led the league in ERA.

•The third-place team in the National League, the Cardinals, also had *their* own rookie relief ace, a guy named Eddie Yuhas. Yuhas went 12–2 with an ERA of 2.73.

Like Bucky Harris, Eddie Sawyer declined to follow through on the logic of his success. Having used Jim Konstanty 74 times in relief in 1950, leading a perennial down-and-out team to the National League pennant, Sawyer took Konstanty to the World Series—as a starting pitcher. Konstanty started the first game of the 1950 World Series. And lost.

Anyway, glance at the won–lost records—11–2 for Kinder, 15–4 for Black, 15–3 for Wilhelm, 12–2 for Yuhas. These lopsided won–lost records tell us something, which is that *these pitchers were not routinely used to protect leads*. A pitcher who is used to protect leads has more opportunities to lose a game than he does to win it, and for that reason will often have a losing record. A pitcher who goes 12–2 in relief is being brought to keep the game close.

Within a very few years, the idea of using some pitchers exclusively in relief swept baseball. In 1946 no major league pitcher pitched 50 games in relief, and only one pitcher (Hugh Casey) pitched 40 times in relief. In 1956, ten years later, more than twenty major league pitchers pitched 40 times in relief, and five of those topped the 60 mark. Casey Stengel continued to use his best pitchers to close out his victories until the late 1950s, when he came up with Ryne Duren. Stengel's relief aces after Joe Page weren't all that good, guys like Tom Morgan and Bob Grim, and he preferred to use Allie Reynolds and Whitey Ford to close out some of his tight victories. When Ryne Duren came along, Stengel stopped using his best starters in relief, effectively ending the strategy which had begun early in the century with Three Finger Brown and Chief Bender, and which had been, for twenty years, the dominant relief strategy of major league managers.

The conditions of the game which had forced managers to use starters as relievers changed in the 1950s. Air travel reduced the number of scheduled travel days, which reduced the number of scheduled doubleheaders. Better groundskeeping reduced the number of *un*scheduled doubleheaders. The four-man starting rotation became standard when the schedule allowed it to become standard.

We could summarize the history of relief pitching, at this point, in three stages:

1906–1926 Experimentation with early relief specialists
1927–1946 Bullpens dominated by off-duty starters
1947–1957 Emergence of the first high-profile relievers

The first stage begins with George (Cecil) Ferguson and ends with Firpo Marberry. From 1927 until the end of World War II, the dominant trend was for victories to be closed out by off-duty starting pitchers. And then, very suddenly, the door swung around the other way, full-time relievers began to dominate bullpens, and the strategy of using starters to close out victories went from dominant to essentially extinct within ten years.

We began with the idea that the starter was *supposed* to finish the game whenever possible; that was his assignment. This idea was very powerful in 1900, and in 1910, and in 1920, and in 1930, and in 1940, and in 1950. And in 1960. And, to a large extent, in 1970. It wasn't dead by 1980. In each generation this idea, this northern star of pitcher usage, was fainter than it had been ten years before, but it was still there.

The idea that a starter was supposed to finish his games atrophied with agonizing slowness, and for each unit of strength that this idea lost, another unit of responsibility was placed on the bullpen. This was the fourth stage in the evolution of relief strategy, the era of ever-expanding responsibilities for the relief ace.

In 1960, when Mike Fornieles pitched 70 times for the Boston Red Sox, this established an American League record for game appearances. The National League (modern) record was still 74 games, by Konstanty. Over the next fifteen years, these records were broken almost annually. Stu Miller pitched 71 games in 1963, a new American League record. Bob Miller pitched 74 games in 1964, tying the National League record, while John Wyatt, Dick Radatz and Hoyt Wilhelm all exceeded the old American League record, with respective totals of 81, 79, and 73. In 1965 Ted Abernathy pushed the National League record to 84 games, while Eddie Fisher extended the American League record to 82. A second National Leaguer, Hal Woodeshick, also pitched 78 games, bettering the old NL mark of 74.

This went on for another decade. Wilbur Wood pitched 88 times in 1968, a new American and Major League record. Wayne Granger upped the ante to 90 (1969), and Mike Marshall to 92 (1973).

And finally, in 1974, Mike Marshall pitched 106 games for the Los Angeles Dodgers. It was shortly after this that John Thorn published his book on relief pitching, *The Relief Pitcher* (1979). "How much can a rescue man pitch?" asked Thorn. "Today we think that Mike Marshall reached— or exceeded—the limit . . . yet 61 years before Marhsall's epic feat, observers thought that Otis Crandall was testing the bounds of endurance by becoming the first man to relieve in 30 or more games. As Dave Danforth passed the 40 mark, Firpo Marberry 50, and Clint Brown 60, baseball brahmins each time proclaimed that forces of nature were being tampered with, that arms could not bear up under the strain. The same remarks accompanied the successive fractures of the 70, 80 and 90 game 'barriers' by, respectively, Jim Konstanty, John Wyatt, and Wayne Granger."

John's a friend, and he knows that I'm not picking on him by quoting back something he was not exactly right about. He had no way of knowing, at that time, that baseball history had planted its pivot foot. The assignment given to top relievers, after thirty years of constant expansion, was about to contract rapidly.

It wasn't the *games;* it was the *innings.* Dick Radatz in 1964 pitched 79 games and 157 innings. Wayne Granger in 1969 pitched 90 games and 145 innings. Mike Marshall pitched 106 games and 208 innings. These are the numbers which, in retrospect, look phenomenal to us. Someday some reliever will pitch 110 games in a season—but he'll pitch 110 games and 85 innings, maybe 65 innings. Marshall pitched 106 games, 2 innings a game.

And, for once, it is absolutely clear who caused baseball history to turn. It was Bruce Sutter.

Bruce Sutter was an amazing pitcher. He threw a split-finger fastball before anyone else did, and better. By June 28, 1977, Sutter had already pitched 37 games, 67 innings, giving up 37 hits and 10 walks. His ERA was 0.67. He had struck out 78 men, and had already recorded 21 saves, moving in on the established major league record of 38. Projected to a full season, he was looking at 87 games, 157 innings, 183 strikeouts, and 49 saves, to go with his 0.67 ERA.

In early season, 1978, he was equally impressive, with an ERA around 1.00 into July. He was more than a good pitcher. Elroy Face was a good pitcher. Johnny Murphy was a good pitcher. Goose Gossage was a great pitcher. Bruce Sutter was a phenomenon. He made the American League All-Star team look like amateurs.

But in both seasons, 1977–1978, he was not the same over the second half. He went on the DL in August 1977. In 1978 he kept pitching, but his ERA skyrocketed over 3.00. Herman Franks was his manager, and Franks hit on a solution. In 1979, he announced, Sutter would be used *only* to protect a lead.

There had long been a feeling that relief aces were being overused. That was what John Thorn was responding to. He was saying, in essence, that most people may think that Mike Marshall was pitched to death in 1974, but then, people have been saying the same thing for sixty years. Each year there were more and more games *not* completed by the starting pitcher, and, since the reliever's job was to pitch in any close game when the starter wasn't available, each year there was more and more work to be done by the relief ace. There was no third clause to the definition of the relief ace's job. Herman Franks wrote the third clause: The relief ace will work when the game is close, the starter is gone, *and it is a "save" situation.*

Within a very few years, this would become the standard definition of a closer's job.

Now, it is very much an open question whether this is an optimal strategy. Does an effective relief ace have the greatest impact on the won–lost record of his team when he is used only to close out narrow *victories*, or might he not have equal impact, or even greater impact, if he was used as Elroy Face was used? I don't know the answer to this question; I don't think anybody else knows, either. There are no studies of the issue. There is no compelling logic. I have never heard any major league manager, executive, or ex-manager explain *why* using his reliever in this way is more effective than using him in some other way.

The manager who defined this practice, Herman Franks, was fired within a year, and never managed again.

Nonetheless, this practice is universally accepted by current major league managers. There is no exception. There is no manager who has continued to use his relief ace in the way that relievers were used from 1950 to 1978. There is something called the "Bullpen by Committee," which means rotating the closer work among several pitchers, but even this, though often talked about, is rare in practice and is really nothing more than a transitional stage while the team attempts to identify the one pitcher who should be The Closer.

This is rather remarkable, isn't it? Nobody studies the issue, nobody explains or defends the strategy in any meaningful way, and there is no dramatic example of a team which adopts this strategy and comes out of nowhere to win a pennant. And yet, within a few years, every major league manager adopts the strategy. How can that happen?

Our language drives our thought.

Jerome Holtzman developed the concept of saves for a reliever, and saves became the standard measure of a relief pitcher's success. There is an intuitive logic which says that if the best relief pitcher is the pitcher who gets the most saves, then the relief pitcher's job is to "save" the game, and therefore the best use of a relief pitcher is to use him in save situations. It's one of those things that seems to make sense unless you actually think about it, at which point you will realize that the caboose is not really hitched to the engine.

The trivial consequence of this change has been a tremendous growth in the number of saves acquired by the top relievers. It's almost become a game for the managers, see how many saves you can get for your relief ace. Elroy Face in his career averaged less than one save every six innings of relief pitching. Dan Quisenberry established a major league record for saves in 1983, averaging less than one save every three innings. The top relievers today are closing in on one save per inning pitched. Quisenberry said, "I thought I was a stud. I thought I'd hold the record a few years, at least." Little more than a decade later, his record 45 saves in a season has been pushed out of the top ten, and will soon enough be pushed out of the top 100.

But at the same time, the slow decay of the expectation that a starting pitcher will finish his games has proceeded. In 1980, starting pitchers still finished 20% of their games. This percentage had gone down in every ten-year period in baseball's history:

YEAR	MLG	GG	CG%
1890	3,213	2,873	89%
1900	1,136	934	82%
1910	2,497	1,550	62%
1920	2,468	1,399	57%
1930	2,468	1,095	44.4%
1940	2,472	1,095	44.3%
1950	2,476	998	40%
1960	2,472	665	27%
1970	3,888	852	22%
1980	4,210	856	20%

Since 1980 it has continued to decline—indeed, the rate of descent has accelerated as the total has approached zero. In 1995, major league starting pitchers completed less than 7% of their starts. The trend line, analyzed without respect to other factors, would suggest that within twenty years there will be a major league season in which no pitcher throws a complete game.

So then we have two things which have happened in the last twenty years.

1) The number of innings pitched by relief aces has declined tremendously.

2) The number of complete games by starters has also declined.

So what does that mean? There has been a tremendous growth in the work assigned to middle relievers. In just fifteen years, there has been a 60% increase in the number of relievers used per game, as was shown in the chart at the beginning of this article.

Which means that roster spots which for sixty years were reserved for third catchers, sixth outfielders, and pure pinch hitters have been suddenly usurped by middle relievers. In 1965 teams normally carried nine pitchers, sometimes eight, and occasionally seven. Now twelve is standard, and sometimes we see thirteen. If you add three pitchers, you've got three less spaces for other players.

One thing you will hear, on almost any baseball broadcast, is a disparaging comment about the quality of pitching today, or about the *shortage* of good pitching nowadays, due to expansion. Now, in general I treat such comments with all the respect I might give to, let us say, the ethical guidance of Ted Kennedy. I can see absolutely no reason why expansion should create a shortage of pitching, as opposed to a shortage of hitting, and there is no evidence that any such thing has happened.

In every baseball game there is one win and one loss. Every hit for a hitter is a hit against a pitcher, and every out recorded by a pitcher is an out charged to some batter. Anything that happens on a baseball field can be presented either as a success or a failure. The people who insist on interpreting everything that happens as a failure tells us how terrible baseball is now and how much better it used to be are just miserable old farts who would do us all a favor if they would shut up and go home.

But let's suppose, for a moment, that there *is* a shortage of pitching. Where would such a shortage come from? Since 1970, the number of major league teams has increased by one-sixth, or 17%. Our population has increased a little more than 20% in the same era, so that hardly explains why we would have a shortage of pitchers.

But in 1970, we had twenty-four teams carrying nine or ten pitchers each. Of the 849 players who played in the major leagues in 1970, 43% were pitchers. Of the 1,133 players who played in the major leagues in 1995, 49% were pitchers. The number of pitchers per team (sometime during the season) has increased from 15.1 to 19.6—while the number of nonpitchers has been essentially constant.

If there is, in fact, a shortage of pitching, couldn't the rapid expansion of bullpens be a primary cause of it? Doesn't that really make more sense, in calm review, than the popular theory that expansion has somehow diluted the quality of pitching, without any effect of the quality of hitting?

In 1965 the Chicago White Sox had an outstanding three-man bullpen:

Pitcher	G	IP	W–L	ERA	Saves
Eddie Fisher	82	165	15–7	2.40	2
Hoyt Wilhelm	66	144	7–7	1.81	20
Bob Locker	51	91	5–2	3.16	2

Three pitchers, who among them pitched 400 innings. In 1995 the Chicago White Sox had a six-man bullpen, in which no one pitched more than 81 innings:

Pitcher	G	IP	W–L	ERA	Saves
Roberto Hernandez	60	60	3–7	3.92	32
Kirk McCaskill	55	81	6–4	4.89	2
Scott Radinsky	46	38	2–1	5.45	1
Matt Karchner	31	32	4–2	1.69	0
Tim Fortugno	37	39	1–3	5.59	0
Jose DeLeon	38	68	5–3	5.19	0

We have many more relief pitchers, making many more game appearances in the aggregate although somewhat fewer as individuals, but pitching dramatically fewer innings per outing, and with the save opportunities all given to a single reliever.

Which leaves us with two large questions:

1) Where are we going? and

2) Does where we are now make any sense?

For more than a hundred years, the number of complete games has been going down, and the number of pitchers per game has been going up. We're now up to two and half pitchers per team per game, and accelerating rapidly. In another generation, will we see three or four or even five pitchers per game?

When a trend has been in motion for more than a hundred years, the forces behind it obviously have a great deal of power, and one should be cautious about predicting that the trend is about to turn around. Nonetheless, I believe that the 2.45 pitchers per game of 1995 is about as high as the average is likely to go, and that this number is as likely to go downward as it is to go upward. The standard bullpen of 2025 may well resemble the bullpen of 1965 more closely than it does the bullpen of 1995.

We will go backward, in my opinion, because:

1) it isn't possible, in some respects, to go forward much further, and

2) the direction in which we have been going doesn't make any sense.

Point a, we have gone, since 1890, from 89% complete games to 7%. We can't go any lower than zero. We've gone about as far as we can go there.

Of course, we could go from starters being lifted in the seventh inning to starters being lifted in the sixth inning to starters being lifted in the fifth inning, so this may be a false argument, but, still on point a, the expansion of the size of the pitching staff has gone as far as it can go. The major league roster has been twenty-five men since before 1920. There is no evidence that the roster is about to expand; in fact, it is very clear that the rosters are *not* about to expand. You can't carry sixteen pitchers and nine position players; that won't work. We've got twelve-man staffs standard now; that's about as far as we can go.

One place we *could* go, and it's not too unlikely that we will, is toward more game appearances per pitcher. The bullpen of the future may consist of six men, but each of those six men may pitch 80 to 120 times per season, as opposed to the 50 to 80 which is standard now. A pitcher pitching 100 games a season, but facing two or three batters per outing, thus pitching only 50 to 70 innings in those 100 games . . . that probably is going to be a *part* of the future bullpen.

But there are two other elements of the 1990s bullpen that I feel strongly are going to break up, simply because the world is ultimately logical, and what major league managers are doing now *isn't* logical. Those two elements are

1) The constant use of left-handed relievers to get out one or two hitters, and

2) The concentration of nearly all save opportunities onto a single reliever.

In 1994 Felipe Alou, manager of the Montreal Expos, did not have a left-hander in the bullpen. He had a five-man bullpen, with Tim Scott, Mel Rojas, John Wetteland, Gil Heredia, and Jeff Shaw. They were all good, but they were all right-handers.

Every time you saw the Expos on TV the announcer would tell you what a tremendous disadvantage Felipe Alou had, not having a left-hander in the bullpen. The Expos had the best record in baseball, 74–40, at the time the season was stopped by Bud Selig's breath.

So I got to wondering, what does this really cost him, not having a left-hander out there? And I worked through the math, how many times does a normal manager have the platoon advantage when he brings in a pitcher, how often did Alou have that advantage, etc. How much does it cost him, per opportunity, and how many opportunities were involved?

And guess what? It doesn't make any difference. Alou's lack of a left-hander in the bullpen cost him the platoon advantage in less than 100 matchups over the course of a season. The normal platoon advantage is about .025, twenty-five points. So the lack of a left-hander in the bullpen probably cost him less than three hits.

We can suppose that the three hits are not all singles; hell, let's suppose one of them is a home run. We can suppose that there might also have been a walk in there, or a situation where an intentional walk was forced by the lack of a lefty to come in. We can suppose that there might have been some hidden situations, situations I didn't find, in which Alou also had a matchup disadvantage when another manager might have had an advantage, although frankly it's hard to understand how. But you can add it up and throw in everything you can think of, and you can't get to five runs.

Now, most 1990s managers feel that you have to have two left-handers in the bullpen, better yet if you have three or even four; gives you maneuverability. But if the disadvantage of having *no* left-hander is only five runs per season, then why in the world are you using two or three roster spots for five runs a year?

Then look at the other side of the equation: What are the costs of doing this? What does it cost you to try to keep two or three lefties in your bullpen?

First, it costs you two or three roster spots. It costs you, let us say, a pinch hitter and a defensive replacement. Any kind of a decent pinch hitter is worth more than five runs a year.

Second, look at the pitchers who are getting major league jobs out of this deal. I've seen countless cases, and I'll bet you have to, where managers will drag in left-hander after left-hander after left-hander, failure after failure after failure, and expose the team to one bad pitcher after another, simply because they are determined to have left-handers in the bullpen.

Wasn't Felipe Alou a lot smarter not to worry about it, just to say, in effect, "These are the best pitchers I've got, they all happen to be right-handers, so what?"

And because his bullpen was all right-handed, Alou was able to *schedule* the work of his relievers to a much greater extent. The left-handed one-out man—he's got to pitch when the opportunity arises. If everybody's right-handed, you can just set up a schedule and rotate them. And he did.

If you ask anybody in baseball about the obsessive use of left-handed spot relievers, he'll say, "Tony LaRussa does it." Well, Tony LaRussa is a smart guy, and a great manager. John McGraw was a smart guy and great manager, too, and he didn't do any of this stuff, so what's that worth?

A key to understanding why managers do what they do is always to remember that *managers like to control the flow of the action.* Any strategy which gives the manager an opportunity to control the flow of the action, such as bunting, will probably be used more often than would be dictated purely by concerns of maximizing optimal expected outcomes.

But this is percentage baseball run amuck. Like Red Rolfe's decision to platoon Vic Wertz, it's percentages promoted ahead of common sense. And as time passes, that will become apparent to more and more managers.

The other 1990s policy, the effort to get as many saves as possible for your relief ace . . . it may be years before that runs its course, and it probably won't happen until the save record is pushed up to around 70. It will break up in this way. Someday a manager will find himself in a tough spot in the sixth inning, and he will ask his closer, a young Lee Smith or John Franco, to go out to the bullpen and get loose. The young pitcher will express displeasure with this. He may even refuse to go to the bullpen, because he's The Closer, and it isn't a save situation. And the manager will say to him, in exactly these words, "I don't give a shit about your personal statistics. Go get ready to pitch."

The logic of it . . . is it more effective to use your best pitcher only in save situations, or more effective to use him the way Elroy Face was used? I don't know the answer to that, and I'm not criticizing the policy on that basis. I'm saying that the belief that only The Closer can finish games is a shibboleth, just like the belief that all of your best pitchers had to be starting pitchers was a shibboleth, and sooner or later it will dissolve into the nothingness of which it is made.

The 1990s use of The Closer presents a manager with two ethical questions for which he has no answer. Those two questions are

1) Why should I manage this team in such a way as to maximize one player's statistics? Why should I care whether my relief ace gets 60 saves or 40 or 25? When did that become my job, to get 50 saves for some overpaid egomaniac?

2) Why should I treat the members of my bullpen unequally on this count? The glory job in relief pitching is getting saves. Why do I give *all* the save opportunities to one pitcher, even though I have other pitchers who are just as good?

A bullpen consists of one guy who's got the big-money job, and four guys who just want a shot at it. That fact will eventually force a manager to face those two questions—why are you managing this team to maximize one guy's statistics, and why are you treating your relievers so inequitably?

And once managers are forced to face those two questions, they'll realize that they have no good answer. The plates will move again. The search for a static equilibrium in relief strategy will go on to its next phase, whatever that might be. Relief strategy has been in constant motion for a hundred years. It is very clear, to me, that we are nowhere near a stopping point.

Games in Relief

In 1876, Harry Wright used twenty-one relievers during the season. The National League was new that year, so this established a new record—a record which would stand, surprisingly enough, for thirteen seasons. It was 1889 before any manager used *more* than twenty-one relievers in a season.

That was the last time that record stood still for as long as thirteen seasons. The record for relievers used in a season since then has been broken and reestablished thirty-seven times, about once every three seasons on the average, as the numbers of relievers used have gone constantly upward.

The terms "left" and "right" in politics date to the French National Assembly during the time of the revolution (1789–1795), when the most radical members made it a point to sit at the far left. As new members came in, they were invariably more radical than those already there, so whoever was sitting on the left tended to be pushed toward the right. The right side became known as "The Pillory," because whoever had been pushed to the right would tend to discover that his next career move was the guillotine.

A low total of games in relief is baseball's pillory. As each new generation of managers comes in, they push the established managers down the chart. Whoever is at the bottom of the chart, his career is about over.

The record for games in relief has generally, but not uniformly, been held by bad teams. Many times, the team which used the most relievers was just whoever had the poorest starters.

This was a record that many managers broke twice—Fred Lake, in 1909 and again in 1910, Fielder Jones, in 1916 and 1917, Branch Rickey, in 1921 and 1922, Burt Shotton, in 1928 and 1929, Bill Rigney, in 1961 and 1962, and Don Baylor, in 1993 and 1995. No one, however, has set the record three times. A history of the record for games in relief:

Year	Team	GIR	Won–Lost	Manager
1876	Boston Red Caps	21	39–31	Harry Wright
1889	Indianapolis Hoosier	29	59–75	Two Managers
1891	St. Louis Browns	38	86–52	Charles Comiskey
1899	Pittsburgh Pirates	39	76–73	Patsy Donovan
1900	Brooklyn Superbas	40	81–54	Ned Hanlon
1905	New York Highlanders	75	71–78	Clark Griffith
1908	Boston Doves	77	63–91	Joe Kelley
1909	Boston Red Sox	94	88–63	Fred Lake
1910	Philadelphia Phillies	107	78–75	Red Dooin
and	Boston Doves	107	53–100	Fred Lake
1911	Boston Rustlers	115	4–107	Fred Tenney
1912	St. Louis Cardinals	134	63–90	Roger Bresnahan
1915	Cleveland Indians	138	57–95	Lee Fohl
1916	St. Louis Browns	141	79–75	Fielder Jones
1917	St. Louis Browns	143	57–97	Fielder Jones
1921	St. Louis Cardinals	155	87–66	Branch Rickey
1922	St. Louis Cardinals	172	85–69	Branch Rickey
1924	St. Louis Browns	174	74–78	George Sisler

1928	Philadelphia Phillies	189	43–109	Burt Shotton
1929	Philadelphia Phillies	204	71–82	Burt Shotton
1935	St. Louis Browns	219	65–87	Rogers Hornsby
1946	Brooklyn Dodgers	223	96–60	Leo Durocher
1948	St. Louis Browns	243	59–94	Zack Taylor
1953	St. Louis Browns	250	54–100	Marty Marion
1954	St. Louis Cardinals	262	72–82	Eddie Stanky
1955	St. Louis Cardinals	274	68–86	Harry Walker
1957	Cincinnati Reds	279	80–74	Birdie Tebbetts
1958	Chicago Cubs	293	72–82	Bob Scheffing
1961	Los Angeles Angels	311	70–91	Bill Rigney
1962	Los Angeles Angels	345	86–76	Bill Rigney
1965	Kansas City A's	378	59–103	Haywood Sullivan
1977	San Diego Padres	382	69–93	Alvin Dark
1987	Cincinnati Reds	392	84–78	Pete Rose
1991	Oakland A's	397	84–78	Tony LaRussa
1992	St. Louis Cardinals	424	83–79	Joe Torre
1993	Colorado Rockies	453	67–96	Don Baylor
1995	Colorado Rockies	456	77–67	Don Baylor

INDEX

Note: Page numbers in *italics* refer to photographs.